FREE Study Skills Videos/DVD Offer

Dear Customer,

Thank you for your purchase from Mometrix! We consider it an honor and a privilege that you have purchased our product and we want to ensure your satisfaction.

As a way of showing our appreciation and to help us better serve you, we have developed Study Skills Videos that we would like to give you for FREE. These videos cover our *best practices* for getting ready for your exam, from how to use our study materials to how to best prepare for the day of the test.

All that we ask is that you email us with feedback that would describe your experience so far with our product. Good, bad, or indifferent, we want to know what you think!

To get your FREE Study Skills Videos, you can use the **QR code** below, or send us an **email** at studyvideos@mometrix.com with *FREE VIDEOS* in the subject line and the following information in the body of the email:

- The name of the product you purchased.
- Your product rating on a scale of 1-5, with 5 being the highest rating.
- Your feedback. It can be long, short, or anything in between. We just want to know your impressions and experience so far with our product. (Good feedback might include how our study material met your needs and ways we might be able to make it even better. You could highlight features that you found helpful or features that you think we should add.)

If you have any questions or concerns, please don't hesitate to contact me directly.

Thanks again!

Sincerely,

Jay Willis
Vice President
jay.willis@mometrix.com
1-800-673-8175

SCAN HERE

Mometrix

TEST PREPARATION

Officer Candidate Tests

Secrets Study Guide

Officer Candidate School Guide for the ASVAB, ASTB, OAR, and AFOQT

Complete Practice Tests

Step-by-Step Review Video Tutorials

Written and edited by the Mometrix Test Prep

Printed in the United States of America

This paper meets the requirements of ANSI/NISO Z39.48-1992 (Permanence of Paper).

Mometrix offers volume discount pricing to institutions. For more information or a price quote, please contact our sales department at sales@mometrix.com or 888-248-1219.

Paperback
ISBN 13: 978-1-5167-1140-6
ISBN 10: 1-5167-1140-8

Ebook
ISBN 13: 978-1-5167-1710-1
ISBN 10: 1-5167-1710-4

Hardback
ISBN 13: 978-1-5167-1387-5
ISBN 10: 1-5167-1387-7

DEAR FUTURE EXAM SUCCESS STORY

First of all, **THANK YOU** for purchasing Mometrix study materials!

Second, congratulations! You are one of the few determined test-takers who are committed to doing whatever it takes to excel on your exam. **You have come to the right place.** We developed these study materials with one goal in mind: to deliver you the information you need in a format that's concise and easy to use.

In addition to optimizing your guide for the content of the test, we've outlined our recommended steps for breaking down the preparation process into small, attainable goals so you can make sure you stay on track.

We've also analyzed the entire test-taking process, identifying the most common pitfalls and showing how you can overcome them and be ready for any curveball the test throws you.

Standardized testing is one of the biggest obstacles on your road to success, which only increases the importance of doing well in the high-pressure, high-stakes environment of test day. Your results on this test could have a significant impact on your future, and this guide provides the information and practical advice to help you achieve your full potential on test day.

Your success is our success

We would love to hear from you! If you would like to share the story of your exam success or if you have any questions or comments in regard to our products, please contact us at **800-673-8175** or **support@mometrix.com**.

Thanks again for your business and we wish you continued success!

Sincerely,
The Mometrix Test Preparation Team

TABLE OF CONTENTS

Introduction

Thank you for purchasing this resource! You have made the choice to prepare yourself for a test that could have a huge impact on your future, and this guide is designed to help you be fully ready for test day. Obviously, it's important to have a solid understanding of the test material, but you also need to be prepared for the unique environment and stressors of the test, so that you can perform to the best of your abilities.

For this purpose, the first section that appears in this guide is the **Secret Keys**. We've devoted countless hours to meticulously researching what works and what doesn't, and we've boiled down our findings to the five most impactful steps you can take to improve your performance on the test. We start at the beginning with study planning and move through the preparation process, all the way to the testing strategies that will help you get the most out of what you know when you're finally sitting in front of the test.

We recommend that you start preparing for your test as far in advance as possible. However, if you've bought this guide as a last-minute study resource and only have a few days before your test, we recommend that you skip over the first two Secret Keys since they address a long-term study plan.

If you struggle with **test anxiety**, we strongly encourage you to check out our recommendations for how you can overcome it. Test anxiety is a formidable foe, but it can be beaten, and we want to make sure you have the tools you need to defeat it.

Secret Key #1 – Plan Big, Study Small

There's a lot riding on your performance. If you want to ace this test, you're going to need to keep your skills sharp and the material fresh in your mind. You need a plan that lets you review everything you need to know while still fitting in your schedule. We'll break this strategy down into three categories.

Information Organization

Start with the information you already have: the official test outline. From this, you can make a complete list of all the concepts you need to cover before the test. Organize these concepts into groups that can be studied together, and create a list of any related vocabulary you need to learn so you can brush up on any difficult terms. You'll want to keep this vocabulary list handy once you actually start studying since you may need to add to it along the way.

Time Management

Once you have your set of study concepts, decide how to spread them out over the time you have left before the test. Break your study plan into small, clear goals so you have a manageable task for each day and know exactly what you're doing. Then just focus on one small step at a time. When you manage your time this way, you don't need to spend hours at a time studying. Studying a small block of content for a short period each day helps you retain information better and avoid stressing over how much you have left to do. You can relax knowing that you have a plan to cover everything in time. In order for this strategy to be effective though, you have to start studying early and stick to your schedule. Avoid the exhaustion and futility that comes from last-minute cramming!

Study Environment

The environment you study in has a big impact on your learning. Studying in a coffee shop, while probably more enjoyable, is not likely to be as fruitful as studying in a quiet room. It's important to keep distractions to a minimum. You're only planning to study for a short block of time, so make the most of it. Don't pause to check your phone or get up to find a snack. It's also important to **avoid multitasking**. Research has consistently shown that multitasking will make your studying dramatically less effective. Your study area should also be comfortable and well-lit so you don't have the distraction of straining your eyes or sitting on an uncomfortable chair.

 The time of day you study is also important. You want to be rested and alert. Don't wait until just before bedtime. Study when you'll be most likely to comprehend and remember. Even better, if you know what time of day your test will be, set that time aside for study. That way your brain will be used to working on that subject at that specific time and you'll have a better chance of recalling information.

Finally, it can be helpful to team up with others who are studying for the same test. Your actual studying should be done in as isolated an environment as possible, but the work of organizing the information and setting up the study plan can be divided up. In between study sessions, you can discuss with your teammates the concepts that you're all studying and quiz each other on the details. Just be sure that your teammates are as serious about the test as you are. If you find that your study time is being replaced with social time, you might need to find a new team.

Secret Key #2 – Make Your Studying Count

You're devoting a lot of time and effort to preparing for this test, so you want to be absolutely certain it will pay off. This means doing more than just reading the content and hoping you can remember it on test day. It's important to make every minute of study count. There are two main areas you can focus on to make your studying count.

Retention

It doesn't matter how much time you study if you can't remember the material. You need to make sure you are retaining the concepts. To check your retention of the information you're learning, try recalling it at later times with minimal prompting. Try carrying around flashcards and glance at one or two from time to time or ask a friend who's also studying for the test to quiz you.

To enhance your retention, look for ways to put the information into practice so that you can apply it rather than simply recalling it. If you're using the information in practical ways, it will be much easier to remember. Similarly, it helps to solidify a concept in your mind if you're not only reading it to yourself but also explaining it to someone else. Ask a friend to let you teach them about a concept you're a little shaky on (or speak aloud to an imaginary audience if necessary). As you try to summarize, define, give examples, and answer your friend's questions, you'll understand the concepts better and they will stay with you longer. Finally, step back for a big picture view and ask yourself how each piece of information fits with the whole subject. When you link the different concepts together and see them working together as a whole, it's easier to remember the individual components.

Finally, practice showing your work on any multi-step problems, even if you're just studying. Writing out each step you take to solve a problem will help solidify the process in your mind, and you'll be more likely to remember it during the test.

Modality

Modality simply refers to the means or method by which you study. Choosing a study modality that fits your own individual learning style is crucial. No two people learn best in exactly the same way, so it's important to know your strengths and use them to your advantage.

For example, if you learn best by visualization, focus on visualizing a concept in your mind and draw an image or a diagram. Try color-coding your notes, illustrating them, or creating symbols that will trigger your mind to recall a learned concept. If you learn best by hearing or discussing information, find a study partner who learns the same way or read aloud to yourself. Think about how to put the information in your own words. Imagine that you are giving a lecture on the topic and record yourself so you can listen to it later.

For any learning style, flashcards can be helpful. Organize the information so you can take advantage of spare moments to review. Underline key words or phrases. Use different colors for different categories. Mnemonic devices (such as creating a short list in which every item starts with the same letter) can also help with retention. Find what works best for you and use it to store the information in your mind most effectively and easily.

Secret Key #3 – Practice the Right Way

Your success on test day depends not only on how many hours you put into preparing, but also on whether you prepared the right way. It's good to check along the way to see if your studying is paying off. One of the most effective ways to do this is by taking practice tests to evaluate your progress. Practice tests are useful because they show exactly where you need to improve. Every time you take a practice test, pay special attention to these three groups of questions:

- The questions you got wrong
- The questions you had to guess on, even if you guessed right
- The questions you found difficult or slow to work through

This will show you exactly what your weak areas are, and where you need to devote more study time. Ask yourself why each of these questions gave you trouble. Was it because you didn't understand the material? Was it because you didn't remember the vocabulary? Do you need more repetitions on this type of question to build speed and confidence? Dig into those questions and figure out how you can strengthen your weak areas as you go back to review the material.

 Additionally, many practice tests have a section explaining the answer choices. It can be tempting to read the explanation and think that you now have a good understanding of the concept. However, an explanation likely only covers part of the question's broader context. Even if the explanation makes perfect sense, **go back and investigate** every concept related to the question until you're positive you have a thorough understanding.

As you go along, keep in mind that the practice test is just that: practice. Memorizing these questions and answers will not be very helpful on the actual test because it is unlikely to have any of the same exact questions. If you only know the right answers to the sample questions, you won't be prepared for the real thing. **Study the concepts** until you understand them fully, and then you'll be able to answer any question that shows up on the test.

It's important to wait on the practice tests until you're ready. If you take a test on your first day of study, you may be overwhelmed by the amount of material covered and how much you need to learn. Work up to it gradually.

On test day, you'll need to be prepared for answering questions, managing your time, and using the test-taking strategies you've learned. It's a lot to balance, like a mental marathon that will have a big impact on your future. Like training for a marathon, you'll need to start slowly and work your way up. When test day arrives, you'll be ready.

Start with the strategies you've read in the first two Secret Keys—plan your course and study in the way that works best for you. If you have time, consider using multiple study resources to get different approaches to the same concepts. It can be helpful to see difficult concepts from more than one angle. Then find a good source for practice tests. Many times, the test website will suggest potential study resources or provide sample tests.

Practice Test Strategy

If you're able to find at least three practice tests, we recommend this strategy:

UNTIMED AND OPEN-BOOK PRACTICE

Take the first test with no time constraints and with your notes and study guide handy. Take your time and focus on applying the strategies you've learned.

TIMED AND OPEN-BOOK PRACTICE

Take the second practice test open-book as well, but set a timer and practice pacing yourself to finish in time.

TIMED AND CLOSED-BOOK PRACTICE

Take any other practice tests as if it were test day. Set a timer and put away your study materials. Sit at a table or desk in a quiet room, imagine yourself at the testing center, and answer questions as quickly and accurately as possible.

Keep repeating timed and closed-book tests on a regular basis until you run out of practice tests or it's time for the actual test. Your mind will be ready for the schedule and stress of test day, and you'll be able to focus on recalling the material you've learned.

5

Secret Key #4 – Pace Yourself

Once you're fully prepared for the material on the test, your biggest challenge on test day will be managing your time. Just knowing that the clock is ticking can make you panic even if you have plenty of time left. Work on pacing yourself so you can build confidence against the time constraints of the exam. Pacing is a difficult skill to master, especially in a high-pressure environment, so **practice is vital**.

Set time expectations for your pace based on how much time is available. For example, if a section has 60 questions and the time limit is 30 minutes, you know you have to average 30 seconds or less per question in order to answer them all. Although 30 seconds is the hard limit, set 25 seconds per question as your goal, so you reserve extra time to spend on harder questions. When you budget extra time for the harder questions, you no longer have any reason to stress when those questions take longer to answer.

Don't let this time expectation distract you from working through the test at a calm, steady pace, but keep it in mind so you don't spend too much time on any one question. Recognize that taking extra time on one question you don't understand may keep you from answering two that you do understand later in the test. If your time limit for a question is up and you're still not sure of the answer, mark it and move on, and come back to it later if the time and the test format allow. If the testing format doesn't allow you to return to earlier questions, just make an educated guess; then put it out of your mind and move on.

On the easier questions, be careful not to rush. It may seem wise to hurry through them so you have more time for the challenging ones, but it's not worth missing one if you know the concept and just didn't take the time to read the question fully. Work efficiently but make sure you understand the question and have looked at all of the answer choices, since more than one may seem right at first.

Even if you're paying attention to the time, you may find yourself a little behind at some point. You should speed up to get back on track, but do so wisely. Don't panic; just take a few seconds less on each question until you're caught up. Don't guess without thinking, but do look through the answer choices and eliminate any you know are wrong. If you can get down to two choices, it is often worthwhile to guess from those. Once you've chosen an answer, move on and don't dwell on any that you skipped or had to hurry through. If a question was taking too long, chances are it was one of the harder ones, so you weren't as likely to get it right anyway.

On the other hand, if you find yourself getting ahead of schedule, it may be beneficial to slow down a little. The more quickly you work, the more likely you are to make a careless mistake that will affect your score. You've budgeted time for each question, so don't be afraid to spend that time. Practice an efficient but careful pace to get the most out of the time you have.

Secret Key #5 – Have a Plan for Guessing

When you're taking the test, you may find yourself stuck on a question. Some of the answer choices seem better than others, but you don't see the one answer choice that is obviously correct. What do you do?

The scenario described above is very common, yet most test takers have not effectively prepared for it. Developing and practicing a plan for guessing may be one of the single most effective uses of your time as you get ready for the exam.

In developing your plan for guessing, there are three questions to address:

- When should you start the guessing process?
- How should you narrow down the choices?
- Which answer should you choose?

When to Start the Guessing Process

Unless your plan for guessing is to select C every time (which, despite its merits, is not what we recommend), you need to leave yourself enough time to apply your answer elimination strategies. Since you have a limited amount of time for each question, that means that if you're going to give yourself the best shot at guessing correctly, you have to decide quickly whether or not you will guess.

Of course, the best-case scenario is that you don't have to guess at all, so first, see if you can answer the question based on your knowledge of the subject and basic reasoning skills. Focus on the key words in the question and try to jog your memory of related topics. Give yourself a chance to bring the knowledge to mind, but once you realize that you don't have (or you can't access) the knowledge you need to answer the question, it's time to start the guessing process.

It's almost always better to start the guessing process too early than too late. It only takes a few seconds to remember something and answer the question from knowledge. Carefully eliminating wrong answer choices takes longer. Plus, going through the process of eliminating answer choices can actually help jog your memory.

Summary: Start the guessing process as soon as you decide that you can't answer the question based on your knowledge.

How to Narrow Down the Choices

The next chapter in this book (**Test-Taking Strategies**) includes a wide range of strategies for how to approach questions and how to look for answer choices to eliminate. You will definitely want to read those carefully, practice them, and figure out which ones work best for you. Here though, we're going to address a mindset rather than a particular strategy.

Your odds of guessing an answer correctly depend on how many options you are choosing from.

Number of options left	5	4	3	2	1
Odds of guessing correctly	20%	25%	33%	50%	100%

You can see from this chart just how valuable it is to be able to eliminate incorrect answers and make an educated guess, but there are two things that many test takers do that cause them to miss out on the benefits of guessing:

- Accidentally eliminating the correct answer
- Selecting an answer based on an impression

We'll look at the first one here, and the second one in the next section.

To avoid accidentally eliminating the correct answer, we recommend a thought exercise called **the $5 challenge**. In this challenge, you only eliminate an answer choice from contention if you are willing to bet $5 on it being wrong. Why $5? Five dollars is a small but not insignificant amount of money. It's an amount you could afford to lose but wouldn't want to throw away. And while losing

$5 once might not hurt too much, doing it twenty times will set you back $100. In the same way, each small decision you make—eliminating a choice here, guessing on a question there—won't by itself impact your score very much, but when you put them all together, they can make a big difference. By holding each answer choice elimination decision to a higher standard, you can reduce the risk of accidentally eliminating the correct answer.

The $5 challenge can also be applied in a positive sense: If you are willing to bet $5 that an answer choice *is* correct, go ahead and mark it as correct.

Summary: Only eliminate an answer choice if you are willing to bet $5 that it is wrong.

Which Answer to Choose

You're taking the test. You've run into a hard question and decided you'll have to guess. You've eliminated all the answer choices you're willing to bet $5 on. Now you have to pick an answer. Why do we even need to talk about this? Why can't you just pick whichever one you feel like when the time comes?

The answer to these questions is that if you don't come into the test with a plan, you'll rely on your impression to select an answer choice, and if you do that, you risk falling into a trap. The test writers know that everyone who takes their test will be guessing on some of the questions, so they intentionally write wrong answer choices to seem plausible. You still have to pick an answer though, and if the wrong answer choices are designed to look right, how can you ever be sure that you're not falling for their trap? The best solution we've found to this dilemma is to take the decision out of your hands entirely. Here is the process we recommend:

Once you've eliminated any choices that you are confident (willing to bet $5) are wrong, select the first remaining choice as your answer.

Whether you choose to select the first remaining choice, the second, or the last, the important thing is that you use some preselected standard. Using this approach guarantees that you will not be enticed into selecting an answer choice that looks right, because you are not basing your decision on how the answer choices look.

This is not meant to make you question your knowledge. Instead, it is to help you recognize the difference between your knowledge and your impressions. There's a huge difference between thinking an answer is right because of what you know, and thinking an answer is right because it looks or sounds like it should be right.

Summary: To ensure that your selection is appropriately random, make a predetermined selection from among all answer choices you have not eliminated.

Test-Taking Strategies

This section contains a list of test-taking strategies that you may find helpful as you work through the test. By taking what you know and applying logical thought, you can maximize your chances of answering any question correctly!

It is very important to realize that every question is different and every person is different: no single strategy will work on every question, and no single strategy will work for every person. That's why we've included all of them here, so you can try them out and determine which ones work best for different types of questions and which ones work best for you.

Question Strategies

⊘ READ CAREFULLY

Read the question and the answer choices carefully. Don't miss the question because you misread the terms. You have plenty of time to read each question thoroughly and make sure you understand what is being asked. Yet a happy medium must be attained, so don't waste too much time. You must read carefully and efficiently.

⊘ CONTEXTUAL CLUES

Look for contextual clues. If the question includes a word you are not familiar with, look at the immediate context for some indication of what the word might mean. Contextual clues can often give you all the information you need to decipher the meaning of an unfamiliar word. Even if you can't determine the meaning, you may be able to narrow down the possibilities enough to make a solid guess at the answer to the question.

⊘ PREFIXES

If you're having trouble with a word in the question or answer choices, try dissecting it. Take advantage of every clue that the word might include. Prefixes and suffixes can be a huge help. Usually, they allow you to determine a basic meaning. *Pre-* means before, *post-* means after, *pro-* is positive, *de-* is negative. From prefixes and suffixes, you can get an idea of the general meaning of the word and try to put it into context.

⊘ HEDGE WORDS

Watch out for critical hedge words, such as *likely, may, can, sometimes, often, almost, mostly, usually, generally, rarely,* and *sometimes*. Question writers insert these hedge phrases to cover every possibility. Often an answer choice will be wrong simply because it leaves no room for exception. Be on guard for answer choices that have definitive words such as *exactly* and *always*.

⊘ SWITCHBACK WORDS

Stay alert for *switchbacks*. These are the words and phrases frequently used to alert you to shifts in thought. The most common switchback words are *but, although,* and *however*. Others include *nevertheless, on the other hand, even though, while, in spite of, despite,* and *regardless of*. Switchback words are important to catch because they can change the direction of the question or an answer choice.

⊘ Face Value

When in doubt, use common sense. Accept the situation in the problem at face value. Don't read too much into it. These problems will not require you to make wild assumptions. If you have to go beyond creativity and warp time or space in order to have an answer choice fit the question, then you should move on and consider the other answer choices. These are normal problems rooted in reality. The applicable relationship or explanation may not be readily apparent, but it is there for you to figure out. Use your common sense to interpret anything that isn't clear.

Answer Choice Strategies

⊘ Answer Selection

The most thorough way to pick an answer choice is to identify and eliminate wrong answers until only one is left, then confirm it is the correct answer. Sometimes an answer choice may immediately seem right, but be careful. The test writers will usually put more than one reasonable answer choice on each question, so take a second to read all of them and make sure that the other choices are not equally obvious. As long as you have time left, it is better to read every answer choice than to pick the first one that looks right without checking the others.

⊘ Answer Choice Families

An answer choice family consists of two (in rare cases, three) answer choices that are very similar in construction and cannot all be true at the same time. If you see two answer choices that are direct opposites or parallels, one of them is usually the correct answer. For instance, if one answer choice says that quantity x increases and another either says that quantity x decreases (opposite) or says that quantity y increases (parallel), then those answer choices would fall into the same family. An answer choice that doesn't match the construction of the answer choice family is more likely to be incorrect. Most questions will not have answer choice families, but when they do appear, you should be prepared to recognize them.

⊘ Eliminate Answers

Eliminate answer choices as soon as you realize they are wrong, but make sure you consider all possibilities. If you are eliminating answer choices and realize that the last one you are left with is also wrong, don't panic. Start over and consider each choice again. There may be something you missed the first time that you will realize on the second pass.

⊘ Avoid Fact Traps

Don't be distracted by an answer choice that is factually true but doesn't answer the question. You are looking for the choice that answers the question. Stay focused on what the question is asking for so you don't accidentally pick an answer that is true but incorrect. Always go back to the question and make sure the answer choice you've selected actually answers the question and is not merely a true statement.

⊘ Extreme Statements

In general, you should avoid answers that put forth extreme actions as standard practice or proclaim controversial ideas as established fact. An answer choice that states the "process should be used in certain situations, if..." is much more likely to be correct than one that states the "process should be discontinued completely." The first is a calm rational statement and doesn't even make a definitive, uncompromising stance, using a hedge word *if* to provide wiggle room, whereas the second choice is far more extreme.

⊘ BENCHMARK

As you read through the answer choices and you come across one that seems to answer the question well, mentally select that answer choice. This is not your final answer, but it's the one that will help you evaluate the other answer choices. The one that you selected is your benchmark or standard for judging each of the other answer choices. Every other answer choice must be compared to your benchmark. That choice is correct until proven otherwise by another answer choice beating it. If you find a better answer, then that one becomes your new benchmark. Once you've decided that no other choice answers the question as well as your benchmark, you have your final answer.

⊘ PREDICT THE ANSWER

Before you even start looking at the answer choices, it is often best to try to predict the answer. When you come up with the answer on your own, it is easier to avoid distractions and traps because you will know exactly what to look for. The right answer choice is unlikely to be word-for-word what you came up with, but it should be a close match. Even if you are confident that you have the right answer, you should still take the time to read each option before moving on.

General Strategies

⊘ TOUGH QUESTIONS

If you are stumped on a problem or it appears too hard or too difficult, don't waste time. Move on! Remember though, if you can quickly check for obviously incorrect answer choices, your chances of guessing correctly are greatly improved. Before you completely give up, at least try to knock out a couple of possible answers. Eliminate what you can and then guess at the remaining answer choices before moving on.

⊘ CHECK YOUR WORK

Since you will probably not know every term listed and the answer to every question, it is important that you get credit for the ones that you do know. Don't miss any questions through careless mistakes. If at all possible, try to take a second to look back over your answer selection and make sure you've selected the correct answer choice and haven't made a costly careless mistake (such as marking an answer choice that you didn't mean to mark). This quick double check should more than pay for itself in caught mistakes for the time it costs.

⊘ PACE YOURSELF

It's easy to be overwhelmed when you're looking at a page full of questions; your mind is confused and full of random thoughts, and the clock is ticking down faster than you would like. Calm down and maintain the pace that you have set for yourself. Especially as you get down to the last few minutes of the test, don't let the small numbers on the clock make you panic. As long as you are on track by monitoring your pace, you are guaranteed to have time for each question.

⊘ DON'T RUSH

It is very easy to make errors when you are in a hurry. Maintaining a fast pace in answering questions is pointless if it makes you miss questions that you would have gotten right otherwise. Test writers like to include distracting information and wrong answers that seem right. Taking a little extra time to avoid careless mistakes can make all the difference in your test score. Find a pace that allows you to be confident in the answers that you select.

⊘ KEEP MOVING

Panicking will not help you pass the test, so do your best to stay calm and keep moving. Taking deep breaths and going through the answer elimination steps you practiced can help to break through a stress barrier and keep your pace.

Final Notes

The combination of a solid foundation of content knowledge and the confidence that comes from practicing your plan for applying that knowledge is the key to maximizing your performance on test day. As your foundation of content knowledge is built up and strengthened, you'll find that the strategies included in this chapter become more and more effective in helping you quickly sift through the distractions and traps of the test to isolate the correct answer.

Now that you're preparing to move forward into the test content chapters of this book, be sure to keep your goal in mind. As you read, think about how you will be able to apply this information on the test. If you've already seen sample questions for the test and you have an idea of the question format and style, try to come up with questions of your own that you can answer based on what you're reading. This will give you valuable practice applying your knowledge in the same ways you can expect to on test day.

Good luck and good studying!

Common Subject: Science

Earth and Space Science

GEOLOGY

Geology is the study of the planet Earth as it pertains to the composition, structure, and origin of its rocks. **Minerals** are naturally occurring, inorganic solids with a definite chemical composition and an orderly internal crystal structure. A **polymorph** is two minerals with the same chemical composition, but a different crystal structure. **Rocks** are aggregates of one or more minerals, and may also contain mineraloids (minerals lacking a crystalline structure) and organic remains. The three types of rocks are sedimentary, igneous, and metamorphic. Rocks are classified based on both their formation and mineral content. Minerals, on the other hand, are classified by their chemical composition. The study of rocks, known as **petrology**, examines their composition, texture, structure, occurrence, mode of formation, and history. **Mineralogy** is the study of minerals.

Sedimentary rocks are formed by the process of lithification, which involves compaction, the expulsion of liquids from pores, and the cementation of the pre-existing rock. Pressure and temperature are responsible for this process. Sedimentary rocks are often formed in layers in the presence of water and may contain organic remains, such as fossils. Sedimentary rocks can be organized into three groups: detrital, biogenic, and chemical. When studying sedimentary rock, scientists use the word *texture* to refer the size, shape, and grains of sedimentary rock. Texture can be used to determine how a particular sedimentary rock was created. Composition refers to the types of minerals present in the rock. The origin of sedimentary rock depends on the type of water that was involved in its creation. Marine deposits, for example, likely involved ocean environments, while continental deposits likely involved dry land and lakes.

Igneous rock is formed from magma, molten material originating from beneath the Earth's surface. Depending upon where the magma cools, the resulting igneous rock can be classified as intrusive, plutonic, hypabyssal, extrusive, or volcanic. Magma that solidifies at a great depth is intrusive, cools slowly, and forms rock with a coarse grain, such as granite. Magma that solidifies at or near the surface is extrusive, cools quickly, and usually forms rock with a fine grain, such as basalt. Magma that actually flows out of the Earth's surface is called **lava**. Some extrusive rock cools so quickly that

15

crystals do not have time to form. These rocks have a glassy appearance, such as obsidian. Hypabyssal rock is igneous rock that is formed at medium depths.

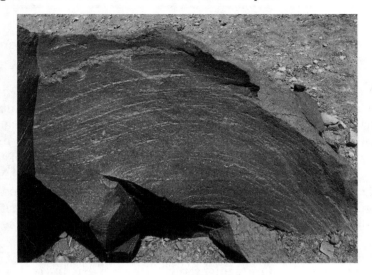

Metamorphic rock is rock which has been changed by great heat and pressure. This results in a variety of outcomes, including deformation, compaction, destruction of the characteristics of the original rock, bending and folding. Some levels of heat and pressure can even cause the formation of new minerals because of chemical reactions and changes in the size and shape of the mineral grain. For example, the igneous rock ferromagnesian can be changed into schist and gneiss. The sedimentary rock carbonaceous can be changed into marble. The texture of metamorphic rocks can be classified as foliated and unfoliated. Foliation, or layering, occurs when rock is compressed along one axis during recrystallization. This can be seen in schist and shale. Unfoliated rock does not include this banding. Rocks that are compressed equally from all sides or lack specific minerals will be unfoliated. Marble is an example of an unfoliated rock.

Fossils are preservations of plant and animal remains or traces that date back to about 10,000 years ago. The fossil record is composed of fossils and where they are found in rock strata. Fossils are formed under a very specific set of conditions. The fossil must not be damaged by predators and scavengers after death, and the fossil must not decompose. Usually, this happens when the organism is quickly covered with sediment. This sediment builds up and molecules in the

16

organism's body are replaced by minerals. Fossils come in an array of sizes, from single-celled organisms to large dinosaurs.

PLATE TECTONICS

The Earth is ellipsoid, not perfectly spherical. This means the diameter is different through the poles and at the equator. Through the poles, the Earth is about 12,715 km in diameter. The approximate center of the Earth is at a depth of 6,378 km. The Earth is divided into a crust, mantle, and core. The core consists of a solid inner portion. Moving outward, the molten outer core occupies the space from about a depth of 5,150 km to a depth of 2,890 km. The mantle consists of a lower and upper layer. The lower layer includes the D' (D prime) and D" (D double-prime) layers. The solid portion of the upper mantle and crust together form the lithosphere, or rocky sphere. Below this, but still within the mantle, is the asthenosphere, or weak sphere. These layers are distinguishable because the lithosphere is relatively rigid, while the asthenosphere resembles a thick liquid.

The theory of plate tectonics states that the lithosphere, the solid portion of the mantle and Earth's crust, consists of major and minor plates. These plates are on top of and move with the viscous upper mantle, which is heated because of the convection cycle that occurs in the interior of the Earth. There are different estimates as to the exact number of major and minor plates. The number of major plates is believed to be between 9 and 15, and it is thought that there may be as many as 40 minor plates. The United States is atop the North American plate. The Pacific Ocean is atop the Pacific plate. The point at which these two plates slide horizontally along the San Andreas fault is an example of a transform plate boundary. The other two types of boundaries are divergent (plates that are spreading apart and forming new crust) and convergent (the process of subduction causes one plate to go under another). The movement of plates is what causes other features of the Earth's crust, such as mountains, volcanoes, and earthquakes.

Volcanoes can occur along any type of tectonic plate boundary. At a divergent boundary, as plates move apart, magma rises to the surface, cools, and forms a ridge, like the mid-Atlantic ridge. Convergent boundaries, where one plate slides under another, are often areas with a lot of volcanic activity. The subduction process creates magma. When it rises to the surface, volcanoes can be created. Volcanoes can also be created in the middle of a plate over hot spots, locations where narrow plumes of magma rise through the mantle in a fixed place over a long period of time. The Hawaiian Islands and Midway Island are examples of how hot spots can create not only volcanoes, but entire islands. As the plate shifts, the island moves and magma can continue to rise through the mantle and produce another island. Volcanoes can be active, dormant, or extinct. Active volcanoes are those that are erupting or about to erupt. Dormant volcanoes are those that might erupt in the future and still have internal volcanic activity. Extinct volcanoes are those that will not erupt.

GEOGRAPHY

For the purposes of tracking time and location, the Earth is divided into sections with imaginary lines. The lines that run vertically around the globe through the poles are lines of longitude, sometimes called meridians. The Prime Meridian is the longitudinal reference point of 0. Longitude is measured in 15-degree increments toward the east or west. Degrees are further divided into 60 minutes, and each minute is divided into 60 seconds. Lines of latitude run horizontally around the Earth parallel to the equator, which is the 0 reference point for latitude and the widest point of the Earth. Latitude is the distance north or south from the equator and is also measured in degrees, minutes, and seconds.

Tropic of Cancer: This is located at 23.5 degrees north. The Sun is directly overhead at noon on June 21st in the Tropic of Cancer, which marks the beginning of summer in the Northern Hemisphere.

Tropic of Capricorn: This is located at 23.5 degrees south. The Sun is directly overhead at noon on December 21st in the Tropic of Capricorn, which marks the beginning of winter in the Northern Hemisphere.

Arctic Circle: This is located at 66.5 degrees north, and marks the start of when the Sun is not visible above the horizon. This occurs on December 21st, the same day the Sun is directly over the Tropic of Capricorn.

Antarctic Circle: This is located at 66.5 degrees south, and marks the start of when the Sun is not visible above the horizon. This occurs on June 21st, which marks the beginning of winter in the Southern Hemisphere and is when the Sun is directly over the Tropic of Cancer.

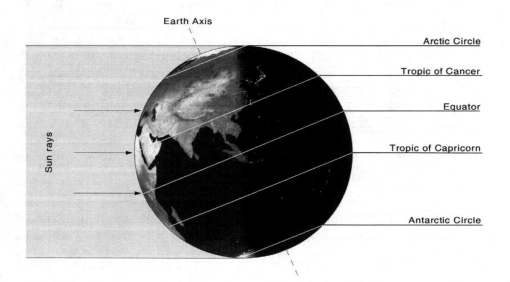

Latitude is a measurement of the distance from the equator. The distance from the equator indicates how much solar radiation a particular area receives. The equator receives more sunlight, while polar areas receive less. The Earth tilts slightly on its rotational axis. This tilt determines the seasons and affects weather. There are eight biomes or ecosystems with particular climates that are associated with latitude. Those in the high latitudes, which get the least sunlight, are tundra and taiga. Those in the mid latitudes are grassland, temperate forest, and chaparral. Those in latitudes closest to the equator, desert and tropical rainforest, are the warmest. The eighth biome is the ocean, which is unique because it consists of water and spans the entire globe. Insolation refers to incoming solar radiation, which is at its peak at noon. Diurnal variations refer to the daily changes in insolation.

The tilt of the Earth on its axis is 23.5°. This tilt causes the seasons and affects the amount of Sun the area receives, which influence temperature. When the Northern or Southern Hemispheres are tilted toward the Sun, the hemisphere tilted toward the sun experiences summer and the other hemisphere experiences winter. This reverses as the Earth revolves around the Sun. Fall and spring occur between the two extremes.

The equator gets the same amount of sunlight every day of the year, about 12 hours, and doesn't experience seasons. Both poles have days during the winter when they are tilted away from the Sun and receive no daylight. The opposite effect occurs during the summer. There are 24 hours of daylight and no night. The summer solstice, the day with the most amount of sunlight, occurs on June 21st in the Northern Hemisphere and on December 21st in the Southern Hemisphere. The winter solstice, the day with the least amount of sunlight, occurs on December 21st in the Northern Hemisphere and on June 21st in the Southern Hemisphere.

WEATHER, ATMOSPHERE, WATER CYCLE

Meteorology is the study of the atmosphere, particularly as it pertains to forecasting the weather and understanding its processes. Weather is the condition of the atmosphere at any given moment. Most weather occurs in the troposphere and includes changing events such as clouds, storms, and temperature, as well as more extreme events such as tornadoes, hurricanes, and blizzards. Climate refers to the average weather for a particular area over time, typically at least 30 years. Latitude is an indicator of climate. Changes in climate occur over long time periods.

The hydrologic, or water, cycle refers to water movement on, above, and in the Earth. Water can be in any one of its three states during different phases of the cycle. The three states of water are liquid water, frozen ice, and water vapor. Processes involved in the hydrologic cycle include precipitation, canopy interception, snow melt, runoff, infiltration, subsurface flow, evaporation, sublimation, advection, condensation, and transpiration. Precipitation is when condensed water vapor falls to Earth as rain, fog drip, and various forms of snow, hail, and sleet.

Canopy interception is when precipitation lands on plant foliage instead of falling to the ground and evaporating. Snow melt is runoff produced by melting snow. Infiltration occurs when water flows from the surface into the ground. Subsurface flow refers to water that flows underground. Evaporation is when water in a liquid state changes to a gas. Sublimation is when water in a solid state (such as snow or ice) changes to water vapor without going through a liquid phase. Advection is the movement of water through the atmosphere. Condensation is when water vapor changes to liquid water. Transpiration is when water vapor is released from plants into the air.

The ocean is the salty body of water that encompasses the Earth. It has a mass of 1.4×10^{24} grams. Geographically, the ocean is divided into three large oceans: the Pacific Ocean, the Atlantic Ocean, and the Indian Ocean. There are also other divisions, such as gulfs, bays, and various types of seas, including Mediterranean and marginal seas. Ocean distances can be measured by latitude, longitude, degrees, meters, miles, and nautical miles. The ocean accounts for 70.8% of the surface of the Earth, amounting to 361,254,000 km². The ocean's depth is greatest at Challenger Deep in the Mariana Trench. The ocean floor here is 10,924 meters below sea level. The depths of the ocean are mapped by echo sounders and satellite altimeter systems. Echo sounders emit a sound pulse from the surface and record the time it takes to return. Satellite altimeters provide better maps of the ocean floor.

The atmosphere consists of 78% nitrogen, 21% oxygen, and 1% argon. It also includes traces of water vapor, carbon dioxide and other gases, dust particles, and chemicals from Earth. The atmosphere becomes thinner the farther it is from the Earth's surface, gradually fading into space. It becomes difficult to breathe at about 3 km above sea level. The lowest layer of the atmosphere is called the troposphere. Its thickness varies at the poles and the equator, varying from about 7 to 17 km. This is where most weather occurs. The stratosphere is next and continues to an elevation of about 51 km. The mesosphere extends from the stratosphere to an elevation of about 81 km. It is the coldest layer and is where meteors tend to ablate, or break down. The next layer is the thermosphere. It is where the International Space Station orbits. The exosphere is the outermost layer, extends to 10,000 km, and mainly consists of hydrogen and helium.

In summary, Earth's atmosphere has five main layers. From lowest to highest, these are the troposphere, the stratosphere, the mesosphere, the thermosphere, and the exosphere. Between each pair of layers is a transition layer called a pause. The troposphere includes the tropopause, which is the transitional layer of the stratosphere. Energy from Earth's surface is transferred to the troposphere. Temperature decreases with altitude in this layer. In the stratosphere, the temperature is inverted, meaning that it increases with altitude. The stratosphere includes the ozone layer, which helps block ultraviolet light from the Sun. The stratopause is the transitional layer to the mesosphere. The temperature of the mesosphere decreases with height. It is considered the coldest place on Earth, and has an average temperature of -85 degrees Celsius. Temperature increases with altitude in the thermosphere, which includes the thermopause. Just past the thermosphere is the exobase, the base layer of the exosphere. Beyond the five main layers are the ionosphere, homosphere, heterosphere, and magnetosphere.

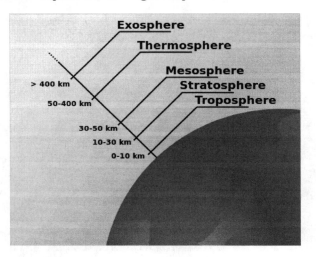

Most clouds can be classified according to the altitude of their base above Earth's surface. High clouds occur at altitudes between 5,000 and 13,000 meters. Middle clouds occur at altitudes between 2,000 and 7,000 meters. Low clouds occur from the Earth's surface to altitudes of 2,000 meters. Types of high clouds include cirrus (Ci), thin wispy mare's tails that consist of ice; cirrocumulus (Cc), small, pillow-like puffs that often appear in rows; and cirrostratus (Cs), thin, sheetlike clouds that often cover the entire sky. Types of middle clouds include altocumulus (Ac), gray-white clouds that consist of liquid water; and altostratus (As), grayish or blue-gray clouds that span the sky. Types of low clouds include stratus (St), gray and fog-like clouds consisting of water droplets that take up the whole sky; stratocumulus (Sc), low-lying, lumpy gray clouds; and nimbostratus (Ns), dark gray clouds with uneven bases that indicate rain or snow. Two types of clouds, cumulus (Cu) and cumulonimbus (Cb), are capable of great vertical growth. They can start at a wide range of altitudes, from the Earth's surface to altitudes of 13,000 meters.

ASTRONOMY

Astronomy is the scientific study of celestial objects and their positions, movements, and structures. Celestial does not refer to the Earth by itself, but does include its movement through space. Other celestial objects include the Sun, the Moon, planets, satellites, asteroids, meteors, comets, stars, galaxies, the universe, and other space phenomena. The term astronomy has its roots in the Greek words "astro" and "nomos," which means "laws of the stars."

What can be seen of the universe is believed to be at least 93 billion light years across. To put this into perspective, the Milky Way galaxy is about 100,000 light years across. Our view of matter in the universe is that it forms into clumps which become stars, galaxies, clusters of galaxies, superclusters, and the Great Wall of galaxies. Galaxies consist of stars, some with planetary systems. Some estimates state that the universe is about 13 billion years old. It is not considered dense and is believed to consist of 73% dark energy, 23% cold dark matter, and 4% regular matter. Cosmology is the study of the universe. Interstellar medium (ISM) is the gas and dust in the interstellar space between a galaxy's stars.

Our solar system is a planetary system of objects that exist in an ecliptic plane. Objects orbit around and are bound by gravity to a star called the Sun. Objects that orbit around the Sun include: planets, dwarf planets, moons, asteroids, meteoroids, cosmic dust, and comets. The definition of planets has changed. At one time, there were nine planets in the solar system, but due to the change in the definition of planets, there are now eight. Planetary objects in the solar system include four inner, terrestrial planets: Mercury, Venus, Earth, and Mars. They are relatively small, dense, rocky, lack rings, and have few or no moons. The four outer, or Jovian, planets are Jupiter, Saturn, Uranus, and Neptune, which are large and have low densities, rings, and moons. They are also known as gas giants. Between the inner and outer planets is the asteroid belt. Beyond Neptune is the Kuiper belt. Within these belts are five dwarf planets: Ceres, Pluto, Haumea, Makemake, and Eris.

The Sun is at the center of the solar system. It is composed of 70% hydrogen (H) and 28% helium (He). The remaining 2% is made up of metals. The Sun is one of 100 billion stars in the Milky Way galaxy. Its diameter is 1,390,000 km, its mass is 1.989×10^{30} kg, its surface temperature is 5,800 K, and its core temperature is 15,600,000 K. The Sun represents more than 99.8% of the total mass of the solar system. At the core, the temperature is 15.6 million K, the pressure is 250 billion atmospheres, and the density is more than 150 times that of water. The surface is called the photosphere. The chromosphere lies above this, and the corona, which extends millions of kilometers into space, is next. Sunspots are relatively cool regions on the surface with a temperature of 3,800 K. Temperatures in the corona are over 1,000,000 K. Its magnetosphere, or heliosphere, extends far beyond Pluto.

Mercury: Mercury is the closest planet to the Sun and is also the smallest planet. It orbits the Sun every 88 days, has no satellites or atmosphere, has a Moon-like surface with craters, appears bright, and is dense and rocky with a large iron core.

Venus: Venus is the second planet from the Sun. It orbits the Sun every 225 days, is very bright, and is similar to Earth in size, gravity, and bulk composition. It has a dense atmosphere composed of carbon dioxide and some sulfur. It is covered with reflective clouds made of sulfuric acid and exhibits signs of volcanism. Lightning and thunder have been recorded on Venus's surface.

Earth: Earth is the third planet from the Sun. It orbits the Sun every 365 days. Approximately 71% of its surface is salt-water oceans. The Earth is rocky, has an atmosphere composed mainly of oxygen and nitrogen, has one moon, and supports millions of species. It contains the only known life in the solar system.

Mars: Mars is the fourth planet from the Sun. It appears reddish due to iron oxide on the surface, has a thin atmosphere, has a rotational period similar to Earth's, and has seasonal cycles. Surface features of Mars include volcanoes, valleys, deserts, and polar ice caps. Mars has impact craters and the tallest mountain, largest canyon, and perhaps the largest impact crater yet discovered.

Jupiter: Jupiter is the fifth planet from the Sun and the largest planet in the solar system. It consists mainly of hydrogen, and 25% of its mass is made up of helium. It has a fast rotation and has clouds in the tropopause composed of ammonia crystals that are arranged into bands sub-divided into lighter-hued zones and darker belts causing storms and turbulence. Jupiter has wind speeds of 100 m/s, a planetary ring, 63 moons, and a Great Red Spot, which is an anticyclonic storm.

Saturn: Saturn is the sixth planet from the Sun and the second largest planet in the solar system. It is composed of hydrogen, some helium, and trace elements. Saturn has a small core of rock and ice, a thick layer of metallic hydrogen, a gaseous outer layer, wind speeds of up to 1,800 km/h, a system of rings, and 61 moons.

Uranus: Uranus is the seventh planet from the Sun. Its atmosphere is composed mainly of hydrogen and helium, and also contains water, ammonia, methane, and traces of hydrocarbons. With a minimum temperature of 49 K, Uranus has the coldest atmosphere. Uranus has a ring system, a magnetosphere, and 13 moons.

Neptune: Neptune is the eighth planet from the Sun and is the planet with the third largest mass. It has 12 moons, an atmosphere similar to Uranus, a Great Dark Spot, and the strongest sustained winds of any planet (wind speeds can be as high as 2,100 km/h). Neptune is cold (about 55 K) and has a fragmented ring system.

The Earth is about 12,765 km (7,934 miles) in diameter. The Moon is about 3,476 km (2,160 mi) in diameter. The distance between the Earth and the Moon is about 384,401 km (238,910 mi). The diameter of the Sun is approximately 1,390,000 km (866,000 mi). The distance from the Earth to the Sun is 149,598,000 km, also known as 1 Astronomical Unit (AU). The star that is nearest to the solar system is Proxima Centauri. It is about 270,000 AU away. Some distant galaxies are so far away that their light takes several billion years to reach the Earth. In other words, people on Earth see them as they looked billions of years ago.

It takes about one month for the Moon to go through all its phases. Waxing refers to the two weeks during which the Moon goes from a new moon to a full moon. About two weeks is spent waning, going from a full moon to a new moon. The lit part of the Moon always faces the Sun.

The phases of waxing are:

- **New moon**, during which the Moon is not illuminated and rises and sets with the Sun.
- **Waxing crescent**, during which a tiny sliver is lit.
- **First quarter**, during which half the Moon is lit and the phase of the Moon is due south on the meridian.

- **Waxing gibbous**, during which more than half of the Moon is lit and has a shape similar to a football.
- **Full moon**, during which the Moon is fully illuminated, rises at sunset, and sets at sunrise.

After a full moon, the Moon is waning. The phases of waning are:

- **Waning gibbous**, during which the left side is lit and the Moon rises after sunset and sets after sunrise.
- **Third quarter**, during which the Moon is half lit and rises at midnight and sets at noon.
- **Waning crescent**, during which a tiny sliver is lit.
- **New moon**, which starts the cycle over.

Biology

CELLS

The main difference between eukaryotic and prokaryotic cells is that eukaryotic cells have a nucleus and prokaryotic cells do not. Eukaryotic cells are considered more complex, while prokaryotic cells are smaller and simpler. Eukaryotic cells have membrane-bound organelles that perform various functions and contribute to the complexity of these types of cells. Prokaryotic cells do not contain membrane-bound organelles.

In prokaryotic cells, the genetic material (DNA) is not contained within a membrane-bound nucleus. Instead, it aggregates in the cytoplasm in a nucleoid. In eukaryotic cells, DNA is mostly contained in chromosomes in the nucleus, although there is some DNA in mitochondria and chloroplasts. Prokaryotic cells usually divide by binary fission and are haploid. Eukaryotic cells divide by mitosis and are diploid. Prokaryotic structures include plasmids, ribosomes, cytoplasm, a cytoskeleton, granules of nutritional substances, a plasma membrane, flagella, and a few others. Prokaryotic cells are single celled organisms, such as bacteria, which are classified as prokaryotes.

The functions of plant and animal cells vary greatly, and the functions of different cells within a single organism can also be vastly different. Animal and plant cells are similar in structure in that they are eukaryotic, which means they contain a nucleus. The nucleus is a round structure that controls the activities of the cell and contains chromosomes. Both types of cells also have cell membranes, cytoplasm, vacuoles, and other structures.

The main difference between plant and animal cells is that plant cells have a cell wall made of cellulose that can handle high levels of pressure within the cell, which can occur when liquid enters a plant cell. Plant cells have chloroplasts that are used during the process of photosynthesis, which is the conversion of sunlight into food. Plant cells usually have one large vacuole, whereas animal cells can have many smaller ones. Plant cells have a regular shape, while the shapes of animal cells can vary.

Plant cells can be much larger than animal cells, ranging from 10 to 100 micrometers. Animal cells are 10 to 30 micrometers in size. Plant cells can have much larger vacuoles that occupy a large portion of the cell. Chloroplasts in plants that perform photosynthesis absorb sunlight and convert it into energy. Mitochondria produce energy from food in animal cells. Plant and animal cells are both eukaryotic, meaning they contain a nucleus. Both plant and animal cells duplicate genetic material, separate it, and then divide in half to reproduce. Plant cells build a cell plate between the two new cells, while animal cells make a cleavage furrow and pinch in half. Microtubules are components of the cytoskeleton in both plant and animal cells. Microtubule organizing centers (MTOCs) make microtubules in plant cells, while centrioles make microtubules in animal cells.

Photosynthesis is the conversion of sunlight into energy in plant cells, and also occurs in some types of bacteria and protists. Carbon dioxide and water are converted into glucose through the use of sunlight during a process called photosynthesis. Cyanobacteria are thought to be the descendants of the first organisms to use photosynthesis about 3.5 billion years ago. Photosynthesis is a form of cellular respiration. It occurs in chloroplasts that use thylakoids, which are structures in the membrane that contain light reaction chemicals. Chlorophyll is a pigment that absorbs light. During the process, water is used and oxygen is released. The equation for the chemical reaction that occurs during photosynthesis is $6H_2O + 6CO_2 \rightarrow C_6H_{12}O_6 + 6O_2$. In other words, during photosynthesis, six molecules of water and six molecules of carbon dioxide react to form one molecule of sugar and six molecules of oxygen.

The term cell cycle refers to the process by which a cell reproduces, which involves cell growth, the duplication of genetic material, and cell division. Complex organisms with many cells use the cell cycle to replace cells as they lose their functionality and wear out. The entire cell cycle in animal cells can take 24 hours. The time required varies among different cell types. Human skin cells, for example, are constantly reproducing. Some other cells only divide infrequently. Once neurons are mature, they do not grow or divide. The two ways that cells can reproduce are through meiosis and mitosis. When cells replicate through mitosis, the "daughter cell" is an exact replica of the parent cell. When cells divide through meiosis, the daughter cells have different genetic coding than the parent cell. Meiosis only happens in specialized reproductive cells called gametes.

Mitosis is the process of cell reproduction in which a eukaryotic cell splits into two separate, but completely identical, cells. This process is divided into a number of different phases.

Interphase: The cell prepares for division by replicating its genetic and cytoplasmic material. Interphase can be further divided into G1, S, and G2.

Prophase: The chromatin thickens into chromosomes and the nuclear membrane begins to disintegrate. Pairs of centrioles move to opposite sides of the cell and spindle fibers begin to form. The mitotic spindle, formed from cytoskeleton parts, moves chromosomes around within the cell.

Metaphase: The spindle moves to the center of the cell and chromosome pairs align along the center of the spindle structure.

Anaphase: The pairs of chromosomes, called sisters, begin to pull apart, and may bend. When they are separated, they are called daughter chromosomes. Grooves appear in the cell membrane.

Telophase: The spindle disintegrates, the nuclear membranes reform, and the chromosomes revert to chromatin. In animal cells, the membrane is pinched. In plant cells, a new cell wall begins to form.

Cytokinesis: This is the physical splitting of the cell (including the cytoplasm) into two cells. Some believe this occurs following telophase. Others say it occurs from anaphase, as the cell begins to furrow, through telophase, when the cell actually splits into two.

Meiosis is another process by which eukaryotic cells reproduce. However, meiosis is used by more complex life forms such as plants and animals and results in four unique cells rather than two identical cells as in mitosis. Meiosis has the same phases as mitosis, but they happen twice. In addition, different events occur during some phases of meiosis than mitosis. The events that occur during the first phase of meiosis are interphase (I), prophase (I), metaphase (I), anaphase (I), telophase (I), and cytokinesis (I). During this first phase of meiosis, chromosomes cross over, genetic material is exchanged, and tetrads of four chromatids are formed. The nuclear membrane dissolves. Homologous pairs of chromatids are separated and travel to different poles. At this point, there has been one cell division resulting in two cells. Each cell goes through a second cell division, which consists of prophase (II), metaphase (II), anaphase (II), telophase (II), and cytokinesis (II). The result is four daughter cells with different sets of chromosomes. The daughter cells are haploid, which means they contain half the genetic material of the parent cell. The second phase of meiosis is similar to the process of mitosis. Meiosis encourages genetic diversity.

GENETICS

Chromosomes consist of genes, which are single units of genetic information. Genes are made up of deoxyribonucleic acid (DNA). DNA is a nucleic acid located in the cell nucleus. There is also DNA in the mitochondria. DNA replicates to pass on genetic information. The DNA in almost all cells is the same. It is also involved in the biosynthesis of proteins. The model or structure of DNA is described as a double helix. A helix is a curve, and a double helix is two congruent curves connected by horizontal members. The model can be likened to a spiral staircase. It is right-handed. The British scientist Rosalind Elsie Franklin is credited with taking the x-ray diffraction image in 1952 that was used by Francis Crick and James Watson to formulate the double-helix model of DNA and speculate about its important role in carrying and transferring genetic information.

DNA has a double helix shape, resembles a twisted ladder, and is compact. It consists of nucleotides. Nucleotides consist of a five-carbon sugar (pentose), a phosphate group, and a nitrogenous base. Two bases pair up to form the rungs of the ladder. The "side rails" or backbone consists of the covalently bonded sugar and phosphate. The bases are attached to each other with hydrogen bonds, which are easily dismantled so replication can occur. Each base is attached to a phosphate and to a sugar. There are four types of nitrogenous bases: adenine (A), guanine (G), cytosine (C), and thymine (T). There are about 3 billion bases in human DNA. The bases are mostly the same in everybody, but their order is different. It is the order of these bases that creates diversity in people. Adenine (A) pairs with thymine (T), and cytosine (C) pairs with guanine (G).

A gene is a portion of DNA that identifies how traits are expressed and passed on in an organism. A gene is part of the genetic code. Collectively, all genes form the genotype of an individual. The genotype includes genes that may not be expressed, such as recessive genes. The phenotype is the physical, visual manifestation of genes. It is determined by the basic genetic information and how

27

genes have been affected by their environment. An allele is a variation of a gene. Also known as a trait, it determines the manifestation of a gene. This manifestation results in a specific physical appearance of some facet of an organism, such as eye color or height. For example, the genetic information for eye color is a gene. The gene variations responsible for blue, green, brown, or black eyes are called alleles. Locus (pl. loci) refers to the location of a gene or alleles.

Mendel's laws are the law of segregation (the first law), the law of independent assortment (the second law), and the law of dominance (the third law). The law of segregation states that there are two alleles and that half of the total number of alleles are contributed by each parent organism. The law of independent assortment states that traits are passed on randomly and are not influenced by other traits. The exception to this is linked traits. A Punnett square can illustrate how alleles combine from the contributing genes to form various phenotypes. One set of a parent's genes are put in columns, while the genes from the other parent are placed in rows. The allele combinations are shown in each cell. The law of dominance states that when two different alleles are present in a pair, the dominant one is expressed. A Punnett square can be used to predict the outcome of crosses.

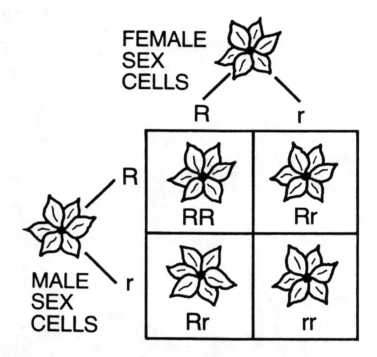

Gene traits are represented in pairs with an upper-case letter for the dominant trait (A) and a lower-case letter for the recessive trait (a). Genes occur in pairs (AA, Aa, or aa). There is one gene on each chromosome half supplied by each parent organism. Since half the genetic material is from each parent, the offspring's traits are represented as a combination of these. A dominant trait only requires one gene of a gene pair for it to be expressed in a phenotype, whereas a recessive trait requires both genes in order to be manifested. For example, if the mother's genotype is Dd and the father's is dd, the possible combinations are Dd and dd. The dominant trait will be manifested if the genotype is DD or Dd. The recessive trait will be manifested if the genotype is dd. Both DD and dd are homozygous pairs. Dd is heterozygous.

EVOLUTION

Scientific evidence supporting the theory of evolution can be found in biogeography, comparative anatomy and embryology, the fossil record, and molecular evidence. Biogeography studies the geographical distribution of animals and plants. Evidence of evolution related to the area of biogeography includes species that are well suited for extreme environments. The fossil record shows that many species lived only for a short time period before becoming extinct. The fossil record can also show the succession of plants and animals. Living fossils are existing species that have not changed much morphologically and are very similar to ancient examples in the fossil record. Examples include the horseshoe crab and ginkgo. Comparative embryology studies how species are similar in the embryonic stage, but become increasingly specialized and diverse as they age. Vestigial organs are those that still exist, but become nonfunctional. Examples include the hind limbs of whales and the wings of birds that can no longer fly, such as ostriches.

The rate of evolution is affected by the variability of a population. Variability increases the likelihood of evolution. Variability in a population can be increased by mutations, immigration, sexual reproduction (as opposed to asexual reproduction), and size. Natural selection, emigration, and smaller populations can lead to decreased variability. Sexual selection affects evolution. If fewer genes are available, it will limit the number of genes passed on to subsequent generations. Some animal mating behaviors are not as successful as others. A male that does not attract a female because of a weak mating call or dull feathers, for example, will not pass on its genes. Mechanical isolation, which refers to sex organs that do not fit together very well, can also decrease successful mating.

Natural selection: This theory developed by Darwin states that traits that help give a species a survival advantage are passed on to subsequent generations. Members of a species that do not have the advantageous trait die before they reproduce. Darwin's four principles are: from generation to generation, there are various individuals within a species; genes determine variations; more individuals are born than survive to maturation; and specific genes enable an organism to better survive.

Gradualism is the idea that evolution proceeds at a steady pace and does not include sudden developments of new species or features from one generation to the next. **Punctuated equilibrium**, in contrast, is the idea that evolution involves long time periods of no change (stasis) accompanied by relatively brief periods (hundreds of thousands of years) of rapid change.

The three types of evolution are divergent, convergent, and parallel. Divergent evolution refers to two species that become different over time. This can be caused by one of the species adapting to a different environment. Convergent evolution refers to two species that start out fairly different but evolve to share many similar traits. Parallel evolution refers to species that are not similar and do not become more or less similar over time. Mechanisms of evolution include descent (the passing on of genetic information), mutation, migration, natural selection, and genetic variation and drift. The biological definition of species refers to a group of individuals that can mate and reproduce. Speciation refers to the evolution of a new biological species. The biological species concept (BSC) basically states that a species is a community of individuals that can reproduce and have a niche in nature.

One theory of how life originated on Earth is that life developed from nonliving materials. The first stage of this transformation happened when abiotic (nonliving) synthesis took place, which is the formation of monomers like amino acids and nucleotides. Next, monomers joined together to create polymers such as proteins and nucleic acids. These polymers are then believed to have formed into protobionts. The last stage was the development of the process of heredity. Supporters of this

29

theory believe that RNA was the first genetic material. Another theory postulates that hereditary systems came about before the origination of nucleic acids. Another theory is that life, or the precursors for it, were transported to Earth from a meteorite or other object from space. There is no real evidence to support this theory.

A number of scientists have made significant contributions to the theory of evolution:

Cuvier (1744-1829): Cuvier was a French naturalist who used the fossil record (paleontology) to compare the anatomies of extinct species and existing species to make conclusions about extinction. He believed in the catastrophism theory more strongly than the theory of evolution.

Lamarck (1769-1832): Lamarck was a French naturalist who believed in the idea of evolution and thought it was a natural occurrence influenced by the environment. He studied medicine and botany. Lamarck put forth a theory of evolution by inheritance of acquired characteristics. He theorized that organisms became more complex by moving up a ladder of progress.

Lyell (1797-1875): Lyell was a British geologist who believed in geographical uniformitarianism, which can be contrasted with catastrophism.

Charles Robert Darwin (1809-1882): Darwin was an English naturalist known for his belief that evolution occurred by natural selection. He believed that species descend from common ancestors.

Alfred Russell Wallace (1823-1913): He was a British naturalist who independently developed a theory of evolution by natural selection. He believed in the transmutation of species (that one species develops into another).

ORGANISM CLASSIFICATION

The most widely accepted system for taxonomy is the three-domain classification system; sometimes called the six-kingdom classification system. The three domains are Archaea, Bacteria, and Eukarya. Both Archaea and Bacteria are made of prokaryotic cells, while Eukarya are made of eukaryotic cells. The domains of Bacteria and Archaea each have a single kingdom Eubacteria and Archaebacteria, respectively. The domain Eukarya has four kingdoms: Protista, Fungi, Plantae, and Animalia. Kingdom Protista includes about 250,000 species of unicellular protozoans and unicellular and multicellular algae. Kingdom Fungi includes about 100,000 species. Kingdom Plantae includes about 320,000 species. Kingdom Animalia is estimated to include more than 1,500,000 species. The groupings in this system, in descending order from broadest to most specific, are: domain, kingdom, phylum/division, class, order, family, genus, and species. A memory aid for this is: Dear King Philip Came Over For Good Soup. According to the three-domain classification system, humans are: domain Eukarya, kingdom Animalia, phylum Chordata, subphylum Vertebrata, class Mammalia, order Primate, family Hominidae, genus Homo, and species Sapiens.

An organism is a living thing. A unicellular organism is an organism that has only one cell. Examples of unicellular organisms are bacteria and paramecium. A multicellular organism is one that consists of many cells. Humans are a good example. By some estimates, the human body is made up of billions of cells. Others think the human body has more than 75 trillion cells. The term microbe refers to small organisms that are only visible through a microscope. Examples include viruses, bacteria, fungi, and protozoa. Microbes are also referred to as microorganisms. Bacteria can be rod shaped, round (cocci), or spiral (spirilla). These shapes are used to differentiate among types of bacteria. Bacteria can be identified by staining them. This particular type of stain is called a gram stain. If bacteria are gram-positive, they absorb the stain and become purple. If bacteria are gram-negative, they do not absorb the stain and become a pinkish color.

Organisms in the Protista kingdom are classified according to their methods of locomotion, their methods of reproduction, and how they get their nutrients. Protists can move by the use of a flagellum, cilia, or pseudopod. Flagellates have flagellum, which are long tails or whip-like structures that are rotated to help the protist move. Ciliates use cilia, which are smaller hair-like structures on the exterior of a cell that wiggle to help move the surrounding matter. Amoeboids use pseudopodia to move. Bacteria reproduce either sexually or asexually. Binary fission is a form of asexual reproduction whereby bacteria divide in half to produce two new organisms that are clones of the parent. In sexual reproduction, genetic material is exchanged. When kingdom members are categorized according to how they obtain nutrients, the three types of protists are photosynthetic, consumers, and saprophytes. Photosynthetic protists convert sunlight into energy. Organisms that use photosynthesis are considered producers. Consumers, also known as heterotrophs, eat or consume other organisms. Saprophytes consume dead or decaying substances.

KINGDOMS FUNGI AND PLANTAE

Mycology is the study of fungi. The Fungi kingdom includes about 100,000 species. They are further delineated as mushrooms, yeasts, molds, rusts, mildews, stinkhorns, puffballs, and truffles. Fungi are characterized by cell walls that have chitin, a long chain polymer carbohydrate. Fungi are different from species in the Plant kingdom, which have cell walls consisting of cellulose. Fungi are thought to have evolved from a single ancestor. Although they are often thought of as a type of plant, they are more similar to animals than plants. Fungi are typically small and numerous, and have a diverse morphology among species. They can have bright red cups and be orange jellylike masses, and their shapes can resemble golf balls, bird nests with eggs, starfish, parasols, and male genitalia. Some members of the stinkhorn family emit odors similar to dog scat to attract flies that help transport spores that are involved in reproduction. Fungi of this family are also consumed by humans.

Chlorophyta are green algae. Bryophyta are nonvascular mosses and liverworts. They have root-like parts called rhizoids. Since they do not have the vascular structures to transport water, they live in moist environments. Lycophyta are club mosses. They are vascular plants. They use spores and need water to reproduce. Equisetopsida (sphenophyta) are horsetails. Like lycophyta, they need water to reproduce with spores. They have rhizoids and needle-like leaves. The pteridophytes (filicopsida) are ferns. They have stems (rhizomes). Spermatopsida are the seed plants. Gymnosperms are a conifer, which means they have cones with seeds that are used in reproduction. Plants with seeds require less water. Cycadophyta are cone-bearing and look like palms. Gnetophyta are plants that live in the desert. Coniferophyta are pine trees, and have both cones and needles. Ginkgophyta are ginkgos. Anthophyta is the division with the largest number of plant species, and includes flowering plants with true seeds.

Only plants in the division bryophyta (mosses and liverworts) are nonvascular, which means they do not have xylem to transport water. All of the plants in the remaining divisions are vascular, meaning they have true roots, stems, leaves, and xylem. Pteridophytes are plants that use spores and not seeds to reproduce. They include the following divisions: Psilophyta (whisk fern), Lycophyta (club mosses), Sphenophyta (horsetails), and Pterophyta (ferns). Spermatophytes are plants that use seeds to reproduce. Included in this category are gymnosperms, which are flowerless plants that use naked seeds, and angiosperms, which are flowering plants that contain seeds in or on a fruit. Gymnosperms include the following divisions: cycadophyta (cycads), ginkgophyta (maidenhair tree), gnetophyta (ephedra and welwitschia), and coniferophyta (which includes pinophyta conifers). Angiosperms comprise the division anthophyta (flowering plants).

Plants are autotrophs, which means they make their own food. In a sense, they are self-sufficient. Three major processes used by plants are photosynthesis, transpiration, and respiration. Photosynthesis involves using sunlight to make food for plants. Transpiration evaporates water out of plants. Respiration is the utilization of food that was produced during photosynthesis.

Two major systems in plants are the shoot and the root system. The shoot system includes leaves, buds, and stems. It also includes the flowers and fruits in flowering plants. The shoot system is located above the ground. The root system is the component of the plant that is underground, and includes roots, tubers, and rhizomes. Meristems form plant cells by mitosis. Cells then differentiate into cell types to form the three types of plant tissues, which are dermal, ground, and vascular. Dermal refers to tissues that form the covering or outer layer of a plant. Ground tissues consist of parenchyma, collenchyma, and/or sclerenchyma cells.

There are at least 230,000 species of flowering plants. They represent about 90 percent of all plants. Angiosperms have a sexual reproduction phase that includes flowering. When growing plants, one may think they develop in the following order: seeds, growth, flowers, and fruit. The reproductive cycle has the following order: flowers, fruit, and seeds. In other words, seeds are the products of successful reproduction. The colors and scents of flowers serve to attract pollinators. Flowers and other plants can also be pollinated by wind. When a pollen grain meets the ovule and is successfully fertilized, the ovule develops into a seed. A seed consists of three parts: the embryo, the endosperm, and a seed coat. The embryo is a small plant that has started to develop, but this development is paused. Germination is when the embryo starts to grow again. The endosperm consists of proteins, carbohydrates, or fats. It typically serves as a food source for the embryo. The seed coat provides protection from disease, insects, and water.

KINGDOM ANIMALIA

The animal kingdom is comprised of more than one million species in about 30 phyla. There about 800,000 species of insects alone, representing half of all animal species. The characteristics that distinguish members of the animal kingdom from members of other kingdoms are that they are multicellular, are heterotrophic, reproduce sexually (there are some exceptions), have cells that do not contain cell walls or photosynthetic pigments, can move at some stage of life, and can rapidly respond to the environment as a result of specialized tissues like nerve and muscle. Heterotrophic refers to the method of getting energy by eating food that has energy releasing substances. Plants, on the other hand, are autotrophs, which mean they make their own energy. During reproduction, animals have a diploid embryo in the blastula stage. This structure is unique to animals. The blastula resembles a fluid-filled ball.

The animal kingdom includes about one million species. Metazoans are multicellular animals. Food is ingested and enters a mesoderm-lined coelom (body cavity). Phylum porifera and coelenterate are exceptions. The taxonomy of animals involves grouping them into phyla according to body symmetry and plan, as well as the presence of or lack of segmentation. The more complex phyla that have a coelom and a digestive system are further classified as protostomes or deuterostomes according to blastula development. In protostomes, the blastula's blastopore (opening) forms a mouth. In deuterostomes, the blastopore forms an anus. Taxonomy schemes vary, but there are about 36 phyla of animals. The most notable phyla include chordata, mollusca, porifera, cnidaria, platyhelminthes, nematoda, annelida, arthropoda, and echinodermata, which account for about 96 percent of all animal species.

The following four animal phyla lack a coelom or have a pseudocoelom.

Porifera: These are sponges. They lack a coelom and get food as water flows through them. They are usually found in marine and sometimes in freshwater environments. They are perforated and diploblastic, meaning there are two layers of cells.

Cnidaria: Members of this phylum are hydrozoa, jellyfish, and obelia. They have radial symmetry, sac-like bodies, and a polyp or medusa (jellyfish) body plan. They are diploblastic, possessing both an ectoderm and an endoderm. Food can get in through a cavity, but members of this phylum do not have an anus.

Platyhelminthes: These are also known as flatworms. Classes include turbellaria (planarian) and trematoda (which include lung, liver, and blood fluke parasites). They have organs and bilateral symmetry. They have three layers of tissue: an ectoderm, a mesoderm, and an endoderm.

Nematoda: These are roundworms. Hookworms and many other parasites are members of this phylum. They have a pseudocoelom, which means the coelom is not completely enclosed within the mesoderm. They also have a digestive tract that runs directly from the mouth to the anus. They are nonsegmented.

Members of the protostomic phyla have mouths that are formed from blastopores.

Mollusca: Classes include bivalvia (organisms with two shells, such as clams, mussels, and oysters), gastropoda (snails and slugs), cephalopoda (octopus, squid, and chambered nautilus), scaphopoda, amphineura (chitons), and monoplacophora.

Annelida: This phylum includes the classes oligochaeta (earthworms), polychaeta (clam worms), and hirudinea (leeches). They have true coeloms enclosed within the mesoderm. They are segmented, have repeating units, and have a nerve trunk.

Arthropoda: This phylum is diverse and populous. Members can be found in all types of environments. They have external skeletons, jointed appendages, bilateral symmetry, and nerve cords. They also have open circulatory systems and sense organs. Subphyla include crustacea (lobster, barnacles, pill bugs, and daphnia), hexapoda (all insects, which have three body segments, six legs, and usual wings), myriapoda (centipedes and millipedes), and chelicerata (the horseshoe crab and arachnids). The subphylum crustacea includes shrimps, crabs, and even pill bugs, which have gills. Bees, ants, and wasps belong to the order hymenoptera. Like several other insect orders, they undergo complete metamorphosis.

Members of the deuterostomic phyla have anuses that are formed from blastopores.

Echinodermata: Members of this phylum have radial symmetry, are marine organisms, and have a water vascular system. Classes include echinoidea (sea urchins and sand dollars), crinoidea (sea lilies), asteroidea (starfish), ophiuroidea (brittle stars), and holothuroidea (sea cucumbers).

Chordata: This phylum includes humans and all other vertebrates, as well as a few invertebrates (urochordata and cephalochordata). Members of this phylum include agnatha (lampreys and hagfish), gnathostomata, chondrichthyes (cartilaginous fish-like sharks, skates, and rays), osteichthyes (bony fishes, including ray-finned fish that humans eat), amphibians (frogs, salamanders, and newts), reptiles (lizards, snakes, crocodiles, and dinosaurs), birds, and mammals.

ANATOMY

Extrinsic refers to homeostatic systems that are controlled from outside the body. In higher animals, the nervous system and endocrine system help regulate body functions by responding to stimuli. Hormones in animals regulate many processes, including growth, metabolism, reproduction, and fluid balance. The names of hormones tend to end in "-one." Endocrine hormones are proteins or steroids. Steroid hormones (anabolic steroids) help control the manufacture of protein in muscles and bones.

Invertebrates do not have a backbone, whereas vertebrates do. The great majority of animal species (an estimated 98 percent) are invertebrates, including worms, jellyfish, mollusks, slugs, insects, and spiders. They comprise 30 phyla in all. Vertebrates belong to the phylum chordata. The vertebrate body has two cavities. The thoracic cavity holds the heart and lungs and the abdominal cavity holds the digestive organs. Animals with exoskeletons have skeletons on the outside. Examples are crabs and turtles. Animals with endoskeletons have skeletons on the inside. Examples are humans, tigers, birds, and reptiles.

The 11 major organ systems are: skeletal, muscular, nervous, digestive, respiratory, circulatory, skin, excretory, immune, endocrine, and reproductive.

Skeletal: This consists of the bones and joints. The skeletal system provides support for the body through its rigid structure, provides protection for internal organs, and works to make organisms motile. Growth hormone affects the rate of reproduction and the size of body cells, and also helps amino acids move through membranes.

Muscular: This includes the muscles. The muscular system allows the body to move and respond to its environment.

Nervous: This includes the brain, spinal cord, and nerves. The nervous system is a signaling system for intrabody communications among systems, responses to stimuli, and interaction within an environment. Signals are electrochemical. Conscious thoughts, memories, and sense interpretation occur in the nervous system. It also controls involuntary muscles and functions, such as breathing and the beating of the heart.

Digestive: This includes the mouth, pharynx, esophagus, stomach, intestines, rectum, anal canal, teeth, salivary glands, tongue, liver, gallbladder, pancreas, and appendix. The system helps change food into a form that the body can process and use for energy and nutrients. Food is eventually eliminated as solid waste. Digestive processes can be mechanical, such as chewing food and churning it in the stomach, and chemical, such as secreting hydrochloric acid to kill bacteria and converting protein to amino acids. The overall system converts large food particles into molecules so the body can use them. The small intestine transports the molecules to the circulatory system. The large intestine absorbs nutrients and prepares the unused portions of food for elimination.

Carbohydrates are the primary source of energy as they can be easily converted to glucose. Fats (oils or lipids) are usually not very water soluble, and vitamins A, D, E, and K are fat soluble. Fats are needed to help process these vitamins and can also store energy. Fats have the highest calorie value per gram (9,000 calories). Dietary fiber, or roughage, helps the excretory system. In humans, fiber can help regulate blood sugar levels, reduce heart disease, help food pass through the digestive system, and add bulk. Dietary minerals are chemical elements that are involved with biochemical functions in the body. Proteins consist of amino acids. Proteins are broken down in the body into amino acids that are used for protein biosynthesis or fuel. Vitamins are compounds that are not made by the body, but obtained through the diet. Water is necessary to prevent dehydration since water is lost through the excretory system and perspiration.

Respiratory: This includes the nose, pharynx, larynx, trachea, bronchi, and lungs. It is involved in gas exchange, which occurs in the alveoli. Fish have gills instead of lungs.

Circulatory: This includes the heart, blood, and blood vessels, such as veins, arteries, and capillaries. Blood transports oxygen and nutrients to cells and carbon dioxide to the lungs.

Skin (integumentary): This includes skin, hair, nails, sense receptors, sweat glands, and oil glands. The skin is a sense organ, provides an exterior barrier against disease, regulates body temperature through perspiration, manufactures chemicals and hormones, and provides a place for nerves from the nervous system and parts of the circulation system to travel through. Skin has three layers: epidermis, dermis, and subcutaneous. The epidermis is the thin, outermost, waterproof layer. Basal cells are located in the epidermis. The dermis contains the sweat glands, oil glands, and hair follicles. The subcutaneous layer has connective tissue, and also contains adipose (fat) tissue, nerves, arteries, and veins.

Excretory: This includes the kidneys, ureters, bladder, and urethra. The excretory system helps maintain the amount of fluids in the body. Wastes from the blood system and excess water are removed in urine. The system also helps remove solid waste.

Immune: This includes the lymphatic system, lymph nodes, lymph vessels, thymus, and spleen. Lymph fluid is moved throughout the body by lymph vessels that provide protection against disease. This system protects the body from external intrusions, such as microscopic organisms and foreign substances. It can also protect against some cancerous cells.

Endocrine: This includes the pituitary gland, pineal gland, hypothalamus, thyroid gland, parathyroids, thymus, adrenals, pancreas, ovaries, and testes. It controls systems and processes by secreting hormones into the blood system. Exocrine glands are those that secrete fluid into ducts. Endocrine glands secrete hormones directly into the blood stream without the use of ducts. Prostaglandin (tissue hormones) diffuses only a short distance from the tissue that created it, and influences nearby cells only. Adrenal glands are located above each kidney. The cortex secretes some sex hormones, as well as mineralocorticoids and glucocorticoids involved in immune suppression and stress response. The medulla secretes epinephrine and norepinephrine. Both elevate blood sugar, increase blood pressure, and accelerate heart rate. Epinephrine also stimulates heart muscle. The islets of Langerhans are clumped within the pancreas and secrete glucagon and insulin, thereby regulating blood sugar levels. The four parathyroid glands at the rear of the thyroid secrete parathyroid hormone.

Reproductive: In the male, this system includes the testes, vas deferens, urethra, prostate, penis, and scrotum. In the female, this system includes the ovaries, fallopian tubes (oviduct and uterine tubes), cervix, uterus, vagina, vulva, and mammary glands. Sexual reproduction helps provide genetic diversity as gametes from each parent contribute half the DNA to the zygote offspring. The system provides a method of transporting the male gametes to the female. It also allows for the growth and development of the embryo. Hormones involved are testosterone, interstitial cell stimulating hormone (ICSH), luteinizing hormone (LH), follicle stimulating hormone (FSH), and estrogen. Estrogens secreted from the ovaries include estradiol, estrone, and estriol. They encourage growth, among other things. Progesterone helps prepare the endometrium for pregnancy.

Based on whether or not and when an organism uses meiosis or mitosis, the three possible cycles of reproduction are haplontic, diplontic, and haplodiplontic. Fungi, green algae, and protozoa are haplontic. Animals and some brown algae and fungi are diplontic. Plants and some fungi are haplodiplontic. Diplontic organisms, like multicelled animals, have a dominant diploid life cycle. The haploid generation is simply the egg and sperm. Monoecious species are bisexual (hermaphroditic). In this case, the individual has both male and female organs: sperm-bearing testicles and egg-bearing ovaries. Hermaphroditic species can self-fertilize. Some worms are hermaphroditic. Cross fertilization is when individuals exchange genetic information. Most animal species are dioecious, meaning individuals are distinctly male or female.

BIOLOGICAL RELATIONSHIPS

As heterotrophs, animals can be further classified as carnivores, herbivores, omnivores, and parasites. Predation refers to a predator that feeds on another organism, which results in its death. Detritivory refers to heterotrophs that consume organic dead matter. Carnivores are animals that are meat eaters. Herbivores are plant eaters, and omnivores eat both meat and plants. A parasite's food source is its host. A parasite lives off of a host, which does not benefit from the interaction. Nutrients can be classified as carbohydrates, fats, fiber, minerals, proteins, vitamins, and water. Each supply a specific substance required for various species to survive, grow, and reproduce. A calorie is a measurement of heat energy. It can be used to represent both how much energy a food can provide and how much energy an organism needs to live.

Biochemical cycles are how chemical elements, required by living organisms, cycle between living and nonliving organisms. Elements that are frequently required are phosphorus, sulfur, oxygen, carbon, gaseous nitrogen, and water. Elements can go through gas cycles, sedimentary cycles, or both. Elements circulate through the air in a gas cycle and from land to water in a sedimentary one.

A food chain is a linking of organisms in a community that is based on how they use each other as food sources. Each link in the chain consumes the link above it and is consumed by the link below it. The exceptions are the organism at the top of the food chain and the organism at the bottom.

Biomagnification (bioamplification): This refers to an increase in concentration of a substance within a food chain. Examples are pesticides or mercury. Mercury is emitted from coal-fired power plants and gets into the water supply, where it is eaten by a fish. A larger fish eats smaller fish, and humans eat fish. The concentration of mercury in humans has now risen. Biomagnification is affected by the persistence of a chemical, whether it can be broken down and negated, food chain energetics, and whether organisms can reduce or negate the substance.

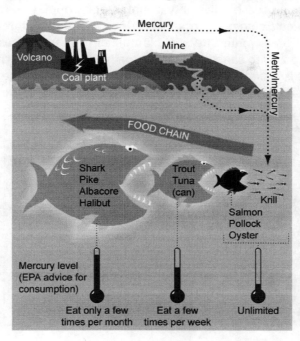

A food web consists of interconnected food chains in a community. The organisms can be linked to show the direction of energy flow. Energy flow in this sense is used to refer to the actual caloric flow through a system from trophic level to trophic level. Trophic level refers to a link in a food chain or a level of nutrition. The 10% rule is that from trophic level to level, about 90% of the energy is lost (in the form of heat, for example). The lowest trophic level consists of primary producers (usually plants), then primary consumers, then secondary consumers, and finally tertiary consumers (large carnivores). The final link is decomposers, which break down the consumers at the top. Food chains usually do not contain more than six links. These links may also be referred to as ecological pyramids.

Ecosystem stability is a concept that states that a stable ecosystem is perfectly efficient. Seasonal changes or expected climate fluctuations are balanced by homeostasis. It also states that interspecies interactions are part of the balance of the system. There are four principles of ecosystem stability: waste disposal and nutrient replenishment by recycling is complete, the system uses sunlight as an energy source, biodiversity remains, and populations are stable in that they do not over consume resources. Ecologic succession is the concept that states that there is an orderly progression of change within a community. An example of primary succession is that over hundreds of years bare rock decomposes to sand, which eventually leads to soil formation, which eventually leads to the growth of grasses and trees. Secondary succession occurs after a disturbance or major event that greatly affects a community, such as a wild fire or construction of a dam.

Population is a measure of how many individuals exist in a specific area. It can be used to measure the size of human, plant, or animal groups. Population growth depends on many factors. Factors that can limit the number of individuals in a population include lack of resources such as food and water, space, habitat destruction, competition, disease, and predators. Exponential growth refers to an unlimited rising growth rate. This kind of growth can be plotted on a chart in the shape of a J. Carrying capacity is the population size that can be sustained. The world's population is about 6.8 billion and growing. The human population has not yet reached its carrying capacity. Population dynamics refers to how a population changes over time and the factors that cause changes. An S-shaped curve shows that population growth has leveled off. Biotic potential refers to the maximum reproductive capacity of a population given ideal environmental conditions.

BIOLOGICAL CONCEPTS

Territoriality: This refers to members of a species protecting areas from other members of their species and from other species. Species members claim specific areas as their own.

Dominance: This refers to the species in a community that is the most populous.

Altruism: This is when a species or individual in a community exhibits behavior that benefit another individual at a cost to itself. In biology, altruism does not have to be a conscious sacrifice.

Threat display: This refers to behavior by an organism that is intended to intimidate or frighten away members of its own or another species.

Competitive exclusion: The principle of competitive exclusion (Gause's Law) states that if there are limited or insufficient resources and species are competing for them, these species will not be able to co-exist. The result is that one of the species will become extinct or be forced to undergo a behavioral or evolutionary change. In other words, complete competitors cannot coexist.

Community: A community is any number of species interacting within a given area. A **niche** is the role of a species within a community. **Species diversity** refers to the number of species within a community and their populations. A **biome** refers to an area in which species are associated because of climate. The six major biomes in North America are desert, tropical rain forest, grassland, coniferous forest, deciduous forest, and tundra.

Biotic: Biotic factors are the living factors, such as other organisms, that affect a community or population. Abiotic factors are nonliving factors that affect a community or population, such as facets of the environment.

Ecology: Ecology is the study of plants, animals, their environments, and how they interact.

Ecosystem: An ecosystem is a community of species and all of the environment factors that affect them.

Biomass: In ecology, biomass refers to the mass of one or all of the species (species biomass) in an ecosystem or area.

Predation, parasitism, commensalism, and mutualism are all types of species interactions that affect species populations. **Intraspecific relationships** are relationships among members of a species. **Interspecific relationships** are relationships between members of different species.

Predation: This is a relationship in which one individual feeds on another (the prey), causing the prey to die. **Mimicry** is an adaptation developed as a response to predation. It refers to an organism that has a similar appearance to another species, which is meant to fool the predator into thinking the organism is more dangerous than it really is. Two examples are the drone fly and the Io moth. The fly looks like a bee, but cannot sting. The Io moth has markings on its wings that make it look like an owl. The moth can startle predators and gain time to escape. Predators can also use mimicry to lure their prey.

Commensalism: This refers to interspecific relationships in which one of the organisms benefits. Mutualism, competition, and parasitism are all types of commensalism.

Mutualism: This is a relationship in which both organisms benefit from an interaction.

Competition: This is a relationship in which both organisms are harmed.

Parasitism: This is a relationship in which one organism benefits and the other is harmed.

Chemistry

ATOMS

Matter refers to substances that have mass and occupy space (or volume). The traditional definition of matter describes it as having three states: solid, liquid, and gas. These different states are caused by differences in the distances and angles between molecules or atoms, which result in differences in the energy that binds them. Solid structures are rigid or nearly rigid and have strong bonds. Molecules or atoms of liquids move around and have weak bonds, although they are not weak enough to readily break. Molecules or atoms of gases move almost independently of each other, are typically far apart, and do not form bonds. The current definition of matter describes it as having four states. The fourth is plasma, which is an ionized gas that has some electrons that are described as free because they are not bound to an atom or molecule.

All matter consists of atoms. Atoms consist of a nucleus and electrons. The nucleus consists of protons and neutrons. The properties of these are measurable; they have mass and an electrical charge. The nucleus is positively charged due to the presence of protons. Electrons are negatively charged and orbit the nucleus. The nucleus has considerably more mass than the surrounding electrons. Atoms can bond together to make molecules. Atoms that have an equal number of protons and electrons are electrically neutral. If the number of protons and electrons in an atom is not equal, the atom has a positive or negative charge and is an ion.

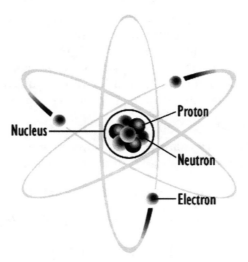

An element is matter with one particular type of atom. It can be identified by its atomic number, or the number of protons in its nucleus. There are approximately 117 elements currently known, 94 of which occur naturally on Earth. Elements from the periodic table include hydrogen, carbon, iron, helium, mercury, and oxygen. Atoms combine to form molecules. For example, two atoms of hydrogen (H) and one atom of oxygen (O) combine to form water (H_2O).

Compounds are substances containing two or more elements. Compounds are formed by chemical reactions and frequently have different properties than the original elements. Compounds are decomposed by a chemical reaction rather than separated by a physical one. Solutions are homogeneous mixtures composed of two or more substances that have become one. Mixtures contain two or more substances that are combined but have not reacted chemically with each other. Mixtures can be separated using physical methods, while compounds cannot.

A solution is a homogeneous mixture. A mixture is two or more different substances that are mixed together, but not combined chemically. Homogeneous mixtures are those that are uniform in their composition. Solutions consist of a solute (the substance that is dissolved) and a solvent (the substance that does the dissolving). An example is sugar water. The solvent is the water and the solute is the sugar. The intermolecular attraction between the solvent and the solute is called solvation. Hydration refers to solutions in which water is the solvent. Solutions are formed when the forces between the molecules of the solute and the solvent are as strong as the forces holding the solute together. An example is that salt (NaCl) dissolves in water to create a solution. The Na^+ and the Cl^- ions in salt interact with the molecules of water and vice versa to overcome the intramolecular forces of the solute.

Elements are represented in upper case letters. If there is no subscript, it indicates there is only one atom of the element. Otherwise, the subscript indicates the number of atoms. In molecular formulas, elements are organized according to the Hill system. Carbon is first, hydrogen comes next, and the remaining elements are listed in alphabetical order. If there is no carbon, all elements are listed alphabetically. There are a couple of exceptions to these rules. First, oxygen is usually listed last in oxides. Second, in ionic compounds the positive ion is listed first, followed by the negative ion. In CO_2, for example, C indicates 1 atom of carbon and O_2 indicates 2 atoms of oxygen. The compound is carbon dioxide. The formula for ammonia (an ionic compound) is NH_3, which is one atom of nitrogen and three of hydrogen. H_2O is two atoms of hydrogen and one of oxygen. Sugar is $C_6H_{12}O_6$, which is 6 atoms of carbon, 12 of hydrogen, and 6 of oxygen.

An **atom** is one of the most basic units of matter. An atom consists of a central nucleus surrounded by electrons. The **nucleus** of an atom consists of protons and neutrons. It is positively charged, dense, and heavier than the surrounding electrons. The plural form of nucleus is nuclei. **Neutrons** are the uncharged atomic particles contained within the nucleus. The number of neutrons in a nucleus can be represented as "N." Along with neutrons, **protons** make up the nucleus of an atom. The number of protons in the nucleus determines the atomic number of an element. Carbon atoms, for example, have six protons. The atomic number of carbon is 6. **Nucleon** refers collectively to neutrons and protons. **Electrons** are atomic particles that are negatively charged and orbit the nucleus of an atom. The number of protons minus the number of electrons indicates the charge of an atom.

> **Review Video: Structure of Atoms**
> Visit mometrix.com/academy and enter code: 905932

The **atomic number** of an element refers to the number of protons in the nucleus of an atom. It is a unique identifier. It can be represented as Z. Atoms with a neutral charge have an atomic number that is equal to the number of electrons. **Atomic mass** is also known as the mass number. The atomic mass is the total number of protons and neutrons in the nucleus of an atom. It is referred to as "A." The atomic mass (A) is equal to the number of protons (Z) plus the number of neutrons (N). This can be represented by the equation $A = Z + N$. The mass of electrons in an atom is basically insignificant because it is so small. **Atomic weight** may sometimes be referred to as "relative atomic mass," but should not be confused with atomic mass. Atomic weight is the ratio of the average mass per atom of a sample (which can include various isotopes of an element) to 1/12 of the mass of an atom of carbon-12.

Chemical properties are qualities of a substance which can't be determined by simply looking at the substance and must be determined through chemical reactions. Some chemical properties of elements include: atomic number, electron configuration, electrons per shell, electronegativity, atomic radius, and isotopes.

In contrast to chemical properties, **physical properties** can be observed or measured without chemical reactions. These include properties such as color, elasticity, mass, volume, and temperature. **Mass** is a measure of the amount of substance in an object. **Weight** is a measure of the gravitational pull of Earth on an object. **Volume** is a measure of the amount of space occupied. There are many formulas to determine volume, depending on the shape being analyzed. For example, the volume of a cube is the length of one side cubed (s^3) and the volume of a rectangular prism is length times width times height ($l \times w \times h$). The volume of an irregular shape can be determined by how much water it displaces. **Density** is a measure of the amount of mass per unit volume. The formula to find density is mass divided by volume ($D = m/V$). It is expressed in terms of mass per cubic unit, such as grams per cubic centimeter (g/cm^3). **Specific gravity** is a measure of the ratio of a substance's density compared to the density of water.

Both physical changes and chemical reactions are everyday occurrences. Physical changes do not result in different substances. For example, when water becomes ice it has undergone a physical change, but not a chemical change. It has changed its form, but not its composition. It is still H_2O. Chemical properties are concerned with the constituent particles that make up the physicality of a substance. Chemical properties are apparent when chemical changes occur. The chemical properties of a substance are influenced by its electron configuration, which is determined in part by the number of protons in the nucleus (the atomic number). Carbon, for example, has 6 protons and 6 electrons. It is an element's outermost valence electrons that mainly determine its chemical properties. Chemical reactions may release or consume energy.

PERIODIC TABLE

The periodic table groups elements with similar chemical properties together. The grouping of elements is based on atomic structure. It shows periodic trends of physical and chemical properties and identifies families of elements with similar properties. It is a common model for organizing and understanding elements. In the periodic table, each element has its own cell that includes varying amounts of information presented in symbol form about the properties of the element. Cells in the table are arranged in rows (periods) and columns (groups or families). At minimum, a cell includes the symbol for the element and its atomic number. The cell for hydrogen, for example, which appears first in the upper left corner, includes an "H" and a "1" above the letter. Elements are ordered by atomic number, left to right, top to bottom.

In the periodic table, the groups are the columns numbered 1 through 18 that group elements with similar outer electron shell configurations. Since the configuration of the outer electron shell is one of the primary factors affecting an element's chemical properties, elements within the same group have similar chemical properties. Previous naming conventions for groups have included the use of Roman numerals and upper-case letters. Currently, the periodic table groups are: Group 1, alkali metals; Group 2, alkaline earth metals; Groups 3-12, transition metals; Group 13, boron family; Group 14; carbon family; Group 15, pnictogens; Group 16, chalcogens; Group 17, halogens; Group 18, noble gases.

In the periodic table, there are seven periods (rows), and within each period there are blocks that group elements with the same outer electron subshell (more on this in the next section). The number of electrons in that outer shell determines which group an element belongs to within a given block. Each row's number (1, 2, 3, etc.) corresponds to the highest number electron shell that is in use. For example, row 2 uses only electron shells 1 and 2, while row 7 uses all shells from 1-7.

Atomic radii will decrease from left to right across a period (row) on the periodic table. In a group (column), there is an increase in the atomic radii of elements from top to bottom. Ionic radii will be smaller than the atomic radii for metals, but the opposite is true for non-metals. From left to right, electronegativity, or an atom's likeliness of taking another atom's electrons, increases. In a group, electronegativity decreases from top to bottom. Ionization energy or the amount of energy needed to get rid of an atom's outermost electron, increases across a period and decreases down a group. Electron affinity will become more negative across a period but will not change much within a group. The melting point decreases from top to bottom in the metal groups and increases from top to bottom in the non-metal groups.

Group →	1	2	3	4	5	6	7	8	9	10	11	12	13	14	15	16	17	18
Period 1	1 H																	2 He
2	3 Li	4 Be											5 B	6 C	7 N	8 O	9 F	10 Ne
3	11 Na	12 Mg											13 Al	14 Si	15 P	16 S	17 Cl	18 Ar
4	19 K	20 Ca	21 Sc	22 Ti	23 V	24 Cr	25 Mn	26 Fe	27 Co	28 Ni	29 Cu	30 Zn	31 Ga	32 Ge	33 As	34 Se	35 Br	36 Kr
5	37 Rb	38 Sr	39 Y	40 Zr	41 Nb	42 Mo	43 Tc	44 Ru	45 Rh	46 Pd	47 Ag	48 Cd	49 In	50 Sn	51 Sb	52 Te	53 I	54 Xe
6	55 Cs	56 Ba	*	72 Hf	73 Ta	74 W	75 Re	76 Os	77 Ir	78 Pt	79 Au	80 Hg	81 Tl	82 Pb	83 Bi	84 Po	85 At	86 Rn
7	87 Fr	88 Ra	**	104 Rf	105 Db	106 Sg	107 Bh	108 Hs	109 Mt	110 Ds	111 Rg	112 Cn	113 Nh	114 Fl	115 Mc	116 Lv	117 Ts	118 Og

*	57 La	58 Ce	59 Pr	60 Nd	61 Pm	62 Sm	63 Eu	64 Gd	65 Tb	66 Dy	67 Ho	68 Er	69 Tm	70 Yb	71 Lu
**	89 Ac	90 Th	91 Pa	92 U	93 Np	94 Pu	95 Am	96 Cm	97 Bk	98 Cf	99 Es	100 Fm	101 Md	102 No	103 Lr

ELECTRONS

Electrons are subatomic particles that orbit the nucleus at various levels commonly referred to as layers, shells, or clouds. The orbiting electron or electrons account for only a fraction of the atom's mass. They are much smaller than the nucleus, are negatively charged, and exhibit wave-like characteristics. Electrons are part of the lepton family of elementary particles. Electrons can occupy orbits that are varying distances away from the nucleus, and tend to occupy the lowest energy level they can. If an atom has all its electrons in the lowest available positions, it has a stable electron arrangement. The outermost electron shell of an atom in its uncombined state is known as the valence shell. The electrons there are called valence electrons, and it is their number that determines bonding behavior. Atoms tend to react in a manner that will allow them to fill or empty their valence shells.

There are seven electron shells. One is closest to the nucleus and seven is the farthest away. Electron shells can also be identified with the letters K, L, M, N, O, P, and Q. Traditionally, there were four subshells identified by the first letter of their descriptive name: s (sharp), p (principal), d (diffuse), and f (fundamental). The maximum number of electrons for each subshell is as follows: s is 2, p is 6, d is 10, and f is 14. Every shell has an s subshell, the second shell and those above also have a p subshell, the third shell and those above also have a d subshell, and so on. Each subshell contains atomic orbitals, which describes the wave-like characteristics of an electron or a pair of electrons expressed as two angles and the distance from the nucleus. Atomic orbital is a concept used to express the likelihood of an electron's position in accordance with the idea of wave-particle duality.

Electron configuration: This is a trend whereby electrons fill shells and subshells in an element in a particular order and with a particular number of electrons. The chemical properties of the elements reflect their electron configurations. Energy levels (shells) do not have to be completely filled before the next one begins to be filled. An example of electron configuration notation is $1s^22s^22p^5$, where the first number is the row (period), or shell. The letter refers to the subshell of the shell, and the number in superscript is the number of electrons in the subshell. A common shorthand method for electron configuration notation is to use a noble gas (in a bracket) to abbreviate the shells that elements have in common. For example, the electron configuration for neon is $1s^22s^22p^6$. The configuration for phosphorus is $1s^22s^22p^63s^23p^3$, which can be written as $[Ne]3s^23p^3$. Subshells are filled in the following manner: 1s, 2s, 2p, 3s, 3p, 4s, 3d, 4p, 5s, 4d, 5p, 6s, 4f, 5d, 6p, 7s, 5f, 6d, and 7p.

Most atoms are neutral since the positive charge of the protons in the nucleus is balanced by the negative charge of the surrounding electrons. Electrons are transferred between atoms when they come into contact with each other. This creates a molecule or atom in which the number of electrons does not equal the number of protons, which gives it a positive or negative charge. A negative ion is created when an atom gains electrons, while a positive ion is created when an atom loses electrons. An ionic bond is formed between ions with opposite charges. The resulting compound is neutral. Ionization refers to the process by which neutral particles are ionized into charged particles. Gases and plasmas can be partially or fully ionized through ionization.

Atoms interact by transferring or sharing the electrons furthest from the nucleus. Known as the outer or valence electrons, they are responsible for the chemical properties of an element. Bonds between atoms are created when electrons are paired up by being transferred or shared. If electrons are transferred from one atom to another, the bond is ionic. If electrons are shared, the bond is covalent. Atoms of the same element may bond together to form molecules or crystalline solids. When two or more different types of atoms bind together chemically, a compound is made. The physical properties of compounds reflect the nature of the interactions among their molecules. These interactions are determined by the structure of the molecule, including the atoms they consist of and the distances and angles between them.

ISOTOPES AND MOLECULES

The number of protons in an atom determines the element of that atom. For instance, all helium atoms have exactly two protons, and all oxygen atoms have exactly eight protons. If two atoms have the same number of protons, then they are the same element. However, the number of neutrons in two atoms can be different without the atoms being different elements. Isotope is the term used to distinguish between atoms that have the same number of protons but a different number of neutrons. The names of isotopes have the element name with the mass number. Recall that the mass number is the number of protons plus the number of neutrons. For example, carbon-

12 refers to an atom that has 6 protons, which makes it carbon, and 6 neutrons. In other words, 6 protons + 6 neutrons = 12. Carbon-13 has six protons and seven neutrons, and carbon-14 has six protons and eight neutrons. Isotopes can also be written with the mass number in superscript before the element symbol. For example, carbon-12 can be written as ^{12}C.

The important properties of water (H_2O) are high polarity, hydrogen bonding, cohesiveness, adhesiveness, high specific heat, high latent heat, and high heat of vaporization. It is essential to life as we know it, as water is one of the main if not the main constituent of many living things. Water is a liquid at room temperature. The high specific heat of water means it resists the breaking of its hydrogen bonds and resists heat and motion, which is why it has a relatively high boiling point and high vaporization point. It also resists temperature change. Water is peculiar in that its solid-state floats in its liquid state. Most substances are denser in their solid forms. Water is cohesive, which means it is attracted to itself. It is also adhesive, which means it readily attracts other molecules. If water tends to adhere to another substance, the substance is said to be hydrophilic. Because of its cohesive and adhesive properties, water makes a good solvent. Substances, particularly those with polar ions and molecules, readily dissolve in water.

> **Review Video: Properties of Water**
> Visit mometrix.com/academy and enter code: 279526

Electrons in an atom can orbit different levels around the nucleus. They can absorb or release energy, which can change the location of their orbit or even allow them to break free from the atom. The outermost layer is the valence layer, which contains the valence electrons. The valence layer tends to have or share eight electrons. Molecules are formed by a chemical bond between atoms, a bond that occurs at the valence level. Two basic types of bonds are covalent and ionic. A covalent bond is formed when atoms share electrons. An ionic bond is formed when an atom transfers an electron to another atom. A cation or positive ion is formed when an atom loses one or more electrons. An anion or negative ion is formed when an atom gains one or more electrons. A hydrogen bond is a weak bond between a hydrogen atom of one molecule and an electronegative atom (such as nitrogen, oxygen, or fluorine) of another molecule. The Van der Waals force is a weak force between molecules. This type of force is much weaker than actual chemical bonds between atoms.

REACTIONS

Chemical reactions measured in human time can take place quickly or slowly. They can take fractions of a second or billions of years. The rates of chemical reactions are determined by how frequently reacting atoms and molecules interact. Rates are also influenced by the temperature and various properties (such as shape) of the reacting materials. Catalysts accelerate chemical reactions, while inhibitors decrease reaction rates. Some types of reactions release energy in the form of heat and light. Some types of reactions involve the transfer of either electrons or hydrogen ions between reacting ions, molecules, or atoms. In other reactions, chemical bonds are broken down by heat or light to form reactive radicals with electrons that will readily form new bonds.

Processes such as the formation of ozone and greenhouse gases in the atmosphere and the burning and processing of fossil fuels are controlled by radical reactions.

Review Video: Chemical Reactions
Visit mometrix.com/academy and enter code: 579876

Chemical equations describe chemical reactions. The reactants are on the left side before the arrow and the products are on the right side after the arrow. The arrow indicates the reaction or change. The coefficient, or stoichiometric coefficient, is the number before the element, and indicates the ratio of reactants to products in terms of moles. The equation for the formation of water from hydrogen and oxygen, for example, is $2H_2(g) + O_2(g) \rightarrow 2H_2O(l)$. The 2 preceding hydrogen and water is the coefficient, which means there are 2 moles of hydrogen and 2 of water. There is 1 mole of oxygen, which does not have to be indicated with the number 1. In parentheses, g stands for gas, l stands for liquid, s stands for solid, and aq stands for aqueous solution (a substance dissolved in water). Charges are shown in superscript for individual ions, but not for ionic compounds. Polyatomic ions are separated by parentheses so the ion will not be confused with the number of ions.

An **unbalanced equation** is one that does not follow the **law of conservation of mass**, which states that matter can only be changed, not created or destroyed. If an equation is unbalanced, the numbers of atoms indicated by the stoichiometric coefficients on each side of the arrow will not be equal. Start by writing the formulas for each species in the reaction. Count the atoms on each side and determine if the number is equal. Coefficients must be whole numbers. Fractional amounts, such as half a molecule, are not possible. Equations can be balanced by adjusting the coefficients of each part of the equation to the smallest possible whole number coefficient. $H_2 + O_2 \rightarrow H_2O$ is an example of an unbalanced equation. The balanced equation is $2H_2 + O_2 \rightarrow 2H_2O$, which indicates that it takes two moles of hydrogen and one of oxygen to produce two moles of water.

One way to organize chemical reactions is to sort them into two categories: oxidation/reduction reactions (also called redox reactions) and metathesis reactions (which include acid/base reactions). Oxidation/reduction reactions can involve the transfer of one or more electrons, or they can occur as a result of the transfer of oxygen, hydrogen, or halogen atoms. The species that loses electrons is oxidized and is referred to as the reducing agent. The species that gains electrons is reduced and is referred to as the oxidizing agent. The element undergoing oxidation experiences an increase in its oxidation number, while the element undergoing reduction experiences a decrease in its oxidation number. Single replacement reactions are types of oxidation/reduction reactions. In a

46

single replacement reaction, electrons are transferred from one chemical species to another. The transfer of electrons results in changes in the nature and charge of the species.

Single substitution, displacement, or **replacement reactions** occur when one reactant is displaced by another to form the final product (A + BC → B + AC). Single substitution reactions can be cationic or anionic. When a piece of copper (Cu) is placed into a solution of silver nitrate ($AgNO_3$), the solution turns blue. The copper appears to be replaced with a silvery-white material. The equation is $2AgNO_3 + Cu \rightarrow Cu(NO_3)_2 + 2Ag$. When this reaction takes place, the copper dissolves and the silver in the silver nitrate solution precipitates (becomes a solid), thus resulting in copper nitrate and silver. Copper and silver have switched places in the nitrate.

In a **combination**, or **synthesis reaction**, two or more reactants combine to form a single product (A + B → C). These reactions are also called synthesis or addition reactions. An example is burning hydrogen in air to produce water. The equation is $2H_2(g) + O_2(g) \rightarrow 2H_2O(l)$. Another example is when water and sulfur trioxide react to form sulfuric acid. The equation is $H_2O + SO_3 \rightarrow H_2SO_4$.

Double displacement, **double replacement**, **substitution**, **metathesis**, or **ion exchange reactions** occur when ions or bonds are exchanged by two compounds to form different compounds (AC + BD → AD + BC). An example of this is that silver nitrate and sodium chloride form two different products (silver chloride and sodium nitrate) when they react. The formula for this reaction is $AgNO_3 + NaCl \rightarrow AgCl + NaNO_3$.

Double replacement reactions are metathesis reactions. In a double replacement reaction, the chemical reactants exchange ions but the oxidation state stays the same. One of the indicators of this is the formation of a solid precipitate. In acid/base reactions, an acid is a compound that can donate a proton, while a base is a compound that can accept a proton. In these types of reactions, the acid and base react to form a salt and water. When the proton is donated, the base becomes water and the remaining ions form a salt. One method of determining whether a reaction is an oxidation/reduction or a metathesis reaction is that the oxidation number of atoms does not change during a metathesis reaction.

A neutralization, acid-base, or **proton transfer reaction** occurs when one compound acquires H^+ from another. These types of reactions are also usually double displacement reactions. The acid has an H^+ that is transferred to the base and neutralized to form a salt.

In **decomposition (desynthesis, decombination**, or **deconstruction) reactions**, a reactant is broken down into two or more products (A → B + C). These reactions are also called analysis reactions. Thermal decomposition is caused by heat. Electrolytic decomposition is due to electricity. An example of this type of reaction is the decomposition of water into hydrogen and oxygen gas. The equation of the decomposition of water is $2H_2O \rightarrow 2H_2 + O_2$. Decomposition is considered a chemical reaction whereby a single compound breaks down into component parts or simpler compounds. When a compound or substance separates into these simpler substances, the byproducts are often substances that are different from the original. Decomposition can be viewed as the opposite of combination reactions. Most decomposition reactions are endothermic. Heat needs to be added for the chemical reaction to occur. Separation processes can be mechanical or chemical and usually involve re-organizing a mixture of substances without changing their chemical nature. The separated products may differ from the original mixture in terms of chemical or physical properties. Types of separation processes include filtration, crystallization, distillation, and chromatography. Basically, decomposition breaks down one compound into two or more compounds or substances that are different from the original; separation sorts the substances from the original mixture into like substances.

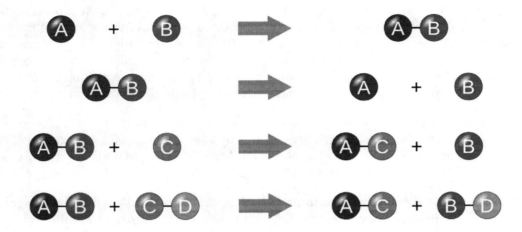

Endothermic reactions are chemical reactions that absorb heat and **exothermic reactions** are chemical reactions that release heat. Reactants are the substances that are consumed during a reaction, while products are the substances that are produced or formed. A balanced equation is one that uses reactants, products, and coefficients in such a way that the number of each type of atom (law of conservation of mass) and the total charge remains the same. The reactants are on the left side of the arrow and the products are on the right. The heat difference between endothermic and exothermic reactions is caused by bonds forming and breaking. If more energy is needed to break the reactant bonds than is released when they form, the reaction is endothermic. Heat is absorbed and the environmental temperature decreases. If more energy is released when product bonds form than is needed to break the reactant bonds, the reaction is exothermic. Heat is released and the environmental temperature increases.

The collision theory states that for a chemical reaction to occur, atoms or molecules have to collide with each other with a certain amount of energy. A certain amount of energy is required to breach the activation barrier. Heating a mixture will raise the energy levels of the molecules and the rate of reaction (the time it takes for a reaction to complete). Generally, the rate of reaction is doubled for every 10 degrees Celsius temperature increase. However, the increase needed to double a reaction rate increases as the temperature climbs. This is due to the increase in collision frequency that occurs as the temperature increases. Other factors that can affect the rate of reaction are surface area, concentration, pressure, and the presence of a catalyst.

The particles of an atom's nucleus (the protons and neutrons) are bound together by nuclear force, also known as residual strong force. Unlike chemical reactions, which involve electrons, nuclear reactions occur when two nuclei or nuclear particles collide. This results in the release or absorption of energy and products that are different from the initial particles. The energy released in a nuclear reaction can take various forms, including the release of kinetic energy of the product particles and the emission of very high energy photons known as gamma rays. Some energy may also remain in the nucleus. **Radioactivity** refers to the particles emitted from nuclei as a result of nuclear instability. There are many nuclear isotopes that are unstable and can spontaneously emit some kind of radiation. The most common types of radiation are alpha, beta, and gamma radiation, but there are several other varieties of radioactive decay.

INORGANIC AND ORGANIC

The terms inorganic and organic have become less useful over time as their definitions have changed. Historically, inorganic molecules were defined as those of a mineral nature that were not created by biological processes. Organic molecules were defined as those that were produced biologically by a "life process" or "vital force." It was then discovered that organic compounds could be synthesized without a life process. Currently, molecules containing carbon are considered organic. Carbon is largely responsible for creating biological diversity, and is more capable than all other elements of forming large, complex, and diverse molecules of an organic nature. Carbon often completes its valence shell by sharing electrons with other atoms in four covalent bonds, which is also known as tetravalence.

The main trait of inorganic compounds is that they lack carbon. Inorganic compounds include mineral salts, alloys, non-metallic compounds such as phosphate, and metal complexes. A metal complex has a central atom (or ion) bonded to surrounding ligands (molecules or anions). The ligands sacrifice the donor atoms (in the form of at least one pair of electrons) to the central atom. Many inorganic compounds are ionic, meaning they form ionic bonds rather than share electrons. They may have high melting points because of this. They may also be colorful, but this is not an absolute identifier of an inorganic compound. Salts, which are inorganic compounds, are an example of inorganic bonding of cations and anions. Some examples of salts are magnesium chloride ($MgCl_2$) and sodium oxide (Na_2O). Oxides, carbonates, sulfates, and halides are classes of inorganic compounds. They are typically poor conductors, are very water soluble, and crystallize easily. Minerals and silicates are also inorganic compounds.

Two of the main characteristics of organic compounds are that they include carbon and are formed by covalent bonds. Carbon can form long chains, double and triple bonds, and rings. While inorganic compounds tend to have high melting points, organic compounds tend to melt at temperatures below 300° C. They also tend to boil, sublimate, and decompose below this temperature. Unlike inorganic compounds, they are not very water soluble. Organic molecules are organized into functional groups based on their specific atoms, which helps determine how they will react chemically. A few groups are alkanes, nitro, alkenes, sulfides, amines, and carbolic acids. The hydroxyl group (-OH) consists of alcohols. These molecules are polar, which increases their solubility. By some estimates, there are more than 16 million organic compounds.

Nomenclature refers to the manner in which a compound is named. First, it must be determined whether the compound is ionic (formed through electron transfer between cations and anions) or molecular (formed through electron sharing between molecules). When dealing with an ionic compound, the name is determined using the standard naming conventions for ionic compounds. This involves indicating the positive element first (the charge must be defined when there is more than one option for the valency) followed by the negative element plus the appropriate suffix. The rules for naming a molecular compound are as follows: write elements in order of increasing group number and determine the prefix by determining the number of atoms. Exclude mono for the first atom. The name for CO_2, for example, is carbon dioxide. The end of oxygen is dropped and "ide" is added to make oxide, and the prefix "di" is used to indicate there are two atoms of oxygen.

ACIDS AND BASES

The potential of hydrogen (pH) is a measurement of the concentration of hydrogen ions in a substance in terms of the number of moles of H^+ per liter of solution. All substances fall between 0 and 14 on the pH scale. A lower pH indicates a higher H^+ concentration, while a higher pH indicates a lower H^+ concentration. Pure water has a neutral pH, which is 7. Anything with a pH lower than water (0-7) is considered acidic. Anything with a pH higher than water (7-14) is a base. Drain cleaner, soap, baking soda, ammonia, egg whites, and sea water are common bases. Urine, stomach acid, citric acid, vinegar, hydrochloric acid, and battery acid are acids. A pH indicator is a substance that acts as a detector of hydrogen or hydronium ions. It is halochromic, meaning it changes color to indicate that hydrogen or hydronium ions have been detected.

> **Review Video: Overview of pH Levels**
> Visit mometrix.com/academy and enter code: 187395

When they are dissolved in aqueous solutions, some properties of acids are that they conduct electricity, change blue litmus paper to red, have a sour taste, react with bases to neutralize them, and react with active metals to free hydrogen. A weak acid is one that does not donate all of its protons or disassociate completely. Strong acids include hydrochloric, hydriodic, hydrobromic, perchloric, nitric, and sulfuric. They ionize completely. Superacids are those that are stronger than 100 percent sulfuric acid. They include fluoroantimonic, magic, and perchloric acids. Acids can be used in pickling, a process used to remove rust and corrosion from metals. They are also used as catalysts in the processing of minerals and the production of salts and fertilizers. Phosphoric acid (H_3PO_4) is added to sodas and other acids are added to foods as preservatives or to add taste.

When they are dissolved in aqueous solutions, some properties of bases are that they conduct electricity, change red litmus paper to blue, feel slippery, and react with acids to neutralize their properties. A weak base is one that does not completely ionize in an aqueous solution, and usually has a low pH. Strong bases can free protons in very weak acids. Examples of strong bases are hydroxide compounds such as potassium, barium, and lithium hydroxides. Most are in the first and second groups of the periodic table. A superbase is extremely strong compared to sodium hydroxide and cannot be kept in an aqueous solution. Superbases are organized into organic, organometallic, and inorganic classes. Bases are used as insoluble catalysts in heterogeneous reactions and as catalysts in hydrogenation.

Some properties of salts are that they are formed from acid base reactions, are ionic compounds consisting of metallic and nonmetallic ions, dissociate in water, and are comprised of tightly bonded ions. Some common salts are sodium chloride (NaCl), sodium bisulfate ($NaHSO_4$), potassium dichromate ($K_2Cr_2O_7$), and calcium chloride ($CaCl_2$). Calcium chloride is used as a drying agent, and may be used to absorb moisture when freezing mixtures. Potassium nitrate (KNO_3) is used to make fertilizer and in the manufacturing of explosives. Sodium nitrate ($NaNO_3$) is also used in the making of fertilizer. Baking soda [sodium bicarbonate ($NaHCO_3$)] is a salt, as are Epsom salts [magnesium sulfate ($MgSO_4$)]. Salt and water can react to form a base and an acid. This is called a hydrolysis reaction.

A buffer is a solution whose pH remains relatively constant when a small amount of an acid or a base is added. It is usually made of a weak acid and its conjugate base (proton receiver) or one of its soluble salts. It can also be made of a weak base and its conjugate acid (proton donator) or one of its salts. A constant pH is necessary in living cells because some living things can only live within a certain pH range. If that pH changes, the cells could die. Blood is an example of a buffer. A pKa is a measure of acid dissociation or the acid dissociation constant. Buffer solutions can help keep enzymes at the correct pH. They are also used in the fermentation process, in dyeing fabrics, and in the calibration of pH meters. An example of a buffer would be a solution of acetic acid (HC_2H_3O) and sodium acetate NaC_2H_3O.

GENERAL CONCEPTS

Lewis formulas: These show the bonding or nonbonding tendency of specific pairs of valence electrons. Lewis dot diagrams use dots to represent valence electrons. Dots are paired around an atom. When an atom forms a covalent bond with another atom, the elements share the dots as they would electrons. Double and triple bonds are indicated with additional adjacent dots. Methane (CH_4), for instance, would be shown as a C with 2 dots above, below, and to the right and left and an H next to each set of dots. In structural formulas, the dots are single lines.

Kekulé diagrams: Like Lewis dot diagrams, these are two-dimensional representations of chemical compounds. Covalent bonds are shown as lines between elements. Double and triple bonds are shown as two or three lines and unbonded valence electrons are shown as dots.

Molar mass: This refers to the mass of one mole of a substance (element or compound), usually measured in grams per mole (g/mol). This differs from molecular mass in that molecular mass is the mass of one molecule of a substance relative to the atomic mass unit (amu).

Atomic mass unit (amu) is the smallest unit of mass, and is equal to 1/12 of the mass of the carbon isotope carbon-12. A mole (mol) is a measurement of molecular weight that is equal to the molecule's amu in grams. For example, carbon has an amu of 12, so a mole of carbon weighs 12 grams. One mole is equal to about 6.0221415×10^{23} elementary entities, which are usually atoms or molecules. This amount is also known as the Avogadro constant or Avogadro's number (N_A). Another way to say this is that one mole of a substance is the same as one Avogadro's number of that substance. Two moles of chlorine, for example, is $2 \times 6.0221415 \times 10^{23}$ or 1.2044283×10^{24} chlorine atoms. The charge on one mole of electrons is referred to as a Faraday.

The kinetic theory of gases assumes that gas molecules are small compared to the distances between them and that they are in constant random motion. The attractive and repulsive forces between gas molecules are negligible. Their kinetic energy does not change with time as long as the temperature remains the same. The higher the temperature is, the greater the motion will be. As the temperature of a gas increases, so does the kinetic energy of the molecules. In other words, gas will occupy a greater volume as the temperature is increased and a lesser volume as the temperature is decreased. In addition, the same amount of gas will occupy a greater volume as the temperature increases, but pressure remains constant. At any given temperature, gas molecules have the same average kinetic energy. The ideal gas law is derived from the kinetic theory of gases.

Charles's law: This law states that gases expand when they are heated. It is also known as the law of volumes.

Boyle's law: This law states that gases contract when pressure is applied to them. It also states that if temperature remains constant, the relationship between absolute pressure and volume is inversely proportional. When one increases, the other decreases. Considered a specialized case of the ideal gas law, Boyle's law is sometimes known as the Boyle-Mariotte law.

The **ideal gas law** is used to explain the properties of a gas under ideal pressure, volume, and temperature conditions. It is best suited for describing monatomic gases (gases in which atoms are not bound together) and gases at high temperatures and low pressures. It is not well-suited for instances in which a gas or its components are close to their condensation point. All collisions are perfectly elastic and there are no intermolecular attractive forces at work. The ideal gas law is a way to explain and measure the macroscopic properties of matter. It can be derived from the kinetic theory of gases, which deals with the microscopic properties of matter. The equation for the ideal gas law is $PV = nRT$, where P is absolute pressure, V is absolute volume, T is absolute temperature, R refers to the universal gas constant, which is 8.3145 J/(mol K), and n is the number of moles of the ideal gas.

Physics

THERMODYNAMICS

Thermodynamics is a branch of physics that studies the conversion of energy into work and heat. It is especially concerned with variables such as temperature, volume, and pressure. Thermodynamic equilibrium refers to objects that have the same temperature because heat is transferred between them to reach equilibrium. Thermodynamics takes places within three different types of systems: open, isolated, and closed systems. Open systems are capable of interacting with a surrounding environment and can exchange heat, work (energy), and matter outside their system boundaries. A closed system can exchange heat and work, but not matter. An isolated system cannot exchange heat, work, or matter with its surroundings. Its total energy and mass stay the same. In physics, surrounding environment refers to everything outside a thermodynamic system. The terms "surroundings" and "environment" are also used. The term "boundary" refers to the division between the system and its surroundings.

The laws of thermodynamics are generalized principles dealing with energy and heat.

- The zeroth law of thermodynamics states that two objects in thermodynamic equilibrium with a third object are also in equilibrium with each other. Being in thermodynamic equilibrium basically means that different objects are at the same temperature.
- The first law deals with conservation of energy. It states that neither mass nor energy can be destroyed, only converted from one form to another.
- The second law states that the entropy (the amount of energy in a system that is no longer available for work or the amount of disorder in a system) of an isolated system can only increase. The second law also states that heat is not transferred from a lower-temperature system to a higher-temperature one unless additional work is done.
- The third law of thermodynamics states that as temperature approaches absolute zero, entropy approaches a constant minimum. It also states that a system cannot be cooled to absolute zero.

> **Review Video: Laws of Thermodynamics**
> Visit mometrix.com/academy and enter code: 253607

Thermal contact refers to energy transferred to a body by a means other than work. A system in thermal contact with another can exchange energy with it through the process of heat transfer. Thermal contact does not necessarily involve direct physical contact. Heat is energy that can be transferred from one body or system to another without work being done. Everything tends to become less organized and less useful over time (entropy). In all energy transfers, therefore, the overall result is that the heat is spread out so that objects are in thermodynamic equilibrium and the heat can no longer be transferred without additional work.

The laws of thermodynamics state that energy can be exchanged between physical systems as heat or work, and that systems are affected by their surroundings. It can be said that the total amount of energy in the universe is constant. The first law is mainly concerned with the conservation of energy and related concepts, which include the statement that energy can only be transferred or converted, not created or destroyed. The formula used to represent the first law is $\Delta U = Q - W$, where ΔU is the change in total internal energy of a system, Q is the heat added to the system, and W is the work done by the system. Energy can be transferred by conduction, convection, radiation, mass transfer, and other processes such as collisions in chemical and nuclear reactions. As transfers

53

occur, the matter involved becomes less ordered and less useful. This tendency towards disorder is also referred to as entropy.

The second law of thermodynamics explains how energy can be used. In particular, it states that heat will not transfer spontaneously from a cold object to a hot object. Another way to say this is that heat transfers occur from higher temperatures to lower temperatures. Also covered under this law is the concept that systems not under the influence of external forces tend to become more disordered over time. This type of disorder can be expressed in terms of entropy. Another principle covered under this law is that it is impossible to make a heat engine that can extract heat and convert it all to useful work. A thermal bottleneck occurs in machines that convert energy to heat and then use it to do work. These types of machines are less efficient than ones that are solely mechanical.

Conduction is a form of heat transfer that occurs at the molecular level. It is the result of molecular agitation that occurs within an object, body, or material while the material stays motionless. An example of this is when a frying pan is placed on a hot burner. At first, the handle is not hot. As the pan becomes hotter due to conduction, the handle eventually gets hot too. In this example, energy is being transferred down the handle toward the colder end because the higher speed particles collide with and transfer energy to the slower ones. When this happens, the original material becomes cooler and the second material becomes hotter until equilibrium is reached. Thermal conduction can also occur between two substances such as a cup of hot coffee and the colder surface it is placed on. Heat is transferred, but matter is not.

Convection refers to heat transfer that occurs through the movement or circulation of fluids (liquids or gases). Some of the fluid becomes or is hotter than the surrounding fluid and is less dense. Heat is transferred away from the source of the heat to a cooler, denser area. Examples of convection are boiling water and the movement of warm and cold air currents in the atmosphere and the ocean. Forced convection occurs in convection ovens, where a fan helps circulate hot air.

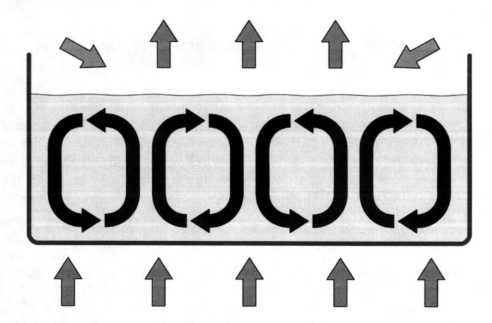

54

Radiation is heat transfer that occurs through the emission of electromagnetic waves, which carry energy away from the emitting object. All objects with temperatures above absolute zero radiate heat.

Temperature is a measurement of an object's stored heat energy. More specifically, temperature is the average kinetic energy of an object's particles. When the temperature of an object increases and its atoms move faster, kinetic energy also increases. Temperature is not energy since it changes and is not conserved. Thermometers are used to measure temperature.

There are three main scales for measuring temperature. Celsius uses the base reference points of water freezing at 0 degrees and boiling at 100 degrees. Fahrenheit uses the base reference points of water freezing at 32 degrees and boiling at 212 degrees. Celsius and Fahrenheit are both relative temperature scales since they use water as their reference point. The Kelvin temperature scale is an absolute temperature scale. Its zero mark corresponds to absolute zero. Water's freezing and boiling points are 273.15 Kelvin and 373.15 Kelvin, respectively. Where Celsius and Fahrenheit are measured is degrees, Kelvin does not use degree terminology.

- Converting Celsius to Fahrenheit: $°F = \frac{9}{5}°C + 32$
- Converting Fahrenheit to Celsius: $°C = \frac{5}{9}(°F - 32)$
- Converting Celsius to Kelvin: $K = °C + 273.15$
- Converting Kelvin to Celsius: $°C = K - 273.15$

Heat capacity, also known as thermal mass, refers to the amount of heat energy required to raise the temperature of an object and is measured in Joules per Kelvin or Joules per degree Celsius. The equation for relating heat energy to heat capacity is $Q = C\Delta T$, where Q is the heat energy transferred, C is the heat capacity of the body, and ΔT is the change in the object's temperature. Specific heat capacity, also known as specific heat, is the heat capacity per unit mass. Each element and compound has its own specific heat. For example, it takes different amounts of heat energy to raise the temperature of the same amounts of magnesium and lead by one degree. The equation for relating heat energy to specific heat capacity is $Q = mc\Delta T$, where m represents the mass of the object, and c represents its specific heat capacity.

Review Video: Specific Heat Capacity
Visit mometrix.com/academy and enter code: 736791

Some discussions of energy consider only two types of energy: kinetic energy (the energy of motion) and potential energy (which depends on relative position or orientation). There are, however, other types of energy. Electromagnetic waves, for example, are a type of energy contained by a field. Another type of potential energy is electrical energy, which is the energy it takes to pull apart positive and negative electrical charges. Chemical energy refers to the manner in which atoms form into molecules, and this energy can be released or absorbed when molecules regroup. Solar energy comes in the form of visible light and non-visible light, such as infrared and ultraviolet rays. Sound energy refers to the energy in sound waves.

Energy is constantly changing forms and being transferred back and forth. An example of a heat to mechanical energy transformation is a steam engine, such as the type used on a steam locomotive. A heat source such as coal is used to boil water. The steam produced turns a shaft, which eventually turns the wheels. A pendulum swinging is an example of both a kinetic to potential and a potential to kinetic energy transformation. When a pendulum is moved from its center point (the point at which it is closest to the ground) to the highest point before it returns, it is an example of a kinetic

55

to potential transformation. When it swings from its highest point toward the center, it is considered a potential to kinetic transformation. The sum of the potential and kinetic energy is known as the total mechanical energy. Stretching a rubber band gives it potential energy. That potential energy becomes kinetic energy when the rubber band is released.

MOTION AND FORCE

Mechanics is the study of matter and motion, and the topics related to matter and motion, such as force, energy, and work. Discussions of mechanics will often include the concepts of vectors and scalars. Vectors are quantities with both magnitude and direction, while scalars have only magnitude. Scalar quantities include length, area, volume, mass, density, energy, work, and power. Vector quantities include displacement, direction, velocity, acceleration, momentum, and force.

Motion is a change in the location of an object and is the result of an unbalanced net force acting on the object. Understanding motion requires an understanding of three basic quantities: displacement, velocity, and acceleration.

DISPLACEMENT

When something moves from one place to another, it has undergone *displacement*. Displacement along a straight line is a very simple example of a vector quantity. If an object travels from position x = -5 cm to x = 5 cm, it has undergone a displacement of 10 cm. If it traverses the same path in the opposite direction, its displacement is -10 cm. A vector that spans the object's displacement in the direction of travel is known as a displacement vector.

VELOCITY

There are two types of velocity to consider: *average velocity* and *instantaneous velocity*. Unless an object has a constant velocity or we are explicitly given an equation for the velocity, finding the instantaneous velocity of an object requires the use of calculus. If we want to calculate the *average velocity* of an object, we need to know two things: the displacement, or the distance it has covered, and the time it took to cover this distance. The formula for average velocity is simply the distance traveled divided by the time required. In other words, the average velocity is equal to the change in position divided by the change in time. Average velocity is a vector and will always point in the same direction as the displacement vector (since time is a scalar and always positive).

ACCELERATION

Acceleration is the change in the velocity of an object. On most test questions, the acceleration will be a constant value. Like position and velocity, acceleration is a vector quantity and will therefore have both magnitude and direction.

Most motion can be explained by Newton's three laws of motion:

NEWTON'S FIRST LAW

An object at rest or in motion will remain at rest or in motion unless acted upon by an external force. This phenomenon is commonly referred to as inertia, the tendency of a body to remain in its present state of motion. In order for the body's state of motion to change, it must be acted on by an unbalanced force.

> **Review Video: Newton's First Law of Motion**
> Visit mometrix.com/academy and enter code: 590367

NEWTON'S SECOND LAW

An object's acceleration is directly proportional to the net force acting on the object, and inversely proportional to the object's mass. This law is generally written in equation form F=ma, where F is the net force acting on a body, *m* is the mass of the body, and *a* is its acceleration. Note that since the mass is always a positive quantity, the acceleration is always in the same direction as the force.

> **Review Video: Newton's Second Law of Motion**
> Visit mometrix.com/academy and enter code: 737975

NEWTON'S THIRD LAW

For every force, there is an equal and opposite force. When a hammer strikes a nail, the nail hits the hammer just as hard. If we consider two objects, *A* and *B*, then we may express any contact between these two bodies with the equation $F_{AB} = -F_{BA}$, where the order of the subscripts denotes which body is exerting the force. At first glance, this law might seem to forbid any movement at all since every force is being countered with an equal opposite force, but these equal opposite forces are acting on different bodies with different masses, so they will not cancel each other out.

> **Review Video: Newton's Third Law of Motion**
> Visit mometrix.com/academy and enter code: 838401

ENERGY

The two types of energy most important in mechanics are potential and kinetic energy. Potential energy is the amount of energy an object has stored within itself because of its position or orientation. There are many types of potential energy, but the most common is gravitational potential energy. It is the energy that an object has because of its height (*h*) above the ground. It can be calculated as $PE = mgh$, where *m* is the object's mass and *g* is the acceleration of gravity. Kinetic energy is the energy of an object in motion, and is calculated as $KE = mv^2/2$, where *v* is the magnitude of its velocity. When an object is dropped, its potential energy is converted into kinetic energy as it falls. These two equations can be used to calculate the velocity of an object at any point in its fall.

> **Review Video: Energy**
> Visit mometrix.com/academy and enter code: 677735
>
> **Review Video: Potential and Kinetic Energy**
> Visit mometrix.com/academy and enter code: 491502

WORK

Work can be thought of as the amount of energy expended in accomplishing some goal. The simplest equation for mechanical work (*W*) is *W* = *Fd*, where *F* is the force exerted and *d* is the displacement of the object on which the force is exerted. This equation requires that the force be applied in the same direction as the displacement. If this is not the case, then the work may be calculated as *W* = *Fd* cos(θ), where θ is the angle between the force and displacement vectors. If force and displacement have the same direction, then work is positive; if they are in opposite directions, then work is negative; and if they are perpendicular, the work done by the force is zero.

As an example, if a man pushes a block horizontally across a surface with a constant force of 10 N for a distance of 20 m, the work done by the man is 200 N-m or 200 J. If instead the block is sliding and the man tries to slow its progress by pushing against it, his work done is -200 J, since he is pushing in the direction opposite the motion. If the man pushes vertically downward on the block

57

while it slides, his work done is zero, since his force vector is perpendicular to the displacement vector of the block.

FRICTION

Friction is a force that arises as a resistance to motion where two surfaces are in contact. The maximum magnitude of the frictional force (f) can be calculated as $f = F_c \mu$, where F_c is the contact force between the two objects and μ is a coefficient of friction based on the surfaces' material composition. Two types of friction are static and kinetic. To illustrate these concepts, imagine a book resting on a table. The force of its weight (W) is equal and opposite to the force of the table on the book, or the normal force (N). If we exert a small force (F) on the book, attempting to push it to one side, a frictional force (f) would arise, equal and opposite to our force. At this point, it is a *static frictional force* because the book is not moving. If we increase our force on the book, we will eventually cause it to move. At this point, the frictional force opposing us will be a *kinetic frictional force*. Generally, the kinetic frictional force is lower than static frictional force (because the frictional coefficient for static friction is larger), which means that the amount of force needed to maintain the movement of the book will be less than what was needed to start it moving.

GRAVITATIONAL FORCE

Gravitational force is a universal force that causes every object to exert a force on every other object. The gravitational force between two objects can be described by the formula, $F = Gm_1 m_2 / r^2$, where m_1 and m_2 are the masses of two objects, r is the distance between them, and G is the gravitational constant, $G = 6.672 \times 10^{-11}$ N m^2/kg^2. In order for this force to have a noticeable effect, one or both of the objects must be extremely large, so the equation is generally only used in problems involving planetary bodies. For problems involving objects on the earth being affected by earth's gravitational pull, the force of gravity is simply calculated as $F = mg$, where g is 9.81 m/s^2 toward the ground.

ELECTRICAL FORCE

Electrical force is a universal force that exists between any two electrically charged objects. Opposite charges attract one another and like charges repel one another. The magnitude of the force is directly proportional to the magnitude of the charges (q) and inversely proportional to the square of the distance (r) between the two objects: $F = kq_1 q_2 / r^2$, where $k = 9 \times 10^9$ N m^2/C^2. Magnetic forces operate on a similar principle.

BUOYANCY

Archimedes' principle states that a buoyant (upward) force on a submerged object is equal to the weight of the liquid displaced by the object. Water has a density of one gram per cubic centimeter. Anything that floats in water has a lower density, and anything that sinks has a higher density. This principle of buoyancy can also be used to calculate the volume of an irregularly shaped object. The mass of the object (m) minus its apparent mass in the water (m_a) divided by the density of water (ρ_w), gives the object's volume: $V = (m - m_a)/\rho_w$.

MACHINES

Simple machines include the inclined plane, lever, wheel and axle, and pulley. These simple machines have no internal source of energy. More complex or compound machines can be formed from them. Simple machines provide a force known as a mechanical advantage and make it easier to accomplish a task. The inclined plane enables a force less than the object's weight to be used to push an object to a greater height. A lever enables a multiplication of force. The wheel and axle allow for movement with less resistance. Single or double pulleys allow for easier direction of force. The wedge and screw are forms of the inclined plane. A wedge turns a smaller force working over a greater distance into a larger force. The screw is similar to an incline that is wrapped around a shaft.

> **Review Video: <u>Simple Machines</u>**
> Visit mometrix.com/academy and enter code: 950789

A certain amount of work is required to move an object. The amount cannot be reduced, but by changing the way the work is performed a mechanical advantage can be gained. A certain amount of work is required to raise an object to a given vertical height. By getting to a given height at an angle, the effort required is reduced, but the distance that must be traveled to reach a given height is increased. An example of this is walking up a hill. One may take a direct, shorter, but steeper route, or one may take a more meandering, longer route that requires less effort. Examples of wedges include doorstops, axes, plows, zippers, and can openers.

A lever consists of a bar or plank and a pivot point or fulcrum. Work is performed by the bar, which swings at the pivot point to redirect the force. There are three types of levers: first, second, and third class. Examples of a first-class lever include balances, see-saws, nail extractors, and scissors (which also use wedges). In a second-class lever the fulcrum is placed at one end of the bar and the work is performed at the other end. The weight or load to be moved is in between. The closer to the fulcrum the weight is, the easier it is to move. Force is increased, but the distance it is moved is decreased. Examples include pry bars, bottle openers, nutcrackers, and wheelbarrows. In a third-class lever the fulcrum is at one end and the positions of the weight and the location where the work is performed are reversed. Examples include fishing rods, hammers, and tweezers.

The center of a wheel and axle can be likened to a fulcrum on a rotating lever. As it turns, the wheel moves a greater distance than the axle, but with less force. Obvious examples of the wheel and axle are the wheels of a car, but this type of simple machine can also be used to exert a greater force. For instance, a person can turn the handles of a winch to exert a greater force at the turning axle to move an object. Other examples include steering wheels, wrenches, faucets, waterwheels, windmills, gears, and belts. Gears work together to change a force. The four basic types of gears are spur, rack and pinion, bevel, and worm gears. The larger gear turns slower than the smaller, but exerts a greater force. Gears at angles can be used to change the direction of forces.

A single pulley consists of a rope or line that is run around a wheel. This allows force to be directed in a downward motion to lift an object. This does not decrease the force required, just changes its direction. The load is moved the same distance as the rope pulling it. When a combination pulley is used, such as a double pulley, the weight is moved half the distance of the rope pulling it. In this way, the work effort is doubled. Pulleys are never 100% efficient because of friction. Examples of pulleys include cranes, chain hoists, block and tackles, and elevators.

ELECTRICAL CHARGES

A glass rod and a plastic rod can illustrate the concept of static electricity due to friction. Both start with no charge. A glass rod rubbed with silk produces a positive charge, while a plastic rod rubbed with fur produces a negative charge. The electron affinity of a material is a property that helps determine how easily it can be charged by friction. Materials can be sorted by their affinity for electrons into a triboelectric series. Materials with greater affinities include celluloid, sulfur, and rubber. Materials with lower affinities include glass, rabbit fur, and asbestos. In the example of a glass rod and a plastic one, the glass rod rubbed with silk acquires a positive charge because glass has a lower affinity for electrons than silk. The electrons flow to the silk, leaving the rod with fewer electrons and a positive charge. When a plastic rod is rubbed with fur, electrons flow to the rod and result in a negative charge.

The attractive force between the electrons and the nucleus is called the electric force. A positive (+) charge or a negative (-) charge creates a field of sorts in the empty space around it, which is known as an electric field. The direction of a positive charge is away from the electric field and the direction of a negative charge is towards it. An electron within the force of the field is pulled towards a positive charge because an electron has a negative charge. A particle with a positive charge is pushed away, or repelled, by another positive charge. Like charges repel each other and opposite charges attract. Lines of force show the paths of charges. The electric force between two objects is directly proportional to the product of the charge magnitudes and inversely proportional to the square of the distance between the two objects. Electric charge is measured with the unit Coulomb (C). It is the amount of charge moved in one second by a steady current of one ampere (1C = 1A × 1s).

Insulators are materials that prevent the movement of electrical charges, while conductors are materials that allow the movement of electrical charges. This is because conductive materials have free electrons that can move through the entire volume of the conductor. This allows an external charge to change the charge distribution in the material. In induction, a neutral conductive material, such as a sphere, can become charged by a positively or negatively charged object, such as a rod. The charged object is placed close to the material without touching it. This produces a force on the free electrons, which will either be attracted to or repelled by the rod, polarizing (or separating) the charge. The sphere's electrons will flow into or out of it when touched by a grounded object. The sphere is now charged. The charge will be opposite that of the charging rod.

Charging by conduction is similar to charging by induction, except that the material transferring the charge actually touches the material receiving the charge. A negatively or positively charged object is touched to an object with a neutral charge. Electrons will either flow into or out of the neutral object and it will become charged. Insulators cannot be used to conduct charges. Charging by conduction can also be called charging by contact. The law of conservation of charge states that the total number of units before and after a charging process remains the same. No electrons have been created. They have just been moved around. The removal of a charge on an object by conduction is called grounding.

CIRCUITS

Electric potential, or electrostatic potential or voltage, is an expression of potential energy per unit of charge. It is measured in volts (V) as a scalar quantity. The formula used is $V = E/Q$, where V is voltage, E is electrical potential energy, and Q is the charge. Voltage is typically discussed in the context of electric potential difference between two points in a circuit. Voltage can also be thought of as a measure of the rate at which energy is drawn from a source in order to produce a flow of electric charge.

Electric current is the sustained flow of electrons that are part of an electric charge moving along a path in a circuit. This differs from a static electric charge, which is a constant non-moving charge rather than a continuous flow. The rate of flow of electric charge is expressed using the ampere (amp or A) and can be measured using an ammeter. A current of 1 ampere means that 1 coulomb of charge passes through a given area every second. Electric charges typically only move from areas of high electric potential to areas of low electric potential. To get charges to flow into a high potential area, you must connect it to an area of higher potential by introducing a battery or other voltage source.

Electric currents experience resistance as they travel through a circuit. Different objects have different levels of resistance. The ohm (Ω) is the measurement unit of electric resistance. The symbol is the Greek letter omega. Ohm's Law, which is expressed as $I = V/R$, states that current flow (I, measured in amps) through an object is equal to the potential difference from one side to the other (V, measured in volts) divided by resistance (R, measured in ohms). An object with a higher resistance will have a lower current flow through it given the same potential difference.

Movement of electric charge along a path between areas of high electric potential and low electric potential, with a resistor or load device between them, is the definition of a simple circuit. It is a closed conducting path between the high and low potential points, such as the positive and negative terminals on a battery. One example of a circuit is the flow from one terminal of a car battery to the other. The electrolyte solution of water and sulfuric acid provides work in chemical form to start the flow. A frequently used classroom example of circuits involves using a D cell (1.5 V) battery, a small light bulb, and a piece of copper wire to create a circuit to light the bulb.

MAGNETS

A magnet is a piece of metal, such as iron, steel, or magnetite (lodestone) that can affect another substance within its field of force that has like characteristics. Magnets can either attract or repel other substances. Magnets have two poles: north and south. Like poles repel and opposite poles (pairs of north and south) attract. The magnetic field is a set of invisible lines representing the paths of attraction and repulsion. Magnetism can occur naturally, or ferromagnetic materials can be magnetized. Certain matter that is magnetized can retain its magnetic properties indefinitely and become a permanent magnet. Other matter can lose its magnetic properties. For example, an iron nail can be temporarily magnetized by stroking it repeatedly in the same direction using one pole of another magnet. Once magnetized, it can attract or repel other magnetically inclined materials, such as paper clips. Dropping the nail repeatedly will cause it to lose its charge.

> **Review Video: Magnets**
> Visit mometrix.com/academy and enter code: 570803

The motions of subatomic structures (nuclei and electrons) produce a magnetic field. It is the direction of the spin and orbit that indicates the direction of the field. The strength of a magnetic field is known as the magnetic moment. As electrons spin and orbit a nucleus, they produce a magnetic field. Pairs of electrons that spin and orbit in opposite directions cancel each other out, creating a net magnetic field of zero. Materials that have an unpaired electron are magnetic. Those with a weak attractive force are referred to as paramagnetic materials, while ferromagnetic materials have a strong attractive force. A diamagnetic material has electrons that are paired, and therefore does not typically have a magnetic moment. There are, however, some diamagnetic materials that have a weak magnetic field.

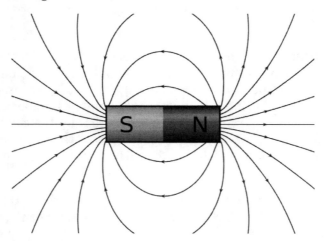

A magnetic field can be formed not only by a magnetic material, but also by electric current flowing through a wire. When a coiled wire is attached to the two ends of a battery, for example, an electromagnet can be formed by inserting a ferromagnetic material such as an iron bar within the coil. When electric current flows through the wire, the bar becomes a magnet. If there is no current, the magnetism is lost. A magnetic domain occurs when the magnetic fields of atoms are grouped and aligned. These groups form what can be thought of as miniature magnets within a material. This is what happens when an object like an iron nail is temporarily magnetized. Prior to magnetization, the organization of atoms and their various polarities are somewhat random with respect to where the north and south poles are pointing. After magnetization, a significant percentage of the poles are lined up in one direction, which is what causes the magnetic force exerted by the material.

WAVES

Waves have energy and can transfer energy when they interact with matter. Although waves transfer energy, they do not transport matter. They are a disturbance of matter that transfers energy from one particle to an adjacent particle. There are many types of waves, including sound, seismic, water, light, micro, and radio waves.

The two basic categories of waves are mechanical and electromagnetic. Mechanical waves are those that transmit energy through matter. Electromagnetic waves can transmit energy through a vacuum. A transverse wave provides a good illustration of the features of a wave, which include crests, troughs, amplitude, and wavelength.

There are a number of important attributes of waves. **Frequency** is a measure of how often particles in a medium vibrate when a wave passes through the medium with respect to a certain point or node. Usually measured in Hertz (Hz), frequency might refer to cycles per second, vibrations per second, or waves per second. One Hz is equal to one cycle per second.

Period is a measure of how long it takes to complete a cycle. It is the inverse of frequency; where frequency is measured in cycles per second, period can be thought of as seconds per cycle, though it is measured in units of time only.

Speed refers to how fast or slow a wave travels. It is measured in terms of distance divided by time. While frequency is measured in terms of cycles per second, speed might be measured in terms of meters per second.

Amplitude is the maximum amount of displacement of a particle in a medium from its rest position and corresponds to the amount of energy carried by the wave. High energy waves have greater amplitudes; low energy waves have lesser amplitudes. Amplitude is a measure of a wave's strength.

Rest position, also called equilibrium, is the point at which there is neither positive nor negative displacement.

Crest, also called the peak, is the point at which a wave's positive or upward displacement from the rest position is at its maximum. **Trough**, also called a valley, is the point at which a wave's negative or downward displacement from the rest position is at its maximum. A wavelength is one complete wave cycle. It could be measured from crest to crest, trough to trough, rest position to rest position, or any point of a wave to the corresponding point on the next wave.

Sound is a pressure disturbance that moves through a medium in the form of mechanical waves, which transfer energy from one particle to the next. Sound requires a medium to travel through, such as air, water, or other matter since it is the vibrations that transfer energy to adjacent particles, not the actual movement of particles over a great distance. Sound is transferred through the movement of atomic particles, which can be atoms or molecules. Waves of sound energy move outward in all directions from the source. Sound waves consist of compressions (particles are forced together) and rarefactions (particles move farther apart and their density decreases). A wavelength consists of one compression and one rarefaction. Different sounds have different wavelengths. Sound is a form of kinetic energy.

> **Review Video: Sound**
> Visit mometrix.com/academy and enter code: 562378

The electromagnetic spectrum is defined by frequency (f) and wavelength (λ). Frequency is typically measured in hertz and wavelength is usually measured in meters. Because light travels at a fairly constant speed, frequency is inversely proportional to wavelength, a relationship expressed by the formula $f = c/\lambda$, where c is the speed of light (about 3.0×10^8 m/s). Frequency multiplied by wavelength equals the speed of the wave; for electromagnetic waves, this is the speed of light, with some variance for the medium in which it is traveling. Electromagnetic waves include (from largest to smallest wavelength) radio waves, microwaves, infrared radiation (radiant heat), visible light, ultraviolet radiation, x-rays, and gamma rays. The energy of electromagnetic waves is carried in packets that have a magnitude inversely proportional to the wavelength. Radio waves have a range of wavelengths, from about 10^{-3} to 10^5 meters, while their frequencies range from 10^3 to about 10^{11} Hz.

Review Video: <u>Electromagnetic Spectrum</u>
Visit mometrix.com/academy and enter code: 771761

Atoms and molecules can gain or lose energy only in particular, discrete amounts. Therefore, they can absorb and emit light only at wavelengths that correspond to these amounts. Using a process known as spectroscopy, these characteristic wavelengths can be used to identify substances.

Light is the portion of the electromagnetic spectrum that is visible because of its ability to stimulate the retina. It is absorbed and emitted by electrons, atoms, and molecules that move from one energy level to another. Visible light interacts with matter through molecular electron excitation (which occurs in the human retina) and through plasma oscillations (which occur in metals). Visible light is between ultraviolet and infrared light on the spectrum. The wavelengths of visible light cover a range from 380 nm (violet) to 760 nm (red). Different wavelengths correspond to different colors. The human brain interprets or perceives visible light, which is emitted from the sun and other stars, as color. For example, when the entire wavelength reaches the retina, the brain perceives the color white. When no part of the wavelength reaches the retina, the brain perceives the color black.

Review Video: <u>Light</u>
Visit mometrix.com/academy and enter code: 900556

When light waves encounter an object, they are either reflected, transmitted, or absorbed. If the light is reflected from the surface of the object, the angle at which it contacts the surface will be the same as the angle at which it leaves on the other side of the perpendicular. If the ray of light is perpendicular to the surface, it will be reflected back in the direction from which it came. When light is transmitted through the object, its direction may be altered upon entering the object. This is known as refraction. The degree to which the light is refracted depends on the speed at which light travels in the object. Light that is neither reflected nor transmitted will be absorbed by the surface and stored as heat energy. Nearly all instances of light hitting an object will involve a combination of two or even all three of these.

When light waves are refracted, or bent, an image can appear distorted. Sound waves and water waves can also be refracted. Diffraction refers to the bending of waves around small objects and the spreading out of waves past small openings. The narrower the opening, the greater the level of diffraction will be. Larger wavelengths also increase diffraction. A diffraction grating can be created by placing a number of slits close together and is used more frequently than a prism to separate light. Different wavelengths are diffracted at different angles. The particular color of an object depends upon what is absorbed and what is transmitted or reflected. For example, a leaf consists of chlorophyll molecules, the atoms of which absorb all wavelengths of the visible light spectrum except for green, which is why a leaf appears green. Certain wavelengths of visible light can be absorbed when they interact with matter. Wavelengths that are not absorbed can be transmitted by transparent materials or reflected by opaque materials.

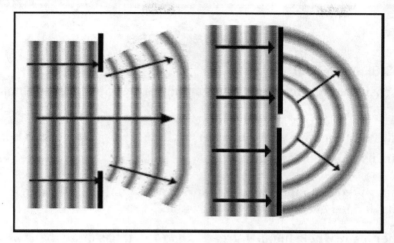

The various properties of light have numerous real-life applications. For example, polarized sunglasses have lenses that help reduce glare, while non-polarized sunglasses reduce the total amount of light that reaches the eyes. Polarized lenses consist of a chemical film of molecules aligned in parallel. This allows the lenses to block wavelengths of light that are intense, horizontal, and reflected from smooth, flat surfaces. The "fiber" in fiber optics refers to a tube or pipe that channels light. Because of the composition of the fiber, light can be transmitted greater distances before losing the signal. The fiber consists of a core, cladding, and a coating. Fibers are bundled, allowing for the transmission of large amounts of data.

Common Subject: Mathematics

Number Sense

CLASSIFICATIONS OF NUMBERS

Numbers are the basic building blocks of mathematics. Specific features of numbers are identified by the following terms:

Integer – any positive or negative whole number, including zero. Integers do not include fractions $\left(\frac{1}{3}\right)$, decimals (0.56), or mixed numbers $\left(7\frac{3}{4}\right)$.

Prime number – any whole number greater than 1 that has only two factors, itself and 1; that is, a number that can be divided evenly only by 1 and itself.

Composite number – any whole number greater than 1 that has more than two different factors; in other words, any whole number that is not a prime number. For example: The composite number 8 has the factors of 1, 2, 4, and 8.

Even number – any integer that can be divided by 2 without leaving a remainder. For example: 2, 4, 6, 8, and so on.

Odd number – any integer that cannot be divided evenly by 2. For example: 3, 5, 7, 9, and so on.

Decimal number – any number that uses a decimal point to show the part of the number that is less than one. Example: 1.234.

Decimal point – a symbol used to separate the ones place from the tenths place in decimals or dollars from cents in currency.

Decimal place – the position of a number to the right of the decimal point. In the decimal 0.123, the 1 is in the first place to the right of the decimal point, indicating tenths; the 2 is in the second place, indicating hundredths; and the 3 is in the third place, indicating thousandths.

The **decimal**, or base 10, system is a number system that uses ten different digits (0, 1, 2, 3, 4, 5, 6, 7, 8, 9). An example of a number system that uses something other than ten digits is the **binary**, or base 2, number system, used by computers, which uses only the numbers 0 and 1. It is thought that the decimal system originated because people had only their 10 fingers for counting.

Rational numbers include all integers, decimals, and fractions. Any terminating or repeating decimal number is a rational number.

Irrational numbers cannot be written as fractions or decimals because the number of decimal places is infinite and there is no recurring pattern of digits within the number. For example, pi (π) begins with 3.141592 and continues without terminating or repeating, so pi is an irrational number.

Real numbers are the set of all rational and irrational numbers.

> **Review Video: Numbers and Their Classifications**
> Visit mometrix.com/academy and enter code: 461071

66

THE NUMBER LINE

A number line is a graph to see the distance between numbers. Basically, this graph shows the relationship between numbers. So, a number line may have a point for zero and may show negative numbers on the left side of the line. Any positive numbers are placed on the right side of the line. For example, consider the points labeled on the following number line:

We can use the dashed lines on the number line to identify each point. Each dashed line between two whole numbers is $\frac{1}{4}$. The line halfway between two numbers is $\frac{1}{2}$.

NUMBERS IN WORD FORM AND PLACE VALUE

When writing numbers out in word form or translating word form to numbers, it is essential to understand how a place value system works. In the decimal or base-10 system, each digit of a number represents how many of the corresponding place value – a specific factor of 10 – are contained in the number being represented. To make reading numbers easier, every three digits to the left of the decimal place is preceded by a comma. The following table demonstrates some of the place values:

Power of 10	10^3	10^2	10^1	10^0	10^{-1}	10^{-2}	10^{-3}
Value	1,000	100	10	1	0.1	0.01	0.001
Place	thousands	hundreds	tens	ones	tenths	hundredths	thousandths

For example, consider the number 4,546.09, which can be separated into each place value like this:

4: thousands
5: hundreds
4: tens
6: ones
0: tenths
9: hundredths

This number in word form would be *four thousand five hundred forty-six and nine hundredths*.

ABSOLUTE VALUE

A precursor to working with negative numbers is understanding what **absolute values** are. A number's absolute value is simply the distance away from zero a number is on the number line. The absolute value of a number is always positive and is written $|x|$. For example, the absolute value of 3, written as $|3|$, is 3 because the distance between 0 and 3 on a number line is three units. Likewise, the absolute value of –3, written as $|-3|$, is 3 because the distance between 0 and –3 on a number line is three units. So, $|3| = |-3|$.

Review Video: <u>Absolute Value</u>
Visit mometrix.com/academy and enter code: 314669

PRACTICE

P1. Write the place value of each digit in 14,059.826

P2. Write out each of the following in words:

(a) 29
(b) 478
(c) 98,542
(d) 0.06
(e) 13.113

P3. Write each of the following in numbers:

(a) nine thousand four hundred thirty-five
(b) three hundred two thousand eight hundred seventy-six
(c) nine hundred one thousandths
(d) nineteen thousandths
(e) seven thousand one hundred forty-two and eighty-five hundredths

PRACTICE SOLUTIONS

P1. The place value for each digit would be as follows:

Digit	Place Value
1	ten-thousands
4	thousands
0	hundreds
5	tens
9	ones
8	tenths
2	hundredths
6	thousandths

P2. Each written out in words would be:

    (a) twenty-nine
    (b) four hundred seventy-eight
    (c) ninety-eight thousand five hundred forty-two
    (d) six hundredths
    (e) thirteen and one hundred thirteen thousandths

P3. Each in numeric form would be:

    (a) 9,435
    (b) 302876
    (c) 0.901
    (d) 0.019
    (e) 7,142.85

OPERATIONS

An **operation** is simply a mathematical process that takes some value(s) as input(s) and produces an output. Elementary operations are often written in the following form: *value operation value*. For instance, in the expression $1 + 2$ the values are 1 and 2 and the operation is addition. Performing the operation gives the output of 3. In this way we can say that $1 + 2$ and 3 are equal, or $1 + 2 = 3$.

ADDITION

Addition increases the value of one quantity by the value of another quantity (both called **addends**). For example, $2 + 4 = 6; 8 + 9 = 17$. The result is called the **sum**. With addition, the order does not matter, $4 + 2 = 2 + 4$.

When adding signed numbers, if the signs are the same simply add the absolute values of the addends and apply the original sign to the sum. For example, $(+4) + (+8) = +12$ and $(-4) + (-8) = -12$. When the original signs are different, take the absolute values of the addends and subtract the smaller value from the larger value, then apply the original sign of the larger value to the difference. For instance, $(+4) + (-8) = -4$ and $(-4) + (+8) = +4$.

SUBTRACTION

Subtraction is the opposite operation to addition; it decreases the value of one quantity (the **minuend**) by the value of another quantity (the **subtrahend**). For example, $6 - 4 = 2; 17 - 8 = 9$. The result is called the **difference**. Note that with subtraction, the order does matter, $6 - 4 \neq 4 - 6$.

For subtracting signed numbers, change the sign of the subtrahend and then follow the same rules used for addition. For example, $(+4) - (+8) = (+4) + (-8) = -4$.

MULTIPLICATION

Multiplication can be thought of as repeated addition. One number (the **multiplier**) indicates how many times to add the other number (the **multiplicand**) to itself. For example, 3×2 (three times two) $= 2 + 2 + 2 = 6$. With multiplication, the order does not matter: $2 \times 3 = 3 \times 2$ or $3 + 3 = 2 + 2 + 2$, either way the result (the **product**) is the same.

If the signs are the same the product is positive when multiplying signed numbers. For example, $(+4) \times (+8) = +32$ and $(-4) \times (-8) = +32$. If the signs are opposite, the product is negative. For example, $(+4) \times (-8) = -32$ and $(-4) \times (+8) = -32$. When more than two factors are multiplied together, the sign of the product is determined by how many negative factors are present. If there are an odd number of negative factors then the product is negative, whereas an even number of negative factors indicates a positive product. For instance, $(+4) \times (-8) \times (-2) = +64$ and $(-4) \times (-8) \times (-2) = -64$.

DIVISION

Division is the opposite operation to multiplication; one number (the **divisor**) tells us how many parts to divide the other number (the **dividend**) into. The result of division is called the **quotient**. For example, $20 \div 4 = 5$; if 20 is split into 4 equal parts, each part is 5. With division, the order of the numbers does matter, $20 \div 4 \neq 4 \div 20$.

The rules for dividing signed numbers are similar to multiplying signed numbers. If the dividend and divisor have the same sign, the quotient is positive. If the dividend and divisor have opposite signs, the quotient is negative. For example, $(-4) \div (+8) = -0.5$.

> **Review Video: Mathematical Operations**
> Visit mometrix.com/academy and enter code: 208095

PARENTHESES

Parentheses are used to designate which operations should be done first when there are multiple operations. Example: $4 - (2 + 1) = 1$; the parentheses tell us that we must add 2 and 1, and then subtract the sum from 4, rather than subtracting 2 from 4 and then adding 1 (this would give us an answer of 3).

> **Review Video: Mathematical Parentheses**
> Visit mometrix.com/academy and enter code: 978600

EXPONENTS

An **exponent** is a superscript number placed next to another number at the top right. It indicates how many times the base number is to be multiplied by itself. Exponents provide a shorthand way to write what would be a longer mathematical expression, for example: $2^4 = 2 \times 2 \times 2 \times 2$. A number with an exponent of 2 is said to be "squared," while a number with an exponent of 3 is said to be "cubed." The value of a number raised to an exponent is called its power. So, 8^4 is read as "8 to the 4th power," or "8 raised to the power of 4."

The properties of exponents are as follows:

Property	Description
$a^1 = a$	Any number to the power of 1 is equal to itself
$1^n = 1$	The number 1 raised to any power is equal to 1
$a^0 = 1$	Any number raised to the power of 0 is equal to 1
$a^n \times a^m = a^{n+m}$	Add exponents to multiply powers of the same base number
$a^n \div a^m = a^{n-m}$	Subtract exponents to divide powers of the same base number
$(a^n)^m = a^{n \times m}$	When a power is raised to a power, the exponents are multiplied
$(a \times b)^n = a^n \times b^n$ $(a \div b)^n = a^n \div b^n$	Multiplication and division operations inside parentheses can be raised to a power. This is the same as each term being raised to that power.
$a^{-n} = \dfrac{1}{a^n}$	A negative exponent is the same as the reciprocal of a positive exponent

Note that exponents do not have to be integers. Fractional or decimal exponents follow all the rules above as well. Example: $5^{\frac{1}{4}} \times 5^{\frac{3}{4}} = 5^{\frac{1}{4}+\frac{3}{4}} = 5^1 = 5$.

Review Video: **Exponents**
Visit mometrix.com/academy and enter code: 600998
Review Video: Laws of Exponents
Visit mometrix.com/academy and enter code: 532558

ROOTS

A **root**, such as a square root, is another way of writing a fractional exponent. Instead of using a superscript, roots use the radical symbol ($\sqrt{}$) to indicate the operation. A radical will have a number underneath the bar, and may sometimes have a number in the upper left: $\sqrt[n]{a}$, read as "the nth root of a." The relationship between radical notation and exponent notation can be described by this equation: $\sqrt[n]{a} = a^{\frac{1}{n}}$. The two special cases of $n = 2$ and $n = 3$ are called square roots and cube roots. If there is no number to the upper left, it is understood to be a square root ($n = 2$). Nearly all of the roots you encounter will be square roots. A square root is the same as a number raised to the one-half power. When we say that a is the square root of b ($a = \sqrt{b}$), we mean that a multiplied by itself equals b: ($a \times a = b$).

A **perfect square** is a number that has an integer for its square root. There are 10 perfect squares from 1 to 100: 1, 4, 9, 16, 25, 36, 49, 64, 81, 100 (the squares of integers 1 through 10).

Review Video: **Roots**
Visit mometrix.com/academy and enter code: 795655

ORDER OF OPERATIONS

The **order of operations** is a set of rules that dictates the order in which we must perform each operation in an expression so that we will evaluate it accurately. If we have an expression that includes multiple different operations, the order of operations tells us which operations to do first. The most common mnemonic for the order of operations is **PEMDAS**, or "Please Excuse My Dear Aunt Sally." PEMDAS stands for parentheses, exponents, multiplication, division, addition, and subtraction. It is important to understand that multiplication and division have equal precedence, as do addition and subtraction, so those pairs of operations are simply worked from left to right in order.

For example, evaluating the expression $5 + 20 \div 4 \times (2 + 3) - 6$ using the correct order of operations would be done like this:

- **P:** Perform the operations inside the parentheses: $(2 + 3) = 5$
- **E:** Simplify the exponents.
  - The equation now looks like this: $5 + 20 \div 4 \times 5 - 6$
- **MD:** Perform multiplication and division from left to right: $20 \div 4 = 5$; then $5 \times 5 = 25$
  - The equation now looks like this: $5 + 25 - 6$
- **AS:** Perform addition and subtraction from left to right: $5 + 25 = 30$; then $30 - 6 = 24$

Review Video: **Order of Operations**
Visit mometrix.com/academy and enter code: 259675

71

SUBTRACTION WITH REGROUPING

A great way to make use of some of the features built into the decimal system would be regrouping when attempting longform subtraction operations. When subtracting within a place value, sometimes the minuend is smaller than the subtrahend, **regrouping** enables you to 'borrow' a unit from a place value to the left in order to get a positive difference. For example, consider subtracting 189 from 525 with regrouping.

> **Review Video: Subtracting Large Numbers**
> Visit mometrix.com/academy and enter code: 603350

First, set up the subtraction problem in vertical form:

$$\begin{array}{r} 525 \\ - \ 189 \\ \hline \end{array}$$

Notice that the numbers in the ones and tens columns of 525 are smaller than the numbers in the ones and tens columns of 189. This means you will need to use regrouping to perform subtraction:

$$\begin{array}{r r r} 5 & 2 & 5 \\ - \quad 1 & 8 & 9 \\ \hline \end{array}$$

To subtract 9 from 5 in the ones column you will need to borrow from the 2 in the tens columns:

$$\begin{array}{r r r} 5 & 1 & 15 \\ - \quad 1 & 8 & 9 \\ \hline & & 6 \end{array}$$

Next, to subtract 8 from 1 in the tens column you will need to borrow from the 5 in the hundreds column:

$$\begin{array}{r r r} 4 & 11 & 15 \\ - \quad 1 & 8 & 9 \\ \hline & 3 & 6 \end{array}$$

Last, subtract the 1 from the 4 in the hundreds column:

$$\begin{array}{r r r} 4 & 11 & 15 \\ - \quad 1 & 8 & 9 \\ \hline 3 & 3 & 6 \end{array}$$

PRACTICE

P1. Demonstrate how to subtract 477 from 620 using regrouping.

P2. Simplify the following expressions with exponents:

(a) 37^0
(b) 1^{30}
(c) $2^3 \times 2^4 \times 2^x$
(d) $(3^x)^3$
(e) $(12 \div 3)^2$

Mometrix

PRACTICE SOLUTIONS

P1. First, set up the subtraction problem in vertical form:

$$\begin{array}{ccc} 6 & 2 & 0 \\ - \ 4 & 7 & 7 \\ \hline \end{array}$$

To subtract 7 from 0 in the ones column you will need to borrow from the 2 in the tens column:

$$\begin{array}{ccc} 6 & 1 & 10 \\ - \ 4 & 7 & 7 \\ \hline & & 3 \end{array}$$

Next, to subtract 7 from the 1 that's still in the tens column you will need to borrow from the 6 in the hundreds column:

$$\begin{array}{ccc} 5 & 11 & 10 \\ - \ 4 & 7 & 7 \\ \hline & 4 & 3 \end{array}$$

Lastly, subtract 4 from the 5 remaining in the hundreds column:

$$\begin{array}{ccc} 5 & 11 & 10 \\ - \ 4 & 7 & 7 \\ \hline 1 & 4 & 3 \end{array}$$

P2. Using the properties of exponents and the proper order of operations:

(a) Any number raised to the power of 0 is equal to 1: $37^0 = 1$
(b) The number 1 raised to any power is equal to 1: $1^{30} = 1$
(c) Add exponents to multiply powers of the same base: $2^3 \times 2^4 \times 2^x = 2^{(3+4+x)} = 2^{(7+x)}$
(d) When a power is raised to a power, the exponents are multiplied: $(3^x)^3 = 3^{3x}$
(e) Perform the operation inside the parentheses first: $(12 \div 3)^2 = 4^2 = 16$

UNITS OF MEASUREMENT

METRIC MEASUREMENT PREFIXES

Giga-: one billion (1 *giga*watt is one billion watts)
Mega-: one million (1 *mega*hertz is one million hertz)
Kilo-: one thousand (1 *kilo*gram is one thousand grams)
Deci-: one tenth (1 *deci*meter is one tenth of a meter)
Centi-: one hundredth (1 *centi*meter is one hundredth of a meter)
Milli-: one thousandth (1 *milli*liter is one thousandth of a liter)
Micro-: one millionth (1 *micro*gram is one millionth of a gram)

MEASUREMENT CONVERSION

When converting between units, the goal is to maintain the same meaning but change the way it is displayed. In order to go from a larger unit to a smaller unit, multiply the number of the known amount by the equivalent amount. When going from a smaller unit to a larger unit, divide the number of the known amount by the equivalent amount.

For complicated conversions, it may be helpful to set up conversion fractions. In these fractions, one fraction is the **conversion factor**. The other fraction has the unknown amount in the numerator.

73

So, the known value is placed in the denominator. Sometimes the second fraction has the known value from the problem in the numerator, and the unknown in the denominator. Multiply the two fractions to get the converted measurement. Note that since the numerator and the denominator of the factor are equivalent, the value of the fraction is 1. That is why we can say that the result in the new units is equal to the result in the old units even though they have different numbers.

It can often be necessary to chain known conversion factors together. As an example, consider converting 512 square inches to square meters. We know that there are 2.54 centimeters in an inch and 100 centimeters in a meter, and that we will need to square each of these factors to achieve the conversion we are looking for.

$$\frac{512 \text{ in}^2}{1} \times \left(\frac{2.54 \text{ cm}}{1 \text{ in}}\right)^2 \times \left(\frac{1 \text{ m}}{100 \text{ cm}}\right)^2 = \frac{512 \text{ in}^2}{1} \times \left(\frac{6.4516 \text{ cm}^2}{1 \text{ in}^2}\right) \times \left(\frac{1 \text{ m}^2}{10000 \text{ cm}^2}\right) = 0.330 \text{ m}^2$$

COMMON UNITS AND EQUIVALENTS
METRIC EQUIVALENTS

1000 µg (microgram)	1 mg
1000 mg (milligram)	1 g
1000 g (gram)	1 kg
1000 kg (kilogram)	1 metric ton
1000 mL (milliliter)	1 L
1000 µm (micrometer)	1 mm
1000 mm (millimeter)	1 m
100 cm (centimeter)	1 m
1000 m (meter)	1 km

DISTANCE AND AREA MEASUREMENT

Unit	Abbreviation	U.S. equivalent	Metric equivalent
Inch	in	1 inch	2.54 centimeters
Foot	ft	12 inches	0.305 meters
Yard	yd	3 feet	0.914 meters
Mile	mi	5280 feet	1.609 kilometers
Acre	ac	4840 square yards	0.405 hectares
Square Mile	mi^2	640 acres	2.590 square kilometers

CAPACITY MEASUREMENTS

Unit	Abbreviation	U.S. equivalent	Metric equivalent
Fluid Ounce	fl oz	8 fluid drams	29.573 milliliters
Cup	cp	8 fluid ounces	0.237 liter
Pint	pt	16 fluid ounces	0.473 liter
Quart	qt	2 pints	0.946 liter
Gallon	gal	4 quarts	3.785 liters
Teaspoon	t or tsp	1 fluid dram	5 milliliters
Tablespoon	T or tbsp	4 fluid drams	15 or 16 milliliters
Cubic Centimeter	cc or cm^3	0.271 drams	1 milliliter

WEIGHT MEASUREMENTS

Unit	Abbreviation	U.S. equivalent	Metric equivalent
Ounce	oz	16 drams	28.35 grams
Pound	lb	16 ounces	453.6 grams
Ton	t	2,000 pounds	907.2 kilograms

VOLUME AND WEIGHT MEASUREMENT CLARIFICATIONS

Always be careful when using ounces and fluid ounces. They are not equivalent.

1 pint = 16 fluid ounces	1 fluid ounce ≠ 1 ounce
1 pound = 16 ounces	1 pint ≠ 1 pound

Having one pint of something does not mean you have one pound of it. In the same way, just because something weighs one pound does not mean that its volume is one pint.

In the United States, the word "ton" by itself refers to a short ton or a net ton. Do not confuse this with a long ton (also called a gross ton) or a metric ton (also spelled *tonne*), which have different measurement equivalents.

$$1 \text{ U.S. ton} = 2000 \text{ pounds} \qquad \neq \qquad 1 \text{ metric ton} = 1000 \text{ kilograms}$$

ROUNDING AND ESTIMATION

Rounding is reducing the digits in a number while still trying to keep the value similar. The result will be less accurate but in a simpler form and easier to use. Whole numbers can be rounded to the nearest ten, hundred, or thousand.

When you are asked to estimate the solution to a problem, you will need to provide only an approximate figure or **estimation** for your answer. In this situation, you will need to round each number in the calculation to the level indicated (nearest hundred, nearest thousand, etc.) or to a level that makes sense for the numbers involved. When estimating a sum **all numbers must be rounded to the same level**. You cannot round one number to the nearest thousand while rounding another to the nearest hundred.

> **Review Video: Rounding and Estimation**
> Visit mometrix.com/academy and enter code: 126243

PRACTICE

P1. Perform the following conversions:

   (a) 1.4 meters to centimeters

   (b) 218 centimeters to meters

   (c) 42 inches to feet

   (d) 15 kilograms to pounds

   (e) 80 ounces to pounds

   (f) 2 miles to kilometers

   (g) 5 feet to centimeters

   (h) 15.14 liters to gallons

   (i) 8 quarts to liters

   (j) 13.2 pounds to grams

P2. Round each number to the indicated degree:

   (a) Round to the nearest ten: 11; 47; 118

   (b) Round to the nearest hundred: 78; 980; 248

   (c) Round each number to the nearest thousand: 302; 1274; 3756

P3. Estimate the solution to 345,932 + 96,369 by rounding each number to the nearest ten thousand.

P4. A runner's heart beats 422 times over the course of six minutes. About how many times did the runner's heart beat during each minute?

PRACTICE SOLUTIONS

P1. (a) $\frac{100 \text{ cm}}{1 \text{ m}} = \frac{x \text{ cm}}{1.4 \text{ m}}$ Cross multiply to get $x = 140$

   (b) $\frac{100 \text{ cm}}{1 \text{ m}} = \frac{218 \text{ cm}}{x \text{ m}}$ Cross multiply to get $100x = 218$, or $x = 2.18$

   (c) $\frac{12 \text{ in}}{1 \text{ ft}} = \frac{42 \text{ in}}{x \text{ ft}}$ Cross multiply to get $12x = 42$, or $x = 3.5$

   (d) 15 kilograms $\times \frac{2.2 \text{ pounds}}{1 \text{ kilogram}} = 33$ pounds

   (e) 80 ounces $\times \frac{1 \text{ pound}}{16 \text{ ounces}} = 5$ pounds

   (f) 2 miles $\times \frac{1.609 \text{ kilometers}}{1 \text{ mile}} = 3.218$ kilometers

   (g) 5 feet $\times \frac{12 \text{ inches}}{1 \text{ foot}} \times \frac{2.54 \text{ centimeters}}{1 \text{ inch}} = 152.4$ centimeters

76

(h) 15.14 liters $\times \frac{1 \text{ gallon}}{3.785 \text{ liters}} = 4$ gallons

(i) 8 quarts $\times \frac{1 \text{ gallon}}{4 \text{ quarts}} \times \frac{3.785 \text{ liters}}{1 \text{ gallon}} = 7.57$ liters

(j) 13.2 pounds $\times \frac{1 \text{ kilogram}}{2.2 \text{ pounds}} \times \frac{1000 \text{ grams}}{1 \text{ kilogram}} = 6000$ grams

P2. (a) When rounding to the nearest ten, anything ending in 5 or greater rounds up. So, 11 rounds to 10, 47 rounds to 50, and 118 rounds to 120.

(b) When rounding to the nearest hundred, anything ending in 50 or greater rounds up. So, 78 rounds to 100, 980 rounds to 1000, and 248 rounds to 200.

(c) When rounding to the nearest thousand, anything ending in 500 or greater rounds up. So, 302 rounds to 0, 1274 rounds to 1000, and 3756 rounds to 4000.

P3. Start by rounding each number to the nearest ten thousand: 345,932 becomes 350,000, and 96,369 becomes 100,000. Then, add the rounded numbers: 350,000 + 100,000 = 450,000. So, the answer is approximately 450,000. The exact answer would be 345,932 + 96,369 = 442,301. So, the estimate of 450,000 is a similar value to the exact answer.

P4. "About how many" indicates that you need to estimate the solution. In this case, look at the numbers you are given. 422 can be rounded down to 420, which is easily divisible by 6. A good estimate is $420 \div 6 = 70$ beats per minute. More accurately, the patient's heart rate was just over 70 beats per minute since his heart actually beat a little more than 420 times in six minutes.

Factoring
Factors and Greatest Common Factor

Factors are numbers that are multiplied together to obtain a **product**. For example, in the equation $2 \times 3 = 6$, the numbers 2 and 3 are factors. A **prime number** has only two factors (1 and itself), but other numbers can have many factors.

A **common factor** is a number that divides exactly into two or more other numbers. For example, the factors of 12 are 1, 2, 3, 4, 6, and 12, while the factors of 15 are 1, 3, 5, and 15. The common factors of 12 and 15 are 1 and 3.

A **prime factor** is also a prime number. Therefore, the prime factors of 12 are 2 and 3. For 15, the prime factors are 3 and 5.

The **greatest common factor (GCF)** is the largest number that is a factor of two or more numbers. For example, the factors of 15 are 1, 3, 5, and 15; the factors of 35 are 1, 5, 7, and 35. Therefore, the greatest common factor of 15 and 35 is 5.

> **Review Video: Factors**
> Visit mometrix.com/academy and enter code: 920086
>
> **Review Video: GCF and LCM**
> Visit mometrix.com/academy and enter code: 838699

MULTIPLES AND LEAST COMMON MULTIPLE

Often listed out in multiplication tables, **multiples** are integer increments of a given factor. In other words, dividing a multiple by the factor number will result in an integer. For example, the multiples of 7 include: $1 \times 7 = 7$, $2 \times 7 = 14$, $3 \times 7 = 21$, $4 \times 7 = 28$, $5 \times 7 = 35$. Dividing 7, 14, 21, 28, or 35 by 7 will result in the integers 1, 2, 3, 4, and 5, respectively.

The least common multiple (**LCM**) is the smallest number that is a multiple of two or more numbers. For example, the multiples of 3 include 3, 6, 9, 12, 15, etc.; the multiples of 5 include 5, 10, 15, 20, etc. Therefore, the least common multiple of 3 and 5 is 15.

> **Review Video: Multiples**
> Visit mometrix.com/academy and enter code: 626738

FRACTIONS

A **fraction** is a number that is expressed as one integer written above another integer, with a dividing line between them $\left(\frac{x}{y}\right)$. It represents the **quotient** of the two numbers "x divided by y." It can also be thought of as x out of y equal parts.

The top number of a fraction is called the **numerator**, and it represents the number of parts under consideration. The 1 in $\frac{1}{4}$ means that 1 part out of the whole is being considered in the calculation. The bottom number of a fraction is called the **denominator**, and it represents the total number of equal parts. The 4 in $\frac{1}{4}$ means that the whole consists of 4 equal parts. A fraction cannot have a denominator of zero; this is referred to as "*undefined*."

Fractions can be manipulated, without changing the value of the fraction, by multiplying or dividing (but not adding or subtracting) both the numerator and denominator by the same number. If you divide both numbers by a common factor, you are **reducing** or simplifying the fraction. Two fractions that have the same value but are expressed differently are known as **equivalent fractions**. For example, $\frac{2}{10}, \frac{3}{15}, \frac{4}{20}$, and $\frac{5}{25}$ are all equivalent fractions. They can also all be reduced or simplified to $\frac{1}{5}$.

When two fractions are manipulated so that they have the same denominator, this is known as finding a **common denominator**. The number chosen to be that common denominator should be the least common multiple of the two original denominators. Example: $\frac{3}{4}$ and $\frac{5}{6}$; the least common multiple of 4 and 6 is 12. Manipulating to achieve the common denominator: $\frac{3}{4} = \frac{9}{12}$; $\frac{5}{6} = \frac{10}{12}$.

PROPER FRACTIONS AND MIXED NUMBERS

A fraction whose denominator is greater than its numerator is known as a **proper fraction**, while a fraction whose numerator is greater than its denominator is known as an **improper fraction**. Proper fractions have values *less than one* and improper fractions have values *greater than one*.

A **mixed number** is a number that contains both an integer and a fraction. Any improper fraction can be rewritten as a mixed number. Example: $\frac{8}{3} = \frac{6}{3} + \frac{2}{3} = 2 + \frac{2}{3} = 2\frac{2}{3}$. Similarly, any mixed number can be rewritten as an improper fraction. Example: $1\frac{3}{5} = 1 + \frac{3}{5} = \frac{5}{5} + \frac{3}{5} = \frac{8}{5}$.

> **Review Video: Fractions and Mixed Numbers**
> Visit mometrix.com/academy and enter code: 211077
>
> **Review Video: Fractions**
> Visit mometrix.com/academy and enter code: 262335

ADDING AND SUBTRACTING FRACTIONS

If two fractions have a common denominator, they can be added or subtracted simply by adding or subtracting the two numerators and retaining the same denominator. If the two fractions do not already have the same denominator, one or both of them must be manipulated to achieve a common denominator before they can be added or subtracted. Example: $\frac{1}{2} + \frac{1}{4} = \frac{2}{4} + \frac{1}{4} = \frac{3}{4}$.

> **Review Video: Adding and Subtracting Fractions**
> Visit mometrix.com/academy and enter code: 378080

MULTIPLYING FRACTIONS

Two fractions can be multiplied by multiplying the two numerators to find the new numerator and the two denominators to find the new denominator. Example: $\frac{1}{3} \times \frac{2}{3} = \frac{1 \times 2}{3 \times 3} = \frac{2}{9}$.

DIVIDING FRACTIONS

Two fractions can be divided by flipping the numerator and denominator of the second fraction and then proceeding as though it were a multiplication. Example: $\frac{2}{3} \div \frac{3}{4} = \frac{2}{3} \times \frac{4}{3} = \frac{8}{9}$.

> **Review Video: Multiplying and Dividing Fractions**
> Visit mometrix.com/academy and enter code: 473632

MULTIPLYING A MIXED NUMBER BY A WHOLE NUMBER OR A DECIMAL

When multiplying a mixed number by something, it is usually best to convert it to an improper fraction first. Additionally, if the multiplicand is a decimal, it is most often simplest to convert it to a fraction. For instance, to multiply $4\frac{3}{8}$ by 3.5, begin by rewriting each quantity as a whole number plus a proper fraction. Remember, a mixed number is a fraction added to a whole number and a decimal is a representation of the sum of fractions, specifically tenths, hundredths, thousandths, and so on:

$$4\frac{3}{8} \times 3.5 = \left(4 + \frac{3}{8}\right) \times \left(3 + \frac{1}{2}\right)$$

Next, the quantities being added need to be expressed with the same denominator. This is achieved by multiplying and dividing the whole number by the denominator of the fraction. Recall that a whole number is equivalent to that number divided by 1:

$$= \left(\frac{4}{1} \times \frac{8}{8} + \frac{3}{8}\right) \times \left(\frac{3}{1} \times \frac{2}{2} + \frac{1}{2}\right)$$

When multiplying fractions, remember to multiply the numerators and denominators separately:

$$= \left(\frac{4 \times 8}{1 \times 8} + \frac{3}{8}\right) \times \left(\frac{3 \times 2}{1 \times 2} + \frac{1}{2}\right)$$
$$= \left(\frac{32}{8} + \frac{3}{8}\right) \times \left(\frac{6}{2} + \frac{1}{2}\right)$$

Now that the fractions have the same denominators, they can be added:

$$= \frac{35}{8} \times \frac{7}{2}$$

Finally, perform the last multiplication and then simplify:

$$= \frac{35 \times 7}{8 \times 2} = \frac{245}{16} = \frac{240}{16} + \frac{5}{16} = 15\frac{5}{16}$$

DECIMALS

Decimals are one way to represent parts of a whole. Using the place value system, each digit to the right of a decimal point denotes the number of units of a corresponding *negative* power of ten. For example, consider the decimal 0.24. We can use a model to represent the decimal. Since a dime is worth one-tenth of a dollar and a penny is worth one-hundredth of a dollar, one possible model to represent this fraction is to have 2 dimes representing the 2 in the tenths place and 4 pennies representing the 4 in the hundredths place:

To write the decimal as a fraction, put the decimal in the numerator with 1 in the denominator. Multiply the numerator and denominator by tens until there are no more decimal places. Then simplify the fraction to lowest terms. For example, converting 0.24 to a fraction:

$$0.24 = \frac{0.24}{1} = \frac{0.24 \times 100}{1 \times 100} = \frac{24}{100} = \frac{6}{25}$$

Review Video: Decimals
Visit mometrix.com/academy and enter code: 837268

ADDING AND SUBTRACTING DECIMALS

When adding and subtracting decimals, the decimal points must always be aligned. Adding decimals is just like adding regular whole numbers. Example: $4.5 + 2 = 6.5$.

If the problem-solver does not properly align the decimal points, an incorrect answer of 4.7 may result. An easy way to add decimals is to align all of the decimal points in a vertical column visually. This will allow you to see exactly where the decimal should be placed in the final answer. Begin adding from right to left. Add each column in turn, making sure to carry the number to the left if a column adds up to more than 9. The same rules apply to the subtraction of decimals.

> **Review Video: Adding and Subtracting Decimals**
> Visit mometrix.com/academy and enter code: 381101

MULTIPLYING DECIMALS

A simple multiplication problem has two components: a **multiplicand** and a **multiplier**. When multiplying decimals, work as though the numbers were whole rather than decimals. Once the final product is calculated, count the number of places to the right of the decimal in both the multiplicand and the multiplier. Then, count that number of places from the right of the product and place the decimal in that position.

For example, 12.3×2.56 has a total of three places to the right of the respective decimals. Multiply 123×256 to get 31488. Now, beginning on the right, count three places to the left and insert the decimal. The final product will be 31.488.

> **Review Video: Multiplying Decimals**
> Visit mometrix.com/academy and enter code: 731574

DIVIDING DECIMALS

Every division problem has a **divisor** and a **dividend**. The dividend is the number that is being divided. In the problem $14 \div 7$, 14 is the dividend and 7 is the divisor. In a division problem with decimals, the divisor must be converted into a whole number. Begin by moving the decimal in the divisor to the right until a whole number is created. Next, move the decimal in the dividend the same number of spaces to the right. For example, 4.9 into 24.5 would become 49 into 245. The decimal was moved one space to the right to create a whole number in the divisor, and then the same was done for the dividend. Once the whole numbers are created, the problem is carried out normally: $245 \div 49 = 5$.

> **Review Video: Dividing Decimals**
> Visit mometrix.com/academy and enter code: 560690

PERCENTAGES

Percentages can be thought of as fractions that are based on a whole of 100; that is, one whole is equal to 100%. The word **percent** means "per hundred." Percentage problems are often presented in three main ways:

- Find what percentage of some number another number is.
  - Example: What percentage of 40 is 8?
- Find what number is some percentage of a given number.
  - Example: What number is 20% of 40?
- Find what number another number is a given percentage of.
  - Example: What number is 8 20% of?

There are three components in each of these cases: a **whole** (W), a **part** (P), and a **percentage** (%). These are related by the equation: $P = W \times \%$. This can easily be rearranged into other forms that may suit different questions better: $\% = \frac{P}{W}$ and $W = \frac{P}{\%}$. Percentage problems are often also word problems. As such, a large part of solving them is figuring out which quantities are what. For example, consider the following word problem:

In a school cafeteria, 7 students choose pizza, 9 choose hamburgers, and 4 choose tacos. What percentage of student choose tacos?

To find the whole, you must first add all of the parts: $7 + 9 + 4 = 20$. The percentage can then be found by dividing the part by the whole ($\% = \frac{P}{W}$): $\frac{4}{20} = \frac{20}{100} = 20\%$.

CONVERTING BETWEEN PERCENTAGES, FRACTIONS, AND DECIMALS

Converting decimals to percentages and percentages to decimals is as simple as moving the decimal point. To *convert from a decimal to a percentage*, move the decimal point **two places to the right**. To *convert from a percentage to a decimal*, move it **two places to the left**. It may be helpful to remember that the percentage number will always be larger than the equivalent decimal number. For example:

$$0.23 = 23\% \quad 5.34 = 534\% \quad 0.007 = 0.7\%$$
$$700\% = 7.00 \quad 86\% = 0.86 \quad 0.15\% = 0.0015$$

To convert a fraction to a decimal, simply divide the numerator by the denominator in the fraction. To convert a decimal to a fraction, put the decimal in the numerator with 1 in the denominator. Multiply the numerator and denominator by tens until there are no more decimal places. Then simplify the fraction to lowest terms. For example, converting 0.24 to a fraction:

$$0.24 = \frac{0.24}{1} = \frac{0.24 \times 100}{1 \times 100} = \frac{24}{100} = \frac{6}{25}$$

Fractions can be converted to a percentage by finding equivalent fractions with a denominator of 100. For example,

$$\frac{7}{10} = \frac{70}{100} = 70\% \quad \frac{1}{4} = \frac{25}{100} = 25\%$$

To convert a percentage to a fraction, divide the percentage number by 100 and reduce the fraction to its simplest possible terms. For example,

$$60\% = \frac{60}{100} = \frac{3}{5} \quad 96\% = \frac{96}{100} = \frac{24}{25}$$

> **Review Video: Converting Fractions to Percentages and Decimals**
> Visit mometrix.com/academy and enter code: 306233
>
> **Review Video: Converting Percentages to Decimals and Fractions**
> Visit mometrix.com/academy and enter code: 287297

RATIONAL NUMBERS

The term **rational** means that the number can be expressed as a ratio or fraction. That is, a number, r, is rational if and only if it can be represented by a fraction $\frac{a}{b}$ where a and b are integers and b does not equal 0. The set of rational numbers includes integers and decimals. If there is no finite way to represent a value with a fraction of integers, then the number is **irrational**. Common examples of irrational numbers include: $\sqrt{5}, (1 + \sqrt{2})$, and π.

> **Review Video: <u>Rational and Irrational Numbers</u>**
> Visit mometrix.com/academy and enter code: 280645

PRACTICE

P1. What is 30% of 120?

P2. What is 150% of 20?

P3. What is 14.5% of 96?

P4. Simplify the following expressions:

(a) $\left(\frac{2}{5}\right)/\left(\frac{4}{7}\right)$
(b) $\frac{7}{8} - \frac{8}{16}$
(c) $\frac{1}{2} + \left(3\left(\frac{3}{4}\right) - 2\right) + 4$
(d) $0.22 + 0.5 - (5.5 + 3.3 \div 3)$
(e) $\frac{3}{2} + (4(0.5) - 0.75) + 2$

P5. Convert the following to a fraction and to a decimal: **(a)** 15%; **(b)** 24.36%

P6. Convert the following to a decimal and to a percentage. **(a)** 4/5; **(b)** $3\frac{2}{5}$

P7. A woman's age is thirteen more than half of 60. How old is the woman?

P8. A patient was given pain medicine at a dosage of 0.22 grams. The patient's dosage was then increased to 0.80 grams. By how much was the patient's dosage increased?

P9. At a hotel, $\frac{3}{4}$ of the 100 rooms are occupied today. Yesterday, $\frac{4}{5}$ of the 100 rooms were occupied. On which day were more of the rooms occupied and by how much more?

P10. At a school, 40% of the teachers teach English. If 20 teachers teach English, how many teachers work at the school?

P11. A patient was given blood pressure medicine at a dosage of 2 grams. The patient's dosage was then decreased to 0.45 grams. By how much was the patient's dosage decreased?

P12. Two weeks ago, $\frac{2}{3}$ of the 60 customers at a skate shop were male. Last week, $\frac{3}{6}$ of the 80 customers were male. During which week were there more male customers?

P13. Jane ate lunch at a local restaurant. She ordered a $4.99 appetizer, a $12.50 entrée, and a $1.25 soda. If she wants to tip her server 20%, how much money will she spend in all?

P14. According to a survey, about 82% of engineers were highly satisfied with their job. If 145 engineers were surveyed, how many reported that they were highly satisfied?

P15. A patient was given 40 mg of a certain medicine. Later, the patient's dosage was increased to 45 mg. What was the percent increase in his medication?

83

P16. Order the following rational numbers from least to greatest: 0.55, 17%, $\sqrt{25}$, $\frac{64}{4}$, $\frac{25}{50}$, 3.

P17. Order the following rational numbers from greatest to least: 0.3, 27%, $\sqrt{100}$, $\frac{72}{9}$, $\frac{1}{9}$, 4.5

P18. Perform the following multiplication. Write each answer as a mixed number.

(a) $\left(1\frac{11}{16}\right) \times 4$

(b) $\left(12\frac{1}{3}\right) \times 1.1$

(c) $3.71 \times \left(6\frac{1}{5}\right)$

P19. Suppose you are making doughnuts and you want to triple the recipe you have. If the following list is the original amounts for the ingredients, what would be the amounts for the tripled recipe?

1 3/4	cup	Flour
1 1/4	tsp	Baking powder
3/4	tsp	Salt
3/8	cup	Sugar
1 1/2	Tbsp	Butter
2	large	Eggs
3/4	tsp	Vanilla extract
3/8	cup	Sour cream

PRACTICE SOLUTIONS

P1. The word *of* indicates multiplication, so 30% of 120 is found by multiplying 120 by 30%. Change 30% to a decimal, then multiply: $120 \times 0.3 = 36$

P2. The word *of* indicates multiplication, so 150% of 20 is found by multiplying 20 by 150%. Change 150% to a decimal, then multiply: $20 \times 1.5 = 30$

P3. Change 14.5% to a decimal before multiplying. $0.145 \times 96 = 13.92$.

P4. Follow the order of operations and utilize properties of fractions to solve each:

(a) Rewrite the problem as a multiplication problem: $\frac{2}{5} \times \frac{7}{4} = \frac{2\times7}{5\times4} = \frac{14}{20}$. Make sure the fraction is reduced to lowest terms. Both 14 and 20 can be divided by 2.

$$\frac{14}{20} = \frac{14 \div 2}{20 \div 2} = \frac{7}{10}$$

(b) The denominators of $\frac{7}{8}$ and $\frac{8}{16}$ are 8 and 16, respectively. The lowest common denominator of 8 and 16 is 16 because 16 is the least common multiple of 8 and 16. Convert the first fraction to its equivalent with the newly found common denominator of 16: $\frac{7 \times 2}{8 \times 2} = \frac{14}{16}$. Now that the fractions have the same denominator, you can subtract them.

$$\frac{14}{16} - \frac{8}{16} = \frac{6}{16} = \frac{3}{8}$$

(c) When simplifying expressions, first perform operations within groups. Within the set of parentheses are multiplication and subtraction operations. Perform the multiplication first to get $\frac{1}{2} + \left(\frac{9}{4} - 2\right) + 4$. Then, subtract two to obtain $\frac{1}{2} + \frac{1}{4} + 4$. Finally, perform addition from left to right:

$$\frac{1}{2} + \frac{1}{4} + 4 = \frac{2}{4} + \frac{1}{4} + \frac{16}{4} = \frac{19}{4} = 4\frac{3}{4}$$

(d) First, evaluate the terms in the parentheses $(5.5 + 3.3 \div 3)$ using order of operations. $3.3 \div 3 = 1.1$, and $5.5 + 1.1 = 6.6$. Next, rewrite the problem: $0.22 + 0.5 - 6.6$. Finally, add and subtract from left to right: $0.22 + 0.5 = 0.72$; $0.72 - 6.6 = -5.88$. The answer is -5.88.

(e) First, simplify within the parentheses, then change the fraction to a decimal and perform addition from left to right:

$$\frac{3}{2} + (2 - 0.75) + 2 =$$
$$\frac{3}{2} + 1.25 + 2 =$$
$$1.5 + 1.25 + 2 = 4.75$$

P5. (a) 15% can be written as $\frac{15}{100}$. Both 15 and 100 can be divided by 5: $\frac{15 \div 5}{100 \div 5} = \frac{3}{20}$

When converting from a percentage to a decimal, drop the percent sign and move the decimal point two places to the left: $15\% = 0.15$

(b) 24.36% written as a fraction is $\frac{24.36}{100}$, or $\frac{2436}{10,000}$, which reduces to $\frac{609}{2500}$. 24.36% written as a decimal is 0.2436. Recall that dividing by 100 moves the decimal two places to the left.

P6. (a) Recall that in the decimal system the first decimal place is one tenth: $\frac{4 \times 2}{5 \times 2} = \frac{8}{10} = 0.8$

Percent means "per hundred." $\frac{4 \times 20}{5 \times 20} = \frac{80}{100} = 80\%$

(b) The mixed number $3\frac{2}{5}$ has a whole number and a fractional part. The fractional part $\frac{2}{5}$ can be written as a decimal by dividing 5 into 2, which gives 0.4. Adding the whole to the part gives 3.4.

To find the equivalent percentage, multiply the decimal by 100. $3.4(100) = 340\%$. Notice that this percentage is greater than 100%. This makes sense because the original mixed number $3\frac{2}{5}$ is greater than 1.

P7. "More than" indicates addition, and "of" indicates multiplication. The expression can be written as $\frac{1}{2}(60) + 13$. So, the woman's age is equal to $\frac{1}{2}(60) + 13 = 30 + 13 = 43$. The woman is 43 years old.

P8. The first step is to determine what operation (addition, subtraction, multiplication, or division) the problem requires. Notice the keywords and phrases "by how much" and "increased." "Increased" means that you go from a smaller amount to a larger amount. This change can be found by subtracting the smaller amount from the larger amount: 0.80 grams– 0.22 grams = 0.58 grams.

Remember to line up the decimal when subtracting:

$$
\begin{array}{r}
0.80 \\
-\ \ 0.22 \\
\hline
0.58
\end{array}
$$

P9. First, find the number of rooms occupied each day. To do so, multiply the fraction of rooms occupied by the number of rooms available:

$$\text{Number occupied} = \text{Fraction occupied} \times \text{Total number}$$
$$\text{Number of rooms occupied today} = \frac{3}{4} \times 100 = 75$$
$$\text{Number of rooms occupied} = \frac{4}{5} \times 100 = 80$$

The difference in the number of rooms occupied is: $80 - 75 = 5$ rooms

P10. To answer this problem, first think about the number of teachers that work at the school. Will it be more or less than the number of teachers who work in a specific department such as English? More teachers work at the school, so the number you find to answer this question will be greater than 20.

40% of the teachers are English teachers. "Of" indicates multiplication, and words like "is" and "are" indicate equivalence. Translating the problem into a mathematical sentence gives $40\% \times t = 20$, where t represents the total number of teachers. Solving for t gives $t = \frac{20}{40\%} = \frac{20}{0.40} = 50$. Fifty teachers work at the school.

P11. The decrease is represented by the difference between the two amounts:

$$2 \text{ grams} - 0.45 \text{ grams} = 1.55 \text{ grams}.$$

Remember to line up the decimal point before subtracting.

$$
\begin{array}{r}
2.00 \\
-\ \ 0.45 \\
\hline
1.55
\end{array}
$$

P12. First, you need to find the number of male customers that were in the skate shop each week. You are given this amount in terms of fractions. To find the actual number of male customers, multiply the fraction of male customers by the number of customers in the store.

Actual number of male customers = fraction of male customers × total customers

$$\text{Number of male customers two weeks ago} = \frac{2}{3} \times 60 = \frac{120}{3} = 40$$

$$\text{Number of male customers last week} = \frac{3}{6} \times 80 = \frac{1}{2} \times 80 = \frac{80}{2} = 40$$

The number of male customers was the same both weeks.

P13. To find total amount, first find the sum of the items she ordered from the menu and then add 20% of this sum to the total.

$$\$4.99 + \$12.50 + \$1.25 = \$18.74$$

$$\$18.74 \times 20\% = (0.20)(\$18.74) = \$3.748 \approx \$3.75$$

$$\text{Total} = \$18.74 + \$3.75 = \$22.49$$

P14. 82% of 145 is 0.82 × 145 = 118.9. Because you can't have 0.9 of a person, we must round up to say that 119 engineers reported that they were highly satisfied with their jobs.

P15. To find the percent increase, first compare the original and increased amounts. The original amount was 40 mg, and the increased amount is 45 mg, so the dosage of medication was increased by 5 mg (45– 40 = 5). Note, however, that the question asks not by how much the dosage increased but by what percentage it increased.

$$\text{Percent increase} = \frac{\text{new amount} - \text{original amount}}{\text{original amount}} \times 100\%$$

$$= \frac{45 \text{ mg} - 40 \text{ mg}}{40 \text{ mg}} \times 100\% = \frac{5}{40} \times 100\% = 0.125 \times 100\% = 12.5\%$$

P16. Recall that the term rational simply means that the number can be expressed as a ratio or fraction. Notice that each of the numbers in the problem can be written as a decimal or integer:

$$17\% = 0.1717$$
$$\sqrt{25} = 5$$
$$\frac{64}{4} = 16$$
$$\frac{25}{50} = \frac{1}{2} = 0.5$$

So, the answer is 17%, $\frac{25}{50}$, 0.55, 3, $\sqrt{25}$, $\frac{64}{4}$.

P17. Converting all the numbers to integers and decimals makes it easier to compare the values:

$$27\% = 0.27$$
$$\sqrt{100} = 10$$
$$\frac{72}{9} = 8$$
$$\frac{1}{9} \approx 0.11$$

So, the answer is $\sqrt{100}, \frac{72}{9}, 4.5, 0.3, 27\%, \frac{1}{9}$.

Review Video: <u>Ordering Rational Numbers</u>
Visit mometrix.com/academy and enter code: 419578

P18. For each, convert improper fractions, adjust to a common denominator, perform the operations, and then simplify:

(a) Sometimes, you can skip converting the denominator and just distribute the multiplication.

$$\left(1\frac{11}{16}\right) \times 4 = \left(1 + \frac{11}{16}\right) \times 4$$
$$= 1 \times 4 + \frac{11}{16} \times 4$$
$$= 4 + \frac{11}{16} \times \frac{4}{1}$$
$$= 4 + \frac{44}{16} = 4 + \frac{11}{4} = 4 + 2\frac{3}{4} = 6\frac{3}{4}$$

(b)

$$\left(12\frac{1}{3}\right) \times 1.1 = \left(12 + \frac{1}{3}\right) \times \left(1 + \frac{1}{10}\right)$$
$$= \left(\frac{12}{1} \times \frac{3}{3} + \frac{1}{3}\right) \times \left(\frac{10}{10} + \frac{1}{10}\right)$$
$$= \left(\frac{36}{3} + \frac{1}{3}\right) \times \frac{11}{10}$$
$$= \frac{37}{3} \times \frac{11}{10}$$
$$= \frac{407}{30} = \frac{390}{30} + \frac{17}{30} = 13\frac{17}{30}$$

(c)

$$3.71 \times \left(6\frac{1}{5}\right) = \left(3 + \frac{71}{100}\right) \times \left(6 + \frac{1}{5}\right)$$
$$= \left(\frac{300}{100} + \frac{71}{100}\right) \times \left(\frac{6}{1} \times \frac{5}{5} + \frac{1}{5}\right)$$
$$= \frac{371}{100} \times \left(\frac{30}{5} + \frac{1}{5}\right)$$
$$= \frac{371}{100} \times \frac{31}{5}$$
$$= \frac{11501}{500} = \frac{11500}{500} + \frac{1}{500} = 23\frac{1}{500}$$

P19. Fortunately, some of the amounts are duplicated, so we do not need to figure out every amount.

$$1\frac{3}{4} \times 3 = (1 \times 3) + \left(\frac{3}{4} \times 3\right) \qquad 1\frac{1}{4} \times 3 = (1 \times 3) + \left(\frac{1}{4} \times 3\right) \qquad \frac{3}{4} \times 3 = \frac{3}{4} \times 3$$
$$= 3 + \frac{9}{4} \qquad\qquad\qquad = 3 + \frac{3}{4} \qquad\qquad\qquad = \frac{9}{4}$$
$$= 3 + 2\frac{1}{4} \qquad\qquad\qquad = 3\frac{3}{4} \qquad\qquad\qquad = 2\frac{1}{4}$$
$$= 5\frac{1}{4}$$

$$\frac{3}{8} \times 3 = \frac{3}{8} \times 3 \qquad\qquad 1\frac{1}{2} \times 3 = 1 \times 3 + \frac{1}{2} \times 3 \qquad\qquad 2 \times 3 = 6$$
$$= \frac{9}{8} \qquad\qquad\qquad = 3 + \frac{3}{2}$$
$$= 1\frac{1}{8} \qquad\qquad\qquad = 3 + 1\frac{1}{2}$$
$$= 4\frac{1}{2}$$

So, the result for the triple recipe is:

$5\frac{1}{4}$	cup	Flour
$3\frac{3}{4}$	tsp	Baking powder
$2\frac{1}{4}$	tsp	Salt
$1\frac{1}{8}$	cup	Sugar
$4\frac{1}{2}$	Tbsp	Butter
6	large	Eggs
$2\frac{1}{4}$	tsp	Vanilla extract
$1\frac{1}{8}$	cup	Sour cream

PROPORTIONS

A proportion is a relationship between two quantities that dictates how one changes when the other changes. A **direct proportion** describes a relationship in which a quantity increases by a set amount for every increase in the other quantity, or decreases by that same amount for every decrease in the other quantity. Example: Assuming a constant driving speed, the time required for a car trip increases as the distance of the trip increases. The distance to be traveled and the time required to travel are directly proportional.

An **inverse proportion** is a relationship in which an increase in one quantity is accompanied by a decrease in the other, or vice versa. Example: the time required for a car trip decreases as the speed increases, and increases as the speed decreases, so the time required is inversely proportional to the speed of the car.

> **Review Video: Proportions**
> Visit mometrix.com/academy and enter code: 505355

RATIOS

A **ratio** is a comparison of two quantities in a particular order. Example: If there are 14 computers in a lab, and the class has 20 students, there is a student to computer ratio of 20 to 14, commonly written as 20:14. Ratios are normally reduced to their smallest whole number representation, so 20:14 would be reduced to 10:7 by dividing both sides by 2.

> **Review Video: Ratios**
> Visit mometrix.com/academy and enter code: 996914

CONSTANT OF PROPORTIONALITY

When two quantities have a proportional relationship, there exists a **constant of proportionality** between the quantities. The product of this constant and one of the quantities is equal to the other quantity. For example, if one lemon costs $0.25, two lemons cost $0.50, and three lemons cost $0.75, there is a proportional relationship between the total cost of lemons and the number of lemons purchased. The constant of proportionality is the **unit price**, namely $0.25/lemon. Notice that the total price of lemons, t, can be found by multiplying the unit price of lemons, p, and the number of lemons, n: $t = pn$.

WORK/UNIT RATE

Unit rate expresses a quantity of one thing in terms of one unit of another. For example, if you travel 30 miles every two hours, a unit rate expresses this comparison in terms of one hour: in one hour you travel 15 miles, so your unit rate is 15 miles per hour. Other examples are how much one ounce of food costs (price per ounce) or figuring out how much one egg costs out of the dozen (price per 1 egg, instead of price per 12 eggs). The denominator of a unit rate is always 1. Unit rates are used to compare different situations to solve problems. For example, to make sure you get the best deal when deciding which kind of soda to buy, you can find the unit rate of each. If soda #1 costs $1.50 for a 1-liter bottle, and soda #2 costs $2.75 for a 2-liter bottle, it would be a better deal to buy soda #2, because its unit rate is only $1.375 per 1-liter, which is cheaper than soda #1. Unit rates can also help determine the length of time a given event will take. For example, if you can paint 2 rooms in 4.5 hours, you can determine how long it will take you to paint 5 rooms by solving for the unit rate per room and then multiplying that by 5.

> **Review Video: Rates and Unit Rates**
> Visit mometrix.com/academy and enter code: 185363

SLOPE

On a graph with two points, (x_1, y_1) and (x_2, y_2), the **slope** is found with the formula $m = \frac{y_2 - y_1}{x_2 - x_1}$; where $x_1 \neq x_2$ and m stands for slope. If the value of the slope is **positive**, the line has an *upward direction* from left to right. If the value of the slope is **negative**, the line has a *downward direction* from left to right. Consider the following example:

A new book goes on sale in bookstores and online stores. In the first month, 5,000 copies of the book are sold. Over time, the book continues to grow in popularity. The data for the number of copies sold is in the table below.

# of Months on Sale	1	2	3	4	5
# of Copies Sold (In Thousands)	5	10	15	20	25

So, the number of copies that are sold and the time that the book is on sale is a proportional relationship. In this example, an equation can be used to show the data: $y = 5x$, where x is the number of months that the book is on sale, and y is the number of copies sold. So, the slope of the corresponding line is $\frac{\text{rise}}{\text{run}} = \frac{5}{1} = 5$.

> **Review Video: Finding the Slope of a Line**
> Visit mometrix.com/academy and enter code: 766664

FINDING AN UNKNOWN IN EQUIVALENT EXPRESSIONS

It is often necessary to apply information given about a rate or proportion to a new scenario. For example, if you know that Jedha can run a marathon (26 miles) in 3 hours, how long would it take her to run 10 miles at the same pace? Start by setting up equivalent expressions:

$$\frac{26 \text{ mi}}{3 \text{ hr}} = \frac{10 \text{ mi}}{x \text{ hr}}$$

Now, cross multiply and, solve for x:

$$26x = 30$$
$$x = \frac{30}{26} = \frac{15}{13}$$
$$x \cong 1.15 \text{ hrs } or \text{ 1 hr 9 min}$$

So, at this pace, Jedha could run 10 miles in about 1.15 hours or about 1 hour and 9 minutes.

> **Review Video: Cross Multiply Fractions**
> Visit mometrix.com/academy and enter code: 893904

PRACTICE

P1. Solve the following for x.

(a) $\frac{45}{12} = \frac{15}{x}$

(b) $\frac{0.50}{2} = \frac{1.50}{x}$

(c) $\frac{40}{8} = \frac{x}{24}$

P2. At a school, for every 20 female students there are 15 male students. This same student ratio happens to exist at another school. If there are 100 female students at the second school, how many male students are there?

P3. In a hospital emergency room, there are 4 nurses for every 12 patients. What is the ratio of nurses to patients? If the nurse-to-patient ratio remains constant, how many nurses must be present to care for 24 patients?

P4. In a bank, the banker-to-customer ratio is 1:2. If seven bankers are on duty, how many customers are currently in the bank?

P5. Janice made $40 during the first 5 hours she spent babysitting. She will continue to earn money at this rate until she finishes babysitting in 3 more hours. Find how much money Janice earns per hour and the total she earned babysitting.

P6. The McDonalds are taking a family road trip, driving 300 miles to their cabin. It took them 2 hours to drive the first 120 miles. They will drive at the same speed all the way to their cabin. Find the speed at which the McDonalds are driving and how much longer it will take them to get to their cabin.

P7. It takes Andy 10 minutes to read 6 pages of his book. He has already read 150 pages in his book that is 210 pages long. Find how long it takes Andy to read 1 page and also find how long it will take him to finish his book if he continues to read at the same speed.

PRACTICE SOLUTIONS

P1. First, cross multiply; then, solve for x:

(a) $45x = 12 \times 15$
$45x = 180$
$x = \frac{180}{45} = 4$

(b) $0.5x = 1.5 \times 2$
$0.5x = 3$
$x = \frac{3}{0.5} = 6$

(c) $8x = 40 \times 24$
$8x = 960$
$x = \frac{960}{8} = 120$

P2. One way to find the number of male students is to set up and solve a proportion.

$$\frac{\text{number of female students}}{\text{number of male students}} = \frac{20}{15} = \frac{100}{\text{number of male students}}$$

Represent the unknown number of male students as the variable x: $\frac{20}{15} = \frac{100}{x}$

Cross multiply and then solve for x:

$$20x = 15 \times 100$$
$$x = \frac{1500}{20}$$
$$x = 75$$

P3. The ratio of nurses to patients can be written as 4 to 12, 4:12, or $\frac{4}{12}$. Because four and twelve have a common factor of four, the ratio should be reduced to 1:3, which means that there is one nurse present for every three patients. If this ratio remains constant, there must be eight nurses present to care for 24 patients.

P4. Use proportional reasoning or set up a proportion to solve. Because there are twice as many customers as bankers, there must be fourteen customers when seven bankers are on duty. Setting up and solving a proportion gives the same result:

$$\frac{\text{number of bankers}}{\text{number of customers}} = \frac{1}{2} = \frac{7}{\text{number of customers}}$$

Represent the unknown number of customers as the variable x: $\frac{1}{2} = \frac{7}{x}$.

To solve for x, cross multiply: $1 \times x = 7 \times 2$, so $x = 14$.

P5. Janice earns $8 per hour. This can be found by taking her initial amount earned, $40, and dividing it by the number of hours worked, 5. Since $\frac{40}{5} = 8$, Janice makes $8 in one hour. This can also be found by finding the unit rate, money earned per hour: $\frac{40}{5} = \frac{x}{1}$. Since cross multiplying yields $5x = 40$, and division by 5 shows that $x = 8$, Janice earns $8 per hour.

Janice will earn $64 babysitting in her 8 total hours (adding the first 5 hours to the remaining 3 gives the 8-hour total). Since Janice earns $8 per hour and she worked 8 hours, $\frac{\$8}{\text{hr}} \times 8 \text{ hrs} = \$64$. This can also be found by setting up a proportion comparing money earned to babysitting hours. Since she earns $40 for 5 hours and since the rate is constant, she will earn a proportional amount in 8 hours: $\frac{40}{5} = \frac{x}{8}$. Cross multiplying will yield $5x = 320$, and division by 5 shows that $x = 64$.

P6. The McDonalds are driving 60 miles per hour. This can be found by setting up a proportion to find the unit rate, the number of miles they drive per one hour: $\frac{120}{2} = \frac{x}{1}$. Cross multiplying yields $2x = 120$ and division by 2 shows that $x = 60$.

Since the McDonalds will drive this same speed for the remaining miles, it will take them another 3 hours to get to their cabin. This can be found by first finding how many miles the McDonalds have left to drive, which is $300-120 = 180$. The McDonalds are driving at 60 miles per hour, so a proportion can be set up to determine how many hours it will take them to drive 180 miles: $\frac{180}{x} = \frac{60}{1}$. Cross multiplying yields $60x = 180$, and division by 60 shows that $x = 3$. This can also be found by using the formula $D = r \times t$ (or distance = rate × time), where $180 = 60 \times t$, and division by 60 shows that $t = 3$.

93

P7. It takes Andy 10 minutes to read 6 pages, $\frac{10}{6} = 1\frac{2}{3}$ minutes, which is 1 minute and 40 seconds.

Next, determine how many pages Andy has left to read, $210 - 150 = 60$. Since it is now known that it takes him $1\frac{2}{3}$ minutes to read each page, then that rate must be multiplied by however many pages he has left to read (60) to find the time he'll need: $60 \times 1\frac{2}{3} = 100$, so it will take him 100 minutes, or 1 hour and 40 minutes, to read the rest of his book.

Algebra

TERMS AND COEFFICIENTS

Mathematical expressions consist of a combination of one or more values arranged in terms that are added together. As such, an expression could be just a single number, including zero. A **variable term** is the product of a real number, also called a **coefficient**, and one or more variables, each of which may be raised to an exponent. Expressions may also include numbers without a variable, called **constants** or **constant terms**. The expression $6s^2$, for example, is a single term where the coefficient is the real number 6 and the variable is s^2. Note that if a term is written as simply a variable to some exponent, like t^2, then the coefficient is 1, because $t^2 = 1t^2$.

LINEAR EXPRESSIONS

A **single variable linear expression** is the sum of a single variable term, where the variable has no exponent, and a constant, which may be zero. For instance, the expression $2w + 7$ has $2w$ as the variable term and 7 as the constant term. It is important to realize that terms are separated by addition or subtraction. Since an expression is a sum of terms, expressions such as $5x - 3$ can be written as $5x + (-3)$ to emphasize that the constant term is negative. A real-world example of a single variable linear expression is the perimeter of a square, four times the side length, often expressed: $4s$.

In general, a **linear expression** is the sum of any number of variable terms so long as none of the variables have an exponent. For example, $3m + 8n - \frac{1}{4}p + 5.5q - 1$ is a linear expression, but $3y^3$ is not. In the same way, the expression for the perimeter of a general triangle, the sum of the side lengths: $a + b + c$, is considered to be linear, but the expression for the area of square, the side length squared: s^2, is not.

LINEAR EQUATIONS

Equations that can be written as $ax + b = 0$, where $a \neq 0$, are referred to as **one variable linear equations**. A solution to such an equation is called a **root**. In the case where we have the equation $5x + 10 = 0$, if we solve for x we get a solution of $x = -2$. In other words, the root of the equation is -2. This is found by first subtracting 10 from both sides, which gives $5x = -10$. Next, simply divide both sides by the coefficient of the variable, in this case 5, to get $x = -2$. This can be checked by plugging -2 back into the original equation $(5)(-2) + 10 = -10 + 10 = 0$.

The **solution set** is the set of all solutions of an equation. In our example, the solution set would simply be -2. If there were more solutions (there usually are in multivariable equations) then they would also be included in the solution set. When an equation has no true solutions, this is referred to as an **empty set**. Equations with identical solution sets are **equivalent equations**. An **identity** is a term whose value or determinant is equal to 1.

Linear equations can be written many ways. Below is a list of some forms linear equations can take:

- **Standard Form**: $Ax + By = C$; the slope is $\frac{-A}{B}$ and the y-intercept is $\frac{C}{B}$
- **Slope Intercept Form**: $y = mx + b$, where m is the slope and b is the y-intercept
- **Point-Slope Form**: $y - y_1 = m(x - x_1)$, where m is the slope and (x_1, y_1) is a point on the line
- **Two-Point Form**: $\frac{y-y_1}{x-x_1} = \frac{y_2-y_1}{x_2-x_1}$, where (x_1, y_1) and (x_2, y_2) are two points on the given line
- **Intercept Form**: $\frac{x}{x_1} + \frac{y}{y_1} = 1$, where $(x_1, 0)$ is the point at which a line intersects the x-axis, and $(0, y_1)$ is the point at which the same line intersects the y-axis

> **Review Video: Slope-Intercept and Point-Slope Forms**
> Visit mometrix.com/academy and enter code: 113216

SOLVING ONE-VARIABLE LINEAR EQUATIONS

Multiply all terms by the lowest common denominator to eliminate any fractions. Look for addition or subtraction to undo so you can isolate the variable on one side of the equal sign. Divide both sides by the coefficient of the variable. When you have a value for the variable, substitute this value into the original equation to make sure you have a true equation. Consider the following example:

Kim's savings are represented by the table below. Represent her savings, using an equation.

X (Months)	Y (Total Savings)
2	$1300
5	$2050
9	$3050
11	$3550
16	$4800

The table shows a function with a constant rate of change, or slope, of 250. Given the points on the table, the slopes can be calculated as $(2050 - 1300)/(5 - 2)$, $(3050 - 2050)/(9 - 5)$, $(3550 - 3050)/(11 - 9)$, and $(4800 - 3550)/(16 - 11)$, each of which equals 250. Thus, the table shows a constant rate of change, indicating a linear function. The slope-intercept form of a linear equation is written as $y = mx + b$, where m represents the slope and b represents the y-intercept. Substituting the slope into this form gives $y = 250x + b$. Substituting corresponding x- and y-values from any point into this equation will give the y-intercept, or b. Using the point, (2, 1300), gives $1300 = 250(2) + b$, which simplifies as b = 800. Thus, her savings may be represented by the equation, $y = 250x + 800$.

RULES FOR MANIPULATING EQUATIONS

LIKE TERMS

Like terms are terms in an equation that have the same variable, regardless of whether or not they also have the same coefficient. This includes terms that *lack* a variable; all constants (i.e. numbers without variables) are considered like terms. If the equation involves terms with a variable raised to different powers, the like terms are those that have the variable raised to the same power.

For example, consider the equation $x^2 + 3x + 2 = 2x^2 + x - 7 + 2x$. In this equation, 2 and –7 are like terms; they are both constants. $3x$, x, and $2x$ are like terms: they all include the variable x raised to the first power. x^2 and $2x^2$ are like terms; they both include the variable x, raised to the second power. $2x$ and $2x^2$ are not like terms; although they both involve the variable x, the variable

95

is not raised to the same power in both terms. The fact that they have the same coefficient, 2, is not relevant.

CARRYING OUT THE SAME OPERATION ON BOTH SIDES OF AN EQUATION

When solving an equation, the general procedure is to carry out a series of operations on both sides of an equation, choosing operations that will tend to simplify the equation when doing so. The reason why the same operation must be carried out on both sides of the equation is because that leaves the meaning of the equation unchanged, and yields a result that is equivalent to the original equation. This would not be the case if we carried out an operation on one side of an equation and not the other. Consider what an equation means: it is a statement that two values or expressions are equal. If we carry out the same operation on both sides of the equation—add 3 to both sides, for example—then the two sides of the equation are changed in the same way, and so remain equal. If we do that to only one side of the equation—add 3 to one side but not the other—then that wouldn't be true; if we change one side of the equation but not the other then the two sides are no longer equal.

ADVANTAGE OF COMBINING LIKE TERMS

Combining like terms refers to adding or subtracting like terms—terms with the same variable—and therefore reducing sets of like terms to a single term. The main advantage of doing this is that it simplifies the equation. Often combining like terms can be done as the first step in solving an equation, though it can also be done later, such as after distributing terms in a product.

For example, consider the equation $2(x + 3) + 3(2 + x + 3) = -4$. The 2 and the 3 in the second set of parentheses are like terms, and we can combine them, yielding $2(x + 3) + 3(x + 5) = -4$. Now we can carry out the multiplications implied by the parentheses, distributing outer 2 and 3 accordingly: $2x + 6 + 3x + 15 = -4$. The $2x$ and the $3x$ are like terms, and we can add them together: $5x + 6 + 15 = -4$. Now, the constants 6, 15, and –4 are also like terms, and we can combine them as well: subtracting 6 and 15 from both sides of the equation, we get $5x = -4 - 6 - 15$, or $5x = -25$, which simplifies further to $x = -5$.

CANCELING TERMS ON OPPOSITE SIDES OF AN EQUATION

Two terms on opposite sides of an equation can be canceled if and only if they *exactly* match each other. They must have the same variable raised to the same power and the same coefficient. For example, in the equation $3x + 2x^2 + 6 = 2x^2 - 6$, $2x^2$ appears on both sides of the equation, and can be canceled, leaving $3x + 6 = -6$. The 6 on each side of the equation can*not* be canceled, because it is added on one side of the equation and subtracted on the other. While they cannot be canceled, however, the 6 and –6 are like terms and can be combined, yielding $3x = -12$, which simplifies further to $x = -4$.

It's also important to note that the terms to be canceled must be independent terms and cannot be part of a larger term. For example, consider the equation $2(x + 6) = 3(x + 4) + 1$. We cannot cancel the xs, because even though they match each other they are part of the larger terms $2(x + 6)$ and $3(x + 4)$. We must first distribute the 2 and 3, yielding $2x + 12 = 3x + 12 + 1$. Now we see that the terms with the x's do not match, but the 12s do, and can be canceled, leaving $2x = 3x + 1$, which simplifies to $x = -1$.

PROCESS FOR MANIPULATING EQUATIONS
ISOLATING VARIABLES

To **isolate a variable** means to manipulate the equation so that the variable appears by itself on one side of the equation, and does not appear at all on the other side. Generally, an equation or inequality is considered to be solved once the variable is isolated and the other side of the equation or inequality is simplified as much as possible. In the case of a two-variable equation or inequality, only one variable need be isolated; it will not usually be possible to simultaneously isolate both variables.

For a linear equation—an equation in which the variable only appears raised to the first power—isolating a variable can be done by first moving all the terms with the variable to one side of the equation and all other terms to the other side. (*Moving* a term really means adding the inverse of the term to both sides; when a term is *moved* to the other side of the equation its sign is flipped.) Then combine like terms on each side. Finally, divide both sides by the coefficient of the variable, if applicable. The steps need not necessarily be done in this order, but this order will always work.

EQUATIONS WITH MORE THAN ONE SOLUTION

Some types of non-linear equation, such as equations involving squares of variables, may have more than one solution. For example, the equation $x^2 = 4$ has two solutions: 2 and –2. Equations with absolute values can also have multiple solutions: $|x| = 1$ has the solutions $x = 1$ and $x = -1$.

It is also possible for a linear equation to have more than one solution, but only if the equation is true regardless of the value of the variable. In this case, the equation is considered to have infinitely many solutions, because any possible value of the variable is a solution. We know a linear equation has infinitely many solutions if when we combine like terms the variables cancel, leaving a true statement. For example, consider the equation $2(3x + 5) = x + 5(x + 2)$. Distributing, we get $6x + 10 = x + 5x + 10$; combining like terms gives $6x + 10 = 6x + 10$, and the $6x$ terms cancel to leave $10 = 10$. This is clearly true, so the original equation is true for any value of x. We could also have canceled the 10s leaving $0 = 0$, but again this is clearly true—in general if both sides of the equation match exactly, it has infinitely many solutions.

EQUATIONS WITH NO SOLUTION

Some types of non-linear equations, such as equations involving squares of variables, may have no solution. For example, the equation $x^2 = -2$ has no solutions in the real numbers, because the square of any real number must be positive. Similarly, $|x| = -1$ has no solution, because the absolute value of a number is always positive.

It is also possible for an equation to have no solution even if does not involve any powers greater than one or absolute values or other special functions. For example, the equation $2(x + 3) + x = 3x$ has no solution. We can see that if we try to solve it. First, we distribute, leaving $2x + 6 + x = 3x$. But now if we try to combine all the terms with the variable, we find that they cancel: we have $3x$ on the left and $3x$ on the right, canceling to leave us with $6 = 0$. This is clearly false. In general, whenever the variable terms in an equation cancel leaving different constants on both sides, it means that the equation has no solution. (If we are left with the *same* constant on both sides, the equation has infinitely many solutions instead.)

FEATURES OF EQUATIONS THAT REQUIRE SPECIAL TREATMENT
LINEAR EQUATIONS

A linear equation is an equation in which variables only appear by themselves; they are not multiplied together, not with exponents other than one, and not inside absolute value signs or any other functions. For example, the equation $x + 1 - 3x = 5 - x$ is a linear equation: while x appears multiple times, it never appears with an exponent other than one, or inside any function. The two-variable equation $2x - 3y = 5 + 2x$ is also a linear equation. In contrast, the equation $x^2 - 5 = 3x$ is *not* a linear equation, because it involves the term x^2. $\sqrt{x} = 5$ is not a linear equation, because it involves a square root. $(x - 1)^2 = 4$ is not a linear equation because even though there's no exponent on the x directly, it appears as part of an expression that is squared. The two-variable equation $x + xy - y = 5$ is not a linear equation because it includes the term xy, where two variables are multiplied together.

Linear equations can always be solved (or shown to have no solution) by combining like terms and performing simple operations on both sides of the equation. Some non-linear equations can also be solved by similar methods, but others may require more advanced methods of solution, if they can be solved analytically at all.

SOLVING EQUATIONS INVOLVING ROOTS

In an equation involving roots, the first step is to isolate the term with the root, if possible, and then raise both sides of the equation to the appropriate power to eliminate it. Consider an example equation, $2\sqrt{x + 1} - 1 = 3$. In this case, begin by adding 1 to both sides, yielding $2\sqrt{x + 1} = 4$, and then dividing both sides by 2, yielding $\sqrt{x + 1} = 2$. Now square both sides, yielding $x + 1 = 4$. Finally, subtracting 1 from both sides yields $x = 3$.

Squaring both sides of an equation may, however, yield a spurious solution—a solution to the squared equation that is *not* a solution of the original equation. It's therefore necessary to plug the solution back into the original equation to make sure it works. In this case, it does: $2\sqrt{3 + 1} - 1 = 2\sqrt{4} - 1 = 2(2) - 1 = 4 - 1 = 3$.

The same procedure applies for roots other than square roots. For example, given the equation $3 + \sqrt[3]{2x} = 5$, we can first subtract 3 from both sides, yielding $\sqrt[3]{2x} = 2$ and isolating the root. Raising both sides to the third power yields $2x = 2^3$, i.e. $2x = 8$. We can now divide both sides by 2 to get $x = 4$.

SOLVING EQUATIONS WITH EXPONENTS

To solve an equation involving an exponent, the first step is to isolate the variable with the exponent. We can then take the appropriate root of both sides to eliminate the exponent. For instance, for the equation $2x^3 + 17 = 5x^3 - 7$, we can subtract $5x^3$ from both sides to get $-3x^3 + 17 = -7$, and then subtract 17 from both sides to get $-3x^3 = -24$. Finally, we can divide both sides by –3 to get $x^3 = 8$. Finally, we can take the cube root of both sides to get $x = \sqrt[3]{8} = 2$.

One important but often overlooked point is that equations with an exponent greater than 1 may have more than one answer. The solution to $x^2 = 9$ isn't simply $x = 3$; it's $x = \pm 3$: that is, $x = 3$ or $x = -3$. For a slightly more complicated example, consider the equation $(x - 1)^2 - 1 = 3$. Adding one to both sides yields $(x - 1)^2 = 4$; taking the square root of both sides yields $x - 1 = 2$. We can then add 1 to both sides to get $x = 3$. However, there's a second solution: we also have the possibility that $x - 1 = -2$, in which case $x = -1$. Both $x = 3$ and $x = -1$ are valid solutions, as can be verified by substituting them both into the original equation.

SOLVING EQUATIONS WITH ABSOLUTE VALUES

When solving an equation with an absolute value, the first step is to isolate the absolute value term. We then consider the two possibilities: when the expression inside the absolute value is positive or when it is negative. In the former case, the expression in the absolute value equals the expression on the other side of the equation; in the latter, it equals the additive inverse of that expression—the expression times negative one. We consider each case separately, and finally check for spurious solutions.

For instance, consider solving $|2x - 1| + x = 5$ for x. We can first isolate the absolute value by moving the x to the other side: $|2x - 1| = -x + 5$. Now, we have two possibilities. First, that $2x - 1$ is positive, and hence $2x - 1 = -x + 5$. Rearranging and combining like terms yields $3x = 6$, and hence $x = 2$. The other possibility is that $2x - 1$ is negative, and hence $2x - 1 = -(-x + 5) = x - 5$. In this case, rearranging and combining like terms yields $x = -4$. Substituting $x = 2$ and $x = -4$ back into the original equation, we see that they are both valid solutions.

Note that the absolute value of a sum or difference applies to the sum or difference as a whole, not to the individual terms: in general, $|2x - 1|$ is not equal to $|2x + 1|$ or to $|2x| - 1$.

SPURIOUS SOLUTIONS

A **spurious solution** may arise when we square both sides of an equation as a step in solving it, or under certain other operations on the equation. It is a solution to the squared or otherwise modified equation that is *not* a solution of the original equation. To identify a spurious solution, it's useful when you solve an equation involving roots or absolute values to plug the solution back into the original equation to make sure it's valid.

CHOOSING WHICH VARIABLE TO ISOLATE IN TWO-VARIABLE EQUATIONS

Similar to methods for a one-variable equation, solving a two-variable equation involves isolating a variable: manipulating the equation so that a variable appears by itself on one side of the equation, and not at all on the other side. However, in a two-variable equation, you will usually only be able to isolate one of the variables; the other variable may appear on the other side along with constant terms, or with exponents or other functions.

Often one variable will be much more easily isolated than the other, and therefore that's the variable you should choose. If one variable appears with various exponents, and the other only raised it to the first power, the latter variable is the one to isolate: given the equation $a^2 + 2b = a^3 + b + 3$, the b only appears to the first power, whereas a appears squared and cubed, so b is the variable that can be solved for: combining like terms and isolating the b on the left side of the equation, we get $b = a^3 - a^2 + 3$. If both variables are equally easy to isolate, then it's best to isolate the independent variable, if one is defined; if the two variables are x and y, the convention is that y is the independent variable.

PRACTICE

P1. Seeing the equation $2x + 4 = 4x + 7$, a student divides the first terms on each side by 2, yielding $x + 4 = 2x + 7$, and then combines like terms to get $x = -3$. However, this is incorrect, as can be seen by substituting –3 into the original equation. Explain what is wrong with the student's reasoning.

P2. Describe the steps necessary to solve the equation $2x + 1 - x = 4 + 3x + 7$.

P3. Describe the steps necessary to solve the equation $2(x + 5) = 7(4 - x)$.

P4. Find all real solutions to the equation $1 - \sqrt{x} = 2$.

P5. Find all real solutions to the equation $|x + 1| = 2x + 5$.

P6. Solve for x: $-x + 2\sqrt{x + 5} + 1 = 3$.

P7. Ray earns $10 an hour at his job. Write an equation for his earnings as a function of time spent working. Determine how long Ray has to work in order to earn $360.

P8. Simplify the following: $3x + 2 + 2y = 5y - 7 + |2x - 1|$

PRACTICE SOLUTIONS

P1. As stated, it's easy to verify that the student's solution is incorrect: $2(-3) + 4 = -2$ and $4(-3) + 7 = -5$; clearly $-2 \neq -5$. The mistake was in the first step, which illustrates a common type of error in solving equations. The student tried to simplify the two variable terms by dividing them by 2. However, it's not valid to multiply or divide only one term on each side of an equation by a number; when multiplying or dividing, the operation must be applied to *every* term in the equation. So, dividing by 2 would yield not $x + 4 = 2x + 7$, but $x + 2 = 2x + \frac{7}{2}$. While this is now valid, that fraction is inconvenient to work with, so this may not be the best first step in solving the equation. Rather, it may have been better to first combine like terms: subtracting $4x$ from both sides yields $-2x + 4 = 7$; subtracting 4 from both sides yields $-2x = 3$; and *now* we can divide both sides by –2 to get $x = -\frac{3}{2}$.

P2. Our ultimate goal is to isolate the variable, x. To that end we first move all the terms containing x to the left side of the equation, and all the constant terms to the right side. Note that when we move a term to the other side of the equation its sign changes. We are therefore now left with $2x - x - 3x = 4 + 7 - 1$.

Next, we combine the like terms on each side of the equation, adding and subtracting the terms as appropriate. This leaves us with $-2x = 10$.

At this point, we're almost done; all that remains is to divide both sides by -2 to leave the x by itself. We now have our solution, $x = -5$. We can verify that this is a correct solution by substituting it back into the original equation.

P3. Generally, in equations that have a sum or difference of terms multiplied by another value or expression, the first step is to multiply those terms, distributing as necessary: $2(x + 5) = 2(x) + 2(5) = 2x + 10$, and $7(4 - x) = 7(4) - 7(x) = 28 - 7x$. So, the equation becomes $2x + 10 = 28 - 7x$. We can now add $7x$ to both sides to eliminate the variable from the right-hand side: $9x + 10 = 28$. Similarly, we can subtract 10 from both sides to move all the constants to the right: $9x = 18$. Finally, we can divide both sides by 9, yielding the final answer, $x = 2$.

P4. It's not hard to isolate the root: subtract one from both sides, yielding $-\sqrt{x} = 1$. Finally, multiply both sides by –1, yielding $\sqrt{x} = -1$. Squaring both sides of the equation yields $x = 1$. However, if we plug this back into the original equation, we get $1 - \sqrt{1} = 2$, which is false. Therefore $x = 1$ is a spurious solution, and the equation has no real solutions.

P5. This equation has two possibilities: $x + 1 = 2x + 5$, which simplifies to $x = -4$; or $x + 1 = -(2x + 5) = -2x - 5$, which simplifies to $x = -2$. However, if we try substituting both values back into the original equation, we see that only $x = -2$ yields a true statement. $x = -4$ is a spurious solution; $x = -2$ is the only valid solution to the equation.

P6. Start by isolating the term with the root. We can do that by moving the $-x$ and the 1 to the other side, yielding $2\sqrt{x + 5} = 3 + x - 1$, or $2\sqrt{x + 5} = x + 2$. Dividing both sides of the equation by 2 would give us a fractional term that could be messy to deal with, so we won't do that for now. Instead, we square both sides of the equation; note that on the left-hand side the 2 is outside the square root sign, so we have to square it. As a result, we get $4(x + 5) = (x + 2)^2$. Expanding both sides gives us $4x + 20 = x^2 + 4x + 4$. In this case, we see that we have $4x$ on both sides, so we can cancel the $4x$ (which is what allows us to solve this equation despite the different powers of x). We now have $20 = x^2 + 4$, or $x^2 = 16$. Since the variable is raised to an even power, we need to take the positive and negative roots, so $x = \pm 4$: that is, $x = 4$ or $x = -4$. Substituting both values into the original equation, we see that $x = 4$ satisfies the equation but $x = -4$ does not; hence $x = -4$ is a spurious solution, and the only solution to the equation is $x = 4$.

P7. The number of dollars that Ray earns is dependent on the number of hours he works, so earnings will be represented by the dependent variable y and hours worked will be represented by the independent variable x. He earns 10 dollars per hour worked, so his earnings can be calculated as $y = 10x$. To calculate the number of hours Ray must work in order to earn \$360, plug in 360 for y and solve for x:

$$360 = 10x$$
$$x = \frac{360}{10} = 36$$

P8. To simplify this equation, we must isolate one of its variables on one side of the equation. In this case, the x appears under an absolute value sign, which makes it difficult to isolate. The y, on the other hand, only appears without an exponent—the equation is linear in y. We will therefore choose to isolate the y. The first step, then, is to move all the terms with y to the left side of the equation, which we can do by subtracting $5y$ from both sides:

$$3x + 2 - 3y = -7 + |2x - 1|$$

We can then move all the terms that do *not* include y to the right side of the equation, by subtracting $3x$ and 2 from both sides of the equation:

$$-3y = -3x - 9 + |2x - 1|$$

Finally, we can isolate the y by dividing both sides by –3.

$$y = x + 3 - \frac{1}{3}|2x - 1|$$

This is as far as we can simplify the equation; we cannot combine the terms inside and outside the absolute value sign. We can therefore consider the equation to be solved.

INEQUALITIES

Commonly in algebra and other upper-level fields of math you find yourself working with mathematical expressions that do not equal each other. The statement comparing such expressions with symbols such as < (less than) or > (greater than) is called an *inequality*. An example of an inequality is $7x > 5$. To solve for x, simply divide both sides by 7 and the solution is shown to be $x > \frac{5}{7}$. Graphs of the solution set of inequalities are represented on a number line. Open circles are used to show that an expression approaches a number but is never quite equal to that number.

> **Review Video: <u>Inequalities</u>**
> Visit mometrix.com/academy and enter code: 347842

Conditional inequalities are those with certain values for the variable that will make the condition true and other values for the variable where the condition will be false. **Absolute inequalities** can have any real number as the value for the variable to make the condition true, while there is no real number value for the variable that will make the condition false. Solving inequalities is done by following the same rules as for solving equations with the exception that when multiplying or dividing by a negative number the direction of the inequality sign must be flipped or reversed. **Double inequalities** are situations where two inequality statements apply to the same variable expression. An example of this is $-c < ax + b < c$.

DETERMINING SOLUTIONS TO INEQUALITIES

To determine whether a coordinate is a solution of an inequality, you can substitute the values of the coordinate into the inequality, simplify, and check whether the resulting statement holds true. For instance, to determine whether $(-2, 4)$ is a solution of the inequality $y \geq -2x + 3$, substitute the values into the inequality, $4 \geq -2(-2) + 3$. Simplify the right side of the inequality and the result is $4 \geq 7$, which is a false statement. Therefore, the coordinate is not a solution of the inequality. You can also use this method to determine which part of the graph of an inequality is shaded. The graph of $y \geq -2x + 3$ includes the solid line $y = -2x + 3$ and, since it excludes the point $(-2, 4)$ to the left of the line, it is shaded to the right of the line.

FLIPPING INEQUALITY SIGNS

When given an inequality, we can always turn the entire inequality around, swapping the two sides of the inequality and changing the inequality sign. For instance, $x + 2 > 2x - 3$ is equivalent to $2x - 3 < x + 2$. Aside from that, normally the inequality does not change if we carry out the same operation on both sides of the inequality. There is, however, one principal exception: if we *multiply* or *divide* both sides of the inequality by a *negative number*, the inequality is flipped. For example, if we take the inequality $-2x < 6$ and divide both sides by -2, the inequality flips and we are left with $x > -3$. This *only* applies to multiplication and division, and only with negative numbers. Multiplying or dividing both sides by a positive number, or adding or subtracting any number regardless of sign, does not flip the inequality.

COMPOUND INEQUALITIES

A **compound inequality** is an equality that consists of two inequalities combined with *and* or *or*. The two components of a proper compound inequality must be of opposite type: that is, one must be greater than (or greater than or equal to), the other less than (or less than or equal to). For instance, "$x + 1 < 2$ or $x + 1 > 3$" is a compound inequality, as is "$2x \geq 4$ and $2x \leq 6$." An *and* inequality can be written more compactly by having one inequality on each side of the common part: "$2x \geq 1$ and $2x \leq 6$," can also be written as $1 \leq 2x \leq 6$.

In order for the compound inequality to be meaningful, the two parts of an *and* inequality must overlap; otherwise no numbers satisfy the inequality. On the other hand, if the two parts of an *or* inequality overlap, then *all* numbers satisfy the inequality and as such is usually not meaningful.

Solving a compound inequality requires solving each part separately. For example, given the compound inequality "$x + 1 < 2$ or $x + 1 > 3$," the first inequality, $x + 1 < 2$, reduces to $x < 1$, and the second part, $x + 1 > 3$, reduces to $x > 2$, so the whole compound inequality can be written as "$x < 1$ or $x > 2$." Similarly, $1 \leq 2x \leq 6$ can be solved by dividing each term by 2, yielding $\frac{1}{2} \leq x \leq 3$.

SOLVING INEQUALITIES INVOLVING ABSOLUTE VALUES

To solve an inequality involving an absolute value, first isolate the term with the absolute value. Then proceed to treat the two cases separately as with an absolute value equation, but flipping the inequality in the case where the expression in the absolute value is negative (since that essentially involves multiplying both sides by -1.) The two cases are then combined into a compound inequality; if the absolute value is on the greater side of the inequality, then it is an *or* compound inequality, if on the lesser side, then it's an *and*.

Consider the inequality $2 + |x - 1| \geq 3$. We can isolate the absolute value term by subtracting 2 from both sides: $|x - 1| \geq 1$. Now, we're left with the two cases $x - 1 \geq 1$ or $x - 1 \leq -1$: note that in the latter, negative case, the inequality is flipped. $x - 1 \geq 1$ reduces to $x \geq 2$, and $x - 1 \leq -1$ reduces to $x \leq 0$. Since in the inequality $|x - 1| \geq 1$ the absolute value is on the greater side, the two cases combine into an *or* compound inequality, so the final, solved inequality is "$x \leq 0$ or $x \geq 2$."

> **Review Video: <u>Solving Absolute Value Inequalities</u>**
> Visit mometrix.com/academy and enter code: 997008

SOLVING INEQUALITIES INVOLVING SQUARE ROOTS

Solving an inequality with a square root involves two parts. First, we solve the inequality as if it were an equation, isolating the square root and then squaring both sides of the equation. Second, we restrict the solution to the set of values of x for which the value inside the square root sign is non-negative.

For example, in the inequality, $\sqrt{x - 2} + 1 < 5$, we can isolate the square root by subtracting 1 from both sides, yielding $\sqrt{x - 2} < 4$. Squaring both sides of the inequality yields $x - 2 < 16$, so $x < 18$. Since we can't take the square root of a negative number, we also require the part inside the square root to be non-negative. In this case, that means $x - 2 \geq 0$. Adding 2 to both sides of the inequality yields $x \geq 2$. Our final answer is a compound inequality combining the two simple inequalities: $x \geq 2$ and $x < 18$, or $2 \leq x < 18$.

Note that we only get a compound inequality if the two simple inequalities are in opposite directions; otherwise we take the one that is more restrictive.

The same technique can be used for other even roots, such as fourth roots. It is *not*, however, used for cube roots or other odd roots—negative numbers *do* have cube roots, so the condition that the quantity inside the root sign cannot be negative does not apply.

SPECIAL CIRCUMSTANCES

Sometimes an inequality involving an absolute value or an even exponent is true for all values of x, and we don't need to do any further work to solve it. This is true if the inequality, once the absolute value or exponent term is isolated, says that term is greater than a negative number (or greater than or equal to zero). Since an absolute value or a number raised to an even exponent is *always* non-negative, this inequality is always true.

PRACTICE

P1. Analyze the following inequalities:

> **(a)** $2 - |x + 1| < 3$
> **(b)** $2(x - 1)^2 + 7 \leq 1$

PRACTICE SOLUTIONS

P1. (a) Subtracting 2 from both sides yields $-|x + 1| < 1$; multiplying by -1—and flipping the inequality, since we're multiplying by a negative number—yields $|x + 1| > -1$. But since the absolute value cannot be negative, it's *always* greater than -1, so this inequality is true for all values of x.

(b) Subtracting 7 from both sides yields $2(x-1)^2 \leq -6$; dividing by 2 yields $(x-1)^2 \leq -3$. But $(x-1)^2$ must be nonnegative, and hence cannot be less than or equal to –3; this inequality has no solution.

POLYNOMIALS

Polynomials are made up of monomials and polynomials. A **monomial** is a single constant, variable, or product of constants and variables, such as 7, x, $2x$, or x^3y. There will never be addition or subtraction symbols in a monomial. Like monomials have like variables, but they may have different coefficients. **Polynomials** are algebraic expressions which use addition and subtraction to combine two or more monomials. Two terms make a **binomial**, three terms make a **trinomial**, etc. The **degree of a monomial** is the sum of the exponents of the variables. The **degree of a polynomial** is the highest degree of any individual term.

> **Review Video: Polynomials**
> Visit mometrix.com/academy and enter code: 305005

SIMPLIFYING POLYNOMIALS

Simplifying polynomials requires combining like terms. The like terms in a polynomial expression are those that have the same variable raised to the same power. It is often helpful to connect the like terms with arrows or lines in order to separate them from the other monomials. Once you have determined the like terms, you can rearrange the polynomial by placing them together. Remember to include the sign that is in front of each term. Once the like terms are placed together, you can apply each operation and simplify. When adding and subtracting polynomials, only add and subtract the **coefficient**, or the number part; the variable and exponent stay the same.

> **Review Video: Adding and Subtracting Polynomials**
> Visit mometrix.com/academy and enter code: 124088

THE FOIL METHOD

In general, multiplying polynomials is done by multiplying each term in one polynomial by each term in the other and adding the results. In the specific case for multiplying binomials, there is useful acronym, FOIL, that can help you make sure to cover each combination of terms. The **FOIL method** for $(Ax + By)(Cx + Dy)$ would be:

F	Multiply the *first* terms of each binomial	$(\overset{first}{\overbrace{Ax}} + By)(\overset{first}{\overbrace{Cx}} + Dy)$	ACx^2
O	Multiply the *outer* terms	$(\overset{outer}{\overbrace{Ax}} + By)(Cx + \overset{outer}{\overbrace{Dy}})$	$ADxy$
I	Multiply the *inner* terms	$(Ax + \underset{inner}{\underbrace{By}})(\underset{inner}{\underbrace{Cx}} + Dy)$	$BCxy$
L	Multiply the *last* terms of each binomial	$(Ax + \underset{last}{\underbrace{By}})(Cx + \underset{last}{\underbrace{Dy}})$	BDy^2

Then add up the result of each and combine like terms: $ACx^2 + (AD + BC)xy + BDy^2$.

For example, using the FOIL method on binomials $(x + 2)$ and $(x - 3)$:

$$\text{First:} \quad (\boxed{x} + 2)(\boxed{x} + (-3)) \quad \rightarrow \quad (x)(x) = x^2$$

$$\text{Outer:} \quad (\boxed{x} + 2)(x + \boxed{(-3)}) \quad \rightarrow \quad (x)(-3) = -3x$$

$$\text{Inner:} \quad (x + \boxed{2})(\boxed{x} + (-3)) \quad \rightarrow \quad (2)(x) = 2x$$

$$\text{Last:} \quad (x + \boxed{2})(x + \boxed{(-3)}) \quad \rightarrow \quad (2)(-3) = -6$$

This results in: $(x^2) + (-3x) + (2x) + (-6)$

Combine like terms: $x^2 + (-3 + 2)x + (-6) = x^2 - x - 6$

DIVIDING POLYNOMIALS

To divide polynomials, set up a long division problem, dividing a polynomial by either a monomial or another polynomial of equal or lesser degree.

When **dividing by a monomial**, divide each term of the polynomial by the monomial.

When **dividing by a polynomial**, begin by arranging the terms of each polynomial in order of one variable. You may arrange in ascending or descending order, but be consistent with both polynomials. To get the first term of the quotient, divide the first term of the dividend by the first term of the divisor. Multiply the first term of the quotient by the entire divisor and subtract that product from the dividend. Repeat for the second and successive terms until you either get a remainder of zero or a remainder whose degree is less than the degree of the divisor. If the quotient has a remainder, write the answer as a mixed expression in the form:

$$\text{quotient} + \frac{\text{remainder}}{\text{divisor}}$$

For example, we can evaluate the following expression in the same way as long division:

$$\frac{x^3 - 3x^2 - 2x + 5}{x - 5}$$

$$
\begin{array}{r}
x^2 + 2x + 8 \\
x - 5 \overline{)\ x^3 - 3x^2 - 2x + 5} \\
\underline{x^3 - 5x^2 } \\
2x^2 - 2x \\
\underline{2x^2 - 10x } \\
8x + 5 \\
\underline{8x + 40} \\
45
\end{array}
$$

$$\frac{x^3 - 3x^2 - 2x + 5}{x - 5} = x^2 + 2x + 8 + \frac{45}{x - 5}$$

When **factoring** a polynomial, first check for a common monomial factor, that is look to see if each coefficient has a common factor or if each term has an x in it. If the factor is a trinomial but not a perfect trinomial square, look for a factorable form, such as one of these:

$$x^2 + (a + b)x + ab = (x + a)(x + b)$$
$$(ac)x^2 + (ad + bc)x + bd = (ax + b)(cx + d)$$

For factors with four terms, look for groups to factor. Once you have found the factors, write the original polynomial as the product of all the factors. Make sure all of the polynomial factors are prime. Monomial factors may be *prime* or *composite*. Check your work by multiplying the factors to make sure you get the original polynomial.

Below are patterns of some special products to remember to help make factoring easier:

- Perfect trinomial squares: $x^2 + 2xy + y^2 = (x + y)^2$ or $x^2 - 2xy + y^2 = (x - y)^2$
- Difference between two squares: $x^2 - y^2 = (x + y)(x - y)$
- Sum of two cubes: $x^3 + y^3 = (x + y)(x^2 - xy + y^2)$
  - Note: the second factor is *not* the same as a perfect trinomial square, so do not try to factor it further.
- Difference between two cubes: $x^3 - y^3 = (x - y)(x^2 + xy + y^2)$
  - Again, the second factor is *not* the same as a perfect trinomial square.
- Perfect cubes: $x^3 + 3x^2y + 3xy^2 + y^3 = (x + y)^3$ and $x^3 - 3x^2y + 3xy^2 - y^3 = (x - y)^3$

RATIONAL EXPRESSIONS

Rational expressions are fractions with polynomials in both the numerator and the denominator; the value of the polynomial in the denominator cannot be equal to zero. Be sure to keep track of values that make the denominator of the original expression zero as the final result inherits the same restrictions. For example, a denominator of $x - 3$ indicates that the expression is not defined when $x = 3$ and as such, regardless of any operations done to the expression, it remains undefined there.

To **add or subtract** rational expressions, first find the common denominator, then rewrite each fraction as an equivalent fraction with the common denominator. Finally, add or subtract the numerators to get the numerator of the answer, and keep the common denominator as the denominator of the answer.

When **multiplying** rational expressions factor each polynomial and cancel like factors (a factor which appears in both the numerator and the denominator). Then, multiply all remaining factors in the numerator to get the numerator of the product, and multiply the remaining factors in the denominator to get the denominator of the product. Remember: cancel entire factors, not individual terms.

To **divide** rational expressions, take the reciprocal of the divisor (the rational expression you are dividing by) and multiply by the dividend.

> **Review Video: Rational Expressions**
> Visit mometrix.com/academy and enter code: 415183

SIMPLIFYING RATIONAL EXPRESSIONS

To simplify a rational expression, factor the numerator and denominator completely. Factors that are the same and appear in the numerator and denominator have a ratio of 1. For example, look at the following expression:

$$\frac{x-1}{1-x^2}$$

The denominator, $(1-x^2)$, is a difference of squares. It can be factored as $(1-x)(1+x)$. The factor $1-x$ and the numerator $x-1$ are opposites and have a ratio of -1. Rewrite the numerator as $-1(1-x)$. So, the rational expression can be simplified as follows:

$$\frac{x-1}{1-x^2}=\frac{-1(1-x)}{(1-x)(1+x)}=\frac{-1}{1+x}$$

Note that since the original expression is only defined for $x \neq \{-1,1\}$, the simplified expression has the same restrictions.

> **Review Video: Reducing Rational Expressions**
> Visit mometrix.com/academy and enter code: 788868

PRACTICE

P1. Expand the following polynomials:

(a) $(x+3)(x-7)(2x)$

(b) $(x+2)^2(x-2)^2$

(c) $(x^2+5x+5)(3x-1)$

P2. Evaluate the following rational expressions:

(a) $\frac{x^3-2x^2-5x+6}{3x+6}$

(b) $\frac{x^2+4x+4}{4-x^2}$

PRACTICE SOLUTIONS

P1. (a) Apply the FOIL method and the distributive property of multiplication:

$$(x+3)(x-7)(2x) = (x^2-7x+3x-21)(2x)$$
$$= (x^2-4x-21)(2x)$$
$$= 2x^3-8x^2-42x$$

(b) Note the difference of squares form:

$$(x+2)^2(x-2)^2 = (x+2)(x+2)(x-2)(x-2)$$
$$= [(x+2)(x-2)][(x+2)(x-2)]$$
$$= (x^2-4)(x^2-4)$$
$$= x^4-8x^2+16$$

(c) Multiply each pair of monomials and combine like terms:

$$(x^2 + 5x + 5)(3x - 1) = 3x^3 + 15x^2 + 15x - x^2 - 5x - 5$$
$$= 3x^3 + 14x^2 + 10x - 5$$

P2. (a) Rather than trying to factor the fourth-degree polynomial, we can use long division:

$$\frac{x^3 - 2x^2 - 5x + 6}{3x + 6} = \frac{x^3 - 2x^2 - 5x + 6}{3(x + 2)}$$

$$
\begin{array}{r}
x^2 - 4x + 3 \\
x + 2 \overline{)\ x^3 - 2x^2 - 5x + 6} \\
\underline{x^3 + 2x^2} \\
-4x^2 - 5x \\
\underline{-4x^2 - 8x} \\
3x + 6 \\
\underline{3x + 6} \\
0
\end{array}
$$

$$\frac{x^3 - 2x^2 - 5x + 6}{3(x + 2)} = \frac{x^2 - 4x + 3}{3}$$

Note that since the original expression is only defined for $x \neq \{-2\}$, the simplified expression has the same restrictions.

(b) The denominator, $(4 - x^2)$, is a difference of squares. It can be factored as $(2 - x)(2 + x)$. The numerator, $(x^2 + 4x + 4)$, is a perfect square. It can be factored as $(x + 2)(x + 2)$. So, the rational expression can be simplified as follows:

$$\frac{x^2 + 4x + 4}{4 - x^2} = \frac{(x + 2)(x + 2)}{(2 - x)(2 + x)} = \frac{(x + 2)}{(2 - x)}$$

Note that since the original expression is only defined for $x \neq \{-2, 2\}$, the simplified expression has the same restrictions.

FACTORIALS

The **factorial** is a function that can be performed on any **non-negative integer**. It is represented by the ! sign written after the integer on which it is being performed. The factorial of an integer is the product of all positive integers less than or equal to the number. For example, 4! (read "4 factorial") is calculated as $4 \times 3 \times 2 \times 1 = 24$.

Since 0 is not itself a positive integer, nor does it have any positive integers less than it, 0! cannot be calculated using this method. Instead, 0! is defined by convention to equal 1. This makes sense if you consider the pattern of descending factorials:

$$5! = 120$$
$$4! = \frac{5!}{5} = \frac{120}{5} = 24$$
$$3! = \frac{4!}{4} = \frac{24}{4} = 6$$
$$2! = \frac{3!}{3} = \frac{6}{3} = 2$$
$$1! = \frac{2!}{2} = \frac{2}{2} = 1$$
$$0! = \frac{1!}{1} = \frac{1}{1} = 1$$

Geometry

LINES AND PLANES

A **point** is a fixed location in space; has no size or dimensions; commonly represented by a dot. A **line** is a set of points that extends infinitely in two opposite directions. It has length, but no width or depth. A line can be defined by any two distinct points that it contains. A **line segment** is a portion of a line that has definite endpoints. A **ray** is a portion of a line that extends from a single point on that line in one direction along the line. It has a definite beginning, but no ending.

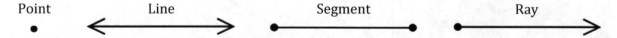

Point   Line   Segment   Ray

Intersecting lines are lines that have exactly one point in common. **Concurrent lines** are multiple lines that intersect at a single point. **Perpendicular lines** are lines that intersect at right angles. They are represented by the symbol ⊥. The shortest distance from a line to a point not on the line is a perpendicular segment from the point to the line. **Parallel lines** are lines in the same plane that have no points in common and never meet. It is possible for lines to be in different planes, have no points in common, and never meet, but they are not parallel because they are in different planes.

Intersecting   Concurrent   Perpendicular   Parallel

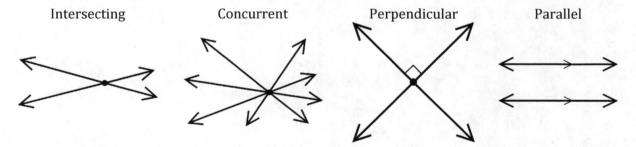

A **transversal** is a line that intersects at least two other lines, which may or may not be parallel to one another. A transversal that intersects parallel lines is a common occurrence in geometry. A **bisector** is a line or line segment that divides another line segment into two equal lengths. A

perpendicular bisector of a line segment is composed of points that are equidistant from the endpoints of the segment it is dividing.

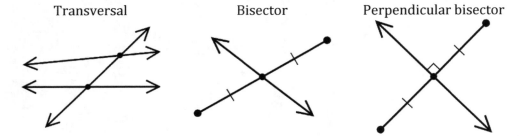

Transversal   Bisector   Perpendicular bisector

The **projection of a point on a line** is the point at which a perpendicular line drawn from the given point to the given line intersects the line. This is also the shortest distance from the given point to the line. The **projection of a segment on a line** is a segment whose endpoints are the points formed when perpendicular lines are drawn from the endpoints of the given segment to the given line. This is similar to the length a diagonal line appears to be when viewed from above.

Projection of a point on a line   Projection of a segment on a line

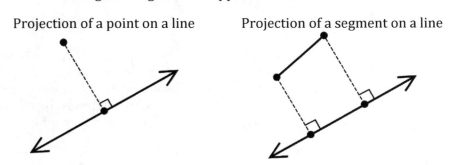

A **plane** is a two-dimensional flat surface defined by three non-collinear points. A plane extends an infinite distance in all directions in those two dimensions. It contains an infinite number of points, parallel lines and segments, intersecting lines and segments, as well as parallel or intersecting rays. A plane will never contain a three-dimensional figure or skew lines, lines that don't intersect and are not parallel. Two given planes are either parallel or they intersect at a line. A plane may intersect a circular conic surface to form **conic sections**, such as a parabola, hyperbola, circle or ellipse.

Review Video: <u>Lines and Planes</u>
Visit mometrix.com/academy and enter code: 554267

ANGLES

An **angle** is formed when two lines or line segments meet at a common point. It may be a common starting point for a pair of segments or rays, or it may be the intersection of lines. Angles are represented by the symbol ∠.

The **vertex** is the point at which two segments or rays meet to form an angle. If the angle is formed by intersecting rays, lines, and/or line segments, the vertex is the point at which four angles are formed. The pairs of angles opposite one another are called vertical angles, and their measures are equal.

- An **acute** angle is an angle with a degree measure less than 90°.
- A **right** angle is an angle with a degree measure of exactly 90°.
- An **obtuse** angle is an angle with a degree measure greater than 90° but less than 180°.
- A **straight angle** is an angle with a degree measure of exactly 180°. This is also a semicircle.
- A **reflex angle** is an angle with a degree measure greater than 180° but less than 360°.

A **full angle** is an angle with a degree measure of exactly 360°. This is also a circle.

Two angles whose sum is exactly 90° are said to be **complementary**. The two angles may or may not be adjacent. In a right triangle, the two acute angles are complementary.

Two angles whose sum is exactly 180° are said to be **supplementary**. The two angles may or may not be adjacent. Two intersecting lines always form two pairs of supplementary angles. Adjacent supplementary angles will always form a straight line.

Two angles that have the same vertex and share a side are said to be **adjacent**. Vertical angles are not adjacent because they share a vertex but no common side.

Adjacent
Share vertex and side

Not adjacent
Share part of side, but not vertex

When two parallel lines are cut by a transversal, the angles that are between the two parallel lines are **interior angles**. In the diagram below, angles 3, 4, 5, and 6 are interior angles.

When two parallel lines are cut by a transversal, the angles that are outside the parallel lines are **exterior angles**. In the diagram below, angles 1, 2, 7, and 8 are exterior angles.

When two parallel lines are cut by a transversal, the angles that are in the same position relative to the transversal and a parallel line are **corresponding angles**. The diagram below has four pairs of corresponding angles: angles 1 and 5; angles 2 and 6; angles 3 and 7; and angles 4 and 8. Corresponding angles formed by parallel lines are congruent.

When two parallel lines are cut by a transversal, the two interior angles that are on opposite sides of the transversal are called **alternate interior angles**. In the diagram below, there are two pairs of alternate interior angles: angles 3 and 6, and angles 4 and 5. Alternate interior angles formed by parallel lines are congruent.

111

When two parallel lines are cut by a transversal, the two exterior angles that are on opposite sides of the transversal are called **alternate exterior angles**.

In the diagram below, there are two pairs of alternate exterior angles: angles 1 and 8, and angles 2 and 7. Alternate exterior angles formed by parallel lines are congruent.

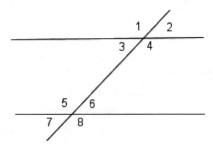

When two lines intersect, four angles are formed. The non-adjacent angles at this vertex are called vertical angles. Vertical angles are congruent. In the diagram, $\angle ABD \cong \angle CBE$ and $\angle ABC \cong \angle DBE$.

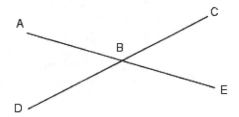

Practice

P1. Find the measure of angles **(a)**, **(b)**, and **(c)** based on the figure with two parallel lines, two perpendicular lines and one transversal:

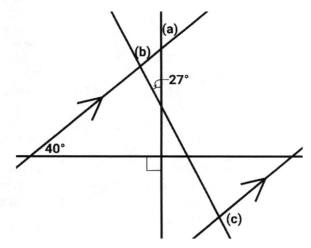

PRACTICE SOLUTIONS

P1. (a) The vertical angle paired with (a) is part of a right triangle with the 40° angle. Thus the measure can be found:

$$90° = 40° + a$$
$$a = 50°$$

(b) The triangle formed by the supplementary angle to (b) is part of a triangle with the vertical angle paired with (a) and the given angle of 27°. Since $a = 50°$:

$$180° = (180° - b) + 50° + 27°$$
$$103° = 180° - b$$
$$-77° = -b$$
$$77° = b$$

(c) As they are part of a transversal crossing parallel lines, angles (b) and (c) are supplementary. Thus $c = 103°$

$$V = \frac{1}{3}\pi r^2 h = \frac{1}{3}\pi(5 \text{ yd})^2(7 \text{ yd}) = \frac{35\pi}{3} \text{ yd}^3 \cong 36.65 \text{ yd}^3$$

TRIANGLES

A triangle is a three-sided figure with the sum of its interior angles being 180° The **perimeter of any triangle** is found by summing the three side lengths; $P = a + b + c$. For an equilateral triangle, this is the same as $P = 3a$, where a is any side length, since all three sides are the same length.

The **area of any triangle** can be found by taking half the product of one side length, referred to as the base and often given the variable b, and the perpendicular distance from that side to the opposite vertex, called the altitude or height and given the variable h. In equation form that is $A = \frac{1}{2}bh$. Another formula that works for any triangle is $A = \sqrt{s(s - a)(s - b)(s - c)}$, where s is the semiperimeter: $\frac{a+b+c}{2}$, and a, b, and c are the lengths of the three sides. Special cases include isosceles triangles: $A = \frac{1}{2}b\sqrt{a^2 - \frac{b^2}{4}}$, where b is the unique side and a is the length of one of the two congruent sides, and equilateral triangles: $A = \frac{\sqrt{3}}{4}a^2$, where a is the length of a side.

> **Review Video: Area and Perimeter of a Triangle**
> Visit mometrix.com/academy and enter code: 853779

QUADRILATERALS

A **quadrilateral** is a closed two-dimensional geometric figure that has four straight sides. The sum of the interior angles of any quadrilateral is 360°.

Trapezoid: A trapezoid is defined as a quadrilateral that has at least one pair of parallel sides. There are no rules for the second pair of sides. So, there are no rules for the diagonals and no lines of symmetry for a trapezoid.

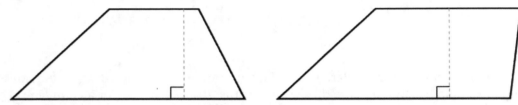

The **area of a trapezoid** is found by the formula $A = \frac{1}{2}h(b_1 + b_2)$, where h is the height (segment joining and perpendicular to the parallel bases), and b_1 and b_2 are the two parallel sides (bases). Do not use one of the other two sides as the height unless that side is also perpendicular to the parallel bases.

The **perimeter of a trapezoid** is found by the formula $P = a + b_1 + c + b_2$, where a, b_1, c, and b_2 are the four sides of the trapezoid.

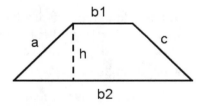

> **Review Video: <u>Area and Perimeter of a Trapezoid</u>**
> Visit mometrix.com/academy and enter code: 587523

Parallelogram: A quadrilateral that has two pairs of opposite parallel sides. As such it is a special type of trapezoid. The sides that are parallel are also congruent. The opposite interior angles are always congruent, and the consecutive interior angles are supplementary. The diagonals of a parallelogram divide each other. Each diagonal divides the parallelogram into two congruent triangles. A parallelogram has no line of symmetry, but does have 180-degree rotational symmetry about the midpoint.

The **area of a parallelogram** is found by the formula $A = bh$, where b is the length of the base, and h is the height. Note that the base and height correspond to the length and width in a rectangle, so this formula would apply to rectangles as well. Do not confuse the height of a parallelogram with the length of the second side. The two are only the same measure in the case of a rectangle.

The **perimeter of a parallelogram** is found by the formula $P = 2a + 2b$ or $P = 2(a + b)$, where a and b are the lengths of the two sides.

> **Review Video: How to Find the Area and Perimeter of a Parallelogram**
> Visit mometrix.com/academy and enter code: 718313

Isosceles trapezoid: A trapezoid with equal base angles. This gives rise to other properties including: the two nonparallel sides have the same length, the two non-base angles are also equal, and there is one line of symmetry through the midpoints of the parallel sides.

Rectangle: A quadrilateral with four right angles. All rectangles are parallelograms and trapezoids, but not all parallelograms or trapezoids are rectangles. The diagonals of a rectangle are congruent. Rectangles have 2 lines of symmetry (through each pair of opposing midpoints) and 180-degree rotational symmetry about the midpoint.

The **area of a rectangle** is found by the formula $A = lw$, where A is the area of the rectangle, l is the length (usually considered to be the longer side) and w is the width (usually considered to be the shorter side). The numbers for l and w are interchangeable.

The **perimeter of a rectangle** is found by the formula $P = 2l + 2w$ or $P = 2(l + w)$, where l is the length, and w is the width. It may be easier to add the length and width first and then double the result, as in the second formula.

Square: A quadrilateral with four right angles and four congruent sides. Squares satisfy the criteria of all other types of quadrilaterals. The diagonals of a square are congruent and perpendicular to each other. Squares have 4 lines of symmetry (through each pair of opposing midpoints and along each of the diagonals) as well as 90-degree rotational symmetry about the midpoint.

The **area of a square** is found by using the formula $A = s^2$, where s is the length of one side. The **perimeter of a square** is found by using the formula $P = 4s$, where s is the length of one side. Because all four sides are equal in a square, it is faster to multiply the length of one side by 4 than to add the same number four times. You could use the formulas for rectangles and get the same answer.

CIRCLES

The **center** of a circle is the single point from which every point on the circle is **equidistant**. The **radius** is a line segment that joins the center of the circle and any one point on the circle. All radii of a circle are equal. Circles that have the same center, but not the same length of radii are **concentric**. The **diameter** is a line segment that passes through the center of the circle and has both endpoints on the circle. The length of the diameter is exactly twice the length of the radius. Point O in the diagram below is the center of the circle, segments $\overline{OX}$, $\overline{OY}$, and $\overline{OZ}$ are radii, and segment $\overline{XZ}$ is a diameter.

The **area of a circle** is found by the formula $A = \pi r^2$, where r is the length of the radius. If the diameter of the circle is given, remember to divide it in half to get the length of the radius before proceeding.

The **circumference** of a circle is found by the formula $C = 2\pi r$, where r is the radius. Again, remember to convert the diameter if you are given that measure rather than the radius.

PRACTICE

P1. Find the area and perimeter of the following quadrilaterals:

(a) A square with side length 2.5 cm.

(b) A parallelogram with height 3 m, base 4 m, and other side 6 m.

P2. Calculate the area of a triangle with side lengths of 7 ft, 8 ft, and 9 ft.

PRACTICE SOLUTIONS

P1. (a) $A = s^2 = (2.5 \text{ cm})^2 = 6.25 \text{ cm}^2$; $P = 4s = 4 \times 2.5 \text{ cm} = 10 \text{ cm}$

(b) $A = bh = (3 \text{ m})(4 \text{ m}) = 12 \text{ m}^2$; $P = 2a + 2b = 2 \times 6 \text{ m} + 2 \times 4 \text{ m} = 20 \text{ m}$

P2. Given only side lengths, we can use the semi perimeter to the find the area based on the formula, $A = \sqrt{s(s-a)(s-b)(s-c)}$, where s is the semiperimeter, $\frac{a+b+c}{2} = \frac{7+8+9}{2} = 12$ ft:

$$A = \sqrt{12(12-7)(12-8)(12-9)}$$
$$= \sqrt{(12)(5)(4)(3)}$$
$$= 12\sqrt{5} \text{ ft}^2$$

TRIANGLE CLASSIFICATION AND PROPERTIES

A **scalene triangle** is a triangle with no congruent sides. A scalene triangle will also have three angles of different measures. The angle with the largest measure is opposite the longest side, and the angle with the smallest measure is opposite the shortest side. An **acute triangle** is a triangle whose three angles are all less than 90°. If two of the angles are equal, the acute triangle is also an **isosceles triangle**. An isosceles triangle will also have two congruent angles opposite the two congruent sides. If the three angles are all equal, the acute triangle is also an **equilateral triangle**. An equilateral triangle will also have three congruent angles, each 60°. All equilateral triangles are also acute triangles. An **obtuse triangle** is a triangle with exactly one angle greater than 90°. The other two angles may or may not be equal. If the two remaining angles are equal, the obtuse triangle is also an isosceles triangle. A **right triangle** is a triangle with exactly one angle equal to

90°. All right triangles follow the Pythagorean theorem. A right triangle can never be acute or obtuse.

The table below illustrates how each descriptor places a different restriction on the triangle:

Sides \ Angles	Acute: All angles < 90°	Obtuse: One angle > 90°	Right: One angle = 90°
Scalene: No equal side lengths	$90° > \angle a > \angle b > \angle c$ $x > y > z$	$\angle a > 90° > \angle b > \angle c$ $x > y > z$	$90° = \angle a > \angle b > \angle c$ $x > y > z$
Isosceles: Two equal side lengths	$90° > \angle a, \angle b,$ or $\angle c$ $\angle b = \angle c, \quad y = z$	$\angle a > 90° > \angle b = \angle c$ $x > y = z$	$\angle a = 90°, \angle b = \angle c$ $= 45°$ $x > y = z$
Equilateral: Three equal side lengths	$60° = \angle a = \angle b = \angle c$ $x = y = z$		

Review Video: <u>Introduction to Types of Triangles</u>
Visit mometrix.com/academy and enter code: 511711

SIMILARITY AND CONGRUENCE RULES

Similar triangles are triangles whose corresponding angles are equal and whose corresponding sides are proportional. Represented by AAA. Similar triangles whose corresponding sides are congruent are also congruent triangles.

The triangles can be shown to be **congruent** in 5 ways:

- **SSS**: Three sides of one triangle are congruent to the three corresponding sides of the second triangle.
- **SAS**: Two sides and the included angle (the angle formed by those two sides) of one triangle are congruent to the corresponding two sides and included angle of the second triangle.

- **ASA**: Two angles and the included side (the side that joins the two angles) of one triangle are congruent to the corresponding two angles and included side of the second triangle.
- **AAS**: Two angles and a non-included side of one triangle are congruent to the corresponding two angles and non-included side of the second triangle.
- **HL**: The hypotenuse and leg of one right triangle are congruent to the corresponding hypotenuse and leg of the second right triangle.

> **Review Video: Similar Triangles**
> Visit mometrix.com/academy and enter code: 398538

GENERAL RULES FOR TRIANGLES

The **triangle inequality theorem** states that the sum of the measures of any two sides of a triangle is always greater than the measure of the third side. If the sum of the measures of two sides were equal to the third side, a triangle would be impossible because the two sides would lie flat across the third side and there would be no vertex. If the sum of the measures of two of the sides was less than the third side, a closed figure would be impossible because the two shortest sides would never meet. In other words, for a triangle with sides lengths A, B, and C: $A + B > C$, $B + C > A$, and $A + C > B$

The sum of the measures of the interior angles of a triangle is always 180°. Therefore, a triangle can never have more than one angle greater than or equal to 90°.

In any triangle, the angles opposite congruent sides are congruent, and the sides opposite congruent angles are congruent. The largest angle is always opposite the longest side, and the smallest angle is always opposite the shortest side.

The line segment that joins the midpoints of any two sides of a triangle is always parallel to the third side and exactly half the length of the third side.

> **Review Video: General Rules (Triangle Inequality Theorem)**
> Visit mometrix.com/academy and enter code: 166488

PRACTICE

P1. Given the following pairs of triangles, determine whether they are similar, congruent, or neither (note that the figures are not drawn to scale):

(a).

(b).

(c).

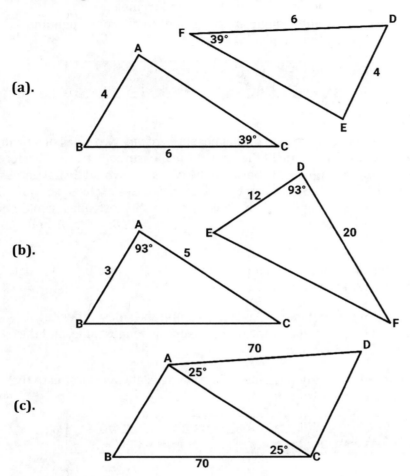

PRACTICE SOLUTIONS

P1. (a). Neither: We are given that two sides lengths and an angle are equal, however, the angle given is not between the given side lengths. That means there are two possible triangles that could satisfy the given measurements. Thus, we cannot be certain of congruence:

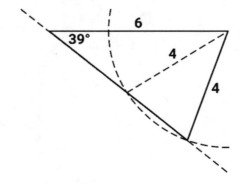

120

(b) Similar: Since we are given a side-angle-side of each triangle and the side lengths given are scaled evenly $\left(\frac{3}{5} \times \frac{4}{4} = \frac{12}{20}\right)$ and the angles are equal. Thus, $\triangle ABC \sim \triangle DEF$. If the side lengths were equal, then they would be congruent.

(c) Congruent: Even though we aren't given a measurement for the shared side of the figure, since it is shared it is equal. So, this is a case of SAS. Thus, $\triangle ABC \cong \triangle CDA$

THREE-DIMENSIONAL SHAPES

The **surface area of a solid object** is the area of all sides or exterior surfaces. For objects such as prisms and pyramids, a further distinction is made between base surface area (B) and lateral surface area (LA). For a prism, the total surface area (SA) is $SA = LA + 2B$. For a pyramid or cone, the total surface area is $SA = LA + B$.

> **Review Video: How to Calculate the Volume of 3D Objects**
> Visit mometrix.com/academy and enter code: 163343

The **surface area of a sphere** can be found by the formula $A = 4\pi r^2$, where r is the radius. The volume is given by the formula $V = \frac{4}{3}\pi r^3$, where r is the radius. Both quantities are generally given in terms of π.

The **volume of any prism** is found by the formula $V = Bh$, where B is the area of the base, and h is the height (perpendicular distance between the bases). The surface area of any prism is the sum of the areas of both bases and all sides. It can be calculated as $SA = 2B + Ph$, where P is the perimeter of the base.

For a **rectangular prism**, the volume can be found by the formula $V = lwh$, where V is the volume, l is the length, w is the width, and h is the height. The surface area can be calculated as $SA = 2lw + 2hl + 2wh$ or $SA = 2(lw + hl + wh)$.

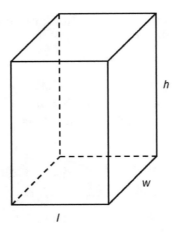

The **volume of a cube** can be found by the formula $V = s^3$, where s is the length of a side. The surface area of a cube is calculated as $SA = 6s^2$, where SA is the total surface area and s is the length of a side. These formulas are the same as the ones used for the volume and surface area of a rectangular prism, but simplified since all three quantities (length, width, and height) are the same.

> **Review Video: Volume and Surface Area of a Cube**
> Visit mometrix.com/academy and enter code: 664455

The **volume of a cylinder** can be calculated by the formula $V = \pi r^2 h$, where r is the radius, and h is the height. The surface area of a cylinder can be found by the formula $SA = 2\pi r^2 + 2\pi rh$. The first term is the base area multiplied by two, and the second term is the perimeter of the base multiplied by the height.

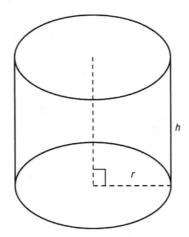

The **volume of a pyramid** is found by the formula $V = \frac{1}{3}Bh$, where B is the area of the base, and h is the height (perpendicular distance from the vertex to the base). Notice this formula is the same as $\frac{1}{3}$ times the volume of a prism. Like a prism, the base of a pyramid can be any shape.

Finding the **surface area of a pyramid** is not as simple as the other shapes we've looked at thus far. If the pyramid is a right pyramid, meaning the base is a regular polygon and the vertex is directly over the center of that polygon, the surface area can be calculated as $SA = B + \frac{1}{2}Ph_s$, where P is the perimeter of the base, and h_s is the slant height (distance from the vertex to the midpoint of one side of the base). If the pyramid is irregular, the area of each triangle side must be calculated individually and then summed, along with the base.

The **volume of a cone** is found by the formula $V = \frac{1}{3}\pi r^2 h$, where r is the radius, and h is the height. Notice this is the same as $\frac{1}{3}$ times the volume of a cylinder. The surface area can be calculated as $SA = \pi r^2 + \pi rs$, where s is the slant height. The slant height can be calculated using the Pythagorean theorem to be $\sqrt{r^2 + h^2}$, so the surface area formula can also be written as $SA = \pi r^2 + \pi r\sqrt{r^2 + h^2}$.

Review Video: <u>Volume and Surface Area of a Right Circular Cone</u>
Visit mometrix.com/academy and enter code: 573574

PRACTICE

P1. Find the surface area and volume of the following solids:

   (a) A cylinder with radius 5 m and height 0.5 m.

   (b) A trapezoidal prism with base area of 254 mm², base perimeter 74 mm, and height 10 mm.

   (c) A half sphere (radius 5 yds) on the base of an inverted cone with the same radius and a height of 7 yds.

PRACTICE SOLUTIONS

P1. (a) $SA = 2\pi r^2 + 2\pi rh = 2\pi(5 \text{ m})^2 + 2\pi(5 \text{ m})(0.5 \text{ m}) = 55\pi \text{ m}^2 \cong 172.79 \text{ m}^2$;
$V = \pi r^2 h = \pi(5 \text{ m})^2(0.5 \text{ m}) = 12.5\pi \text{ m}^3 \cong 39.27 \text{ m}^3$

(b) $SA = 2B + Ph = 2(254 \text{ mm}^2) + (74 \text{ mm})(10 \text{ mm}) = 1248 \text{ mm}^2$;
$V = Bh = (254 \text{ mm}^2)(10 \text{ mm}) = 2540 \text{ mm}^3$

(c) We can find s, the slant height using Pythagoras' theorem, and since this solid is made of parts of simple solids, we can combine the formulas to find surface area and volume:

$$s = \sqrt{r^2 + h^2} = \sqrt{(5 \text{ yd})^2 + (7 \text{ yd})^2} = \sqrt{74} \text{ yd}$$
$$SA = \frac{4\pi r^2}{2} + \pi rs = \frac{4\pi(5 \text{ yd})^2}{2} + \pi(5 \text{ yd})(\sqrt{74} \text{ yd}) = \left(5\pi + 5\pi\sqrt{74}\right) \text{ yd}^2 \cong 150.83 \text{ yd}^2$$
$$V = \frac{1}{3}\pi r^2 h = \frac{1}{3}\pi(5 \text{ yd})^2(7 \text{ yd}) = \frac{35\pi}{3} \text{ yd}^3 \cong 36.65 \text{ yd}^3$$

Probability and Data Analysis

Probability is the likelihood of a certain outcome occurring for a given event. An **event** is a situation that produces a result; that could be something as simple as flipping a coin or as complex as launching a rocket. Determining the probability of an outcome for an event can be equally simple or complex. As such there are specific terms used in the study of probability that need to be understood:

- **Compound event**—an event that involves two or more independent events (rolling a pair of dice and taking the sum)
- **Desired outcome** (or success)—an outcome that meets a particular set of criteria (a roll of 1 or 2 if we are looking for numbers less than 3)
- **Independent events**—two or more events whose outcomes do not affect one another (two coins tossed at the same time)
- **Dependent events**—two or more events whose outcomes affect one another (two cards drawn consecutively from the same deck)
- **Certain outcome**—probability of outcome is 100% or 1
- **Impossible outcome**—probability of outcome is 0% or 0
- **Mutually exclusive outcomes**—two or more outcomes whose criteria cannot all be satisfied in a single event (a coin coming up heads and tails on the same toss)
- **Random variable**—refers to all possible outcomes of a single event which may be discrete or continuous.

> **Review Video: Intro to Probability**
> Visit mometrix.com/academy and enter code: 212374

Theoretical probability can usually be determined without actually performing the event. The likelihood of a outcome occurring, or the probability of an outcome occurring, is given by the formula:

$$P(A) = \frac{\text{Number of acceptable outcomes}}{\text{Number of possible outcomes}}$$

Note that $P(A)$ is the probability of an outcome A occurring, and each outcome is just as likely to occur as any other outcome. If each outcome has the same probability of occurring as every other possible outcome, the outcomes are said to be equally likely to occur. The total number of acceptable outcomes must be less than or equal to the total number of possible outcomes. If the two are equal, then the outcome is certain to occur and the probability is 1. If the number of acceptable outcomes is zero, then the outcome is impossible and the probability is 0. For example, if there are 20 marbles in a bag and 5 are red, then the theoretical probability of randomly selecting a red marble is 5 out of 20, ($\frac{5}{20} = \frac{1}{4}$, 0.25, or 25%).

COMPLEMENT OF AN EVENT

Sometimes it may be easier to calculate the possibility of something not happening, or the **complement of an event**. Represented by the symbol $\bar{A}$, the complement of A is the probability that event A does not happen. When you know the probability of event A occurring, you can use the formula $P(\bar{A}) = 1 - P(A)$, where $P(\bar{A})$ is the probability of event A not occurring, and $P(A)$ is the probability of event A occurring.

ADDITION RULE

The **addition rule** for probability is used for finding the probability of a compound event. Use the formula $P(A \text{ or } B) = P(A) + P(B) - P(A \text{ and } B)$, where $P(A \text{ and } B)$ is the probability of both events occurring to find the probability of a compound event. The probability of both events occurring at the same time must be subtracted to eliminate any overlap in the first two probabilities.

CONDITIONAL PROBABILITY

Given two events A and B, the **conditional probability** $P(A|B)$ is the probability that event A will occur, given that event B has occurred. The conditional probability cannot be calculated simply from $P(A)$ and $P(B)$; these probabilities alone do not give sufficient information to determine the conditional probability. It can, however, be determined if you are also given the probability of the intersection of events A and B, $P(A \cap B)$, the probability that events A and B both occur. Specifically, $P(A|B) = \frac{P(A \cap B)}{P(B)}$. For instance, suppose you have a jar containing two red marbles and two blue marbles, and you draw two marbles at random. Consider event A being the event that the first marble drawn is red, and event B being the event that the second marble drawn is blue. $P(A)$ is $\frac{1}{2}$, and $P(A \cap B)$ is $\frac{1}{3}$. (The latter may not be obvious, but may be determined by finding the product of $\frac{1}{2}$ and $\frac{2}{3}$). Therefore $P(A|B) = \frac{1/3}{1/2} = \frac{2}{3}$.

CONDITIONAL PROBABILITY IN EVERYDAY SITUATIONS

Conditional probability often arises in everyday situations in, for example, estimating the risk or benefit of certain activities. The conditional probability of having a heart attack given that you exercise daily may be smaller than the overall probability of having a heart attack. The conditional probability of having lung cancer given that you are a smoker is larger than the overall probability of having lung cancer. Note that changing the order of the conditional probability changes the meaning: the conditional probability of having lung cancer given that you are a smoker is a very different thing from the probability of being a smoker given that you have lung cancer. In an extreme case, suppose that a certain rare disease is caused only by eating a certain food, but even then, it is unlikely. Then the conditional probability of having that disease given that you eat the dangerous food is nonzero but low, but the conditional probability of having eaten that food given that you have the disease is 100%!

INDEPENDENCE

The conditional probability $P(A|B)$ is the probability that event A will occur given that event B occurs. If the two events are independent, we do not expect that whether or not event B occurs should have any effect on whether or not event A occurs. In other words, we expect $P(A|B) = P(A)$.

This can be proven using the usual equations for conditional probability and the joint probability of independent events. The conditional probability $P(A|B) = \frac{P(A \cap B)}{P(B)}$. If A and B are independent, then $P(A \cap B) = P(A)P(B)$. So $P(A|B) = \frac{P(A)P(B)}{P(B)} = P(A)$. By similar reasoning, if A and B are independent then $P(B|A) = P(B)$.

MULTIPLICATION RULE

The **multiplication rule** can be used to find the probability of two independent events occurring using the formula $P(A \text{ and } B) = P(A) \times P(B)$, where $P(A \text{ and } B)$ is the probability of two independent events occurring, $P(A)$ is the probability of the first event occurring, and $P(B)$ is the probability of the second event occurring.

The multiplication rule can also be used to find the probability of two dependent events occurring using the formula $P(A \text{ and } B) = P(A) \times P(B|A)$, where $P(A \text{ and } B)$ is the probability of two dependent events occurring and $P(B|A)$ is the probability of the second event occurring after the first event has already occurred. Before using the multiplication rule, you MUST first determine whether the two events are *dependent* or *independent*.

Use a **combination of the multiplication** rule and the rule of complements to find the probability that at least one outcome of the element will occur. This given by the general formula $P(\text{at least one event occurring}) = 1 - P(\text{no outcomes occurring})$. For example, to find the probability that at least one even number will show when a pair of dice is rolled, find the probability that two odd numbers will be rolled (no even numbers) and subtract from one. You can always use a tree diagram or make a chart to list the possible outcomes when the sample space is small, such as in the dice-rolling example, but in most cases, it will be much faster to use the multiplication and complement formulas.

PRACTICE

P1. Determine the theoretical probability of the following events:

(a) Rolling an even number on a regular 6-sided die.

(b) Not getting a red ball when selecting one from a bag of 3 red balls, 4 black balls, and 2 green balls.

(c) Rolling a standard die and then selecting a card from a standard deck that is less than the value rolled.

PRACTICE SOLUTIONS

P1. (a). The values on the faces of a regular die are 1, 2, 3, 4, 5, and 6. Since three of these are even numbers (2, 4, 6), The probability of rolling an even number is $\frac{3}{6} = \frac{1}{2} = 0.5 = 50\%$.

(b) The bag contains a total of 9 balls, 6 of which are not red, so the probability of selecting one non-red ball would be $\frac{6}{9} = \frac{2}{3} \cong 0.667 \cong 66.7\%$.

(c) In this scenario, we need to determine how many cards could satisfy the condition for each possible value of the die roll. If a one is rolled, there is no way to achieve the desired outcome, since no cards in a standard deck are less than 1. If a two is rolled, then any of the four aces would achieve the desired result. If a three is rolled, then either an ace or a two would satisfy the condition, and so on. Note that any value on the die is equally likely to occur, meaning that the probability of each roll is $\frac{1}{6}$. Putting all this in a table can help:

Roll	Cards< Roll	Probability of Card	Probability of Event
1	-	$\frac{0}{52} = 0$	$\frac{1}{6} \times 0 = 0$
2	1	$\frac{4}{52} = \frac{1}{13}$	$\frac{1}{6} \times \frac{1}{13} = \frac{1}{78}$
3	1,2	$\frac{8}{52} = \frac{2}{13}$	$\frac{1}{6} \times \frac{2}{13} = \frac{2}{78}$
4	1,2,3	$\frac{12}{52} = \frac{3}{13}$	$\frac{1}{6} \times \frac{3}{13} = \frac{3}{78}$
5	1,2,3,4	$\frac{16}{52} = \frac{4}{13}$	$\frac{1}{6} \times \frac{4}{13} = \frac{4}{78}$
6	1,2,3,4,5	$\frac{20}{52} = \frac{5}{13}$	$\frac{1}{6} \times \frac{5}{13} = \frac{5}{78}$

Assuming that each value of the die is equally likely, then the probability of selecting a card less than the value of the die is the sum of the probabilities of each way to achieve the desired outcome: $\frac{0+1+2+3+4+5}{78} = \frac{15}{78} = \frac{5}{26} \cong 0.192 \cong 19.2\%$.

DATA ANALYSIS

MEAN

The **statistical mean** of a group of data is the same as the arithmetic average of that group. To find the mean of a set of data, first convert each value to the same units, if necessary. Then find the sum of all the values, and count the total number of data values, making sure you take into consideration each individual value. If a value appears more than once, count it more than once. Divide the sum of the values by the total number of values and apply the units, if any. Note that the mean does not have to be one of the data values in the set, and may not divide evenly.

$$\text{mean} = \frac{\text{sum of the data values}}{\text{quantity of data values}}$$

For instance, the mean of the data set {88, 72, 61, 90, 97, 68, 88, 79, 86, 93, 97, 71, 80, 84, 89} would be the sum of the fifteen numbers divided by 15:

$$\frac{88 + 72 + 61 + 90 + 97 + 68 + 88 + 79 + 86 + 93 + 97 + 71 + 80 + 84 + 88}{15} = \frac{1242}{15}$$
$$= 82.8$$

While the mean is relatively easy to calculate and averages are understood by most people, the mean can be very misleading if it is used as the sole measure of central tendency. If the data set has outliers (data values that are unusually high or unusually low compared to the rest of the data values), the mean can be very distorted, especially if the data set has a small number of values. If unusually high values are countered with unusually low values, the mean is not affected as much. For example, if five of twenty students in a class get a 100 on a test, but the other 15 students have an average of 60 on the same test, the class average would appear as 70. Whenever the mean is skewed by outliers, it is always a good idea to include the median as an alternate measure of central tendency.

A **weighted mean**, or weighted average, is a mean that uses "weighted" values. The formula is weighted mean $= \frac{w_1x_1+w_2x_2+w_3x_3...+w_nx_n}{w_1+w_2+w_3+\cdots+w_n}$. Weighted values, such as $w_1, w_2, w_3, ... w_n$ are assigned to each member of the set $x_1, x_2, x_3, ... x_n$. When calculating the weighted mean, make sure a weight value for each member of the set is used.

MEDIAN

The **statistical median** is the value in the middle of the set of data. To find the median, list all data values in order from smallest to largest or from largest to smallest. Any value that is repeated in the set must be listed the number of times it appears. If there are an odd number of data values, the median is the value in the middle of the list. If there is an even number of data values, the median is the arithmetic mean of the two middle values.

For example, the median of the data set {88, 72, 61, 90, 97, 68, 88, 79, 86, 93, 97, 71, 80, 84, 88} is 86 since the ordered set is {61, 68, 71, 72, 79, 80, 84, **86**, 88, 88, 88, 90, 93, 97, 97}.

The big disadvantage of using the median as a measure of central tendency is that is relies solely on a value's relative size as compared to the other values in the set. When the individual values in a set of data are evenly dispersed, the median can be an accurate tool. However, if there is a group of rather large values or a group of rather small values that are not offset by a different group of values, the information that can be inferred from the median may not be accurate because the distribution of values is skewed.

MODE

The **statistical mode** is the data value that occurs the greatest number of times in the data set. It is possible to have exactly one mode, more than one mode, or no mode. To find the mode of a set of data, arrange the data like you do to find the median (all values in order, listing all multiples of data values). Count the number of times each value appears in the data set. If all values appear an equal number of times, there is no mode. If one value appears more than any other value, that value is the mode. If two or more values appear the same number of times, but there are other values that appear fewer times and no values that appear more times, all of those values are the modes.

For example, the mode of the data set {**88**, 72, 61, 90, 97, 68, **88**, 79, 86, 93, 97, 71, 80, 84, **88**} is 88.

The main disadvantage of the mode is that the values of the other data in the set have no bearing on the mode. The mode may be the largest value, the smallest value, or a value anywhere in between in the set. The mode only tells which value or values, if any, occurred the greatest number of times. It does not give any suggestions about the remaining values in the set.

> **Review Video: <u>Mean, Median, and Mode</u>**
> Visit mometrix.com/academy and enter code: 286207

RANGE

The **range** of a set of data is the difference between the greatest and lowest values of the data in the set. To calculate the range, you must first make sure the units for all data values are the same, and then identify the greatest and lowest values. If there are multiple data values that are equal for the highest or lowest, just use one of the values in the formula. Write the answer with the same units as the data values you used to do the calculations.

Common Subject: Word Knowledge

The Word Knowledge Test on the ASVAB consists of an 11-minute section with 35 questions.

You will be given a sentence that has an underlined, boldfaced word. From the four answer choices provided, you must choose which answer choice most nearly means the same as the underlined word. In other words, you have to identify a synonym of the underlined word.

Determining Word Meaning

An understanding of the basics of language is helpful, and often vital, to understanding what you read. The term *structural analysis* refers to looking at the parts of a word and breaking it down into its different components to determine the word's meaning. Parts of a word include prefixes, suffixes, and the root word. By learning the meanings of prefixes, suffixes, and other word fundamentals, you can decipher the meaning of words which may not yet be in your vocabulary. Prefixes are common letter combinations at the beginning of words, while suffixes are common letter combinations at the end. The main part of the word is known as the root. Visually, it would look like this: prefix + root word + suffix. Look first at the individual meanings of the root word, prefix and/or suffix. Use knowledge of the meaning(s) of the prefix and/or suffix to see what information it adds to the root. Even if the meaning of the root is unknown, one can use knowledge of the prefix's and/or suffix's meaning(s) to determine an approximate meaning of the word. For example, if one sees the word *uninspired* and does not know what it means, they can use the knowledge that *un-* means 'not' to know that the full word means "not inspired." Understanding the common prefixes and suffixes can illuminate at least part of the meaning of an unfamiliar word.

> **Review Video: Determining Word Meanings**
> Visit mometrix.com/academy and enter code: 894894

The following is a list of common prefixes and their meanings:

Prefix	Definition	Examples
a	in, on, of, up, to	abed, afoot
a-	without, lacking	atheist, agnostic
ab-	from, away, off	abdicate, abjure
ad-	to, toward	advance
am-	friend, love	amicable, amatory
ante-	before, previous	antecedent, antedate
anti-	against, opposing	antipathy, antidote
auto-	self	autonomy, autobiography
belli-	war, warlike	bellicose
bene-	well, good	benefit, benefactor
bi-	two	bisect, biennial
bio-	life	biology, biosphere
cata-	down, away, thoroughly	catastrophe, cataclysm
chron-	time	chronometer, synchronize
circum-	around	circumspect, circumference
com-	with, together, very	commotion, complicate

130

Prefix	Definition	Examples
contra-	against, opposing	contradict, contravene
cred-	belief, trust	credible, credit
de-	from	depart
dem-	people	demographics, democracy
dia-	through, across, apart	diameter, diagnose
dis-	away, off, down, not	dissent, disappear
epi-	upon	epilogue
equi-	equal, equally	equivalent
ex-	out	extract
for-	away, off, from	forget, forswear
fore-	before, previous	foretell, forefathers
homo-	same, equal	homogenized
hyper-	excessive, over	hypercritical, hypertension
hypo-	under, beneath	hypodermic, hypothesis
in-	in, into	intrude, invade
in-	not, opposing	incapable, ineligible
inter-	among, between	intercede, interrupt
intra-	within	intramural, intrastate
magn-	large	magnitude, magnify
mal-	bad, poorly, not	malfunction
micr-	small	microbe, microscope
mis-	bad, poorly, not	misspell, misfire
mono-	one, single	monogamy, monologue
mor-	die, death	mortality, mortuary
neo-	new	neolithic, neoconservative
non-	not	nonentity, nonsense
ob-	against, opposing	objection
omni-	all, everywhere	omniscient
ortho-	right, straight	orthogonal, orthodox
over-	above	overbearing
pan-	all, entire	panorama, pandemonium
para-	beside, beyond	parallel, paradox
per-	through	perceive, permit
peri-	around	periscope, perimeter
phil-	love, like	philosophy, philanthropic
poly-	many	polymorphous, polygamous
post-	after, following	postpone, postscript
pre-	before, previous	prevent, preclude
prim-	first, early	primitive, primary
pro-	forward, in place of	propel, pronoun
re-	back, backward, again	revoke, recur
retro-	back, backward	retrospect, retrograde
semi-	half, partly	semicircle, semicolon

Prefix	Definition	Examples
sub-	under, beneath	subjugate, substitute
super-	above, extra	supersede, supernumerary
sym-	with, together	sympathy, symphony
trans-	across, beyond, over	transact, transport
ultra-	beyond, excessively	ultramodern, ultrasonic, ultraviolet
un-	not, reverse of	unhappy, unlock
uni-	one	uniform, unity
vis-	to see	visage, visible

The following is a list of common suffixes and their meanings:

Suffix	Definition	Examples
-able	able to, likely	capable, tolerable
-age	process, state, rank	passage, bondage
-ance	act, condition, fact	acceptance, vigilance
-arch	to rule	monarch
-ard	one that does excessively	drunkard, wizard
-ate	having, showing	separate, desolate
-ation	action, state, result	occupation, starvation
-cy	state, condition	accuracy, captaincy
-dom	state, rank, condition	serfdom, wisdom
-en	cause to be, become	deepen, strengthen
-er	one who does	teacher
-esce	become, grow, continue	convalesce, acquiesce
-esque	in the style of, like	picturesque, grotesque
-ess	feminine	waitress, lioness
-fic	making, causing	terrific, beatific
-ful	full of, marked by	thankful, zestful
-fy	make, cause, cause to have	glorify, fortify
-hood	state, condition	manhood, statehood
-ible	able, likely, fit	edible, possible, divisible
-ion	action, result, state	union, fusion
-ish	suggesting, like	churlish, childish
-ism	act, manner, doctrine	barbarism, socialism
-ist	doer, believer	monopolist, socialist
-ition	action, state, result	sedition, expedition
-ity	state, quality, condition	acidity, civility
-ize	make, cause to be, treat with	sterilize, mechanize, criticize
-less	lacking, without	hopeless, countless
-like	like, similar	childlike, dreamlike
-logue	type of written/spoken language	prologue
-ly	like, of the nature of	friendly, positively
-ment	means, result, action	refreshment, disappointment
-ness	quality, state	greatness, tallness

132

Suffix	Definition	Examples
-or	doer, office, action	juror, elevator, honor
-ous	marked by, given to	religious, riotous
-ship	the art or skill of	statesmanship
-some	apt to, showing	tiresome, lonesome
-th	act, state, quality	warmth, width
-tude	quality, state, result	magnitude, fortitude
-ty	quality, state	enmity, activity
-ward	in the direction of	backward, homeward

When defining words in a text, words often have a meaning that is more than the dictionary definition. The **denotative** meaning of a word is the literal meaning. The **connotative** meaning goes beyond the denotative meaning to include the emotional reaction a word may invoke. The connotative meaning often takes the denotative meaning a step further due to associations which the reader makes with the denotative meaning. The reader can differentiate between the denotative and connotative meanings by first recognizing when authors use each meaning. Most non-fiction, for example, is fact-based, the authors not using flowery, figurative language. The reader can assume that the writer is using the denotative, or literal, meaning of words. In fiction, on the other hand, the author may be using the connotative meaning. Connotation is one form of figurative language. The reader should use context clues to determine if the author is using the denotative or connotative meaning of a word.

> **Review Video: Denotation and Connotation**
> Visit mometrix.com/academy and enter code: 310092

Readers of all levels will encounter words with which they are somewhat unfamiliar. The best way to define a word in **context** is to look for nearby words that can help. For instance, unfamiliar nouns are often accompanied by examples that furnish a definition. Consider the following sentence: "Dave arrived at the party in hilarious garb: a leopard-print shirt, buckskin trousers, and high heels." If a reader was unfamiliar with the meaning of garb, he could read the examples and quickly determine that the word means "clothing." Examples will not always be this obvious. For instance, consider this sentence: "Parsley, lemon, and flowers were just a few of items he used as garnishes." Here, the possibly unfamiliar word *garnishes* is exemplified by parsley, lemon, and flowers. Readers who have eaten in a few restaurants will probably be able to identify a garnish as something used to decorate a plate.

In addition to looking at the context of a passage, readers can often use contrasts to define an unfamiliar word in context. In many sentences, the author will not describe the unfamiliar word directly, but will instead describe the opposite of the unfamiliar word. Of course, this provides information about the word the reader needs to define. Consider the following example: "Despite his intelligence, Hector's low brow and bad posture made him look obtuse." The author suggests that Hector's appearance was opposite to his actual intelligence. Therefore, *obtuse* must mean unintelligent or stupid. Here is another example: "Despite the horrible weather, we were beatific about our trip to Alaska." The word *despite* indicates that the speaker's feelings were at odds with the weather. Since the weather is described as "horrible," *beatific* must mean something good.

In some cases, there will be very few contextual clues to help a reader define the meaning of an unfamiliar word. When this happens, one strategy the reader may employ is substitution. A good reader will brainstorm some possible synonyms for the given word and then substitute these words into the sentence. If the sentence and the surrounding passage continue to make sense, the

133

substitution has revealed at least some information about the unfamiliar word. Consider the sentence, "Frank's admonition rang in her ears as she climbed the mountain." A reader unfamiliar with *admonition* might come up with some substitutions like "vow," "promise," "advice," "complaint," or "compliment." All of these words make general sense of the sentence, though their meanings are diverse. The process has suggested, however, that an admonition is some sort of message. The substitution strategy is rarely able to pinpoint a precise definition, but can be effective as a last resort.

It is sometimes possible to define an unfamiliar word by looking at the descriptive words in the context. Consider the following sentence: "Fred dragged the recalcitrant boy kicking and screaming up the stairs." *Dragged*, *kicking*, and *screaming* all suggest that the boy does not want to go up the stairs. The reader may assume that *recalcitrant* means something like unwilling or protesting. In that example, an unfamiliar adjective was identified. It is perhaps more typical to use description to define an unfamiliar noun, as in this sentence: "Don's wrinkled frown and constantly shaking fist identified him as a curmudgeon of the first order." Don is described as having a "wrinkled frown and constantly shaking fist," suggesting that a *curmudgeon* must be a grumpy old man. Contrasts do not always provide detailed information about the unfamiliar word, but they at least give the reader some clues.

When a word has more than one meaning, it can be tricky to determine how it is being used in a given sentence. Consider the verb *cleave*, which bizarrely can mean either "join" or "separate." When a reader comes upon this word, she will have to select the definition that makes the most sense. So, take as an example the following sentence: "The birds cleaved together as they flew from the oak tree." Immediately, the presence of the word *together* should suggest that in this sentence *cleave* is being used to mean "*join*." A slightly more difficult example would be the sentence, "Hermione's knife cleaved the bread cleanly." It doesn't make sense for a knife to join bread together, so the word must be meant to indicate separation. Discovering the meaning of a word with multiple meanings requires the same tricks as defining an unknown word: looking for contextual clues and evaluating substituted words.

LITERARY DEVICES

Understanding how words relate to each other can often add meaning to a passage. This is explained by understanding **synonyms** (words that mean the same thing) and **antonyms** (words that mean the opposite of one another). As an example, *dry* and *arid* are synonyms, and *dry* and *wet* are antonyms. There are many pairs of words in English that can be considered synonyms, despite having slightly different definitions. For instance, the words *friendly* and *collegial* can both be used to describe a warm interpersonal relationship, so it would be correct to call them synonyms. However, *collegial* (kin to *colleague*) is more often used in reference to professional or academic relationships, while *friendly* has no such connotation. Nevertheless, it would be appropriate to call these words synonyms. If the difference between the two words is too great, however, they may not be called synonyms. *Hot* and *warm* are not synonyms, for instance, because their meanings are too distinct. A good way to determine whether two words are synonyms is to substitute one for the other and see if the sentence means the same thing. Substituting *warm* for *hot* in a sentence would convey a different meaning.

Antonyms are opposites. *Light* and *dark*, *up* and *down*, *right* and *left*, *good* and *bad*: these are all sets of antonyms. It is important to distinguish between antonyms and pairs of words that are simply different. *Black* and *gray*, for instance, are not antonyms because gray is not the opposite of black. *Black* and *white*, on the other hand, are antonyms. Not every word has an antonym. For instance, many nouns do not. What would be the antonym of *chair*, after all? On a standardized test, the questions related to antonyms are more likely to concern adjectives. Remember that adjectives are words that describe a noun. Some common adjectives include *red*, *fast*, *skinny*, and *sweet*. Of these four examples, only *red* lacks a group of obvious antonyms.

There are many types of language devices that authors use to convey their meaning in a more descriptive or interesting way. Understanding these concepts will help you understand what you read. These types of devices are called **figurative language**—language that goes beyond the literal meaning of the words. **Descriptive language** that evokes imagery in the reader's mind is one type of figurative language. **Exaggeration** is also one type of figurative language. Comparing two things typically also uses figurative language. Similes and **metaphors** are ways of comparing things, and both are types of figurative language commonly found in poetry. An example of figurative language (a simile in this case) is: "The child howled like a coyote when her mother told her to pick up the toys." In this example, the child's howling is compared to that of a coyote. Figurative language is descriptive in nature and helps the reader understand the sound being made in this sentence.

Alliteration is a stylistic device, or literary technique, in which successive words (more strictly, stressed syllables) begin with the same sound or letter. Alliteration is a frequent tool in poetry but it is also common in prose, particularly to highlight short phrases. An example of alliteration could be "thundering through the thickets," in which the initial *th* sound is used in four consecutive words. Especially in poetry, alliteration contributes to the euphony of the passage, lending it a musical air. It also may act to humorous effect. Alliteration draws attention to itself, which may be a good or a bad thing. Authors should be conscious of the character of the sound to be repeated. In the above example, a *th* sound is somewhat difficult to make quickly in four consecutive words, so the phrase conveys a little of the difficulty of moving through tall grass. If the author is indeed trying to suggest this difficulty, then the alliteration is a success. Consider, however, the description of eyes as "glassy globes of glitter." This is definitely alliteration, since the initial *gl* sound is used three times. However, one might question whether this awkward sound is appropriate for a description of pretty eyes. The phrase is not especially pleasant to the ear, and therefore is probably not effective as alliteration. Related to alliteration are **assonance**, the repetition of vowel sounds, and **consonance**, the repetition of consonant sounds.

A **figure of speech**, sometimes termed a rhetorical figure or device is a word or phrase that departs from straightforward, literal language. Figures of speech are often used and crafted for emphasis, freshness of expression, or clarity. However, clarity may also suffer from their use.

Note that not all theories of meaning necessarily have a concept of "literal language" (see literal and figurative language). Under theories that do not, figure of speech is not an entirely coherent concept.

As an example of the figurative use of a word, consider the sentence, "I am going to crown you." It may mean:

I am going to place a literal crown on your head.

I am going to symbolically exalt you to the place of kingship.

I am going to punch you in the head with my clenched fist.

I am going to put a second checker on top of your checker to signify that it has become a king.

A **metaphor** is a type of figurative language in which the writer equates one thing with a different thing. For instance, in the sentence "The bird was an arrow arcing through the sky," the arrow is serving as a metaphor for the bird. The point of a metaphor is to encourage the reader to think about the thing being described in a different way. Using this example, we are being asked to envision the bird's flight as being similar to the arc of an arrow, so we will imagine it to be swift, bending, etc. Metaphors are a more lyrical way for the author to describe or provide information without being direct and obvious. Note that the thing to which a metaphor refers will not always be mentioned explicitly by the author. For instance, consider the following description of a forest in winter: "Swaying skeletons reached for the sky and groaned as the wind blew through them." The author is clearly using *skeletons* as a metaphor for leafless trees. This metaphor creates a spooky tone while inspiring the reader's imagination.

> **Review Video: Metaphor**
> Visit mometrix.com/academy and enter code: 133295

Metonymy is referring to one thing in terms of another, closely related thing. This is similar to metaphor, but there is less distance between the description and the thing being described. An example of metonymy is referring to the news media as the "press," when of course the press is only the device by which newspapers are printed. Metonymy is a way of referring to something without having to repeat its name constantly. **Synecdoche**, on the other hand, is referring to a whole by one of its parts. An example of synecdoche would be calling a police officer a "badge." Synecdoche, like metonymy, is a handy way of referring without having to overuse certain words. It also allows the writer to emphasize aspects of the thing being described. For instance, referring to businessmen as "suits" suggests professionalism, conformity, and drabness.

Hyperbole is overstatement for effect. The following sentence is an example of hyperbole: *He jumped ten feet in the air when he heard the good news*. Obviously, no person has the ability to jump ten feet in the air. The author hyperbolizes not because he believes the statement will be taken literally, but because the exaggeration conveys the extremity of emotion. Consider how much less colorful the sentence would be if the author simply said, "He jumped when he heard the good news." Hyperbole can be dangerous if the author does not exaggerate enough. For instance, if the author wrote, "He jumped two feet in the air when he heard the good news," the reader might not be sure whether this is actually true or just hyperbole. Of course, in many situations this distinction will not really matter. However, an author should avoid confusing or vague hyperbole when he needs to maintain credibility or authority with readers.

> **Review Video: Hyperbole and Understatement**
> Visit mometrix.com/academy and enter code: 308470

Understatement is the opposite of hyperbole; that is, it is describing something as less than it is, for effect. As an example, consider a person who climbs Mount Everest and then describes the journey as "a little stroll." This is an almost extreme example of understatement. Like other types of figurative language, understatement has a range of uses. It may convey self-deprecation or modesty, as in the above example. Of course, some people might interpret understatement as false modesty, a deliberate attempt to call attention to the magnitude of what is being discussed. For example, a woman is complimented on her enormous diamond engagement ring and says, "Oh, this little thing?" Her understatement might be viewed as snobby or insensitive. Understatement can have various effects, but it always calls attention to itself.

A **simile** is a figurative expression similar to a metaphor, though it requires the use of a distancing word such as *like* or *as*. Some examples are "The sun was like an orange," "eager as a beaver," and "nimble as a mountain goat." Because a simile includes *like* or a*s*, it creates a little space between the description and the thing being described. If an author says that a house was "like a shoebox," the tone is slightly different than if the author said that the house *was* a shoebox. In a simile, the author indicates an awareness that the description is not the same thing as the thing being described. In a metaphor, there is no such distinction, even though one may safely assume that the author is aware of it. This is a subtle difference, but authors will alternately use metaphors and similes depending on their intended tone.

Another type of figurative language is **personification.** This is the description of the nonhuman as if it were human. Literally, the word means the process of making something into a person. There is a wide range of approaches to personification, from common expressions like "whispering wind" to full novels like *Animal Farm*, by George Orwell, in which the Bolshevik Revolution is reenacted by farmyard animals. The general intent of personification is to describe things in a manner that will be comprehensible to readers. When an author states that a tree "groans" in the wind, she of course does not mean that the tree is emitting a low, pained sound from its mouth. Instead, she means that the tree is making a noise similar to a human groan. Of course, this personification establishes a tone of sadness or suffering. A different tone would be established if the author said the tree was "swaying" or "dancing."

Irony is a statement that suggests its opposite. In other words, it is when an author or character says one thing but means another. For example, imagine a man walks in his front door, covered in mud and in tattered clothes. His wife asks him, "How was your day?" and he says "Great!" The man's comment is an example of irony. As in this example, irony often depends on information the reader obtains elsewhere. There is a fine distinction between irony and sarcasm. Irony is any statement in which the literal meaning is opposite from the intended meaning, while sarcasm is a statement of this type that is also insulting to the person at whom it is directed. A sarcastic statement suggests that the other person is stupid enough to believe an obviously false statement is true. Irony is a bit more subtle than sarcasm.

> **Review Video: Irony**
> Visit mometrix.com/academy and enter code: 374204

The more words a person is exposed to, the greater their vocabulary will become. By reading on a regular basis, a person can increase the number of ways they have seen a word in context. Based on experience, a person can recall how a word was used in the past and apply that knowledge to a new context. For example, a person may have seen the word *gull* used to mean a bird that is found near the seashore. However, a *gull* can also be a person who is easily tricked. If the word is used in context in reference to a character, the reader can recognize that the character is being called a bird that is not seen as extremely intelligent. Using what the reader knows about a word can be useful when making comparisons or figuring out the meaning of a new use of a word, as in figurative language, idioms, analogies, and multiple-meaning words.

Testing Tips

NEARLY AND PERFECT SYNONYMS

You must determine which of five provided choices has the best similar definition as a certain word. Nearly similar may often be more correct, because the goal is to test your understanding of the nuances, or little differences, between words. A perfect match may not exist, so don't be concerned if your answer choice is not a complete synonym. Focus upon edging closer to the word. Eliminate the words that you know aren't correct first. Then narrow your search. Cross out the words that are the least similar to the main word until you are left with the one that is the most similar.

PREFIXES

Take advantage of every clue that the word might include. Prefixes and suffixes can be a huge help. Usually they allow you to determine a basic meaning. Pre- means before, post- means after, pro- is positive, de- is negative. From these prefixes and suffixes, you can get an idea of the general meaning of the word and look for its opposite. Beware though of any traps. Just because con is the opposite of pro, doesn't necessarily mean congress is the opposite of progress! A list of the most common prefixes and suffixes is included in the appendix.

POSITIVE VS. NEGATIVE

Many words can be easily determined to be a positive word or a negative word. Words such as despicable, gruesome, and bleak are all negative. Words such as ecstatic, praiseworthy, and magnificent are all positive. You will be surprised at how many words can be viewed as either positive or negative. Once that is determined, you can quickly eliminate any other words with an opposite meaning and focus on those that have the same characteristic, whether positive or negative.

WORD STRENGTH

Part of the challenge is determining which answer is the most nearly similar word to the word in the question. This is particularly true when two of the words in the answer choices seem to be similar. When analyzing a word, determine how strong it is. For example, stupendous and good are both positive words. However, stupendous is a much stronger positive adjective than good. Also, towering and gigantic are stronger words than tall and large. Search for an answer choice that is similar and also has the same strength. If the main word is weak, look for similar words that are also weak. If the main word is strong, look for similar words that are also strong.

TYPE AND TOPIC

Another key is what type of word is the main word. If the main word is an adjective describing height, then look for the answer to be an adjective describing height as well. Match both the type and topic of the main word. The type refers to the parts of speech, whether the word is an adjective, adverb, or verb. The topic refers to what the definition of the word includes, such as sizes or fashion styles.

FORM A SENTENCE

Many words seem more natural in a sentence. *Specious* reasoning, *irresistible* force, and *uncanny* resemblance are just a few of the word combinations that usually go together. When faced with an uncommon word that you barely understand (and on the ASVAB there will be many), try to put the word in a sentence that makes sense. It will help you to understand the word's meaning and make it easier to determine its opposite. Once you have a good descriptive sentence that utilizes the main

139

word properly, plug in the answer choices and see if the sentence still has the same meaning with each answer choice. The answer choice that maintains the meaning of the sentence is correct!

USE REPLACEMENTS

Using a sentence is a great help because it puts the word into a proper perspective. Since ASVAB actually gives you a sentence, sometimes you don't always have to create your own (though in many cases the sentence won't be helpful). Read the provided sentence with the underlined word. Then read the sentence again and again, each time replacing the underlined word with one of the answer choices. The correct answer should "sound" right and fit.

Example: The desert landscape was **desolate**.

1. cheerful
2. creepy
3. excited
4. forlorn

After reading the example sentence, begin replacing "desolate" with each of the answer choices. Does "the desert landscape was cheerful, creepy, excited, or forlorn" sound right? Deserts are typically hot, empty, and rugged environments, probably not cheerful, or excited. While creepy might sound right, that word would certainly be more appropriate for a haunted house. But "the desert landscape was forlorn" has a certain ring to it and would be correct.

ELIMINATE SIMILAR CHOICES

If you don't know the word, don't worry. Look at the answer choices and just use them. Remember that three of the answer choices will always be wrong. If you can find a common relationship between a set of answer choices, then you know they are wrong. Find the answer choice that does not have a common relationship to the other answer choices and it will be the correct answer.

Example: **Laconic** most nearly means

1. wordy
2. talkative
3. expressive
4. quiet

In this example the first three choices are all similar. Even if you don't know that laconic means the same as quiet, you know that "quiet" must be correct, because the other three choices were all virtually the same, so they must all be wrong. The one that is different must be correct. So, don't worry if you don't know a word. Focus on the answer choices that you do understand and see if you can identify similarities. Even identifying two words that are similar will allow you to eliminate those two answer choices, for they are both wrong, because they are either both right or both wrong (they're similar, remember), so since they can't both be right, they both must be wrong.

THE TRAP OF FAMILIARITY

Don't choose a word just because you recognize it. On difficult questions, you may only recognize one or two words. ASVAB doesn't put "make-believe" words on the test, so don't think that just because you only recognize one word means that word must be correct. If you don't recognize four words, then focus on the one that you do recognize. Is it correct? Try your best to determine if it fits the sentence. If it does, that is great, but if it doesn't, eliminate it. Each word you eliminate increases your chances of getting the question correct.

READ CAREFULLY

Be sure to read all of the choices. You may find an answer choice that seems right at first, but continue reading and you may find a better choice.

Difficult words are usually synonyms or antonyms (opposites). Whenever you have extremely difficult words that you don't understand, look at the answer choices. Try and identify whether two or more of the answer choices are either synonyms or antonyms. Remember that if you can find two words that have the same relationship (for example, two answer choices are synonyms) then you can eliminate them both.

WORK QUICKLY

Since you have 35 questions to answer in only 11 minutes, that means that you have between 18 and 19 seconds to spend per question. This section faces a greater time crunch that any other test you will take on the ASVAB. If you are stuck on one word, don't waste too much time. Eliminate the answers you could bet a quick $5 on and then pick the first one that remains. You can make a note in your book and if you have time you can always come back, but don't waste your time. You must work quickly!

Common Subject: Reading Comprehension

The Paragraph Comprehension Test on the ASVAB consists of a 13-minute section with 15 questions.

You will be given one or more paragraphs of information to read followed by a question or incomplete statement. From the four answer choices provided, you must choose which answer choice best completes the statement or answers the question.

Comprehension Skills

One of the most important skills in reading comprehension is the identification of **topics** and **main ideas.** There is a subtle difference between these two features. The topic is the subject of a text, or what the text is about. The main idea, on the other hand, is the most important point being made by the author. The topic is usually expressed in a few words at the most, while the main idea often needs a full sentence to be completely defined. As an example, a short passage might have the topic of penguins and the main idea *Penguins are different from other birds in many ways.* In most nonfiction writing, the topic and the main idea will be stated directly, often in a sentence at the very beginning or end of the text. When being tested on an understanding of the author's topic, the reader can quickly skim the passage for the general idea, stopping to read only the first sentence of each paragraph. A paragraph's first sentence is often (but not always) the main topic sentence, and it gives you a summary of the content of the paragraph. However, there are cases in which the reader must figure out an unstated topic or main idea. In these instances, the student must read every sentence of the text and try to come up with an overarching idea that is supported by each of those sentences.

> **Review Video: Topics and Main Ideas**
> Visit mometrix.com/academy and enter code: 407801

While the main idea is the overall premise of a story, **supporting details** provide evidence and backing for the main point. In order to show that a main idea is correct, or valid, the author needs to add details that prove their point. All texts contain details, but they are only classified as supporting details when they serve to reinforce some larger point.

Supporting details are most commonly found in informative and persuasive texts. In some cases, they will be clearly indicated with words like *for example* or *for instance*, or they will be enumerated with words like *first*, *second*, and *last*. However, they may not be indicated with special words.

As a reader, it is important to consider whether the author's supporting details really back up his or her main point. Supporting details can be factual and correct but still not relevant to the author's point. Conversely, supporting details can seem pertinent but be ineffective because they are based on opinion or assertions that cannot be proven.

> **Review Video: Supporting Details**
> Visit mometrix.com/academy and enter code: 396297

An example of a main idea is: "Giraffes live in the Serengeti of Africa." A supporting detail about giraffes could be: "A giraffe uses its long neck to reach twigs and leaves on trees." The main idea gives the general idea that the text is about giraffes. The supporting detail gives a specific fact about how the giraffes eat.

As opposed to a main idea, themes are seldom expressed directly in a text, so they can be difficult to identify. A **theme** is an issue, an idea, or a question raised by the text. For instance, a theme of William Shakespeare's *Hamlet* is indecision, as the title character explores his own psyche and the results of his failure to make bold choices. A great work of literature may have many themes, and the reader is justified in identifying any for which he or she can find support. One common characteristic of themes is that they raise more questions than they answer. In a good piece of fiction, the author is not always trying to convince the reader, but is instead trying to elevate the reader's perspective and encourage him to consider the themes more deeply. When reading, one can identify themes by constantly asking what general issues the text is addressing. A good way to evaluate an author's approach to a theme is to begin reading with a question in mind (for example, how does this text approach the theme of love?) and then look for evidence in the text that addresses that question.

> **Review Video: Theme**
> Visit mometrix.com/academy and enter code: 732074

PURPOSES FOR WRITING

In order to be an effective reader, one must pay attention to the author's **position** and purpose. Even those texts that seem objective and impartial, like textbooks, have some sort of position and bias. Readers need to take these positions into account when considering the author's message. When an author uses emotional language or clearly favors one side of an argument, his position is clear. However, the author's position may be evident not only in what he writes, but in what he doesn't write. For this reason, it is sometimes necessary to review some other texts on the same topic in order to develop a view of the author's position. If this is not possible, then it may be useful to acquire a little background personal information about the author. When the only source of information is the text, however, the reader should look for language and argumentation that seems to indicate a particular stance on the subject.

> **Review Video: Author's Position**
> Visit mometrix.com/academy and enter code: 827954

Identifying the **purpose** of an author is usually easier than identifying her position. In most cases, the author has no interest in hiding his or her purpose. A text that is meant to entertain, for instance, should be obviously written to please the reader. Most narratives, or stories, are written to entertain, though they may also inform or persuade. Informative texts are easy to identify as well. The most difficult purpose of a text to identify is persuasion, because the author has an interest in making this purpose hard to detect. When a person knows that the author is trying to convince him, he is automatically more wary and skeptical of the argument. For this reason, persuasive texts often try to establish an entertaining tone, hoping to amuse the reader into agreement, or an informative tone, hoping to create an appearance of authority and objectivity.

An author's purpose is often evident in the organization of the text. For instance, if the text has headings and subheadings, if key terms are in bold, and if the author makes his main idea clear from the beginning, then the likely purpose of the text is to inform. If the author begins by making a claim and then makes various arguments to support that claim, the purpose is probably to persuade. If the author is telling a story, or is more interested in holding the attention of the reader than in making a particular point or delivering information, then his purpose is most likely to entertain. As a reader, it is best to judge an author on how well he accomplishes his purpose. In other words, it is not entirely fair to complain that a textbook is boring: if the text is clear and easy to understand, then the author has done his job. Similarly, a storyteller should not be judged too harshly for getting some facts wrong, so long as he is able to give pleasure to the reader.

> **Review Video: Purpose**
> Visit mometrix.com/academy and enter code: 511819

The author's purpose for writing will affect his writing style and the response of the reader. In a **persuasive essay**, the author is attempting to change the reader's mind or convince him of something he did not believe previously. There are several identifying characteristics of persuasive writing. One is opinion presented as fact. When an author attempts to persuade the reader, he often presents his or her opinions as if they were fact. A reader must be on guard for statements that sound factual but which cannot be subjected to research, observation, or experiment. Another characteristic of persuasive writing is emotional language. An author will often try to play on the reader's emotion by appealing to his sympathy or sense of morality. When an author uses colorful or evocative language with the intent of arousing the reader's passions, it is likely that he is attempting to persuade. Finally, in many cases a persuasive text will give an unfair explanation of opposing positions, if these positions are mentioned at all.

An **informative text** is written to educate and enlighten the reader. Informative texts are almost always nonfiction and are rarely structured as a story. The intention of an informative text is to deliver information in the most comprehensible way possible, so the structure of the text is likely to be very clear. In an informative text, the thesis statement is often in the first sentence. The author may use some colorful language, but is likely to put more emphasis on clarity and precision. Informative essays do not typically appeal to the emotions. They often contain facts and figures, and rarely include the opinion of the author. Sometimes a persuasive essay can resemble an informative essay, especially if the author maintains an even tone and presents his or her views as if they were established fact.

> **Review Video: Informative Text**
> Visit mometrix.com/academy and enter code: 924964

The success or failure of an author's intent to **entertain** is determined by those who read the author's work. Entertaining texts may be either fiction or nonfiction, and they may describe real or imagined people, places, and events. Entertaining texts are often narratives, or stories. A text that is written to entertain is likely to contain colorful language that engages the imagination and the emotions. Such writing often features a great deal of figurative language, which typically enlivens its subject matter with images and analogies. Though an entertaining text is not usually written to persuade or inform, it may accomplish both of these tasks. An entertaining text may appeal to the reader's emotions and cause him or her to think differently about a particular subject. In any case, entertaining texts tend to showcase the personality of the author more so than other types of writing.

When an author intends to **express feelings,** she may use colorful and evocative language. An author may write emotionally for any number of reasons. Sometimes, the author will do so because she is describing a personal situation of great pain or happiness. Sometimes an author is attempting to persuade the reader, and so will use emotion to stir up the passions. It can be easy to identify this kind of expression when the writer uses phrases like *I felt* and *I sense*. However, sometimes the author will simply describe feelings without introducing them. As a reader, it is important to recognize when an author is expressing emotion, and not to become overwhelmed by sympathy or passion. A reader should maintain some detachment so that he or she can still evaluate the strength of the author's argument or the quality of the writing.

In a sense, almost all writing is descriptive, insofar as it seeks to describe events, ideas, or people to the reader. Some texts, however, are primarily concerned with **description**. A descriptive text focuses on a particular subject and attempts to depict it in a way that will be clear to the reader. Descriptive texts contain many adjectives and adverbs, words that give shades of meaning and create a more detailed mental picture for the reader. A descriptive text fails when it is unclear or vague to the reader. On the other hand, however, a descriptive text that compiles too much detail can be boring and overwhelming to the reader. A descriptive text will certainly be informative, and it may be persuasive and entertaining as well. Descriptive writing is a challenge for the author, but when it is done well, it can be fun to read.

WRITING DEVICES

Authors will use different stylistic and writing devices to make their meaning more clearly understood. One of those devices is comparison and contrast. When an author describes the ways in which two things are alike, he or she is **comparing** them. When the author describes the ways in which two things are different, he or she is **contrasting** them. The "compare and contrast" essay is one of the most common forms in nonfiction. It is often signaled with certain words: a comparison may be indicated with such words as *both, same, like, too,* and *as well*; while a contrast may be indicated by words like *but, however, on the other hand, instead,* and *yet*. Of course, comparisons and contrasts may be implicit without using any such signaling language. A single sentence may both compare and contrast. Consider the sentence *Brian and Sheila love ice cream, but Brian prefers vanilla and Sheila prefers strawberry*. In one sentence, the author has described both a similarity (love of ice cream) and a difference (favorite flavor).

> ### Review Video: <u>Compare and Contrast</u>
> Visit mometrix.com/academy and enter code: 171799

One of the most common text structures is **cause and effect**. A cause is an act or event that makes something happen, and an effect is the thing that happens as a result of that cause. A cause-and-effect relationship is not always explicit, but there are some words in English that signal causality, such as *since, because,* and *as a result*. As an example, consider the sentence *Because the sky was clear, Ron did not bring an umbrella*. The cause is the clear sky, and the effect is that Ron did not bring an umbrella. However, sometimes the cause-and-effect relationship will not be clearly noted. For instance, the sentence *He was late and missed the meeting* does not contain any signaling words, but it still contains a cause (he was late) and an effect (he missed the meeting). It is possible for a single cause to have multiple effects, or for a single effect to have multiple causes. Also, an effect can in turn be the cause of another effect, in what is known as a cause-and-effect chain.

Authors often use analogies to add meaning to the text. An **analogy** is a comparison of two things. The words in the analogy are connected by a certain, often undetermined relationship. Look at this analogy: moo is to cow as quack is to duck. This analogy compares the sound that a cow makes with the sound that a duck makes. Even if the word 'quack' was not given, one could figure out it is the correct word to complete the analogy based on the relationship between the words 'moo' and 'cow'. Some common relationships for analogies include synonyms, antonyms, part to whole, definition, and actor to action.

Another element that impacts a text is the author's point of view. The **point of view** of a text is the perspective from which it is told. The author will always have a point of view about a story before he draws up a plot line. The author will know what events they want to take place, how they want the characters to interact, and how the story will resolve. An author will also have an opinion on the topic, or series of events, which is presented in the story, based on their own prior experience and beliefs.

The two main points of view that authors use are first person and third person. If the narrator of the story is also the main character, or *protagonist*, the text is written in first-person point of view. In first person, the author writes with the word *I*. Third-person point of view is probably the most common point of view that authors use. Using third person, authors refer to each character using the words *he* or *she*. In third-person omniscient, the narrator is not a character in the story and tells the story of all of the characters at the same time.

> **Review Video: Point of View**
> Visit mometrix.com/academy and enter code: 383336

A good writer will use **transitional words** and phrases to guide the reader through the text. You are no doubt familiar with the common transitions, though you may never have considered how they operate. Some transitional phrases (*after, before, during, in the middle of*) give information about time. Some indicate that an example is about to be given (*for example, in fact, for instance*). Writers use them to compare (*also, likewise*) and contrast (*however, but, yet*). Transitional words and phrases can suggest addition (*and, also, furthermore, moreover*) and logical relationships (*if, then, therefore, as a result, since*). Finally, transitional words and phrases can demarcate the steps in a process (*first, second, last*). You should incorporate transitional words and phrases where they will orient your reader and illuminate the structure of your composition.

> **Review Video: Transitional Words and Phrases**
> Visit mometrix.com/academy and enter code: 197796

TYPES OF PASSAGES

A **narrative** passage is a story. Narratives can be fiction or nonfiction. However, there are a few elements that a text must have in order to be classified as a narrative. To begin with, the text must have a plot. That is, it must describe a series of events. If it is a good narrative, these events will be interesting and emotionally engaging to the reader. A narrative also has characters. These could be people, animals, or even inanimate objects, so long as they participate in the plot. A narrative passage often contains figurative language, which is meant to stimulate the imagination of the reader by making comparisons and observations. A metaphor, which is a description of one thing in terms of another, is a common piece of figurative language. *The moon was a frosty snowball* is an example of a metaphor: it is obviously untrue in the literal sense, but it suggests a certain mood for the reader. Narratives often proceed in a clear sequence, but they do not need to do so.

An **expository** passage aims to inform and enlighten the reader. It is nonfiction and usually centers around a simple, easily defined topic. Since the goal of exposition is to teach, such a passage should be as clear as possible. It is common for an expository passage to contain helpful organizing words, like *first, next, for example*, and *therefore*. These words keep the reader oriented in the text. Although expository passages do not need to feature colorful language and artful writing, they are often more effective when they do. For a reader, the challenge of expository passages is to maintain steady attention. Expository passages are not always about subjects in which a reader will naturally be interested, and the writer is often more concerned with clarity and comprehensibility than with engaging the reader. For this reason, many expository passages are dull. Making notes is a good way to maintain focus when reading an expository passage.

A **technical** passage is written to describe a complex object or process. Technical writing is common in medical and technological fields, in which complicated mathematical, scientific, and engineering ideas need to be explained simply and clearly. To ease comprehension, a technical passage usually proceeds in a very logical order. Technical passages often have clear headings and subheadings, which are used to keep the reader oriented in the text. It is also common for these passages to break sections up with numbers or letters. Many technical passages look more like an outline than a piece of prose. The amount of jargon or difficult vocabulary will vary in a technical passage depending on the intended audience. As much as possible, technical passages try to avoid language that the reader will have to research in order to understand the message. Of course, it is not always possible to avoid jargon.

A persuasive passage is meant to change the reader's mind or lead her into agreement with the author. The persuasive intent may be obvious, or it may be quite difficult to discern. In some cases, a persuasive passage will be indistinguishable from an informative passage: it will make an assertion and offer supporting details. However, a persuasive passage is more likely to make claims based on opinion and to appeal to the reader's emotions. Persuasive passages may not describe alternate positions and, when they do, they often display significant bias. It may be clear that a persuasive passage is giving the author's viewpoint, or the passage may adopt a seemingly objective tone. A persuasive passage is successful if it can make a convincing argument and win the trust of the reader.

A persuasive essay will likely focus on one central argument, but it may make many smaller claims along the way. These are subordinate arguments with which the reader must agree if he or she is going to agree with the central argument. The central argument will only be as strong as the subordinate claims. These claims should be rooted in fact and observation, rather than subjective judgment. The best persuasive essays provide enough supporting detail to justify claims without overwhelming the reader. Remember that a fact must be susceptible to independent verification: that is, it must be something the reader could confirm. Also, statistics are only effective when they take into account possible objections. For instance, a statistic on the number of foreclosed houses would only be useful if it was taken over a defined interval and in a defined area. Most readers are wary of statistics, because they are so often misleading. If possible, a persuasive essay should always include references so that the reader can obtain more information. Of course, this means that the writer's accuracy and fairness may be judged by the inquiring reader.

Opinions are formed by emotion as well as reason, and persuasive writers often appeal to the feelings of the reader. Although readers should always be skeptical of this technique, it is often used in a proper and ethical manner. For instance, there are many subjects that have an obvious emotional component, and therefore cannot be completely treated without an appeal to the emotions. Consider an article on drunk driving: it makes sense to include some specific examples that will alarm or sadden the reader. After all, drunk driving often has serious and tragic consequences. Emotional appeals are not appropriate, however, when they attempt to mislead the reader. For instance, in political advertisements it is common to emphasize the patriotism of the preferred candidate, because this will encourage the audience to link their own positive feelings about the country with their opinion of the candidate. However, these ads often imply that the other candidate is unpatriotic, which in most cases is far from the truth. Another common and improper emotional appeal is the use of loaded language, as for instance referring to an avidly religious person as a "fanatic" or a passionate environmentalist as a "tree hugger." These terms introduce an emotional component that detracts from the argument.

HISTORY AND CULTURE

Historical context has a profound influence on literature: the events, knowledge base, and assumptions of an author's time color every aspect of his or her work. Sometimes, authors hold opinions and use language that would be considered inappropriate or immoral in a modern setting, but that was acceptable in the author's time. As a reader, one should consider how the historical context influenced a work and also how today's opinions and ideas shape the way modern readers read the works of the past. For instance, in most societies of the past, women were treated as second-class citizens. An author who wrote in 18th-century England might sound sexist to modern readers, even if that author was relatively feminist in his time. Readers should not have to excuse the faulty assumptions and prejudices of the past, but they should appreciate that a person's thoughts and words are, in part, a result of the time and culture in which they live or lived, and it is perhaps unfair to expect writers to avoid all of the errors of their times.

> **Review Video: Historical Context**
> Visit mometrix.com/academy and enter code: 169770

Even a brief study of world literature suggests that writers from vastly different cultures address similar themes. For instance, works like the *Odyssey* and *Hamlet* both tackle the individual's battle for self-control and independence. In every culture, authors address themes of personal growth and the struggle for maturity. Another universal theme is the conflict between the individual and society. In works as culturally disparate as *Native Son*, the *Aeneid*, and *1984*, authors dramatize how people struggle to maintain their personalities and dignity in large, sometimes oppressive groups. Finally, many cultures have versions of the hero's (or heroine's) journey, in which an adventurous person must overcome many obstacles in order to gain greater knowledge, power, and perspective. Some famous works that treat this theme are the *Epic of Gilgamesh*, Dante's *Divine Comedy*, and *Don Quixote.*

Authors from different genres (for instance poetry, drama, novel, short story) and cultures may address similar themes, but they often do so quite differently. For instance, poets are likely to address subject matter obliquely, through the use of images and allusions. In a play, on the other hand, the author is more likely to dramatize themes by using characters to express opposing viewpoints. This disparity is known as a dialectical approach. In a novel, the author does not need to express themes directly; rather, they can be illustrated through events and actions. Different movements and styles become popular in different regions. For example, in Greece and England, authors tend to use more irony. In the 1950s Latin American authors popularized the use of unusual and surreal events to show themes about real life in the genre of magical realism. Japanese authors use the well-established poetic form of the haiku to organize their treatment of common themes.

RESPONDING TO LITERATURE

When reading good literature, the reader is moved to engage actively in the text. One part of being an active reader involves making predictions. A **prediction** is a guess about what will happen next. Readers are constantly making predictions based on what they have read and what they already know. Consider the following sentence: *Staring at the computer screen in shock, Kim blindly reached over for the brimming glass of water on the shelf to her side.* The sentence suggests that Kim is agitated and that she is not looking at the glass she is going to pick up, so a reader might predict that she is going to knock the glass over. Of course, not every prediction will be accurate; perhaps Kim will pick the glass up cleanly. Nevertheless, the author has certainly created the expectation that the water might be spilled. Predictions are always subject to revision as the reader acquires more information.

Readers are often required to understand text that claims and suggests ideas without stating them directly. An **inference** is a piece of information that is implied but not written outright by the author. For instance, consider the following sentence: *Mark made more money that week than he had in the previous year.* From this sentence, the reader can infer that Mark either has not made much money in the previous year or made a great deal of money that week. Often, a reader can use information he or she already knows to make inferences. Take as an example the sentence *When his coffee arrived, he looked around the table for the silver cup.* Many people know that cream is typically served in a silver cup, so using their own base of knowledge they can infer that the subject of this sentence takes his coffee with cream. Making inferences requires concentration, attention, and practice.

Test-taking tip: While being tested on his ability to make correct inferences, the student must look for contextual clues. An answer can be *true* but not *correct*. The contextual clues will help you find the answer that is the best answer out of the given choices. Understand the context in which a phrase is stated. When asked for the implied meaning of a statement made in the passage, the student should immediately locate the statement and read the context in which it was made. Also, look for an answer choice that has a similar phrase to the statement in question.

A reader must be able to identify a text's **sequence**, or the order in which things happen. Often, and especially when the sequence is very important to the author, it is indicated with signal words like *first, then, next,* and *last.* However, sometimes a sequence is merely implied and must be noted by the reader. Consider the sentence *He walked in the front door and switched on the hall lamp.* Clearly, the man did not turn the lamp on before he walked in the door, so the implied sequence is that he first walked in the door and then turned on the lamp. Texts do not always proceed in an orderly sequence from first to last; sometimes, they begin at the end and then start over at the beginning. As a reader, it can be useful to make brief notes to clarify the sequence.

In addition to inferring and predicting things about the text, the reader must often **draw conclusions** about the information he has read. When asked for a *conclusion* that may be drawn, look for critical "hedge" phrases, such as *likely, may, can,* and *will often,* among many others. When you are being tested on this knowledge, remember that question writers insert these hedge phrases to cover every possibility. Often an answer will be wrong simply because it leaves no room for exception. Extreme positive or negative answers (such as *always, never,* etc.) are usually not correct. The reader should not use any outside knowledge that is not gathered from the reading passage to answer the related questions. Correct answers can be derived straight from the reading passage.

LITERARY GENRES

Literary genres refer to the basic generic types of poetry, drama, fiction, and nonfiction. Literary genre is a method of classifying and analyzing literature. There are numerous subdivisions within genre, including such categories as novels, novellas, and short stories in fiction. Drama may also be subdivided into comedy, tragedy, and many other categories. Poetry and nonfiction have their own distinct divisions.

Genres often overlap, and the distinctions among them are blurred, such as that between the nonfiction novel and docudrama, as well as many others. However, the use of genres is helpful to the reader as a set of understandings that guide our responses to a work. The generic norm sets expectations and forms the framework within which we read and evaluate a work. This framework will guide both our understanding and interpretation of the work. It is a useful tool for both literary criticism and analysis.

Fiction is a general term for any form of literary narrative that is invented or imagined rather than being factual. For those individuals who equate fact with truth, the imagined or invented character of fiction tends to render it relatively unimportant or trivial among the genres. Defenders of fiction are quick to point out that the fictional mode is an essential part of being. The ability to imagine or discuss what-if plots, characters, and events is clearly part of the human experience.

Prose is derived from the Latin and means "straightforward discourse." Prose fiction, although having many categories, may be divided into three main groups:

- **Short stories**: a fictional narrative, the length of which varies, usually under 20,000 words. Short stories usually have only a few characters and generally describe one major event or insight. The short story began in magazines in the late 1800s and has flourished ever since.
- **Novels**: a longer work of fiction, often containing a large cast of characters and extensive plotting. The emphasis may be on an event, action, social problems, or any experience. There is now a genre of nonfiction novels pioneered by Truman Capote's *In Cold Blood* in the 1960s. Novels may also be written in verse.
- **Novellas**: a work of narrative fiction longer than a short story but shorter than a novel. Novellas may also be called short novels or novelettes. They originated from the German tradition and have become common forms in all of the world's literature.

Many elements influence a work of prose fiction. Some important ones are:

- **Speech and dialogue**: Characters may speak for themselves or through the narrator. Dialogue may be realistic or fantastic, depending on the author's aim.
- **Thoughts and mental processes**: There may be internal dialogue used as a device for plot development or character understanding.
- **Dramatic involvement**: Some narrators encourage readers to become involved in the events of the story, whereas others attempt to distance readers through literary devices.
- **Action**: This is any information that advances the plot or involves new interactions between the characters.
- **Duration**: The time frame of the work may be long or short, and the relationship between described time and narrative time may vary.
- **Setting and description**: Is the setting critical to the plot or characters? How are the action scenes described?

150

- **Themes**: This is any point of view or topic given sustained attention.
- **Symbolism**: Authors often veil meanings through imagery and other literary constructions.

Fiction is much wider than simply prose fiction. Songs, ballads, epics, and narrative poems are examples of non-prose fiction. A full definition of fiction must include not only the work itself but also the framework in which it is read. Literary fiction can also be defined as not true rather than nonexistent, as many works of historical fiction refer to real people, places, and events that are treated imaginatively as if they were true. These imaginary elements enrich and broaden literary expression.

When analyzing fiction, it is important for the reader to look carefully at the work being studied. The plot or action of a narrative can become so entertaining that the language of the work is ignored. The language of fiction should not simply be a way to relate a plot—it should also yield many insights to the judicious reader. Some prose fiction is based on the reader's engagement with the language rather than the story. A studious reader will analyze the mode of expression as well as the narrative. Part of the reward of reading in this manner is to discover how the author uses different language to describe familiar objects, events, or emotions. Some works focus the reader on an author's unorthodox use of language, whereas others may emphasize characters or storylines. What happens in a story is not always the critical element in the work. This type of reading may be difficult at first but yields great rewards.

The **narrator** is a central part of any work of fiction, and can give insight about the purpose of the work and its main themes and ideas. The following are important questions to address to better understand the voice and role of the narrator and incorporate that voice into an overall understanding of the novel:

- Who is the narrator of the novel? What is the narrator's perspective, first person or third person? What is the role of the narrator in the plot? Are there changes in narrators or the perspective of narrators?
- Does the narrator explain things in the novel, or does meaning emerge from the plot and events? The personality of the narrator is important. She may have a vested interest in a character or event described. Some narratives follow the time sequence of the plot, whereas others do not. A narrator may express approval or disapproval about a character or events in the work.
- Tone is an important aspect of the narration. Who is actually being addressed by the narrator? Is the tone familiar or formal, intimate or impersonal? Does the vocabulary suggest clues about the narrator?

Review Video: The Narrator
Visit mometrix.com/academy and enter code: 742528

A **character** is a person intimately involved with the plot and development of the novel. Development of the novel's characters not only moves the story along but will also tell the reader a lot about the novel itself. There is usually a physical description of the character, but this is often omitted in modern and postmodern novels. These works may focus on the psychological state or motivation of the character. The choice of a character's name may give valuable clues to his role in the work.

Characters are said to be flat or round. Flat characters tend to be minor figures in the story, changing little or not at all. Round characters (those understood from a well-rounded view) are more central to the story and tend to change as the plot unfolds. Stock characters are similar to flat characters, filling out the story without influencing it.

Modern literature has been greatly affected by Freudian psychology, giving rise to such devices as the interior monologue and magical realism as methods of understanding characters in a work. These give the reader a more complex understanding of the inner lives of the characters and enrich the understanding of relationships between characters.

Another important genre is that of **drama**: a play written to be spoken aloud. The drama is, in many ways, inseparable from performance. Reading drama ideally involves using imagination to visualize and re-create the play with characters and settings. The reader stages the play in his imagination, watching characters interact and developments unfold. Sometimes this involves simulating a theatrical presentation; other times it involves imagining the events. In either case, the reader is imagining the setting and action to re-create the dramatic experience. Novels require a use similar use of imagination, but a narrator will provide much more information about the setting, characters, inner dialogues, and many other supporting details. In drama, much of this is missing, and we are required to use our powers of projection and imagination to taste the full flavor of the dramatic work. There are many empty spaces in dramatic texts that must be filled by the reader to fully appreciate the work.

When reading drama in this way, there are some advantages over watching the play performed (though there is much criticism in this regard):

- Freedom of point of view and perspective: Text is free of interpretations of actors, directors, producers, and technical staging.
- Additional information: The text of a drama may be accompanied by notes or prefaces placing the work in a social or historical context. Stage directions may also provide relevant information about the author's purpose. None of this is typically available at live or filmed performances.
- Study and understanding: Difficult or obscure passages may be studied at leisure and supplemented by explanatory works. This is particularly true of older plays with unfamiliar language, which cannot be fully understood without an opportunity to study the material.

Critical elements of drama, especially when it is being read aloud or performed, include dialect, speech, and dialogue. Analysis of speech and dialogue is important in the critical study of drama. Some playwrights use speech to develop their characters. Speeches may be long or short, and written in as normal prose or blank verse. Some characters have a unique way of speaking which illuminates aspects of the drama. Emphasis and tone are both important, as well. Does the author make clear the tone in which lines are to be spoken, or is this open to interpretation? Sometimes there are various possibilities in tone with regard to delivering lines.

Dialect is any distinct variety of a language, especially one spoken in a region or part of a country. The criterion for distinguishing dialects from languages is that of mutual understanding. For example, people who speak Dutch cannot understand English unless they have learned it. But a speaker from Amsterdam can understand one from Antwerp; therefore, they speak different dialects of the same language. This is, however, a matter of degree; there are languages in which different dialects are unintelligible.

Dialect mixtures are the presence in one form of speech with elements from different neighboring dialects. The study of speech differences from one geographical area to another is called dialect geography. A dialect atlas is a map showing distribution of dialects in a given area. A dialect continuum shows a progressive shift in dialects across a territory, such that adjacent dialects are understandable, but those at the extremes are not.

Dramatic dialogue can be difficult to interpret and changes depending upon the tone used and which words are emphasized. Where the stresses, or meters, of dramatic dialogue fall can determine meaning. Variations in emphasis are only one factor in the manipulability of dramatic speech. Tone is of equal or greater importance and expresses a range of possible emotions and feelings that cannot be readily discerned from the script of a play. The reader must add tone to the words to understand the full meaning of a passage. Recognizing tone is a cumulative process as the reader begins to understand the characters and situations in the play. Other elements that influence the interpretation of dialogue include the setting, possible reactions of the characters to the speech, and possible gestures or facial expressions of the actor. There are no firm rules to guide the interpretation of dramatic speech. An open and flexible attitude is essential in interpreting dramatic dialogue.

Action is a crucial element in the production of a dramatic work. Many dramas contain little dialogue and much action. In these cases, it is essential for the reader to carefully study stage directions and visualize the action on the stage. Benefits of understanding stage directions include knowing which characters are on the stage at all times, who is speaking to whom, and following these patterns through changes of scene.

Stage directions also provide additional information, some of which is not available to a live audience. The nature of the physical space where the action occurs is vital, and stage directions help with this. The historical context of the period is important in understanding what the playwright was working with in terms of theaters and physical space. The type of staging possible for the author is a good guide to the spatial elements of a production.

Asides and soliloquies are devices that authors use in plot and character development. **Asides** indicate that not all characters are privy to the lines. This may be a method of advancing or explaining the plot in a subtle manner. **Soliloquies** are opportunities for character development, for plot enhancement, and to give insight to characters' motives, feelings, and emotions. Careful study of these elements provides a reader with an abundance of clues to the major themes and plot of the work.

Art, music, and literature all interact in ways that contain many opportunities for the enrichment of all of the arts. Students could apply their knowledge of art and music by creating illustrations for a work or creating a musical score for a text.

Understanding the art and music of a period can make the experience of literature a richer, more rewarding experience. Students should be encouraged to use the knowledge of art and music to illuminate the text. Examining examples of dress, architecture, music, and dance of a period may be helpful in a fuller engagement of the text. Much of period literature lends itself to the analysis of the prevailing taste in art and music of an era, which helps place the literary work in a more meaningful context.

Critical Thinking Skills

OPINIONS, FACTS, & FALLACIES

Critical thinking skills are mastered through understanding various types of writing and the different purposes that authors have for writing the way they do. Every author writes for a purpose.

Understanding that purpose, and how they accomplish their goal, will allow you to critique the writing and determine whether or not you agree with their conclusions.

Readers must always be conscious of the distinction between fact and opinion. A **fact** can be subjected to analysis and can be either proved or disproved. An **opinion**, on the other hand, is the author's personal feeling, which may not be alterable by research, evidence, or argument. If the author writes that the distance from New York to Boston is about two hundred miles, he is stating a fact. But if he writes that New York is too crowded, then he is giving an opinion, because there is no objective standard for overpopulation. An opinion may be indicated by words like *believe*, *think*, or *feel*. Also, an opinion may be supported by facts: for instance, the author might give the population density of New York as a reason for why it is overcrowded. An opinion supported by fact tends to be more convincing. When authors support their opinions with other opinions, the reader is unlikely to be moved.

> **Review Video: Fact or Opinion**
> Visit mometrix.com/academy and enter code: 870899

Facts should be presented to the reader from reliable sources. An opinion is what the author thinks about a given topic. An opinion is not common knowledge or proven by expert sources, but it is information that the author believes and wants the reader to consider. To distinguish between fact and opinion, a reader needs to look at the type of source that is presenting information, what information backs-up a claim, and whether or not the author may be motivated to have a certain point of view on a given topic. For example, if a panel of scientists has conducted multiple studies on the effectiveness of taking a certain vitamin, the results are more likely to be factual than if a company selling a vitamin claims that taking the vitamin can produce positive effects. The company is motivated to sell its product, while the scientists are using the scientific method to prove a theory. If the author uses words such as "I think...", the statement is an opinion.

In their attempt to persuade, writers often make mistakes in their thinking patterns and writing choices. It's important to understand these so you can make an informed decision. Every author has a point of view, but when an author ignores reasonable counterarguments or distorts opposing viewpoints, she is demonstrating a **bias**. A bias is evident whenever the author is unfair or inaccurate in his or her presentation. Bias may be intentional or unintentional, but it should always alert the reader to be skeptical of the argument being made. It should be noted that a biased author may still be correct. However, the author will be correct in spite of her bias, not because of it. A **stereotype** is like a bias, except that it is specifically applied to a group or place. Stereotyping is considered to be particularly abhorrent because it promotes negative generalizations about people. Many people are familiar with some of the hateful stereotypes of certain ethnic, religious, and cultural groups. Readers should be very wary of authors who stereotype. These faulty assumptions typically reveal the author's ignorance and lack of curiosity.

> **Review Video: Bias and Stereotype**
> Visit mometrix.com/academy and enter code: 644829

Sometimes, authors will **appeal to the reader's emotions** in an attempt to persuade or to distract the reader from the weakness of the argument. For instance, the author may try to inspire the pity of the reader by delivering a heart-rending story. An author also might use the bandwagon approach, in which he suggests that his opinion is correct because it is held by the majority. Some authors resort to name-calling, in which insults and harsh words are delivered to the opponent in an attempt to distract. In advertising, a common appeal is the testimonial, in which a famous person endorses a product. Of course, the fact that a celebrity likes something should not really mean anything to the reader. These and other emotional appeals are usually evidence of poor reasoning and a weak argument.

Certain *logical fallacies* are frequent in writing. A logical fallacy is a failure of reasoning. As a reader, it is important to recognize logical fallacies, because they diminish the value of the author's message. The four most common logical fallacies in writing are the false analogy, circular reasoning, false dichotomy, and overgeneralization. In a **false analogy**, the author suggests that two things are similar, when in fact they are different. This fallacy is often committed when the author is attempting to convince the reader that something unknown is like something relatively familiar. The author takes advantage of the reader's ignorance to make this false comparison. One example might be the following statement: *Failing to tip a waitress is like stealing money out of somebody's wallet.* Of course, failing to tip is very rude, especially when the service has been good, but people are not arrested for failing to tip as they would for stealing money from a wallet. To compare stingy diners with thieves is a false analogy.

Circular reasoning is one of the more difficult logical fallacies to identify, because it is typically hidden behind dense language and complicated sentences. Reasoning is described as circular when it offers no support for assertions other than restating them in different words. Put another way, a circular argument refers to itself as evidence of truth. A simple example of circular argument is when a person uses a word to define itself, such as saying *Niceness is the state of being nice.* If the reader does not know what *nice* means, then this definition will not be very useful. In a text, circular reasoning is usually more complex. For instance, an author might say *Poverty is a problem for society because it creates trouble for people throughout the community.* It is redundant to say that poverty is a problem because it creates trouble. When an author engages in circular reasoning, it is often because he or she has not fully thought out the argument, or cannot come up with any legitimate justifications.

One of the most common logical fallacies is the **false dichotomy**, in which the author creates an artificial sense that there are only two possible alternatives in a situation. This fallacy is common when the author has an agenda and wants to give the impression that his view is the only sensible one. A false dichotomy has the effect of limiting the reader's options and imagination. An example of a false dichotomy is the statement *You need to go to the party with me, otherwise you'll just be bored at home.* The speaker suggests that the only other possibility besides being at the party is being bored at home. But this is not true, as it is perfectly possible to be entertained at home, or even to go somewhere other than the party. Readers should always be wary of the false dichotomy: when an author limits the alternatives, it is always wise to ask whether his argument valid.

Overgeneralization is a logical fallacy in which the author makes a claim that is so broad it cannot be proved or disproved. In most cases, overgeneralization occurs when the author wants to create an illusion of authority, or when he is using sensational language to sway the opinion of the reader. For instance, in the sentence *Everybody knows that she is a terrible teacher*, the author makes an assumption that cannot really be believed. This kind of statement is made when the author wants to create the illusion of consensus when none actually exists: it may be that most people have a negative view of the teacher, but to say that *everybody* feels that way is an exaggeration. When a reader spots overgeneralization, she should become skeptical about the argument that is being made, because an author will often try to hide a weak or unsupported assertion behind authoritative language.

Review Video: Reading Logical Fallacies
Visit mometrix.com/academy and enter code: 644845

Two other types of logical fallacies are **slippery slope** arguments and **hasty generalizations**. In a slippery slope argument, the author says that if something happens, it automatically means that something else will happen as a result, even though this may not be true. (i.e., just because you study hard does not mean you are going to ace the test). "Hasty generalization" is drawing a conclusion too early, without finishing analyzing the details of the argument. Writers of persuasive texts often use these techniques because they are very effective. In order to **identify logical fallacies**, readers need to read carefully and ask questions as they read. Thinking critically means not taking everything at face value. Readers need to critically evaluate an author's argument to make sure that the logic used is sound.

ORGANIZATION OF THE TEXT

The way a text is organized can help the reader to understand more clearly the author's intent and his conclusions. There are various ways to organize a text, and each one has its own purposes and uses.

Some nonfiction texts are organized to **present a problem** followed by a solution. In this type of text, it is common for the problem to be explained before the solution is offered. In some cases, as when the problem is well known, the solution may be briefly introduced at the beginning. The entire passage may focus on the solution, and the problem will be referenced only occasionally. Some texts will outline multiple solutions to a problem, leaving the reader to choose among them. If the author has an interest or an allegiance to one solution, he may fail to mention or may inaccurately describe some of the other solutions. Readers should be careful of the author's agenda when reading a problem-solution text. Only by understanding the author's point of view and interests can one develop a proper judgment of the proposed solution.

Authors need to organize information logically so the reader can follow it and locate information within the text. Two common organizational structures are cause and effect and chronological order. When using **chronological order**, the author presents information in the order that it happened. For example, biographies are written in chronological order; the subject's birth and childhood are presented first, followed by their adult life, and lastly by the events leading up to the person's death.

In **cause and effect**, an author presents one thing that makes something else happen. For example, if one were to go to bed very late, they would be tired. The cause is going to bed late, with the effect of being tired the next day.

It can be tricky to identify the cause-and-effect relationships in a text, but there are a few ways to approach this task. To begin with, these relationships are often signaled with certain terms. When an author uses words like *because*, *since*, *in order*, and *so*, she is likely describing a cause-and-effect relationship. Consider the sentence, "He called her because he needed the homework." This is a simple causal relationship, in which the cause was his need for the homework and the effect was his phone call. Not all cause-and-effect relationships are marked in this way, however. Consider the sentences, "He called her. He needed the homework." When the cause-and-effect relationship is not indicated with a keyword, it can be discovered by asking why something happened. He called her: why? The answer is in the next sentence: He needed the homework.

Persuasive essays, in which an author tries to make a convincing argument and change the reader's mind, usually include cause-and-effect relationships. However, these relationships should not always be taken at face value. An author frequently will assume a cause or take an effect for granted. To read a persuasive essay effectively, one needs to judge the cause-and-effect relationships the author is presenting. For instance, imagine an author wrote the following: "The parking deck has been unprofitable because people would prefer to ride their bikes." The relationship is clear: the cause is that people prefer to ride their bikes, and the effect is that the parking deck has been unprofitable. However, a reader should consider whether this argument is conclusive. Perhaps there are other reasons for the failure of the parking deck: a down economy, excessive fees, etc. Too often, authors present causal relationships as if they are fact rather than opinion. Readers should be on the alert for these dubious claims.

Thinking critically about ideas and conclusions can seem like a daunting task. One way to make it easier is to understand the basic elements of ideas and writing techniques. Looking at the way different ideas relate to each other can be a good way for the reader to begin his analysis. For instance, sometimes writers will write about two different ideas that are in opposition to each other. The analysis of these opposing ideas is known as **contrast**. Contrast is often marred by the author's obvious partiality to one of the ideas. A discerning reader will be put off by an author who does not engage in a fair fight. In an analysis of opposing ideas, both ideas should be presented in their clearest and most reasonable terms. If the author does prefer a side, he should avoid indicating this preference with pejorative language. An analysis of opposing ideas should proceed through the major differences point by point, with a full explanation of each side's view. For instance, in an analysis of capitalism and communism, it would be important to outline each side's view on labor, markets, prices, personal responsibility, etc. It would be less effective to describe the theory of communism and then explain how capitalism has thrived in the West. An analysis of opposing views should present each side in the same manner.

Many texts follow the **compare-and-contrast** model, in which the similarities and differences between two ideas or things are explored. Analysis of the similarities between ideas is called comparison. In order for a comparison to work, the author must place the ideas or things in an equivalent structure. That is, the author must present the ideas in the same way. Imagine an author wanted to show the similarities between cricket and baseball. The correct way to do so would be to summarize the equipment and rules for each game. It would be incorrect to summarize the equipment of cricket and then lay out the history of baseball, since this would make it impossible for the reader to see the similarities. It is perhaps too obvious to say that an analysis of similar ideas should emphasize the similarities. Of course, the author should take care to include any differences that must be mentioned. Often, these small differences will only reinforce the more general similarity.

DRAWING CONCLUSIONS

Authors should have a clear purpose in mind while writing. Especially when reading informational texts, it is important to understand the logical conclusion of the author's ideas. **Identifying this logical conclusion** can help the reader understand whether he agrees with the writer or not. Identifying a logical conclusion is much like making an inference: it requires the reader to combine the information given by the text with what he already knows to make a supportable assertion. If a passage is written well, then the conclusion should be obvious even when it is unstated. If the author intends the reader to draw a certain conclusion, then all of his argumentation and detail should be leading toward it. One way to approach the task of drawing conclusions is to make brief notes of all the points made by the author. When these are arranged on paper, they may clarify the logical conclusion. Another way to approach conclusions is to consider whether the reasoning of the author raises any pertinent questions. Sometimes it will be possible to draw several conclusions from a passage, and on occasion these will be conclusions that were never imagined by the author. It is essential, however, that these conclusions be supported directly by the text.

Review Video: Identifying Logical Conclusions
Visit mometrix.com/academy and enter code: 281653

The term **text evidence** refers to information that supports a main point or points in a story, and can help lead the reader to a conclusion. Information used as *text evidence* is precise, descriptive, and factual. A main point is often followed by supporting details that provide evidence to back-up a claim. For example, a story may include the claim that winter occurs during opposite months in the Northern and Southern hemispheres. *Text evidence* based on this claim may include countries where winter occurs in opposite months, along with reasons that winter occurs at different times of the year in separate hemispheres (due to the tilt of the Earth as it rotates around the sun).

Review Video: Text Evidence
Visit mometrix.com/academy and enter code: 486236

Readers interpret text and respond to it in a number of ways. Using textual support helps defend your response or interpretation because it roots your thinking in the text. You are interpreting based on information in the text and not simply your own ideas. When crafting a response, look for important quotes and details from the text to help bolster your argument. If you are writing about a character's personality trait, for example, use details from the text to show that the character acted in such a way. You can also include statistics and facts from a nonfiction text to strengthen your response. For example, instead of writing, "A lot of people use cell phones," use statistics to provide the exact number. This strengthens your argument because it is more precise.

The text used to support an argument can be the argument's downfall if it is not credible. A text is **credible**, or believable, when the author is knowledgeable and objective, or unbiased. The author's motivations for writing the text play a critical role in determining the credibility of the text and must be evaluated when assessing that credibility. The author's motives should be for the dissemination of information. The purpose of the text should be to inform or describe, not to persuade. When an author writes a persuasive text, he has the motivation that the reader will do what they want. The extent of the author's knowledge of the topic and their motivation must be evaluated when assessing the credibility of a text. Reports written about the Ozone layer by an environmental scientist and a hairdresser will have a different level of credibility.

Review Video: Credible
Visit mometrix.com/academy and enter code: 827257

After determining your own opinion and evaluating the credibility of your supporting text, it is sometimes necessary to communicate your ideas and findings to others. When **writing a response to a text**, it is important to use elements of the text to support your assertion or defend your position. Using supporting evidence from the text strengthens the argument because the reader can see how in depth the writer read the original piece and based their response on the details and facts within that text. Elements of text that can be used in a response include: facts, details, statistics, and direct quotations from the text. When writing a response, one must make sure they indicate which information comes from the original text and then base their discussion, argument, or defense around this information.

A reader should always be drawing conclusions from the text. Sometimes conclusions are implied from written information, and other times the information is **stated directly** within the passage. It is always more comfortable to draw conclusions from information stated within a passage, rather than to draw them from mere implications. At times an author may provide some information and then describe a counterargument. The reader should be alert for direct statements that are subsequently rejected or weakened by the author. The reader should always read the entire passage before drawing conclusions. Many readers are trained to expect the author's conclusions at either the beginning or the end of the passage, but many texts do not adhere to this format.

Drawing conclusions from information implied within a passage requires confidence on the part of the reader. **Implications** are things the author does not state directly, but which can be assumed based on what the author does say. For instance, consider the following simple passage: "I stepped outside and opened my umbrella. By the time I got to work, the cuffs of my pants were soaked." The author never states that it is raining, but this fact is clearly implied. Conclusions based on implication must be well supported by the text. In order to draw a solid conclusion, a reader should have multiple pieces of evidence, or, if he only has one, must be assured that there is no other possible explanation than his conclusion. A good reader will be able to draw many conclusions from information implied by the text, which enriches the reading experience considerably.

As an aid to drawing conclusions, the reader should be adept at **outlining** the information contained in the passage; an effective outline will reveal the structure of the passage, and will lead to solid conclusions. An effective outline will have a title that refers to the basic subject of the text, though it need not recapitulate the main idea. In most outlines, the main idea will be the first major section. It will have each major idea of the passage established as the head of a category. For instance, the most common outline format calls for the main ideas of the passage to be indicated with Roman numerals. In an effective outline of this kind, each of the main ideas will be represented by a Roman numeral and none of the Roman numerals will designate minor details or secondary ideas. Moreover, all supporting ideas and details should be placed in the appropriate place on the outline. An outline does not need to include every detail listed in the text, but it should feature all of those that are central to the argument or message. Each of these details should be listed under the appropriate main idea.

> **Review Video: Outlining**
> Visit mometrix.com/academy and enter code: 584445

It is also helpful to **summarize** the information you have read in a paragraph or passage format. This process is similar to creating an effective outline. To begin with, a summary should accurately define the main idea of the passage, though it does not need to explain this main idea in exhaustive detail. It should continue by laying out the most important supporting details or arguments from the passage. All of the significant supporting details should be included, and none of the details included should be irrelevant or insignificant. Also, the summary should accurately report all of these details. Too often, the desire for brevity in a summary leads to the sacrifice of clarity or veracity. Summaries are often difficult to read, because they omit all of the graceful language, digressions, and asides that distinguish great writing. However, if the summary is effective, it should contain much the same message as the original text.

> **Review Video: Summarizing Text**
> Visit mometrix.com/academy and enter code: 172903

Paraphrasing is another method the reader can use to aid in comprehension. When paraphrasing, one puts what they have read into their own words, rephrasing what the author has written to make it their own, to "translate" all of what the author says to their own words, including as many details as they can.

Testing Tips

SKIMMING

Your first task when you begin reading is to answer the question "What is the topic of the selection?" This can best be answered by quickly skimming the passage for the general idea, stopping to read only the first sentence of each paragraph. A paragraph's first sentence is usually the main topic sentence, and it gives you a summary of the content of the paragraph.

Once you've skimmed the passage, stopping to read only the first sentences, you will have a general idea about what it is about, as well as what is the expected topic in each paragraph.

Each question will contain clues as to where to find the answer in the passage. Do not just randomly search through the passage for the correct answer to each question. Search scientifically. Find key words or ideas in the question that are going to either contain or be near the correct answer. These are typically nouns, verbs, numbers, or phrases in the question that will probably be duplicated in the passage. Once you have identified the key words or ideas, skim the passage quickly to find where the key words or ideas appear. The correct answer choice will be nearby.

    Example: What caused Martin to suddenly return to Paris?

The key word is *Paris*. Skim the passage quickly to find where this word appears. The answer will be close by that word.

However, sometimes key words in the question are not repeated in the passage. In those cases, search for the general idea of the question.

    Example: Which of the following was the psychological impact of the author's childhood upon the remainder of his life?

Key words are *childhood* or *psychology*. While searching for those words, be alert for other words or phrases that have similar meaning, such as *emotional effect* or *mentally* which could be used in the passage, rather than the exact word *psychology*.

Numbers or years can be particularly good key words to skim for, as they stand out from the rest of the text.

    Example: Which of the following best describes the influence of Newton's work in the 20th century?

The adjective *20th* contains numbers and will easily stand out from the rest of the text. Use *20th* as the key word to skim for in the passage.

Other good key words may be in quotation marks. These identify a word or phrase that is copied directly from the passage. In those cases, the words in quotation marks are exactly duplicated in the passage.

    Example: In her college years, what was meant by Margaret's "drive for excellence"?

"Drive for excellence" is a direct quote from the passage and should be easy to find.

Once you've quickly found the correct section of the passage to find the answer, focus upon the answer choices. Sometimes a choice will repeat word for word a portion of the passage near the answer. However, beware of such duplication – it may be a trap! More than likely, the correct choice will paraphrase or summarize the related portion of the passage, rather than being exactly the same wording.

For the answers that you think are correct, read them carefully and make sure that they answer the question. An answer can be factually correct, but it MUST answer the question asked. Additionally, two answers can both be seemingly correct, so be sure to read all of the answer choices, and make sure that you get the one that BEST answers the question.

Some questions will not have a key word.

Example: Which of the following would the author of this passage likely agree with?

In these cases, look for key words in the answer choices. Then, skim the passage to find where the answer choice occurs. By skimming to find where to look, you can minimize the time required.

Sometimes, it may be difficult to identify a good key word in the question to skim for in the passage. In those cases, look for a key word in one of the answer choices to skim for. Often, the answer choices can all be found in the same paragraph, which can quickly narrow your search.

PARAGRAPH FOCUS

Focus upon the first sentence of each paragraph, which is the most important. The main topic of the paragraph is usually there.

Once you've read the first sentence in the paragraph, you should have a general idea about what each paragraph will be about. As you read the questions, try to determine which paragraph will have the answer. Paragraphs have a concise topic. The answer should either obviously be there or obviously not. It will save time if you can jump straight to the paragraph, so try to remember what you learned from the first sentences.

Example: The first paragraph is about radiation; the second is about cancer. If a question asks about cancer, where will the answer be? The second paragraph.

The main idea of a passage is typically spread across all or most of its paragraphs. Whereas the main idea of a paragraph may be completely different than the main idea of the very next paragraph, a main idea for a passage affects all of the paragraphs in one form or another.

Example: What is the main idea of the passage?

For each answer choice, try to see how many paragraphs are related. It can help to count how many sentences are affected by each choice, but it is best to see how many paragraphs are affected by the choice. Typically, the answer choices will include incorrect choices that are main ideas of individual paragraphs, but not the entire passage. That is why it is crucial to choose ideas that are supported by the most paragraphs possible.

ELIMINATE CHOICES

Some choices can quickly be eliminated. "Albert Einstein lived there." Is Albert Einstein even mentioned in the passage? If not, quickly eliminate it.

When trying to answer a question such as "the passage indicates all of the following EXCEPT," quickly skim the paragraph searching for references to each choice. If the reference exists, scratch it off as a choice. Similar choices may be crossed off simultaneously if they are close enough.

161

Copyright © Mometrix Media. You have been licensed one copy of this document for personal use only. Any other reproduction or redistribution is strictly prohibited. All rights reserved.

In choices that ask you to choose "which answer choice does NOT describe?" or "all of the following answer choices are identifiable characteristics, EXCEPT which?", look for answers that are similarly worded. Since only one answer can be correct, if there are two answers that appear to mean the same thing, they must BOTH be incorrect and can be eliminated.

Example:
A.) changing values and attitudes
B.) a large population of mobile or uprooted people

These answer choices are similar; they both describe a fluid culture. Because of their similarity, they can be linked together. Since the answer can have only one choice, they can also be eliminated together.

CONTEXTUAL CLUES

Look for contextual clues. An answer can be right but not correct. The contextual clues will help you find the answer that is most right and is correct. Understand the context in which a phrase is stated.

When asked for the implied meaning of a statement made in the passage, immediately go find the statement and read the context it was made in. Also, look for an answer choice that has a similar phrase to the statement in question.

Example: In the passage, what is implied by the phrase "Scientists have become more or less part of the furniture"?

Find an answer choice that is similar or describes the phrase "part of the furniture," as that is the key phrase in the question. "Part of the furniture" is a saying that means something is fixed, immovable, or set in its ways. Those are all similar ways of saying "part of the furniture." As such, the correct answer choice will probably include a similar rewording of the expression.

Example: Why was John described as "morally desperate"?

The answer will probably have some sort of definition of morals in it. "Morals" refers to a code of right and wrong behavior, so the correct answer choice will likely have words that mean something like that.

FACT/OPINION

When asked about which statement is a fact or opinion, remember that answer choices that are facts will typically have no ambiguous words. For example, how long is a long time? What defines an ordinary person? These ambiguous words of *long* and *ordinary* should not be in a factual statement. However, if all of the choices have ambiguous words, go to the context of the passage. Often, a factual statement may be set out as a research finding.

Example: "The scientist found that the eye reacts quickly to change in light."

Opinions may be set out in the context of words like *thought, believed, understood,* or *wished.*

Example: "He thought the Yankees should win the World Series."

OPPOSITES

Answer choices that are direct opposites are usually correct. The paragraph will often contain established relationships (when this goes up, that goes down). The question may ask you to draw conclusions for this and will give two similar answer choices that are opposites.

> Example:
> A.) a decrease in housing starts
> B.) an increase in housing starts

TIME MANAGEMENT

In technical passages, do not get lost on the technical terms. Skip them and move on. You want a general understanding of what is going on, not a mastery of the passage.

When you encounter material in the selection that seems difficult to understand, it often may not be necessary and can be skipped. Only spend time trying to understand it if it is going to be relevant for a question. Understand difficult phrases only as a last resort.

Answer general questions before detail questions. A reader with a good understanding of the whole passage can often answer general questions without rereading a word. Get the easier questions out of the way before tackling the more time-consuming ones.

Identify each question by type. Usually, the wording of a question will tell you whether you can find the answer by referring directly to the passage or by using your reasoning powers. You alone know which question types you customarily handle with ease and which give you trouble and will require more time. Save the difficult questions for last.

HEDGE PHRASES REVISITED

Once again, watch out for critical "hedge" phrases, such as likely, may, can, will often, sometimes, etc., often, almost, mostly, usually, generally, rarely, sometimes. Question writers insert these hedge phrases, to cover every possibility. Often an answer will be wrong simply because it leaves no room for exception.

> Example: Animals live longer in cold places than animals in warm places.

This answer choice is wrong, because there are exceptions in which certain warm climate animals live longer. This answer choice leaves no possibility of exception. It states that every animal species in cold places live longer than animal species in warm places. Correct answer choices will typically have a key hedge word to leave room for exceptions.

> Example: In severe cold, a polar bear cub is likely to survive longer than an adult polar bear.

This answer choice is correct, because not only does the paragraph imply that younger animals survive better in the cold, it also allows for exceptions to exist. The use of the word *likely* leaves room for cases in which a polar bear cub might not survive longer than the adult polar bear.

WORD USAGE QUESTIONS

When asked how a word is used in the passage, don't use your existing knowledge of the word. The question is being asked precisely because there is some strange or unusual usage of the word in the passage. Go to the passage and use contextual clues to determine the answer. Don't simply use the popular definition you already know.

SWITCHBACK WORDS

Stay alert for "switchbacks". These are the words and phrases frequently used to alert you to shifts in thought. The most common switchback word is "but". Others include although, however, nevertheless, on the other hand, even though, while, in spite of, despite, regardless of.

AVOID "FACT TRAPS"

Once you know which paragraph the answer will be in, focus on that paragraph. However, don't get distracted by a choice that is factually true about the paragraph. Your search is for the answer that answers the question, which may be about a tiny aspect in the paragraph. Stay focused and don't fall for an answer that describes the larger picture of the paragraph. Always go back to the question and make sure you're choosing an answer that actually answers the question and is not just a true statement.

MILK THE PARAGRAPH

Some of the paragraphs may throw you completely off. They might deal with a subject you have not been exposed to, or one that you haven't reviewed in years. While your lack of knowledge about the subject will be a hindrance, the paragraph itself can give you many clues that will help you find the correct answer. Read the paragraph carefully, and look for clues. Watch particularly for adjectives and nouns describing difficult terms or words that you don't recognize. Regardless of if you understand a word or not, replacing it with the synonyms used for it in the paragraph may help you to understand what the questions are asking.

Example: A bacteriophage is a virus that infects bacteria.

While you may not know much about the characteristics of a bacteriophage, the fifth word into the sentence told you that a bacteriophage is a virus. Wherever you see the word *bacteriophage*, you can mentally replace it with the word *virus*. Your more general knowledge of viruses may enable you to answer the question.

Look carefully for these descriptive synonyms (nouns) and adjectives and use them to help you understand the difficult terms. Rather than wracking your mind about specific detail information concerning a difficult term in the paragraph, use the more general description or synonym provided to make it easier for you.

MAKE PREDICTIONS

As you read and understand the passage and then the question, try to guess what the answer will be. Remember that all but one of the answer choices are wrong, and once you read them, your mind will immediately become cluttered with answer choices designed to throw you off. Your mind is typically the most focused immediately after you have read the passage and question and digested its contents. If you can, try to predict what the correct answer will be. You may be surprised at what you can predict.

Quickly scan the choices and see if your prediction is in the listed answer choices. If it is, then you can be quite confident that you have the right answer. It still won't hurt to check the other answer choices, but most of the time, you've got it!

ANSWER THE QUESTION

It may seem obvious to only pick answer choices that answer the question, but the test can create some excellent answer choices that are wrong. Don't pick an answer just because it sounds right, or you believe it to be true. It MUST answer the question. Once you've made your selection, always go back and check it against the question and make sure that you didn't misread the question, and the answer choice does answer the question posed.

BENCHMARK

After you read the first answer choice, decide if you think it sounds correct or not. If it doesn't, move on to the next answer choice. If it does, make a mental note about that choice. This doesn't mean that you've definitely selected it as your answer choice, it just means that it's the best you've seen thus far. Go ahead and read the next choice. If the next choice is worse than the one you've already selected, keep going to the next answer choice. If the next choice is better than the choice you've already selected, then make a mental note about that answer choice.

As you read through the list, you are mentally noting the choice you think is right. That is your new standard. Every other answer choice must be benchmarked against that standard. That choice is correct until proven otherwise by another answer choice beating it out. Once you've decided that no other answer choice seems as good, do one final check to ensure that it answers the question posed.

NEW INFORMATION

Correct answers will usually contain the information listed in the paragraph and question. Rarely will completely new information be inserted into a correct answer choice. Occasionally the new information may be related in a manner that the test is asking for you to interpret, but seldom.

> Example:
> The argument above is dependent upon which of the following assumptions?
> A.) Charles's Law was used

If Charles's Law is not mentioned at all in the referenced paragraph and argument, then it is unlikely that this choice is correct. All of the information needed to answer the question is provided for you, so you should not have to make guesses that are unsupported or choose answer choices that have unknown information that cannot be reasoned.

VALID INFORMATION

Don't discount any of the information provided in the passage, particularly shorter ones. Every piece of information may be necessary to determine the correct answer. None of the information in the paragraph is there to throw you off (while the answer choices will certainly have information to throw you off). If two seemingly unrelated topics are discussed, don't ignore either. You can be confident there is a relationship, or it wouldn't be included in the paragraph, and you are probably going to have to determine what is that relationship for the answer.

DON'T FALL FOR THE OBVIOUS

When in doubt of the answer, it is easy to go with what you are familiar with. If you are familiar with one of the answer choices and know it is correct, then you may be inclined to guess at that term. Be careful though, and don't go with familiar answers simply because they are familiar.

Example: What happened when the temperature changed to 212° F?

A.) The solution began to boil.
B.) The reaction would become stabilized.
C.) The solution would become saturated.
D.) The reaction would be more easily controlled.

You know that 212° F is the boiling point of pure water. Therefore, choice A is familiar, because there is a link between the temperature 212° F and the word "boiling". If you are unsure of the correct answer, you may decide upon choice A simply because of its familiarity. Don't be deceived though. Think through the other answer choices before making your final selection. Just because you have a mental link between the question and an answer choice, doesn't make that answer choice correct.

RANDOM TIPS

- For questions that you're not clear on the answer, use the process of elimination. Weed out the answer choices that you know are wrong before choosing an answer.
- Don't fall for "bizarre" choices, mentioning things that are not relevant to the paragraph. Also avoid answers that sound "smart." Again, if you're willing to bet $5, ignore the tips and go with your bet.

Common Subject: Mechanical Comprehension

In order to succeed on the mechanical concepts section of the exam, you will need to be familiar with basic concepts in physics and mechanics. Don't worry: the exam does not dwell on obscure theories or require you to make complicated calculations. The equations that are included in this section of the book are meant to illustrate the relationships of physics, not to show you how to solve numerical problems. You do, however, need to understand the essential properties of physics, and how they apply to real-life situations. In order to help you along, we have included a full primer on all of the concepts that may come up on this section of the exam. Important terms and concepts are placed in bold. Finally, although we have tried to make this section of the guidebook as easy to read as possible, we still recommend that you take your time and avoid reading in a hurry. You may need to read some of this information a few times before fully absorbing it. Whenever possible, try to imagine some everyday examples for the concepts we discuss; after all, applying the theories of physics to the materials of everyday life is one way to define mechanics.

Kinematics

To begin, we will look at the basics of physics. At its heart, physics is just a set of explanations for the ways in which matter and energy behave. There are three key concepts used to describe how matter moves:

1. Displacement
2. Velocity
3. Acceleration

DISPLACEMENT

Concept: Where and how far an object has gone

Calculation: Final position – initial position

When something changes its location from one place to another, it is said to have undergone displacement. If a golf ball is hit across a sloped green into the hole, the displacement only takes into account the final and initial locations, not the path of the ball.

Displacement along a straight line is a very simple example of a vector quantity; it has both a magnitude and a direction. Direction is as important as magnitude in many measurements. If we can determine the original and final position of the object, then we can determine the total displacement with this simple equation:

$$\text{Displacement} = \text{final position} - \text{original position}$$

The hole (final position) is at the Cartesian coordinate location (2,0) and the ball is hit from the location (1,0). The displacement is:

$$\text{Displacement} = (2,0) - (1,0)$$

$$\text{Displacement} = (1,0)$$

The displacement has a magnitude of 1 and a direction of the positive x-direction.

> **Review Video: Displacement**
> Visit mometrix.com/academy and enter code: 236197

VELOCITY

Concept: The rate of moving from one position to another

Calculation: Change in position / change in time

Velocity answers the question, "How quickly is an object moving?" For example, if a car and a plane travel between two cities that are a hundred miles apart, but the car takes two hours and the plane takes one hour, the car has the same displacement as the plane but a smaller velocity.

In order to solve some of the problems on the exam, you may need to assess the velocity of an object. If we want to calculate the average velocity of an object, we must know two things. First, we must know its displacement. Second, we must know the time it took to cover this distance. The formula for average velocity is quite simple:

$$\text{average velocity} = \frac{\text{displacement}}{\text{change in time}}$$

Or

$$\text{average velocity} = \frac{\text{final position} - \text{original position}}{\text{final time} - \text{original time}}$$

To complete the example, the velocity of the plane is calculated to be:

$$\text{plane average velocity } = \frac{100 \text{ miles}}{1 \text{ hour}} = 100 \text{ miles per hour}$$

The velocity of the car is less:

$$\text{car average velocity } = \frac{100 \text{ miles}}{2 \text{ hours}} = 50 \text{ miles per hour}$$

Often, people confuse the words *speed* and *velocity*. There is a significant difference. The average velocity is based on the amount of displacement, a vector. Alternately, the average speed is based on the distance covered or the path length. The equation for speed is:

$$\textbf{average speed } = \frac{\textbf{total distance traveled}}{\textbf{change in time}}$$

Notice that we used total distance and *not* change in position, because speed is path-dependent.

If the plane traveling between cities had needed to fly around a storm on its way, making the distance traveled 50 miles greater than the distance the car traveled, the plane would still have the same total displacement as the car.

For this reason, the average speed can be calculated:

$$\text{plane average speed } = \frac{150 \text{ miles}}{1 \text{ hour}} = 150 \text{ miles per hour}$$

$$\text{car average speed } = \frac{100 \text{ miles}}{2 \text{ hours}} = 50 \text{ miles per hour}$$

ACCELERATION

Concept: How quickly something changes from one velocity to another

Calculation: Change in velocity / change in time

Acceleration is the rate of change of the velocity of an object. If a car accelerates from zero velocity to 60 miles per hour (88 feet per second) in two seconds, the car has an impressive acceleration.

But if a car performs the same change in velocity in eight seconds, the acceleration is much lower and not as impressive.

To calculate average acceleration, we may use the equation:

$$\text{average acceleration} = \frac{\text{change in velocity}}{\text{change in time}}$$

The acceleration of the cars is found to be:

$$\text{Car \#1 average acceleration} = \frac{88 \text{ feet per second}}{2 \text{ seconds}} = 44 \frac{\text{feet}}{\text{second}^2}$$

$$\text{Car \#2 average acceleration} = \frac{88 \text{ feet per second}}{8 \text{ seconds}} = 11 \frac{\text{feet}}{\text{second}^2}$$

Acceleration will be expressed in units of distance divided by time squared; for instance, meters per second squared or feet per second squared.

> **Review Video: <u>Velocity and Acceleration</u>**
> Visit mometrix.com/academy and enter code: 671849

PROJECTILE MOTION

A specific application of the study of motion is projectile motion. Simple projectile motion occurs when an object is in the air and experiencing only the force of gravity. We will disregard drag for this topic. Some common examples of projectile motion are thrown balls, flying bullets, and falling rocks. The characteristics of projectile motion are:

4. The horizontal component of velocity doesn't change
5. The vertical acceleration due to gravity affects the vertical component of velocity

Because gravity only acts downwards, objects in projectile motion only experience acceleration in the y-direction (vertical). The horizontal component of the object's velocity does not change in

170

flight. This means that if a rock is thrown out off a cliff, the horizontal velocity (think of the shadow if the sun is directly overhead) will not change until the ball hits the ground.

The velocity in the vertical direction is affected by gravity. Gravity imposes an acceleration of $g = 9.8 \frac{m}{s^2}$ or $32 \frac{ft}{s^2}$ downward on projectiles. The vertical component of velocity at any point is equal to:

vertical velocity = original vertical velocity − g × time

When these characteristics are combined, there are three points of particular interest in a projectile's flight. At the beginning of a flight, the object has a horizontal component and a vertical component giving it a large speed. At the top of a projectile's flight, the vertical velocity equals zero, making the top the slowest part of travel. When the object passes the same height as the launch, the vertical velocity is opposite of the initial vertical velocity, making the speed equal to the initial speed.

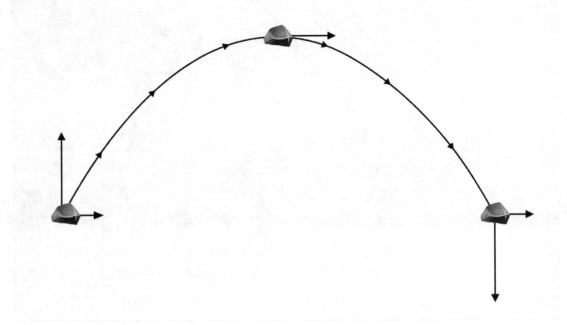

If the object continues falling below the initial height from which it was launched (e.g., it was launched from the edge of a cliff), it will have an even greater velocity than it did initially from that point until it hits the ground.

Review Video: Projectile Motion
Visit mometrix.com/academy and enter code: 719700

Rotational Kinematics

Concept: Increasing the radius increases the linear speed

Calculation: Linear speed = radius × rotational speed

Another interesting application of the study of motion is rotation. In practice, simple rotation is when an object rotates around a point at a constant speed. Most questions covering rotational kinematics will provide the distance from a rotating object to the center of rotation (radius) and ask about the linear speed of the object. A point will have a greater linear speed when it is farther from the center of rotation.

If a potter is spinning his wheel at a constant speed of one revolution per second, the clay six inches away from the center will be going faster than the clay three inches from the center. The clay directly in the center of the wheel will not have any linear velocity.

To find the linear speed of rotating objects using radians, we use the equation:

linear speed = (rotational speed [in radians]) × (radius)

Using degrees, the equation is:

$$\textbf{linear speed} = \textbf{(rotational speed [in degrees])} \times \frac{\boldsymbol{\pi} \textbf{ radians}}{\textbf{180 degrees}} \times \textbf{(radius)}$$

To find the speed of the pieces of clay, we use the known values (rotational speed of 1 revolution per second, radii of 0 inches, 3 inches, and 6 inches) and the knowledge that one revolution = 2π.

$$\text{clay \#1 speed} = \left(2\pi \frac{\text{rad}}{\text{s}}\right) \times (0 \text{ inches}) = 0 \frac{\text{inches}}{\text{second}}$$

$$\text{clay \#2 speed} = \left(2\pi \frac{\text{rad}}{\text{s}}\right) \times (3 \text{ inches}) = 18.8 \frac{\text{inches}}{\text{second}}$$

$$\text{clay \#3 speed} = \left(2\pi \frac{\text{rad}}{\text{s}}\right) \times (6 \text{ inches}) = 37.7 \frac{\text{inches}}{\text{second}}$$

Review Video: Linear Speed
Visit mometrix.com/academy and enter code: 327101

CAMS

In the study of motion, a final application often tested is the cam. A cam and follower system allows mechanical systems to have timed, specified, and repeating motion. Although cams come in varied forms, tests focus on rotary cams. In engines, a cam shaft coordinates the valves for intake and exhaust. Cams are often used to convert rotational motion into repeating linear motion.

Cams rotate around one point. The follower sits on the edge of the cam and moves along with the edge. To understand simple cams, count the number of bumps on the cam. Each bump will cause the follower to move outwards.

Another way to consider cams is to unravel the cam profile into a straight object. The follower will then follow the top of the profile.

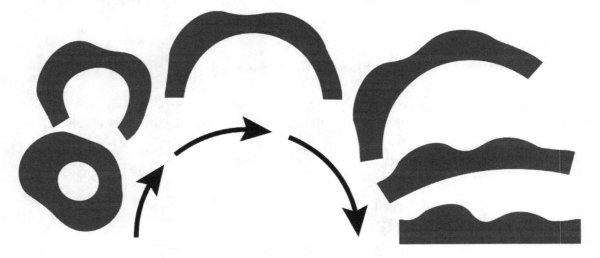

Kinetics

NEWTON'S THREE LAWS OF MECHANICS

The questions on the exam may require you to demonstrate familiarity with the concepts expressed in Newton's three laws of motion which relate to the concept of force.

Newton's first law – A body at rest tends to remain at rest, while a body in motion tends to remain in motion, unless acted upon by an external force.

Newton's second law – The acceleration of an object is directly proportional to the force being exerted on it and inversely proportional to its mass.

Newton's third law – For every force, there is an equal and opposite force.

FIRST LAW

Concept: Unless something interferes, an object won't start or stop moving

Although intuition supports the idea that objects do not start moving until a force acts on them, the idea of an object continuing forever without any forces can seem odd. Before Newton formulated his laws of mechanics, general thought held that some force had to act on an object continuously in order for it to move at a constant velocity. This seems to make sense; when an object is briefly pushed, it will eventually come to a stop. Newton, however, determined that unless some other force acted on the object (most notably friction or air resistance), it would continue in the direction it was pushed at the same velocity forever.

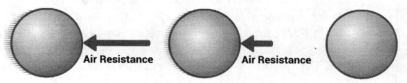

As time moves forward, the air resistance stops one ball, but the ball without air resistance has no stopping force.

SECOND LAW

Concept: Acceleration increases linearly with force.

Although Newton's second law can be conceptually understood as a series of relationships describing how an increase in one factor will decrease another factor, the law can be understood best in equation format:

$$\text{Force} = \text{mass} \times \text{acceleration}$$

Or

$$\text{Acceleration} = \frac{\text{force}}{\text{mass}}$$

Or

$$\text{Mass} = \frac{\text{force}}{\text{acceleration}}$$

Each of the forms of this equation allows for a different look at the same relationships. To examine the relationships, change one factor and observe the result. If a steel ball with a diameter of 6.3 cm has a mass of 1 kg and an acceleration of 1 m/s², then the net force on the ball will be 1 Newton.

THIRD LAW
Concept: Nothing can push or pull without being pushed or pulled in return.

When any object exerts a force on another object, the other object exerts the opposite force back on the original object. To observe this, consider two spring-based fruit scales, both tipped on their sides as shown with the weighing surfaces facing each other. If fruit scale #1 is pressing fruit scale #2 into the wall, it exerts a force on fruit scale #2, measurable by the reading on scale #2. However, because fruit scale #1 is exerting a force on scale #2, scale #2 is exerting a force on scale #1 with an opposite direction, but the same magnitude.

FORCE
Concept: A push or pull on an object

Calculation: Force = mass × acceleration

A force is a vector that causes acceleration of a body. Force has both magnitude and direction. Furthermore, multiple forces acting on one object combine in vector addition. This can be demonstrated by considering an object placed at the origin of the coordinate plane. If it is pushed along the positive direction of the x-axis, it will move in this direction. If the force acting on it is in the positive direction of the y-axis, it will move in that direction.

176

However, if both forces are applied at the same time, then the object will move at an angle to both the *x*- and *y*-axes, an angle determined by the relative amount of force exerted in each direction. In this way, we may see that the resulting force is a vector sum; a net force that has both magnitude and direction.

Resultant vectors from applied forces:

Review Video: **Forces: Push-Pull**
Visit mometrix.com/academy and enter code: 104731

MASS

Concept: The amount of matter

Mass can be defined as the quantity of matter in an object. If we apply the same force to two objects of different mass, we will find that the resulting acceleration is different. In other words, the acceleration of an object is directly proportional to the force being exerted on it and inversely proportional to its mass.

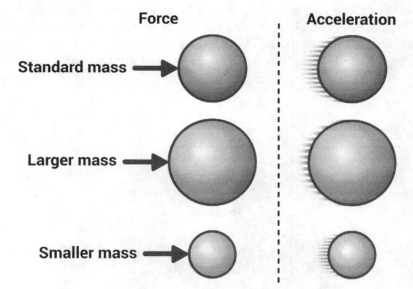

GRAVITY

Gravity is a force that exists between all objects with matter. Gravity is a pulling force between objects, meaning that the forces on the objects point toward the opposite object. When Newton's third law is applied to gravity, the force pairs from gravity are shown to be equal in magnitude and opposite in direction.

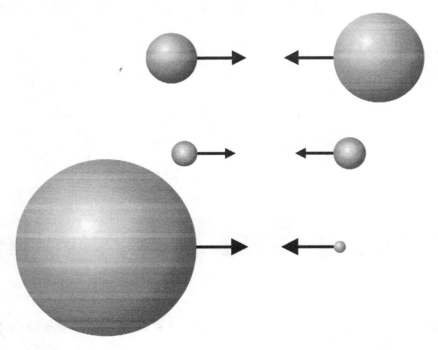

WEIGHT

Weight is sometimes confused with mass. While mass is the amount of matter, weight is the force exerted by the earth on an object with matter by gravity. The earth pulls every object of mass toward its center while every object of mass pulls the earth toward its center. The object's pull on the earth is equal in magnitude to the pull which the earth exerts, but, because the mass of the earth is very large in comparison (5.97×10^{24} kg), only the object appears to be affected by the force.

The gravity of the earth causes a constant acceleration due to gravity (g) at a specific altitude. For most earthbound applications, the acceleration due to gravity is 32.2 ft/s^2 or 9.8 m/s^2 in a downward direction. The equation for the force of gravity (weight) on an object is the equation from Newton's Second Law with the constant acceleration due to gravity (g).

Weight = mass × acceleration due to gravity

W = m × g

The SI (International Standard of Units) unit for weight is the Newton $\left(\frac{kg \times m}{s^2}\right)$. The English Engineering unit system uses the pound, or lb, as the unit for weight and force $\left(\frac{slug \times ft}{s^2}\right)$. Thus, a 2 kg object under the influence of gravity would have a weight of:

$$W = 2 \text{ kg} \times 9.8\frac{m}{s^2} = 19.6 \text{ N downward}$$

> **Review Video: Mass, Weight, Volume, Density, and Specific Gravity**
> Visit mometrix.com/academy and enter code: 920570

NORMAL FORCE
Concept: The force perpendicular to a contact surface

The word *normal* is used in mathematics to mean perpendicular, and so the force known as normal force should be remembered as the perpendicular force exerted on an object that is resting on some other surface. For instance, if a box is resting on a horizontal surface, we may say that the normal force is directed upwards through the box (the opposite, downward force is the weight of the box). If the box is resting on a wedge, the normal force from the wedge is not vertical but is perpendicular to the wedge edge.

TENSION
Concept: A pulling force like that from a cord or rope.

Another force that may come into play on the exam is called tension. Anytime a cord is attached to a body and pulled so that it is taut, we may say that the cord is under tension. The cord in tension applies a pulling tension force on the connected objects. This force is pointed away from the body and along the cord at the point of attachment. In simple considerations of tension, the cord is assumed to be both without mass and incapable of stretching. In other words, its only role is as the connector between two bodies. The cord is also assumed to pull on both ends with the same magnitude of tension force.

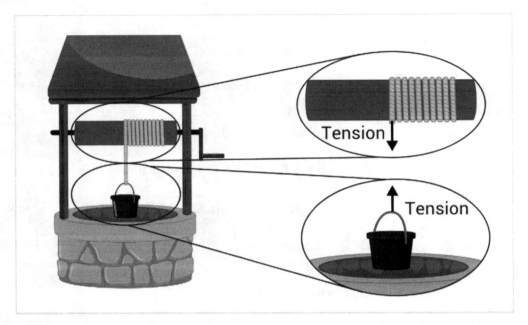

FRICTION

Concept: Friction is a resistance to motion between contacting surfaces

In order to illustrate the concept of friction, let us imagine a book resting on a table. As it sits, the force of its weight is equal to and opposite of the normal force. If, however, we were to exert a force on the book, attempting to push it to one side, a frictional force would arise, equal and opposite to our force. This kind of frictional force is known as static frictional force.

As we increase our force on the book, however, we will eventually cause it to accelerate in the direction of our force. At this point, the frictional force opposing us will be known as kinetic friction. For many combinations of surfaces, the magnitude of the kinetic frictional force is lower than that of the static frictional force, and consequently, the amount of force needed to maintain the movement of the book will be less than that needed to initiate the movement.

Review Video: Friction
Visit mometrix.com/academy and enter code: 716782

ROLLING FRICTION

Occasionally, a question will ask you to consider the amount of friction generated by an object that is rolling. If a wheel is rolling at a constant speed, then the point at which it touches the ground will not slide, and there will be no friction between the ground and the wheel inhibiting movement. In fact, the friction at the point of contact between the wheel and the ground is static friction necessary to propel with wheels. When a vehicle accelerates, the static friction between the wheels and the ground allows the vehicle to achieve acceleration. Without this friction, the vehicle would spin its wheels and go nowhere.

Although the static friction does not impede movement for the wheels, a combination of frictional forces can resist rolling motion. One such frictional force is bearing friction. Bearing friction is the kinetic friction between the wheel and an object it rotates around, such as a stationary axle.

Static Friction

Bearing Friction

DRAG FORCE

Friction can also be generated when an object is moving through air or liquid. A drag force occurs when a body moves through some fluid (either liquid or gas) and experiences a force that opposes the motion of the body. The drag force is greater if the air or fluid is thicker or is moving in the direction opposite to the object. Obviously, the higher the drag force, the greater amount of positive force required to keep the object moving forward.

BALANCED FORCES

An object is in equilibrium when the sum of all forces acting on the object is zero. When the forces on an object sum to zero, the object does not accelerate. Equilibrium can be obtained when forces in the y-direction sum to zero, forces in the x-direction sum to zero, or forces in both directions sum to zero.

In most cases, a problem will provide one or more forces acting on an object and ask for a force to balance the system. The force will be the opposite of the current force or sum of current forces.

Balance the forces

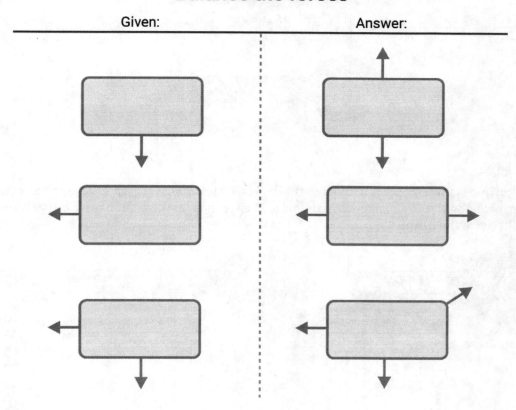

ROTATIONAL KINETICS

Many equations and concepts in linear kinematics and kinetics transfer to rotation. For example, angular position is an angle. Angular velocity, like linear velocity, is the change in the position (angle) divided by the time. Angular acceleration is the change in angular velocity divided by time. Although most tests will not require you to perform angular calculations, they will expect you to understand the angular version of force: torque.

Concept: Torque is a twisting force on an object

Calculation: Torque = radius × force

Torque, like force, is a vector and has magnitude and direction. As with force, the sum of torques on an object will affect the angular acceleration of that object. The key to solving problems with torque is understanding the lever arm. A better description of the torque equation is:

Torque = force × the distance perpedicular to the force from the center of rotation

Because torque is directly proportional to the radius, or lever arm, a greater lever arm will result in a greater torque with the same amount of force. The wrench on the right has twice the radius and, as a result, twice the torque.

Alternatively, a greater force also increases torque. The wrench on the right has twice the force and twice the torque.

Work/Energy

WORK

Concept: Work is the transfer of energy from one object to another

Calculation: Work = force × displacement

The equation for work in one dimension is fairly simple: W = F × d In the equation, the force and the displacement are the magnitude of the force exerted and the total change in position of the object on which the force is exerted, respectively. If force and displacement have the same direction, then the work is positive. If they are in opposite directions, however, the work is negative.

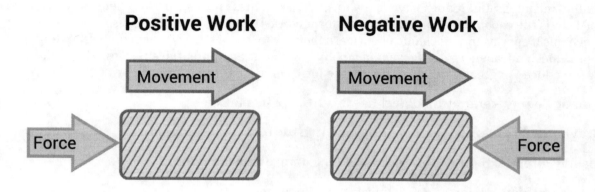

For two-dimensional work, the equation is a bit more complex:

Work = Force × displacement × cos(θ between displacement and force)

$$W = F \times d \times \cos(\theta)$$

The angle in the equation is the angle between the direction of the force and the direction of the displacement. Thus, the work done when a box is pulled at a 20 degree angle with a force of 100 lb for 20 ft will be less than the work done when a differently weighted box is pulled horizontally with a force of 100 lb for 20 ft.

$$W_1 = 100\text{lb} \times 20\text{ft} \times \cos(20°) = 1880 \text{ ft} \cdot \text{lb}$$

$$W_2 = 100\text{lb} \times 20\text{ft} \times \cos(0°) = 2000 \text{ ft} \cdot \text{lb}$$

The unit ft · lb is the unit for both work and energy.

Review Video: Work
Visit mometrix.com/academy and enter code: 681834

ENERGY
Concept: The ability of a body to do work on another object

Energy is a word that has developed several different meanings in the English language, but in physics, it refers to the measure of a body's ability to do work. In physics, energy may not have a million meanings, but it does have many forms. Each of these forms, such as chemical, electric, and nuclear, is the capability of an object to perform work. However, for the purpose of most tests, mechanical energy and mechanical work are the only forms of energy worth understanding in depth. Mechanical energy is the sum of an object's kinetic and potential energies. Although they will be introduced in greater detail, these are the forms of mechanical energy:

Kinetic Energy – energy an object has by virtue of its motion

Gravitational Potential Energy – energy by virtue of an object's height

Elastic Potential Energy – energy stored in compression or tension

Neglecting frictional forces, mechanical energy is conserved.

As an example, imagine a ball moving perpendicular to the surface of the earth, in other words straight up and down, with its weight being the only force acting on it. As the ball rises, the weight will be doing work on the ball, decreasing its speed and its kinetic energy and slowing it down until it momentarily stops. During this ascent, the potential energy of the ball will be rising. Once the ball begins to fall back down, it will lose potential energy as it gains kinetic energy. Mechanical energy is conserved throughout; the potential energy of the ball at its highest point is equal to the kinetic energy of the ball at its lowest point prior to impact.

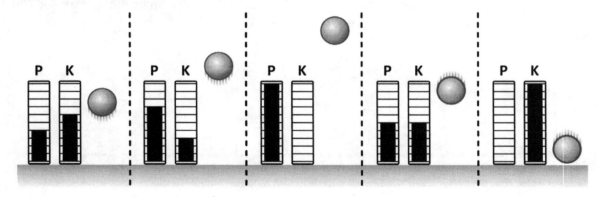

In systems where friction and air resistance are not negligible, we observe a different sort of result. For example, imagine a block sliding across the floor until it comes to a stop due to friction. Unlike a compressed spring or a ball flung into the air, there is no way for this block to regain its energy with a return trip. Therefore, we cannot say that the lost kinetic energy is being stored as potential energy. Instead, it has been dissipated and cannot be recovered. The total mechanical energy of the block-floor system has been not conserved in this case but rather reduced. The total energy of the system has not decreased, since the kinetic energy has been converted into thermal energy, but that energy is no longer useful for work.

Energy, though it may change form, will be neither created nor destroyed during physical processes. However, if we construct a system and some external force performs work on it, the result may be slightly different. If the work is positive, then the overall store of energy is increased; if it is negative, however, we can say that the overall energy of the system has decreased.

KINETIC ENERGY

The kinetic energy of an object is the amount of energy it possesses by reason of being in motion. Kinetic energy cannot be negative. Changes in kinetic energy will occur when a force does work on an object, such that the motion of the object is altered. This change in kinetic energy is equal to the amount of work that is done. This relationship is commonly referred to as the work-energy theorem.

One interesting application of the work-energy theorem is that of objects in a free fall. To begin with, let us assert that the force acting on such an object is its weight, which is equal to its mass times g (the force of gravity). The work done by this force will be positive, as the force is exerted in the direction in which the object is traveling. Kinetic energy will, therefore, increase, according to the work-kinetic energy theorem.

If the object is dropped from a great enough height, it eventually reaches its terminal velocity, where the drag force is equal to the weight, so the object is no longer accelerating and its kinetic energy remains constant.

GRAVITATIONAL POTENTIAL ENERGY

Gravitational potential energy is simply the potential for a certain amount of work to be done by one object on another using gravity. For objects on earth, the gravitational potential energy is equal to the amount of work which the earth can act on the object. The work which gravity performs on objects moving entirely or partially in the vertical direction is equal to the force exerted by the earth (weight) times the distance traveled in the direction of the force (height above the ground or reference point): Work from gravity = weight × height above the ground. Thus, the gravitational potential energy is the same as the potential work.

Gravitational Potential Energy = weight × height

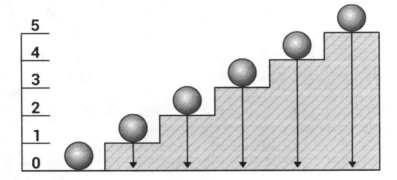

ELASTIC POTENTIAL ENERGY

Elastic potential energy is the potential for a certain amount of work to be done by one object on another using elastic compression or tension. The most common example is the spring. A spring will resist any compression or tension away from its equilibrium position (natural position). A small buggy is pressed into a large spring. The spring contains a large amount of elastic potential energy. If the buggy and spring are released, the spring will exert a force on the buggy, pushing it for a distance. This work will put kinetic energy into the buggy. The energy can be imagined as a liquid poured from one container into another. The spring pours its elastic energy into the buggy, which receives the energy as kinetic energy.

POWER

Concept: The rate of work

Calculation: Work/time

On occasion, you may need to demonstrate an understanding of power as it is defined in applied physics. Power is the rate at which work is done. Power, like work and energy, is a scalar quantity. Power can be calculated by dividing the amount of work performed by the amount of time in which the work was performed: $\textbf{Power} = \frac{\textbf{work}}{\textbf{time}}$. If more work is performed in a shorter amount of time, more power has been exerted. Power can be expressed in a variety of units. The preferred metric expression is one of watts or joules per seconds. Engine power is often expressed in horsepower.

Machines

SIMPLE MACHINES

Concept: Tools which transform forces to make tasks easier.

As their job is to transform forces, simple machines have an input force and an output force or forces. Simple machines transform forces in two ways: direction and magnitude. A machine can change the direction of a force, with respect to the input force, like a single stationary pulley which only changes the direction of the output force. A machine can also change the magnitude of the force like a lever.

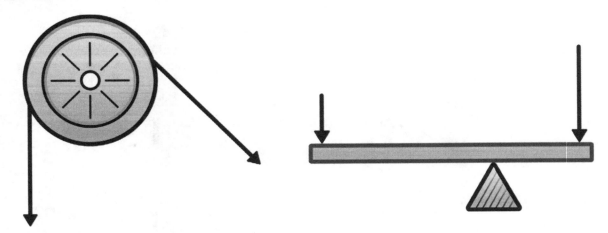

Simple machines include the inclined plane, the wedge, the screw, the pulley, the lever, and the wheel.

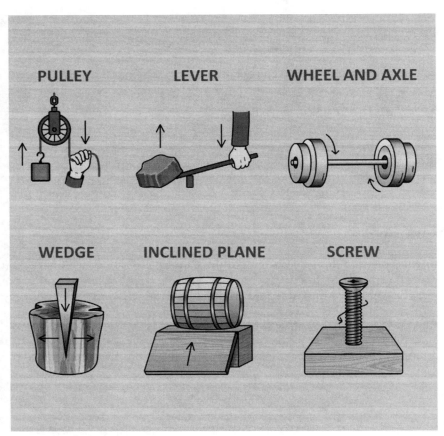

MECHANICAL ADVANTAGE

Concept: The amount of change a simple machine provides to the magnitude of a force

Calculation: Output force/input force

Mechanical advantage is the measure of the output force divided by the input force. Thus, mechanical advantage measures the change performed by a machine. Machines cannot create energy, only transform it. Thus, in frictionless, ideal machines, the input work equals the output work.

$$\text{Work}_{input} = \text{Work}_{output}$$

$$\text{force}_{input} \times \text{distance}_{input} = \text{force}_{output} \times \text{distance}_{output}$$

This means that a simple machine can increase the force of the output by decreasing the distance which the output travels or it can increase the distance of the output by decreasing the force at the output.

By moving parts of the equation for work, we can arrive at the equation for mechanical advantage.

$$\text{Mechanical Advantage} = \frac{\text{force}_{output}}{\text{force}_{input}} = \frac{\text{distance}_{input}}{\text{distance}_{output}}$$

If the mechanical advantage is greater than one, the output force is greater than the input force and the input distance is greater than the output distance. Conversely, if the mechanical advantage is less than one, the input force is greater than the output force and the output distance is greater than the input distance. In equation form this is:

If Mechanical Advantage > 1:

$$\text{force}_{input} < \text{force}_{output} \text{ and distance}_{output} < \text{distance}_{input}$$

If Mechanical Advantage < 1:

$$\text{force}_{input} > \text{force}_{output} \text{ and distance}_{output} > \text{distance}_{input}$$

INCLINED PLANE

The inclined plane is perhaps the most common of the simple machines. It is simply a flat surface that elevates as you move from one end to the other; a ramp is an easy example of an inclined plane. Consider how much easier it is for an elderly person to walk up a long ramp than to climb a shorter but steeper flight of stairs; this is because the force required is diminished as the distance increases. Indeed, the longer the ramp, the easier it is to ascend.

On the exam, this simple fact will most often be applied to moving heavy objects. For instance, if you have to move a heavy box onto the back of a truck, it is much easier to push it up a ramp than to lift it directly onto the truck bed. The longer the ramp, the greater the mechanical advantage, and the easier it will be to move the box. The mechanical advantage of an inclined plane is equal to the slant length divided by the rise of the plane.

$$\text{Mechanical Advantage} = \frac{\text{slant length}}{\text{rise}}$$

As you solve this kind of problem, however, remember that the same amount of work is being performed whether the box is lifted directly or pushed up a twenty-foot ramp; a simple machine only changes the force and the distance.

WEDGE

A wedge is a variation on the inclined plane, in which the wedge moves between objects or parts and forces them apart. The unique characteristic of a wedge is that, unlike an inclined plane, it is designed to move. Perhaps the most familiar use of the wedge is in splitting wood. A wedge is driven into the wood by hitting the flat back end. The thin end of a wedge is easier to drive into the wood since it has less surface area and, therefore, transmits more force per area. As the wedge is driven in, the increased width helps to split the wood.

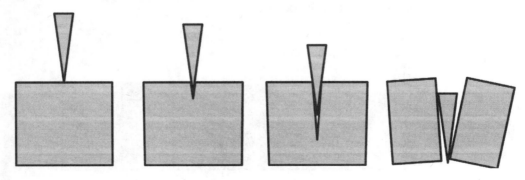

The exam may require you to select the wedge that has the highest mechanical advantage. This should be easy: the longer and thinner the wedge, the greater the mechanical advantage. The equation for mechanical advantage is:

$$\text{Mechanical Advantage} = \frac{\text{Length}}{\text{Width}}$$

SCREW

A screw is simply an inclined plane that has been wound around a cylinder so that it forms a sort of spiral.

When it is placed into some medium, as for instance wood, the screw will move either forward or backward when it is rotated. The principle of the screw is used in a number of different objects, from jar lids to flashlights. On the exam, you are unlikely to see many questions regarding screws, though you may be presented with a given screw rotation and asked in which direction the screw will move. However, for consistency's sake, the equation for the mechanical advantage is a modification of the inclined plane's equation. Again, the formula for an inclined plane is:

$$\text{Mechanical Advantage} = \frac{\text{slant length}}{\text{rise}}$$

Because the rise of the inclined plane is the length along a screw, length between rotations = rise. Also, the slant length will equal the circumference of one rotation = 2πr.

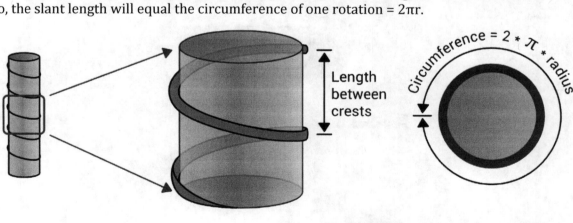

$$\text{Mechanical Advantage} = \frac{2 \times \pi \times \text{radius}}{\text{length between crests}}$$

LEVER

The lever is the most common kind of simple machine. See-saws, shovels, and baseball bats are all examples of levers. There are three classes of levers which are differentiated by the relative orientations of the fulcrum, resistance, and effort. The fulcrum is the point at which the lever rotates, the effort is the point on the lever where force is applied, and the resistance is the part of the lever that acts in response to the effort.

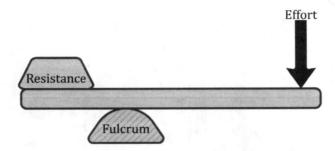

The mechanical advantage of a lever depends on the distances of the effort and resistance from the fulcrum.

$$\textbf{Mechanical Advantage} = \frac{\textbf{effort distance}}{\textbf{resistance distance}}$$

Each class of lever has a different arrangement of effort, fulcrum, and resistance:

First-Class Lever

First-Class Lever

Second-Class Lever

Second-Class Lever

Third-Class Lever

Third-Class Lever

In a first-class lever, the fulcrum is between the effort and the resistance. A seesaw is a good example of a first-class lever when effort is applied to force one end up, the other end goes down, and vice versa. The shorter the distance between the fulcrum and the resistance, the easier it will be to move the resistance. As an example, consider whether it is easier to lift another person on a see-saw when they are sitting close to the middle or all the way at the end. A little practice will show you that it is much more difficult to lift a person the farther away he or she is on the see-saw.

In a second-class lever, the resistance is in between the fulcrum and the effort. While a first-class lever is able to increase force and distance through mechanical advantage, a second-class lever is only able to increase force. A common example of a second-class lever is the wheelbarrow; the force exerted by your hand at one end of the wheelbarrow is magnified at the load. Basically, with a second-class lever, you are trading distance for force; by moving your end of the wheelbarrow a bit farther, you produce greater force at the load.

Third-class levers are used to produce greater distance. In a third-class lever, the force is applied in between the fulcrum and the resistance. A baseball bat is a classic example of a third-class lever; the bottom of the bat, below where you grip it, is considered the fulcrum. The end of the bat, where the ball is struck, is the resistance. By exerting effort at the base of the bat, close to the fulcrum, you are able to make the end of the bat fly quickly through the air. The closer your hands are to the base of the bat, the faster you will be able to make the other end of the bat travel.

Review Video: <u>Levers</u>
Visit mometrix.com/academy and enter code: 103910

PULLEY

The pulley is a simple machine in which a rope is carried by the rotation of a wheel. Another name for a pulley is a block. Pulleys are typically used to allow the force to be directed from a convenient location. For instance, imagine you are given the task of lifting a heavy and tall bookcase. Rather than tying a rope to the bookcase and trying to lift it, it would make sense to tie a pulley system to a rafter above the bookcase and run the rope through it, so that you could pull down on the rope and lift the bookcase. Pulling down allows you to incorporate your weight (normal force) into the act of lifting, thereby making it easier.

If there is just one pulley above the bookcase, you have created a first-class lever that will not diminish the amount of force that needs to be applied to lift the bookcase. There is another way to use a pulley, however, that can make the job of lifting a heavy object considerably easier. First, tie the rope directly to the rafter. Then, attach a pulley to the top of the bookcase and run the rope through it. If you can then stand so that you are above the bookcase, you will have a much easier time lifting this heavy object. Why? Because the weight of the bookcase is now being distributed: half of it is acting on the rafter, and half of it is acting on you. In other words, this arrangement allows you to lift an object with half the force. This simple pulley system, therefore, has a mechanical advantage of 2. Note that in this arrangement, the unfixed pulley is acting like a second-class lever. The price you pay for your mechanical advantage is that whatever distance you raise your end of the rope, the bookcase will only be lifted half as much.

Of course, it might be difficult for you to find a place high enough to enact this system. If this is the case, you can always tie another pulley to the rafter and run the rope through it and back down to the floor. Since this second pulley is fixed, the mechanical advantage will remain the same.

There are other, slightly more complex ways to obtain an even greater mechanical advantage with a system of pulleys. On the exam, you may be required to determine the pulley and tackle (rope) arrangement that creates the greatest mechanical advantage. The easiest way to determine the answer is to count the number of ropes that are going to and from the unfixed pulley; the more ropes coming and going, the greater the mechanical advantage.

WHEEL AND AXLE

Another basic arrangement that makes use of simple machines is called the wheel and axle. When most people think of a wheel and axle, they immediately envision an automobile tire. The steering wheel of the car, however, operates on the same mechanical principle, namely that the force required to move the center of a circle is much greater than the force required to move the outer rim of a circle. When you turn the steering wheel, you are essentially using a second-class lever by increasing the output force by increasing the input distance. The force required to turn the wheel from the outer rim is much less than would be required to turn the wheel from its center. Just imagine how difficult it would be to drive a car if the steering wheel was the size of a saucer!

Conceptually, the mechanical advantage of a wheel is easy to understand. For instance, all other things being equal, the mechanical advantage created by a system will increase along with the radius. In other words, a steering wheel with a radius of 12 inches has a greater mechanical advantage than a steering wheel with a radius of ten inches; the same amount of force exerted on the rim of each wheel will produce greater force at the axis of the larger wheel.

The equation for the mechanical advantage of a wheel and axle is:

$$\text{Mechanical Advantage} = \frac{\text{radius}_{\text{wheel}}}{\text{radius}_{\text{axle}}}$$

Thus, the mechanical advantage of the steering wheel with a larger radius will be:

$$\text{Mechanical Advantage} = \frac{12 \text{ inches}}{2 \text{ inches}} = 6$$

GEARS

The exam may ask you questions involving some slightly more complex mechanisms. It is very common, for instance, for there to be a couple of questions concerning gears. Gears are a system of interlocking wheels that can create immense mechanical advantages. The amount of mechanical advantage, however, will depend on the gear ratio; that is, on the relation in size between the gears.

When a small gear is driving a big gear, the speed of the big gear is relatively slow; when a big gear is driving a small gear, the speed of the small gear is relatively fast.

The equation for the mechanical advantage is:

$$\text{Mechanical Advantage} = \frac{\text{Torque}_{output}}{\text{Torque}_{input}} = \frac{r_{output}}{r_{input}} = \frac{\#\text{ of teeth}_{output}}{\#\text{ of teeth}_{input}}$$

Note that mechanical advantage is greater than 1 when the output gear is larger. In these cases, the output velocity (**ω**) will be lower. The equation for the relative speed of a gear system is:

$$\frac{\omega_{input}}{\omega_{output}} = \frac{r_{output}}{r_{input}}$$

USES OF GEARS

Gears are used to change the direction, location, and amount of output torque, as well as change the angular velocity of output.

Change output direction

Change torque location

Change torque amount

Change output velocity

GEAR RATIOS

A gear ratio is a measure of how much the speed and torque are changing in a gear system. It is the ratio of output speed to input speed. Because the number of teeth is directly proportional to the speed in meshing gears, a gear ratio can also be calculated using the number of teeth on the gears. When the driving gear has 30 teeth and the driven gear has 10 teeth, the gear ratio is 3:1.

$$\text{Gear Ratio} = \frac{\#\text{ of teeth}_{driving}}{\#\text{ of teeth}_{driven}} = \frac{30}{10} = \frac{3}{1} = 3:1$$

This means that the smaller, driven gear rotates 3 times for every 1 rotation of the driving gear.

The Hydraulic Jack

The hydraulic jack is a simple machine using two tanks and two pistons to change the amount of an output force.

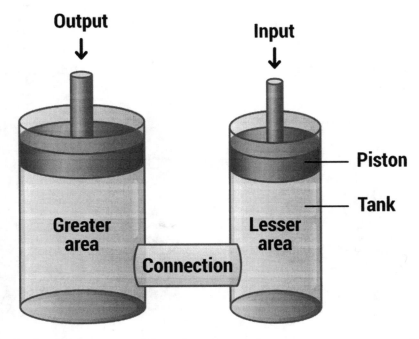

Since fluids are effectively incompressible, when you apply pressure to one part of a contained fluid, that pressure will have to be relieved in equal measure elsewhere in the container. Suppose the input piston has half the surface area of the output piston (10 in² compared to 20 in²), and it is being pushed downward with 50 pounds of force. The pressure being applied to the fluid is 50 lb ÷ 10 in² = $5\frac{\text{lb}}{\text{in}^2}$ or 5 psi. When that 5 psi of pressure is applied to the output piston, it pushes that piston upward with a force of $5\frac{\text{lb}}{\text{in}^2} \times 20$ in² = 100 lb.

The hydraulic jack functions similarly to a first-class lever, but with the important factor being the area of the pistons rather than the length of the lever arms. Note that the mechanical advantage is based on the relative areas, not the relative radii, of the pistons. The radii must be squared to compute the relative areas.

$$\textbf{Mechanical Advantage} = \frac{\textbf{Force}_{\text{output}}}{\textbf{Force}_{\text{input}}} = \frac{\textbf{area}_{\text{output}}}{\textbf{area}_{\text{input}}} = \frac{\textbf{radius}_{\text{output}}^2}{\textbf{radius}_{\text{input}}^2}$$

Pulleys and Belts

Another system involves two pulleys connected by a drive belt (a looped band that goes around both pulleys). The operation of this system is similar to that of gears, with the exception that the pulleys will rotate in the same direction, while interlocking gears will rotate in opposite directions.

A smaller pulley will always spin faster than a larger pulley, though the larger pulley will generate more torque.

The speed ratio between the pulleys can be determined by comparing their radii; for instance, a 4-inch pulley and a 12-inch pulley will have a speed ratio of 3:1.

Momentum/Impulse

LINEAR MOMENTUM

Concept: How much a body will resist stopping

Calculation: Momentum = mass × velocity

In physics, linear momentum can be found by multiplying the mass and velocity of an object. Momentum and velocity will always be in the same direction. Newton's second law describes momentum, stating that the rate of change of momentum is proportional to the force exerted and is in the direction of the force. If we assume a closed and isolated system (one in which no objects leave or enter, and upon which the sum of external forces is zero), then we can assume that the momentum of the system will neither increase nor decrease. That is, we will find that the momentum is a constant. The law of conservation of linear momentum applies universally in physics, even in situations of extremely high velocity or with subatomic particles.

COLLISIONS

This concept of momentum takes on new importance when we consider collisions. A collision is an isolated event in which a strong force acts between each of two or more colliding bodies for a brief period of time. However, a collision is more intuitively defined as one or more objects hitting each other.

When two bodies collide, each object exerts a force on the opposite member. These equal and opposite forces change the linear momentum of the objects. However, when both bodies are considered, the net momentum in collisions is conserved.

There are two types of collisions: elastic and inelastic. The difference between the two lies in whether kinetic energy is conserved. If the total kinetic energy of the system is conserved, the collision is elastic. Visually, elastic collisions are collisions in which objects bounce perfectly. If some of the kinetic energy is transformed into heat or another form of energy, the collision is inelastic. Visually, inelastic collisions are collisions in which the objects stick to each other or bounce but do not return to their original height.

If the two bodies involved in an elastic collision have the same mass, then the body that was moving will stop completely, and the body that was at rest will begin moving at the same velocity as the projectile was moving before the collision.

Fluids

FLUIDS
Concept: Liquids and gasses

A few of the questions on the exam will probably require you to consider the behavior of fluids. It sounds obvious, perhaps, but fluids can best be defined as substances that flow. A fluid will conform, slowly or quickly, to any container in which it is placed. Both liquids and gasses are considered to be fluids. Fluids are essentially those substances in which the atoms are not arranged in any permanent, rigid way. In ice, for instance, atoms are all lined up in what is known as a crystalline lattice, while in water and steam, the only intermolecular arrangements are haphazard connections between neighboring molecules.

FLOW RATES

When liquids flow in and out of containers at certain rates, the change in volume is the volumetric flow in minus the volumetric flow out. Volumetric flow is essentially the amount of volume moved past some point divided by the time it took for the volume to pass.

$$\text{Volumetric flow rate} = \frac{\text{volume moved}}{\text{time for the movement}}$$

If the flow into a container is greater than the flow out, the container will fill with the fluid. However, if the flow out of a container is greater than the flow into a container, the container will drain of the fluid.

DENSITY

Concept: How much mass is in a specific volume of a substance

Calculation: Density $= \rho = \dfrac{\text{mass}}{\text{volume}}$

Density is essentially how much stuff there is in a volume or space. The density of a fluid is generally expressed with the symbol ρ (the Greek letter *rho*). Density is a scalar property, meaning that it has no direction component.

PRESSURE

Concept: The amount of force applied per area

Calculation: Pressure $= \dfrac{\text{force}}{\text{area}}$

Pressure, like fluid density, is a scalar and does not have a direction. The equation for pressure is concerned only with the magnitude of that force, not with the direction in which it is pointing. The SI unit of pressure is the Newton per square meter, or Pascal.

As every deep-sea diver knows, the pressure of water becomes greater the deeper you go below the surface; conversely, experienced mountain climbers know that air pressure decreases as they gain a higher altitude. These pressures are typically referred to as hydrostatic pressures because they involve fluids at rest.

PASCAL'S PRINCIPLE

The exam may also require you to demonstrate some knowledge of how fluids move. Anytime you squeeze a tube of toothpaste, you are demonstrating the idea known as Pascal's principle. This principle states that a change in the pressure applied to an enclosed fluid is transmitted undiminished to every portion of the fluid as well as to the walls of the containing vessel.

BUOYANT FORCE

If an object is submerged in water, it will have a buoyant force exerted on it in the upward direction. Often, of course, this buoyant force is much too small to keep an object from sinking to the bottom. Buoyancy is summarized in Archimedes' principle; a body wholly or partially submerged in a fluid will be buoyed up by a force equal to the weight of the fluid that the body displaces.

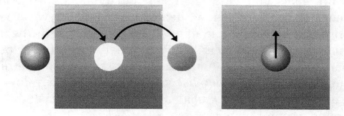

If the buoyant force is greater than the weight of an object, the object will go upward. If the weight of the object is greater than the buoyant force, the object will sink. When an object is floating on the surface, the buoyant force has the same magnitude as the weight.

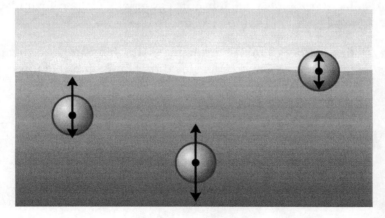

Even though the weight of a floating object is precisely balanced by a buoyant force, these forces will not necessarily act at the same point. The weight will act from the center of mass of the object, while the buoyancy will act from the center of mass of the hole in the water made by the object (known as the center of buoyancy). If the floating object is tilted, then the center of buoyancy will shift and the object may be unstable. In order to remain in equilibrium, the center of buoyancy must always shift in such a way that the buoyant force and weight provide a restoring torque, one that will restore the body to its upright position. This concept is, of course, crucial to the construction of boats which must always be made to encourage restoring torque.

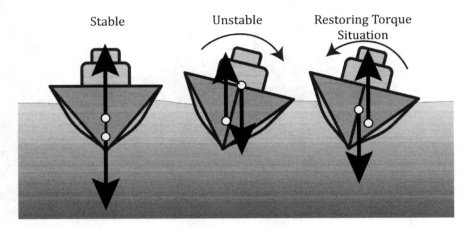

IDEAL FLUIDS

Because the motion of actual fluids is extremely complex, the exam usually assumes ideal fluids when they set up their problems. Using ideal fluids in fluid dynamics problems is like discounting friction in other problems. Therefore, when we deal with ideal fluids, we are making four assumptions. It is important to keep these in mind when considering the behavior of fluids on the exam. First, we are assuming that the flow is steady; in other words, the velocity of every part of the fluid is the same. Second, we assume that fluids are incompressible and therefore have a consistent density. Third, we assume that fluids are nonviscous, meaning that they flow easily and without resistance. Fourth, we assume that the flow of ideal fluids is irrotational: that is, particles in the fluid will not rotate around a center of mass.

BERNOULLI'S PRINCIPLE

When fluids move, they do not create or destroy energy; this modification of Newton's second law for fluid behavior is called Bernoulli's principle. It is essentially just a reformulation of the law of conservation of mechanical energy for fluid mechanics.

The most common application of Bernoulli's principle is that pressure and speed are inversely related, assuming constant altitude. Thus, if the elevation of the fluid remains constant and the speed of a fluid particle increases as it travels along a streamline, the pressure will decrease. If the fluid slows down, the pressure will increase.

Heat Transfer

HEAT TRANSFER

Heat is a type of energy. Heat transfers from the hot object to the cold object through the three forms of heat transfer: conduction, convection, and radiation.

Conduction is the transfer of heat by physical contact. When you touch a hot pot, the pot transfers heat to your hand by conduction.

Convection is the transfer of heat by the movement of fluids. When you put your hand in steam, the steam transfers heat to your hand by convection.

Radiation is the transfer of heat by electromagnetic waves. When you put your hand near a campfire, the fire heats your hand by radiation.

> **Review Video: <u>Heat Transfer</u>**
> Visit mometrix.com/academy and enter code: 451646

PHASE CHANGES

Materials exist in four phases or states: solid, liquid, gas, and plasma. However, as most tests will not cover plasma, we will focus on solids, liquids, and gases. The solid state is the densest in almost all cases (water is the most notable exception), followed by liquid, and then gas.

The catalyst for phase change (changing from one phase to another) is heat. When a solid is heated, it will change into a liquid. The same process of heating will change a liquid into a gas.

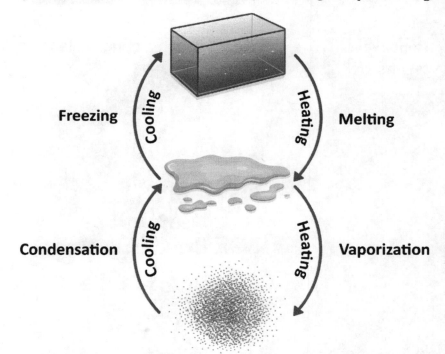

Review Video: **States of Matter**
Visit mometrix.com/academy and enter code: 742449

Optics

OPTICS

Lenses change the way light travels. Lenses are able to achieve this by the way in which light travels at different speeds in different mediums. The essentials to optics with lenses deal with concave and convex lenses. Concave lenses make objects appear smaller, while convex lenses make objects appear larger.

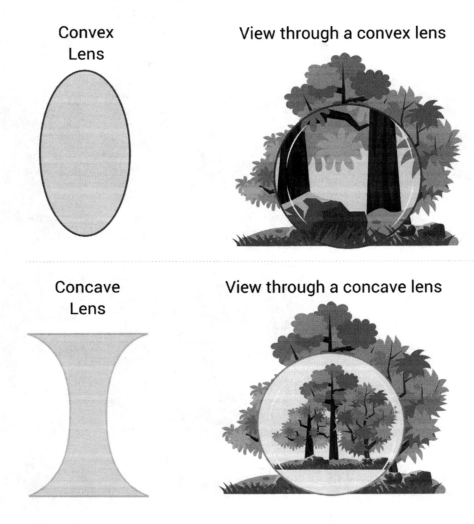

Convex Lens

View through a convex lens

Concave Lens

View through a concave lens

Electricity

ELECTRIC CHARGE

Much like gravity, electricity is an everyday observable phenomenon which is very complex, but may be understood as a set of behaviors. As the gravitational force exists between objects with mass, the electric force exists between objects with electrical charge. In all atoms, the protons have a positive charge, while the electrons have a negative charge. An imbalance of electrons and protons in an object results in a net charge. Unlike gravity, which only pulls, electrical forces can push objects apart as well as pull them together.

Similar electric charges repel each other. Opposite charges attract each other.

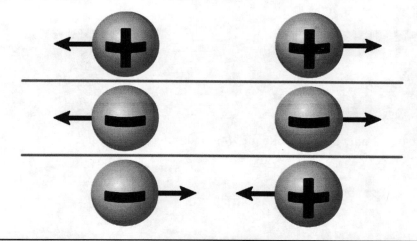

CURRENT

Electrons (and electrical charge with it) move through conductive materials by switching quickly from one atom to another. This electrical flow can manipulate energy like mechanical systems.

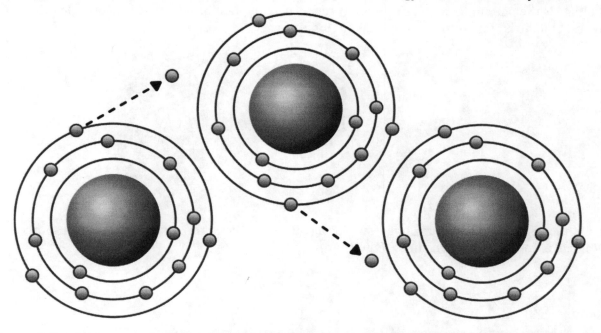

The term for the rate at which the charge flows through a conductive material is *current*. Because each electron carries a specific charge, current can be thought of as the number of electrons passing a point in a length of time. Current is measured in Amperes (A), each unit of which is approximately 6.24×10^{18} electrons per second.

Electric current carries energy much like moving balls carry energy.

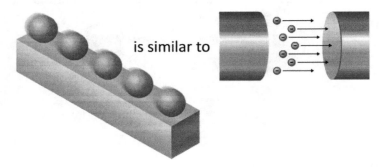

VOLTAGE

Voltage is the potential for electric work. It can also be thought of as the *push* behind electrical work. Voltage is similar to gravitational potential energy.

Anything used to generate a voltage, such as a battery or a generator, is called a voltage source. Voltage is conveniently measured in Volts (V).

RESISTANCE

Resistance is the amount something hinders the flow of electrical current. Electrical resistance is much like friction, resisting flow and dissipating energy.

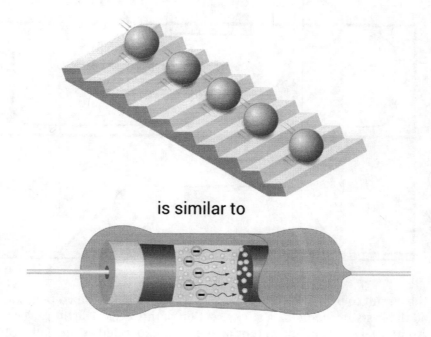

is similar to

Different objects have different resistances. A resistor is an electrical component designed to have a specific resistance, measured in Ohms (Ω).

> **Review Video: <u>Resistance of Electric Currents</u>**
> Visit mometrix.com/academy and enter code: 668423

BASIC CIRCUITS

A circuit is a closed loop through which current can flow. A simple circuit contains a voltage source and a resistor. The current flows from the positive side of the voltage source through the resistor to the negative side of the voltage source.

If we plot the voltage of a simple circuit, the similarities to gravitational potential energy appear.

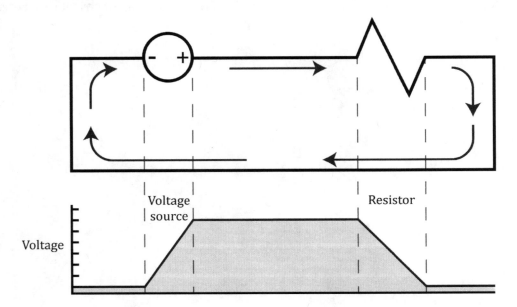

If we consider the circuit to be a track, the electrons would be balls, the voltage source would be a powered lift, and the resistor would be a sticky section of the track. The lift raises the balls, increasing their potential energy. This potential energy is expended as the balls roll down the sticky section of the track.

216

OHM'S LAW

A principle called Ohm's Law explains the relationship between the voltage, current, and resistance. The voltage drop over a resistance is equal to the amount of current times the resistance:

$$\textbf{Voltage (V)} = \textbf{current (I)} \times \textbf{resistance (R)}$$

We can gain a better understanding of this equation by looking at a reference simple circuit and then changing one variable at a time to examine the results.

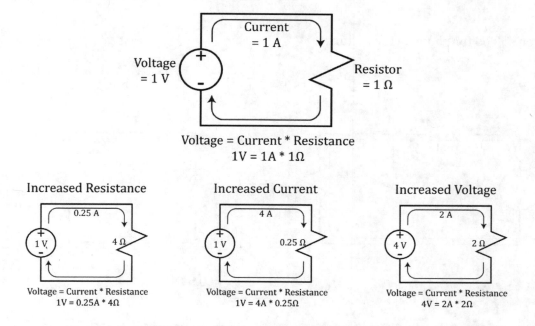

Review Video: <u>Ohm's Law and Power</u>
Visit mometrix.com/academy and enter code: 784016

SERIES CIRCUITS

A series circuit is a circuit with two or more resistors on the same path. The same current runs through both resistors. However, the total voltage drop splits between the resistors. The resistors in series can be added together to make an equivalent basic circuit.

$$R_{equiv} = R_1 + R_2$$

PARALLEL CIRCUITS

A parallel circuit is a circuit with two or more resistors on different, parallel paths. Unlike the series circuit, the current splits between the different paths in a parallel circuit. Resistors in parallel can be reduced to an equivalent circuit, but not by simply adding the resistances. The inverse of the equivalent resistance of parallel resistors is equal to the sum of the inverses of the resistance of each leg of the parallel circuit. In equation form that means:

$$\frac{1}{R_{equiv}} = \frac{1}{R_1} + \frac{1}{R_2}$$

Or when solved for equivalent resistance:

$$R_{equiv} = \frac{1}{\frac{1}{R_1} + \frac{1}{R_2}}$$

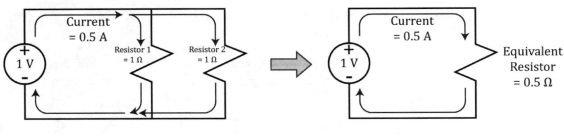

$$R_{equiv} = \frac{1}{\frac{1}{1\,\Omega} + \frac{1}{1\,\Omega}} = 0.5\ \Omega$$

ELECTRICAL POWER

Electrical power, or the energy output over time, is equal to the current resulting from a voltage source times the voltage of that source:

$$\textbf{Power(P)} = \textbf{current (I)} \times \textbf{voltage (V)}$$

Thanks to Ohm's Law, we can write this relation in two other ways:

$$P = I^2 R$$

$$P = \frac{V^2}{R}$$

For instance, if a circuit is composed of a 9 Volt battery and a 3 Ohm resistor, the power output of the battery will be:

$$Power = \frac{V^2}{R} = \frac{9^2}{3} = 27\ Watts$$

AC VS. DC

Up until this point, current has been assumed to flow in one direction. One directional flow is called Direct Current (DC). However, there is another type of electric current: Alternating Current (AC).

Many circuits use AC power sources, in which the current flips back and forth rapidly between directions.

Direct Current (DC)   Alternating Current (AC)

CAPACITORS

Capacitors are electrical components which store voltage. Capacitors are made from two conductive surfaces separated from each other by a space and/or insulation. Capacitors resist changes to voltage. Capacitors don't stop AC circuits (although they do affect the current flow), but they do stop DC circuits, acting as open circuits.

Conductive Plates   Circuit Diagram Symbol

Air or insulation

Open Circuit

INDUCTORS

Inductors are electrical components which effectively store current. Inductors use the relationship between electricity and magnetism to resist changes in current by running the current through coils of wire. Inductors don't stop DC circuits, but they do resist AC circuits as AC circuits utilize changing currents.

Coils   Circuit Diagram Symbol

Magnetic Field

Doesn't impede current

DIODES

Diodes are electrical components which limit the flow of electricity to one direction. If current flows through a diode in the intended direction, the diode will allow the flow. However, a diode will stop current if it runs the wrong way.

Circuit Diagram Symbol

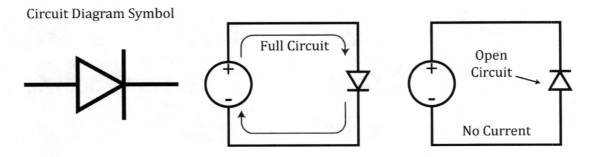

Magnetism

MAGNETISM

Magnetism is an attraction between opposite poles of magnetic materials and a repulsion between similar poles of magnetic materials. Magnetism can be natural or induced with the use of electric currents. Magnets almost always exist with two polar sides: north and south. A magnetic force exists between two poles on objects. Different poles attract each other. Like poles repel each other.

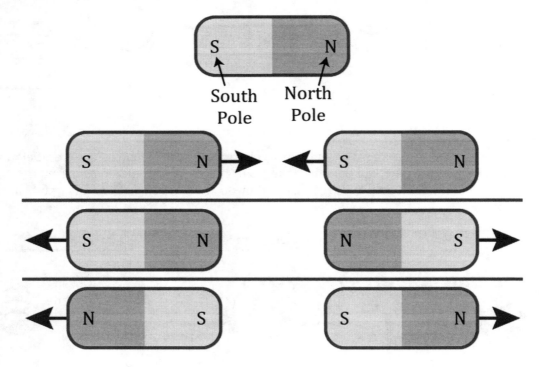

ASVAB: Auto Information

The Internal Combustion Engine Systems

INTERNAL COMBUSTION ENGINES

Combustion is the chemical reaction between fuel and air to release energy; spark ignition (SI)/gasoline **internal combustion engines** ignite gasoline (or a gasoline mixture) and air with a spark to do work. Diesel engines are also internal combustion engines, but they utilize compression ignition (CI) to ignite diesel, rather than a spark for gasoline. Core engine components are housed in the **engine block**.

Most gasoline engines operate with reciprocating pistons in cylinders. They use either a four-stroke or a two-stroke cycle, and most automobiles in the United States utilize the four-stroke cycle. Four piston strokes make up the four-stroke cycle: intake, compression, power, and exhaust. In one cycle, the piston moves down and back up twice.

ELECTRICAL SYSTEM

When a driver turns a key (or pushes a button) to start a car, an electrical circuit is completed. Electricity runs from the **battery** to the **starter motor (starter)**, which turns the crankshaft. In turn, the engine uses a pully system to turn the **alternator**, which recharges the battery and produces most of the electricity to the vehicle while it runs. The **solenoid** acts as a heavy-duty relay between the battery and the starter motor.

The electrical system also simultaneously fires up the fuel pump (in newer cars) and spark plugs (via a coil).

COMMON ELECTRICAL PROBLEMS

If a car won't start when the key is turned, this could be the result of a dead battery, faulty battery connections, or a problem with the starter motor or solenoid. If the alternator is bad, this may lead to a battery without a charge or headlights that are dim at low engine speeds.

Battery connections can be checked and improved by cleaning off corrosion with a wire brush and applying specialized grease to prevent further corrosion. A dead battery can be jumped to attempt to get the car running and help troubleshoot electrical problems. If it won't jump start, the problem might be with the starter; if it will start but won't stay running, the problem could be with the battery; if it will start and stays running, the problem could be with the alternator, or a light might have been left on in the vehicle.

FUEL SYSTEM

When a gasoline car is started, the electrical system starts the fuel system, which stores and delivers fuel (gasoline or gasoline mixture, in this case) to the engine. In newer cars, the **fuel pump** is housed in the **fuel tank**. **Fuel filters** protect fuel injectors or carburetors by ensuring clean fuel, and they can be found on either side of the fuel pump. In newer cars, computer-controlled **fuel injectors** atomize fuel into the cylinder (part of the engine) through a tiny electric valve in order to feed the combustion process; the computerization allows for better fuel economy and lower emissions. Older vehicles use **carburetors**, which mix fuel and air without a computer.

COMMON FUEL SYSTEM PROBLEMS

Fuel filters can clog and should be replaced at regular intervals. Clogged filters can prevent the vehicle from starting or cause it to sputter when traveling at high speed. Faulty fuel pumps can also prevent the car from starting: this could be an electrical problem or a problem with the pump itself due to regular wear-and-tear, contamination, or overheating. Fuel injectors can also clog, even with regular changing of the fuel filter. Signs of dirty or clogged injectors include increased emissions, decreased fuel economy, and poor idling and performance.

IGNITION SYSTEM

When a gasoline car is started, the electrical system starts the ignition system. **Ignition** is the generation of a spark or heating of an electrode to initiate combustion of fuel and air. The battery provides low voltage to a **coil**, which acts as a transformer and electromagnetically converts it to high voltage for use by the corresponding spark plug. **Spark plugs** force electricity to jump between electrodes across a gap, creating a spark. The alternator continues to produce electricity while the car is running, which allows the spark plugs to continue firing. There is one spark plug per cylinder in a spark-ignition internal combustion engine.

COMMON IGNITION PROBLEMS

One of the most common ignition problems is spark plug fouling, which occurs when carbon builds up at the ignition point; it will cause engine misfiring and increased carbon emissions. Driving at highway speeds is good for spark plugs because the increased temperature of the engine helps burn off the excess fuel or ash. Spark plug fouling is more common with prolonged idling and city driving because the engine doesn't get as hot.

Common signs of faulty ignition coils include: backfiring as a result of excess fuel in the combustion chamber, poor fuel economy, vibration when idling, and stalling.

ENGINE SYSTEM
PISTON AND CYLINDER

Most gasoline engines utilize a reciprocating piston and cylinder system for combustion, which functions to combust fuel (in this case, gasoline) and air. **Pistons**, together with their **rings**, act as plungers to take in and compress gas within the **cylinder**. Pistons are connected to the crankshaft via a hinged **connecting rod**. The **combustion chamber** is the space created by a piston where fuel and air mix and are ignited by the spark plug. Fuel delivery occurs by way of either a **fuel injector** or a **carburetor**.

ENGINE BLOCK

Once the gasoline vehicle is started, the electrical, fuel, and ignition systems converge in the engine. The electrical system starts turning the crankshaft, fuel injectors atomize gasoline pre-combustion, and spark plugs create a spark.

The **valvetrain** coordinates opening and closing of valves so that air-fuel entry and exhaust release is timed properly. The **camshaft** is a rotating shaft surrounded by oil with **cams** (specially shaped nodes) that depress or allow the release of the intake and exhaust valves as they rotate with the shaft. **Intake valves** regulate air-fuel mixture entry into the combustion chamber. **Exhaust valves** release gas byproducts of combustion to the exhaust manifold.

The **crankcase** is full of oil and houses the crankshaft and connecting rods. Each piston is hinged to a **connecting rod**, which is hinged to the crankshaft. The **crankshaft** rotates by combined, alternating motion of the pistons and their connecting rods. As it rotates, the crankshaft drives the camshaft by way of a **timing belt** or chain and gears.

COMMON ENGINE PROBLEMS

Problems with the engine and process of combustion can occur within the piston and cylinder unit or with the components that coordinate their functions. A broken or faulty timing belt will likely result in a ticking noise from the engine and will cause the vehicle to rough idle or misfire. It can also lead to a decrease in oil pressure, smoke coming from the engine, or broken pistons or valves. Crankshaft problems will lead to difficulty starting the vehicle or intermittent stalling; camshaft problems may cause rough idling, frequent stalling, poor fuel economy, slow accelerations, and difficulty starting. If the piston rings fail, oil will leak into the combustion chamber, causing the engine to smoke. Backfiring occurs when combustion takes place outside of the cylinders and can be the result of bad engine timing or improper fuel-air mixture ratios.

EXHAUST SYSTEM

The **exhaust system** transports gas products (exhaust) from the combustion process away from the engine and the vehicle. Exhaust from the combustion chamber is released by the exhaust valve towards the **exhaust manifold**, which collects gas byproducts from each cylinder and helps with noise control. Through the exhaust pipe, gas travels to the **catalytic converter**, which filters out pollutants and converts them to water vapor and carbon dioxide. From the catalytic converter, exhaust travels through the exhaust pipe to the **muffler**, which further reduces noise. From the muffler, the **tail pipe** releases gas away from the vehicle.

COMMON EXHAUST PROBLEMS

Consistently short trips of less than 15 miles, such as driving in town without getting on the highway, don't allow the water condensed in the exhaust system to vaporize and escape, which can cause corrosion and rusting of the exhaust system.

Mometrix

Fluids such as coolant or oil can leak from the engine if there is a faulty gasket and clog the catalytic converter, causing poor engine performance or preventing it from running properly. Excessive heat or unused fuel coming off the engine can cause the catalytic converter to overheat. Other symptoms of catalytic converter trouble include: reduced acceleration, dark exhaust smoke, more heat than usual under the vehicle, or exhaust that smells like sulfur.

LUBRICATION SYSTEM

Motor oil is used to prevent friction and corrosion within the engine. The **oil pan** is below the engine block and holds oil for pressurized distribution by the **oil pump** through the **oil galleries**, specialized channels throughout the engine. An **oil filter** helps keep the oil free of debris so that the moving parts in the engine don't get clogged. In addition to the galleries, the camshaft and the crankshaft are lubricated by motor oil; piston rings keep oil below the piston head and out of the combustion chamber.

COMMON LUBRICATION PROBLEMS

Besides friction reduction, oil also keeps the engine parts clean, and vehicles should have the oil and oil filter changed every 3,000 miles to prevent overheating and wearing out of the engine. Motor oil is labelled with viscosity ratings at both low temperatures (example: 5W or 10W) and high temperatures (SAE 30 or SAE 40) so that it will be thin enough to be functional when it is very cold outside and thick enough when the engine is very hot. **Synthetic motor oil** is manufactured and is more consistent and will last longer than conventional motor oil.

COOLING SYSTEM

While running, the average engine temperature is 200 °F; the walls of the cylinders are between 350 °F and 600 °F, and the combustion chamber is roughly 3000 °F. The cooling system helps keep the engine running within its ideal temperature range without overheating. **Coolant**, commonly made up of half antifreeze and half water, prevents overheating by circulating through **channels** throughout the engine by way of the **water pump**. The **thermostat** helps control engine temperature by sending coolant either to the engine or to the radiator if it needs to be cooled further. The **radiator** is a series of thin channels that allow air to remove heat from the coolant, aided by the **cooling fan**.

COMMON COOLING PROBLEMS

Problems with the cooling system can lead to engine overheating and damage. Broken or cracked coolant or radiator hoses can allow coolant to leak. Coolant breaks down over time and should be replaced according to the schedule given by the vehicle manufacturer. A thermostat stuck open will cause the engine to run cold and result in bad gas mileage; a thermostat stuck closed will cause the engine to overheat. The water pump and radiator cap both maintain the correct pressure range of the coolant in the system; a problem with either will prevent proper temperature regulation and lead to overheating. A broken or faulty fan belt or cooling fan will prevent the pumping of air into the radiator; if the car overheats, both should be checked for proper function.

Chassis Systems

DRIVETRAIN SYSTEM

The **drivetrain** translates power from the engine in order to move the vehicle forward. The crankshaft is attached to the **flywheel**, which stores rotational energy from the engine and smooths the motion of the pistons. The **clutch** allows for disengaging and re-engaging of the transmission and the flywheel/engine so that stopping the motion of the wheels doesn't also stop the engine. The

225

transmission multiplies engine torque to allow for a wide range of vehicle speeds, as well as acceleration and deceleration; it consists of a series of gears, and more gears translate to better engine efficiency. Most modern transmissions are automatic, but they can also be manual or constant velocity (CV). The **differential** splits the torque of the engine to allow the inside and outside wheels to spin at different speeds, as when turning.

DRIVETRAIN CONFIGURATIONS

Drivetrains power the turning of the wheels of the vehicle through the transmission and axles in the following configurations:

- **Rear wheel drive (RWD)** is found in trucks and older cars, and the transmission delivers power to the rear axle via the **driveshaft**.
- **Front wheel drive (FWD)** is found in most modern economy or compact cars; the **transaxle** combines the functionality of the transmission, front axle, and differential into one component. The engine weight is over the drive wheels, which allows for better traction.
- **All wheel drive (AWD)** is in most newer cars and SUVs and powers both axles using a **transfer case**, which distributes the engine torque to both the front and rear axles.
- **Four-wheel drive (4WD)** utilizes a specialized transfer case to accommodate different driving conditions: Two-wheel drive (2WD) offers better gas mileage for city and highway driving; four-wheel drive high (4WD-HI) allows for intermediate torque for off-road driving at higher speeds; four-wheel drive low (4WD-LO) provides maximum torque for off-road driving at lower speeds.

COMMON DRIVETRAIN SYSTEM PROBLEMS

In a manual transmission, hard shifting or grinding may be the result of clashing gears and worn out synchronizers. Automatic transmissions also wear out, which leads to transmission slipping and poor shifting. Transmission fluid should also be changed and levels maintained to prevent gear slippage and shifting problems. The clutch can jam, which may cause violent vehicle shaking and overheating in the transmission. Transfer case problems can lead to difficulty shifting gears, grinding noises, or jumping in and out of four-wheel drive.

SUSPENSION SYSTEM

The suspension system allows for a smooth, comfortable ride when driving, prevents components from stress or vibrating loose, keeps the vehicle upright, and allows for pivoting when steering. **Springs**, installed between the chassis or frame and the axels, absorb the impact of the road on the vehicle; most vehicles use coil springs or layered leaf springs:

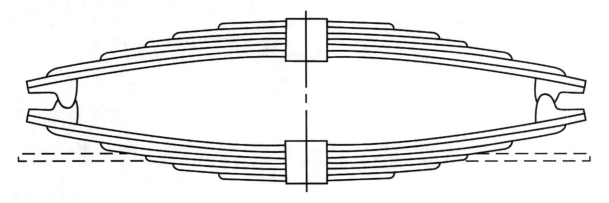

Shocks (shock absorbers or dampers) oppose the oscillating motion of the springs and dampen road vibration. **Struts** are a combination of springs and shocks. The **anti-roll bar** or **sway bar** keeps the vehicle from rolling over when turning and allows for better handling. The **spindles**, which should be parallel to the ground, are the center point of each wheel that connects to the upper and lower control arms via a sealed and greased ball joint. **Control arms** connect the suspension system to the frame of the vehicle through **bushings**, which are insulated joint linings that protect the jointed components from vibration or wear.

COMMON SUSPENSION PROBLEMS

Worn shocks and struts can cause excessive bumping and bouncing, and oil leaking from either is a sign of wear. The bushings of the sway bar can also wear out, signaled by thumping or knocking when turning or taking bumps. Pickup trucks should normally sit with their bed slightly higher than the body of the truck to allow for heavy loads; if it sits level (without modifications), it could be a sign of a faulty spring. The same is true if one corner of the vehicle sits lower than the rest while on level ground.

STEERING SYSTEM

The steering system directs the vehicle while driving and minimizes the force required for such movement. The steering system engages either the modern, highly precise **rack-and-pinion system** or the older, less precise **steering-box system** to translate the turning of the **steering wheel** via small gears to the front wheels. **Power steering** supplies pressurized engine oil from a pump to the steering rack or steering box so that steering is easier and more responsive.

Car alignment, though it involves the suspension system, impacts vehicle steering; proper alignment is required for the vehicle to continue to travel straight when the steering wheel is temporarily released.

COMMON STEERING PROBLEMS

Power steering fluid sometimes gets low and needs to be refilled. However, hoses associated with the steering system, like all vehicle hoses, can wear and crack over time and lead to leaking power steering fluid and require replacement. Low or leaking power steering fluid, a problem with the power steering pump, and even some suspension problems such as worn control arm bushings can result in difficulty turning the steering wheel and steering the vehicle. Power steering problems can also cause a grinding or squealing noise when turning. Improper alignment can also cause passive steering problems: when the steering wheel is temporarily released, the vehicle will pull to one side.

BRAKE SYSTEM

The brake system is vital for motorist safety as it allows for slowing and stopping, even at high speeds. When the **brake pedal** is depressed, **brake fluid** is pushed from the **master cylinder** through the brake lines to each wheel's **brake caliper**. The fluid pressure causes friction, which forces the wheels to stop turning.

Most vehicles have **disc brakes** on the front wheels, and some have them on the rear wheels as well. When the brake fluid flows through the brake lines, it depresses a piston in the brake caliper, squeezing the inner and outer **brake pads**, which are materially hard and designed to withstand heat and friction. Brake pads squeeze against the cast iron **disc rotor**, which is held to the wheel at the wheel hub.

Vehicles that do not have disc brakes on the rear tires use **drum brakes**. The **wheel cylinder** forces the paired **brake shoes** against the inside walls of the bowl-shaped, cast iron **drum**.

COMMON BRAKE PROBLEMS

Brake pads encounter lots of friction, wear out and need to be replaced; symptoms of this include grinding, squealing, and slow stopping when the brake pedal is applied. Rotors also encounter a lot of friction and can warp. If the vehicle experiences pulsing when slowing or stopping, it might be due to warped rotors. Sponginess or softness when the brake pedal is applied could signal a problem with the master cylinder or low brake fluid levels and requires immediate attention. If the car pulls to one side when braking, the brake calipers might not be applying equal pressure to the tires. A stuck brake caliper or engaged parking brake while driving can lead to overheating, will likely cause a sharp odor, and should also be addressed immediately.

ASVAB: Shop Information

Measuring Tools

RULERS & TAPE MEASURES

A **ruler** is a device with a straight edge used to measure length, generally in both centimeters (cm) and inches (in); these are generally subdivided into millimeters and sixteenths, respectively. Standard lengths for rulers are 12 inches (30 cm).

A **tape measure** is a flexible, often retractable, ruler used to measure length. Standard tape measures are measured in centimeters (with millimeter increments) on one edge of the tape and inches (with quarter-, eighth-, and sixteenth-inch increments) on the other. Some tape measures may include thirty-seconds or even smaller increments, which are required for more detailed projects.

CALIPERS

Calipers are precise measuring devices with sliding jaws used to measure two-dimensional **inside measurements** (an empty distance between two points) and **outside measurements** (the width or thickness of an object). Calipers can be digital or analog; analog calipers measure relatively precisely using a vernier (a graduated, sliding measuring device) or a dial (using a rack and pinion). Both calipers pictured have jaws for inside and outside measurements.

Calipers are used widely in mechanical engineering, woodworking, machining, and metalworking.

Vernier caliper

Dial caliper

MICROMETERS

A type of caliper, **micrometers** are jawed devices used to measure the distance between two points. However, micrometers are much more precise, specialized, and difficult to use; they are most commonly used in machining applications and mechanical engineering. Micrometers can measure to 1/20,000 of an inch, which makes them sensitive to even temperature, and they must be handled with skill and caution. Like calipers, they can measure inside and outside measurements, but with their specialized jaws, they can be used for other, more difficult, measurements as well. Ball micrometers measure the thickness of curved parts, and offset centerline micrometers accurately measure the distance between the center of two holes.

Simple outside micrometer

LEVELS

Levels are used to determine if an object's surface is horizontal (level; 0°) or vertical (plumb; 90°) relative to the earth's surface, though this does not necessarily mean relative to the ground in the immediate area. There are several different types of levels:

- Spirit or bubble level: a tool containing or consisting of a small, clear tube filled with alcohol or another liquid and a small air bubble. The tube is very slightly bowed so that when the level is perfectly horizontal, the bubble will be in the middle; the less bow the tube has, the more accurate the level will be.
- Laser level: a tool utilizing a laser or series of lasers to establish a horizontal plane on the desired surface.
- Optical level: a tool used by builders to establish grade (a level base or specific slope) across a large area, such as for foundations of buildings.
- Water level: clear, flexible tubing filled with water used to create a horizontal line between distant objects (such as fence posts) or a large surface (such as a deck). When both ends are held steady and upright, the water lines in each tube will be in line with one another horizontally.

Diagram of water level

PLUMB BOB

A **plumb bob** is a tool used to establish a vertical (plumb; 90°) reference line relative to the earth's surface, though this does not necessarily mean the ground in the immediate area. Laser plumb bobs work much like laser levels, but the simpler plumb bob, a weight with a point on the bottom hung from a string, can also be used to find the plumb-line or vertical reference line. To use the plumb bob, attach the end of the string to the upper point being measured. For example, tie the end of the string to a long nail at the top of a fence post. To be sure the fence post is upright, let the plumb bob swing unhindered until still. The bottom tip of the bob will hang perfectly vertically below the knot in the string above, and the line will be parallel to the fence post if it is plumb.

SQUARES

Squares consist of two straight edges set at 90° to each other and are used by carpenters, builders, and machinists, among others, to check for exact right (90°) angles. Perfect right angles are essential to the proper function of doors and windows and the soundness of buildings and other structures, among other things. There are several different types of squares, depending on the project at hand. For example:

- Speed square: a small, right triangle-shaped tool commonly used for guiding saw cuts, marking angles, and squaring lines. It can also be used as a substitute level and to assist with **ripping wood** (cutting wood parallel to the grain).
- Framing or steel square: an L-shaped square with graduated edges used for cutting stair stringers and laying out rafters.
- Combination square: a tool consisting of a ruler and interchangeable, sliding heads used most commonly in woodworking, stonemasonry, and metalworking. The square or standard head is the most common and is used to check 90° and 45° angles.
- Drywall square: used for marking and cutting drywall for hanging, this T-shaped tool has graduated edges, the longest of which is 48 inches in order to accommodate squaring a standard sheet of drywall.

Striking Tools

HAMMERS

Hammers are tools with a weighted head on a handle used to strike with concentrated force on a small surface area, such as a nail head when driving it into wood. There are many different types of hammers, but some of the most common are:

- Claw hammer: highly versatile, this hammer has a curved claw on the back side of the weighted head used for prying. Several other hammer variations include the claw, as well.
- Rubber mallet: commonly used in woodworking and upholstery, the rubber head delivers more insulated force so as not to damage the work surface.
- Sledge hammer: With a long handle and a heavy head, the sledge hammer is designed for driving stakes, breaking up masonry, and other jobs requiring maximum force and heavy blows.
- Nail gun: Drives nails, powered most commonly by electricity or an air compressor.

CHISELS

A **chisel** is a hand tool commonly used in woodworking with a long blade used to cut or shape wood, as well as stone, metal, or other hard materials. To use a chisel, be sure to have a firm, 2-handed grip: one hand guides while the other drives the chisel. If more force is needed, a rubber mallet can be used to deliver the force to the end of the handle, but chiseling should always occur with the grain of the wood. Different types of chisels include:

- Beveled edge chisels: The most basic of chisels, beveled edge chisels have a relatively thin blade with a flat back. Its square blade end has 3 acute beveled edges on the front side.

- Mortise chisels: Sturdier than beveled edge chisels, mortise chisels have a thicker blade with a flat back. Its square end has just 1 beveled edge on the front side, which is less acute than that of a beveled edge chisel.

Beveled edge chisel

Mortise chisel

PUNCHES

Used in conjunction with a hammer and sometimes a chisel, a **punch tool or punch** is a hard metal hand tool with a blunted end and a specialized pointed end used to mark the center for drawing circles, punch precise holes in hard material such as sheet metal or leather, start holes for drilling, and more. Hollow punches have a hollow interior and are used to create holes in the workpiece, and solid punches have a solid interior and are used for marking, to remove material from an area, or to drive small components such as pins precisely into place.

Turning Tools

SCREWDRIVERS

Screwdrivers are hand tools used to apply torque (a twisting force used to cause rotation); most commonly, they are used to turn screws using the groove patterns on the screw head with the corresponding shape at the end of the screwdriver:

Common screwdriver types

On the left, the **Phillips-head screwdriver** forms a cross at the end of the screwdriver. The **flat head screwdriver** is a simple wedge shape.

Power drills and **power screwdrivers** are battery powered or corded tools used to drive screws, among other things. They are required when the project requires many screws or the materials being attached are hard to penetrate. Power or electric screwdrivers are more lightweight than drills and are easier to maneuver, but they are less powerful and therefore less versatile.

WRENCHES

Wrenches are hand tools used to apply torque, usually by gripping the outside of the bolt, nut or screw with relative specificity.

Image	Tool Variation	Description & Uses
	Crescent or adjustable wrench	Jaw diameter can be adjusted by turning the threaded worm to engage the corrugated edge of the non-fixed jaw. **Crescent wrenches** are highly versatile.
	Pipe wrench	With serrated and adjustable jaws, the F-shaped **pipe wrench** is sturdy and commonly used for metal pipes.
	Lug wrench	Used to remove or replace lug nuts on cars, **lug wrenches** are either L-shaped (with a socket on one end) or X-shaped (with 4 different sockets).
	Allen wrench or Allen key	Used to apply torque to screws with a hexagonal recess in their head, **Allen wrenches** are L-shaped and have a hexagonal cross-section. They usually come in sets of various sizes.
	Box-ended wrench	The closed loops at either end of the **box wrench** can be used for square or hexagonal bolts, and the (sometimes present) raised ends allow for gripping of recessed nuts or bolts. The two ends are slightly different sizes. They usually come in sets of various sizes.

233

Image	Tool Variation	Description & Uses
	Open-ended wrench	A very common type of wrench, **open-ended wrenches** have U-shaped openings at each end, and the ends are slightly different sizes. The open ends are more likely to round the edges of a nut or bolt than closed ends. They usually come in sets of various sizes.
	Combination wrench	A combination of box-ended and open-ended wrenches, **combination wrenches** have an open and a closed end. They usually come in sets of various sizes.
	Ratcheting wrench	At least one end of the **ratcheting wrench** contains a ratcheting device so that loosening or tightening doesn't require a complete circular motion or removing and resetting the wrench if something is in the way. These wrenches are helpful in tight spaces.
	Socket wrench	**Socket wrenches** have a drive (the square-shaped fitting) attached to a ratchet on one end; various sockets can be attached to the drive to accommodate different size bolt heads. Sockets come in sets of various sizes.
	Torque wrench	Manual and digital **torque wrenches** help prevent overtightening because they can be calibrated in accordance with manufactured specifications. These are commonly used in automotive work, among other things.

Wrench sizes for sets come in standard and metric, and size-range and specificity depend on the trade or project for which they are used. Common metric wrench sizes start at 4 millimeters (mm) and increase by 1 mm increments; common standard wrench sizes start at $\frac{5}{32}$ of an inch and increase by $\frac{1}{32}$ " increments.

Like other wrenches, **Allen wrenches** come in fractional inch and metric sizes.

Socket sizes depend on the **drive size**, which is the square-shaped fitting on the ratchet at the end of the socket wrench. The larger the drive, the more torque it can handle, therefore the sockets will be larger. The most common drive sizes are $\frac{1}{4}$ inch, $\frac{3}{8}$ inch, and $\frac{1}{2}$ inch.

IMPACT TOOLS

Impact drivers operate much like power drills or power screwdrivers, but they sense when additional torque is needed and internally employ a spring, hammer, and anvil to provide more rotational force. Because of the additional torque, drill bits must have a **hex shank**, meaning the end of the bit inserted into the **chuck** (the drill's specialized clamp used to hold bits) must be hexagonal. Hex shanks are designed to withstand the stress of impact drivers. An example of when an impact driver might be necessary is when attempting to remove a screw that has rusted into place. They can be cordless with a battery or powered by an air compressor.

Impact wrenches use sockets (like the socket wrench) to remove stubborn nuts or bolts with the same spring, hammer, and anvil mechanism as impact drivers. They can be cordless with a battery or powered by an air compressor.

An **air compressor** pressurizes gas by reducing its volume, therefore converting power from a motor or an engine into pressurized air. They can be used to power pneumatic tools such as nail guns or impact wrenches and to air up tires.

NUTS, BOLTS & WASHERS

A **nut** is a piece of hardware with a threaded hole and a typically hexagonal perimeter used in conjunction with a bolt; a **bolt** is a threaded rod with a head capable of being securely grasped. Together, a nut and a bolt are used to fasten multiple parts together. **Washers** are used when the hole through which the bolt passes is too large for the bolt head or the nut or when the force of the nut-bolt load needs to be more widely distributed; they are flat, typically circular plates with circular holes in the center. The outside edge should be larger than the holes passing through the pieces to be attached; the hole in the middle of the washer should be just large enough for the bolt to pass through.

Fastening Tools

RIVETING TOOLS

Riveting is the process of joining plates of metal by use of **rivets**, which are short metal pins with a head and a stem (may be solid or hollow) that act as mechanical fasteners. Once passed through both metal sheets by drilling, placing, or punching, the rivets are smashed or pounded so as to flatten the head and expand the stem to complete the rivet joint.

Rivets support tensile loads (force that occurs in opposite directions along the same axis) and shear loads (force that produces sliding, which is a failure in the plane parallel to the direction of force), and the most common modern applications include: residential gutter construction, HVAC duct work, and aircraft manufacturing.

Tensile   Shear

RETAINING RINGS

Retaining rings are a class of hardware used to reduce motion by stretching or compressing between mating pieces by fitting either on the inside of the exterior component or around the outside of the interior component. Common variations include:

- **Circlip rings** allow axial rotation while preventing lateral motion by snapping into a groove or onto a shaft.
- **Grooveless rings** do not require a groove to function properly and often have a low profile.
- **Spiral rings** are coiled into a groove and allow flexibility.
- **Beveled rings** are specifically beveled to provide a rigid, sturdy joint when complementary ends are locked.
- **Bowed rings** have one central tab and two projecting tabs so that they function like a spring.

SOLDERING TOOLS

Soldering is the process of melting **solder** (a metal alloy commonly made of lead and tin) to create a joint between two different metals without melting either of them; this process requires applying heat at roughly 600-840°F. Solder comes as wire with common diameters of 0.032 and 0.062 inches, and it can be purchased with or without lead as part of the alloy. Soldering is commonly used to connect components on electronic circuit boards.

Soldering irons are hand tools used to apply heat to melt solder.

Soldering guns are heavier than soldering irons, but they heat and cool more quickly. They are used when soldering stained-glass windows and in heavy electronics.

A **soldering station** allows precise temperature adjusting for soldering irons and include other safety features such as temperature sensors and password protection, depending on the device.

A **solder sucker** or **de-soldering pump** is used to removed excess solder or to correct mistakes when soldering, even after the solder has solidified.

WELDING & WELDING TOOLS

Welding is the process of fusing two metals into one by melting the **base metal** (material to be welded or cut) through use of extreme heat (6500°F) and sometimes other metals or gases, depending on the welding method.

Goggles, a helmet (auto-dimming is best), gloves, and long sleeves should be worn while welding to protect from heat and radiation. Never look at the welding arc with the naked eye; this could cause permanent eye damage.

Common arc welding processes include: Tungsten inert gas (TIG) welding, flux-cored arc welding (FCAW), stick welding, and metal inert gas (MIG) welding.

COMMON WELDING TERMINOLOGY & TOOLS

A **cutting torch** is a tool that uses gas to pre-heat and cut metal.

Electrodes in welding refer to the various current-conducting metals used between the electrode holder/stinger and welding arc.

Flux is a cleaner used before welding or soldering to dissolve oxidation (rust); it can also be used during high-temperature welding to prevent oxidation.

External **shielding gases** are inert or semi-inert gases that protect the welding arc and molten weld from atmospheric contamination.

Slag is the solidified byproduct of some arc welding processes after the area cools.

A **stinger** or **electrode holder** is an insulated clamp that holds the electrode securely in position.

A **welder** or **welding machine** is the power source for the electrical current and heat source.

The **welding arc** is the discharge of electrons between the electrode and the base metal.

Gripping Tools

PLIERS

Pliers are a class of hinged hand tool with handles and specialized jaws used especially for gripping and pulling. There are many different types of pliers, including:

Image	Tool Variation	Description & Uses
	Slip Joint Pliers	Highly versatile, the adjustable fulcrum allows the corrugated jaws to lock at varying widths.
	Needle Nose Pliers	Elongated, often corrugated jaws allow for increased precision when bending and shaping wire.
	Bent Nose Pliers	A variation of needle nose pliers with bent jaws, they are used for delicate tasks or working at difficult angles.
	Crimping pliers	Specialized jaws allow for breaking plastic coating on wire and crimping wires together; this makes them ideal for telecommunications technicians.

Image	Tool Variation	Description & Uses
	Diagonal pliers (Wire cutters)	Acutely angled jaws enable cutting of wire and nails.
	Tongue and Groove Pliers (Channel Locks)	Various grooves on the upper jaw allow for an adjustable, locking fulcrum and a highly versatile tool.

CLAMPS

Clamps are devices used to secure objects together tightly for woodworking, plumbing, and countless other tasks. Clamps are specialized, and there are many common varieties, including:

Image	Tool Variation	Description & Uses
	C-clamp or G-clamp	The screw section is used to increase and decrease jaw-width and applied pressure of this very common clamp.
	Pipe clamp	This clamp has jaws that form a circle so as to be fit around a pipe.
	Hose clamp	An adjustable, circular band allows for tightening over a hose fitting to prevent leakage of fluid.

Image	Tool Variation	Description & Uses
	Bar clamp, F-clamp, speed clamp	The upper jaw is attached to a long bar, and the lower jaw can be adjusted to varying widths making it ideal for holding larger projects.
	Spring clamp, pinch clamp, hand clamp	Built like pliers, jaws are usually padded and pressure originates from a spring, making it ideal for stabilizing while glue sets.
	Toolmakers parallel jaw clamp	Double, parallel screws likewise hold the jaws parallel for maximum stability.
	Bench clamp	A clamp built to be mounted on a workbench.

VISE-GRIPS

Vise-grips (which can also be spelled **vice-grips**), also known as **locking pliers,** are part clamp and part pliers. With handles, corrugated jaws, and a fulcrum between the two like pliers, they can also be locked into a clamped position. A lever in one of the handles allows for the release of the clamping action.

Vise-grips can be used as clamps, pliers, wrenches, and more; their versatility makes them useful for most trades and projects.

Cutting Tools

MANUAL SAWS

A **saw** is a hand tool used to cut wood, metal, pipe, or other materials with a serrated edge using a back-and-forth motion. Different saws have specialized blades and handles for different jobs, including:

Image	Tool Variation	Description & Uses
	Hand saw, rip cut saw, ripsaw	With a long, flexible, slightly tapered blade and sharpened, relatively wide set teeth, the hand saw is common in framing and other woodworking jobs. Can be used to roughly rip wood (cut wood with the grain).
	Back saw, tenon saw	A square, thin blade with a reinforced upper edge and small teeth that are set close together, making it ideal for straight, fine cuts.
	Bow saw	Shaped like a bow, the narrow blade with jagged teeth is used commonly to prune or trim trees.
	Crosscut saw, lumberjack saw	Large teeth sit on the curved edge of a thick blade made for large, rough cuts of wood. Traditional forms have two handles so that two people can work together with one tool; common versions designed for one person have one handle with an extra sometimes placed on the back of the leading edge.
	Hacksaw	Very common and ideal for metalworking and cutting pipes, the blade has hard teeth.

Image	Tool Variation	Description & Uses
	Coping saw	Good for precision and intricacy, the thin blade is held tight by the frame and is used commonly for cutting curves in wood.
	Keyhole saw, pad saw, jab saw, drywall saw	The blade is dagger shaped and most commonly used to cut small circles or odd shapes in drywall.

POWERED SAWS

Powered saws are specialized cutting tools that can be hand-held, stand-alone, or mounted on a work surface in order to cut various surfaces including wood, plastics, metal, and masonry.

Image	Tool Variation	Description & Uses
	Chainsaw	Used for felling or trimming trees, chainsaws have a continuous chain of specialized teeth that feeds around a metal bar and is ideal for ripping and cutting wood.
	Band saw	Stationary or portable, this saw has aa continuous band that is used to make cuts that are intricate, though relatively shallow.
	Circular saw, buzz saw, Skilsaw	The most common type of power saw, circular saws have a circular blade with teeth around the edge; specialized blade materials can be used to cut wood, metal, stone, and plastic. They are easily portable and can be used to rip (cut wood with the grain) or cross cut (cut perpendicular to the grain) wood.

241

Image	Tool Variation	Description & Uses
	Miter saw	A miter saw is a circular saw that can be mounted to a work bench, and its blade can make straight (90°) cuts or be locked at an angle to make highly specific cuts (commonly the 45° cut for making corners in wood trim).
	Table saw	A table saw is a circular blade mounted in the middle of a table; wood (or other materials, depending on the makeup of the blade) is fed into to the blade in order to make the cut.
	Jigsaw, saber saw	A narrow, easily maneuverable blade on a hand-held jigsaw allows for easy cutting of non-straight details and curves.
	Reciprocating saw, Sawzall	Frequently used in construction and demolition, the reciprocating saw can cut both nails and wood, as well as plastics, bricks, and tiles.
	Oscillating saw, oscillating multi-tool	Certain blade attachments change the functionality of the oscillating saw so that it can grind, scrape, or remove grout or caulk. Its saw form utilizes a serrated blade that oscillates side to side; this design allows for cuts that plunge straight into the work surface without requiring an approach from the side or drilling a starter hole first.

DRILLING TOOLS

Drilling tools cut new, circular holes in wood, metal, plastic, or other materials using **bits**, which are specialized tips that both cut and remove material as they move. Common drill bits used for wood are characterized by a spiral-shaped blade with recessed flutes that make up the body of the bit and a shank, which feeds into and is held by the radially gripping **chuck** of the drill. Drills are

242

most commonly hand-held, but some can be mounted on a work bench or can stand on the floor; impact varieties also exist, which sense when additional torque is needed and internally employ a spring, hammer, and anvil to provide more rotational force.

Drill bit

Boring Tools

Common in machining, a boring bar is used in conjunction with a lathe following the drilling process to **bore** a workpiece (enlarging an existing hole). A **lathe** is a machine tool that rotates a workpiece radially in order to sand, cut, drill, bore, and more. A **boring bar** is used in conjunction with a lathe to bore a pre-drilled hole into a workpiece to exact specifications. **Line boring** is when the boring bar is supported on both ends and the hole being enlarged must pass completely through the workpiece. With **back boring** only one end of the boring bar fixed and supported. This can be used for blind holes, which do not pass completely through the workpiece, or holes that pass all the way through the workpiece.

Surface Preparing & Finishing Tools

Planes

Planing is the woodworking process of smoothing, shaping, flattening, and straightening the surface of a wooden workpiece. **Hand planers** are the hand-held, manual tools traditionally used for this task; they are still used for small jobs such as slightly reshaping a door that sticks. However, **power planers** are used commonly to handle bulk jobs of adjusting board thickness or flatness, such as planing boards so that they are uniform for a building project, repurposing old lumber, or downsizing larger dimensional lumber into smaller, custom, or more expensive pieces.

Files and Rasps

Files and rasps are manual, hand-held tools used for removing material from workpieces, most commonly of wood or metal.

Files produce a finer finish but cut more slowly than rasps. They can be single cut, with parallel ridges, or double cut, with two sets of parallel ridges set at an angle to each other; double cut files are rougher on a workpiece than single cut. Files come in four grades from smoothest to coarsest: smooth, second cut, bastard, and coarse.

Mill files are used to sharpen metal blades.

Rasps have raised teeth instead of ridges like a file, and they have various levels of coarseness: wood (the roughest), cabinet, and patternmaker (the smoothest).

GRINDERS

Grinders are powered, hand-held tools used for cutting, rough and fine shaping, smoothing, brushing, and polishing many different types of materials including wood, metal, stone, and plastic. They can sometimes be used for sanding jobs, whereas sanders cannot be typically be used for grinding jobs.

Angle grinders are the most common form of grinders and are highly versatile. They can be used to clean metal (with the wire brush attachment); cut metal bolts (with the metal cutoff wheel attachment); cut masonry (with the diamond wheel attachment); and sharpen blades (with the grinding wheel).

Belt grinders can be used to finish surfaces and sharpen metal blades, among other things, using an abrasive belt.

Bench grinders can be mounted on a work bench and are used for grinding off large amounts of material or rust, sharpening metal blades, buffing and polishing surfaces, and cutting wood and other hard materials.

SANDERS

Sanding is the process of smoothing a surface, commonly wood or metal, using an abrasive material such as sandpaper. **Sandpaper** comes in varying grit levels, the higher the number, the finer the sandpaper grit. Fine-grit sandpaper should be used for more detailed jobs, such as the final sanding step before staining wood.

Sanding blocks are hand-held, manual tools used to prevent high spots and ridges on the wood surface, and they are useful when a powered sander might do damage to the project. Removable sandpaper is attached to the side of the block opposite to where it is handled.

Orbital sanders (also known as **palm sanders** or **circular sanders**) are hand-held, powered tools that vibrates the square-shaped sanding pad in small, circular motions. They are relatively gentle and lightweight and work better for delicate projects than heavy ones. **Random orbital sanders** operate the same way, but their sanding pads are round, thus eliminating the minor scarring that can happen with the square-shaped pads of an orbital sanders.

Some sanders utilize a sanding belt, such as the **belt sander** and the **file sander**, which has a narrower belt used for fitting into small spaces.

ASVAB: Assembling Objects

This section of the test measures your ability to imagine the way an object will look when its pieces are joined together properly. The questions that make up this section will begin with a picture of five separate parts. Each of these parts will be marked with one or more letters. These letters will be assigned to places on the part. Sometimes the letter will appear directly over part of the object, and sometimes a line will be drawn from the letter to the appropriate spot on the object. If there is a dotted line drawn from the letter to the object, this means that the letter corresponds to a place on the side of the object that cannot be seen. Your task will be to imagine how the object will look when all of the parts are connected such that the letters touch one another. In other words, all of the parts marked with an *A* will need to touch; all of the parts marked with a *B* will need to touch, and so on. You will be given five assembled objects from which to choose your answer. This format will be the same for all twenty questions in the assembly section.

The format of the assembly questions, then, is fairly straightforward. However, you will need to be able to work efficiently. This means approaching the assembly questions with a strategy in mind. There are a couple of different ways to proceed. Perhaps the best way to approach assembly questions is to proceed in order and work methodically. In other words, begin by mentally connecting the *A*s; once you have this assembly in mind, move on to the *B*s, and so forth. One mistake that many test-takers make is to attempt the entire assembly all at once. Many of these problems will involve four or five parts, and it will be too easy to get confused if you do not work in order. Indeed, the test administrator will be sure to include a few close-but-incorrect answers designed to trip up people who work too fast. The best way to proceed through an assembly question is to firmly decide on the arrangement of the object one piece at a time.

In tandem with this strategy, you can use the process of elimination to quickly reduce the number of possible answers. After you have mentally connected the *A*s, for instance, you can go through and rule out all of those answers that do not have the *A*s connected properly. You can then proceed through the *B*s, ruling out a few more answers, until you are left with a single possible right answer, which you can then take a moment to confirm.

There are a few things to keep in mind when considering possible solutions to an assembly problem. To begin with, remember that the pieces can be turned in any way. They may be rotated, spun, and flipped. They may not, however, be folded, bent, or twisted. Furthermore, they may not change in size; each piece should be the same size in the answer as it is in the original picture. Occasionally, the makers of the exam will place the pieces in the correct configuration but will drastically alter the sizes of one or more pieces. This automatically invalidates the answer. It is best to imagine the pieces as solid three-dimensional objects, which can be manipulated in all directions but cannot have their fundamental size and shape altered.

Similarly, make sure that the answer you select has the appropriate number of pieces. If there are five different components in the original drawing, there must be five connected parts in the answer. It is common for the exam to leave out a piece or include an extra piece in one or more of the possible answers; even if these answers are right in all other respects, they cannot be correct if they include more or fewer pieces than the original drawing.

Once you have worked through the problem in this systematic manner and have selected your answer, go back and double-check your work. To begin with, make sure that all of the letters are joined properly in the answer you have chosen. Then, make sure that your answer has the right

245

number of pieces. Finally, make sure that the pieces in the assembled object are similar in size to the pieces in the original drawing. If all of these factors check out, you can be comfortable that you have selected the right answer.

This methodical way of working through assembly problems may seem too time-consuming given the limits of the exam, but with a little bit of practice you can speed through the process within the time given. In fact, by adhering to this organized way of solving assembly problems, you will actually save time, since you will never get confused or lost in a problem and have to go back to the beginning. All it takes to master these problems is a little strategic knowledge and a little preparation. Having covered the strategy, let's now take a look at a few ways to prepare for this section of the exam.

There are a few common activities you can use to prepare for the assembly section of the exam. For instance, even though jigsaw puzzles do not offer an exact replication of the items you will encounter on the exam, they still exercise your spatial reasoning skills. Envisioning which pieces of the puzzle will fit together, and how the resulting arrangement will look, is a great way to hone your assembly skills. For an even greater challenge, try turning all the pieces of the puzzle face down, so that you cannot use the picture to guide your work: this will force you to rely more on your sense of orientation and arrangement.

Another way to prepare for this section of the exam is to take apart a small piece of machinery and study its configuration. Yard sales and junk bins are great places to find old appliances and electronics equipment. With the help of a screwdriver, wrench, and pair of pliers, you should be able to take apart most any appliance with ease. Once you have broken the item down into a pile of parts, see if you can put those parts back together into a functional whole. Even better, have someone else take apart the item and then see if you can put it back together. Of course, it is not recommended that you try this with valuable or expensive pieces of hardware. Also, some electronic appliances contain small batteries which should not be handled by non-professionals; always obey any warnings listed on the equipment. Nevertheless, taking apart and putting together small machines can be a fantastic way to improve your assembly skills.

Finally, there is a wealth of spatial intelligence exercises to be found on the Internet. Just by entering "spatial intelligence" into a search engine, you should receive listings for dozens of simple, free puzzles and games that strengthen your ability to visualize and perform basic assemblies. Some of these programs are so sophisticated that they allow you to manipulate three-dimensional objects on your computer screen! While for many people working on a computer is no substitute for direct contact with an object, these online exercises are a clean, fast way to stretch your mental muscles.

Whatever method you choose, be sure to prepare for at least a few hours before sitting for the examination. For most students, the most difficult thing about the assembly questions is getting comfortable with the format and learning how to approach the problem. By remembering the strategies discussed above, and utilizing some of the suggested practice exercises, you can make sure that you will be ready to attack assembly problems immediately.

AFOQT: Verbal Analogies

WHAT ARE ANALOGIES QUESTIONS?

Analogies are pairs of terms that have a common relationship. Analogy questions are presented in the format, "A is to B as C is to D," meaning that terms A and B are related to one another in the same or similar way that terms C and D are related to each other. Terms A and B do not have to be related to terms C and D at all, though they usually will be.

Usually in the question, you will be given terms A, B, and C, and will have to supply term D from the choices given. Occasionally, you may be given only terms A and B, and you will have to select a pair of terms for C and D.

WHAT SORT OF RELATIONSHIPS WILL THERE BE?

Below are some examples of the types of analogies that may appear on the exam. Most of the questions you encounter will be relatively simple relationships, but here is an extensive list of the types of analogies that might show up.

CHARACTERISTIC

Some characteristic analogies will focus on a characteristic of something else.

- Dog : Paw – The foot of a dog is its paw.
- Lady : Lovely – A lady has a lovely personality.
- Outrageous : Lies – Lies can be described as being outrageous.

Some characteristic analogies will focus on something that is NOT a characteristic of something else.

- Desert : Humidity – A desert does not have humidity.
- Job : Unemployed – A person without a job is unemployed.
- Quick : Considered – A quick decision is often not very considered.

SOURCE

- Casting : Metal – A casting is made from metal.
- Forest : Trees – A forest is composed of trees.
- Slogans : Banners – A slogan is printed on banners.

LOCATION

- Eiffel Tower : Paris – The Eiffel Tower is a structure in Paris.
- Welsh : Wales – The Welsh are the inhabitants of Wales.
- Pound : England – The pound is the monetary unit of England.

SEQUENTIAL

- One : Two – These are consecutive numbers.
- Birth : Death – These are the first and last events of a life or project.
- Spring : Summer – The season of spring immediately precedes summer.

CAUSE/EFFECT

- Storm : Hail – Hail can be caused by a storm.
- Heat : Fire – Heat results from a fire.
- Monotony : Boredom – Boredom is a consequence of monotony.

CREATOR/CREATION

- Carpenter : House – A carpenter builds a house.
- Painter : Portrait – A painter makes a portrait.
- Burroughs : Tarzan – Edgar Rice Burroughs wrote the novel Tarzan.

PROVIDER/PROVISION

- Job : Salary – A job provides a salary.
- Therapist : Treatment – A therapist treats patients.
- Army : Defense – An army enables national defense.

OBJECT/FUNCTION

- Pencil : Write – A pencil is used to write.
- Pressure : Barometer – A barometer measures pressure.
- Frown : Unhappy – A frown shows unhappiness.

USER/TOOL

- Carpenter : Hammer – A carpenter uses a hammer.
- Teacher : Chalk – A teacher uses chalk.
- Farmer : Tractor – A farmer drives a tractor.

WHOLE/PART

- Door : House – A door is part of a house.
- State : Country – A country is made up of states.
- Day : Month – A month consists of many days.

GRAMMATICAL TRANSFORMATION

- Ran : Run – These are different tenses of the same verb.
- Die : Dice – These are singular and plural forms.
- We : Our – These are pronouns related to groups.

TRANSLATION

- Satan : Lucifer – These are both names for the devil.
- Bon Voyage : Farewell – These are the French and English words for goodbye.
- Japan : Nippon – These are two names for the same country.

CATEGORY

- Door : Window – Both a door and a window are parts of a house.
- Thigh : Shin – Both a thigh and a shin are parts of a leg.
- Measles : Mumps – Both measles and mumps are types of diseases.

SYNONYM OR DEFINITION

These are analogies in which both terms have a similar meaning.

- Chase : Pursue – Both of these terms mean to "go after".
- Achieve : Accomplish – Both of these terms refer to the successful attainment of a goal.
- Satiate : Satisfy – Both of these terms mean to gratify a desire.

ANTONYM OR CONTRAST

These are analogies in which both terms have an opposite meaning.

- Disguise : Reveal – To disguise something is not to reveal it, but to conceal it.
- Peace : War – Peace is a state in which there is no war.
- Forget : Remember – The word "remember" means not to forget something.

INTENSITY

These are analogies in which either one term expresses a higher degree of something than the other term.

- Exuberant : Happy – To be exuberant is to be extremely happy.
- Break : Shatter – To shatter is to strongly break.
- Deluge : Rain – A deluge is a heavy rain.

WHAT STRATEGIES CAN I USE?

A huge vocabulary is not necessary to succeed on analogy questions (though it certainly doesn't hurt). In most cases though, you can determine the answer even if you don't recognize all the words. The strategies listed here will help you develop the ability to recognize basic relationships and apply simple steps and methods to solving them.

DETERMINE THE RELATIONSHIP

Don't focus on the meanings, but rather the relationship between the two words.

To understand the relationship, first create a sentence that links the two words and puts them into perspective. The sentence that you use to connect the words can be simple at first.

- Example:
- WOOD is to FIRE
- *Wood* feeds a *fire*.

Then go through each answer choice and replace the words with the answer choices. If the question is easy, then that may be all that is necessary. If the question is hard, you might have to fine-tune your sentence.

- Example:
- FIRE is to WOOD as COW is to (*a.* GRASS, *b.* FARMER)

Using the initial sentence, you would state "Grass feeds a cow." This is correct, but then so is the next answer choice "Farmer feeds a cow." So, which is right? Modify the sentence to be more specific.

- Example: "Wood feeds a fire and is consumed."

This modified sentence makes answer choice B incorrect and answer choice A clearly correct, because while "grass feeds a cow and is consumed" is correct, "farmer feeds a cow and is consumed" is definitely wrong.

If your initial sentence seems correct with more than one answer choice, then keep modifying it until only one answer choice makes sense.

SIMILAR CHOICES

If you don't know the word, don't worry. Look at the answer choices and just use them. Remember that three of the answer choices will always be wrong. If you can find a common relationship between any three answer choices, then you know they are all wrong. Find the answer choice that does not have a common relationship to the other answer choices and it will be the correct answer.

- Example:
- TOUGH is to RUGGED as HARD is to (*a*. SOFT, *b*. EASY, *c*. DELICATE, *d*. RIGID)

In this example the first three choices are all opposites of the term "hard". Even if you don't know that rigid means the same as hard, you know it must be correct, because the other three all had the same relationship. They were all opposites, so they must all be wrong. The one that has a different relationship from the other three must be correct. So, don't worry if you don't know a word. Focus on the answer choices that you do understand and see if you can identify common relationships. Even identifying two word pairs with the same relationship (for example, two word pairs that are both opposites) will allow you to eliminate those two answer choices, for they are both wrong.

A simple way to remember this is that if you have two or more answer choices with the exact same relationship, then they are both or all wrong.

- Example: (a. neat, *b*. orderly)

Since the two answer choices above are synonyms and therefore have the same relationship with the matching term, then you know that they both must be wrong, because they both can't be correct, and for all intents and purposes they are the same word.

Be sure to read all of the choices. You may find an answer choice that seems right at first, but continue reading and you may find a better choice.

Difficult words are usually synonyms or antonyms (opposites). Whenever you have extremely difficult words that you don't understand, look at the answer choices. Try and identify whether two or more of the answer choices are either synonyms or antonyms. Remember that if you can find two word pairs that have the same relationship (for example, they are both synonyms) then you can eliminate them both.

ELIMINATE ANSWERS

Eliminate choices as soon as you realize they are wrong, but be careful! Make sure you consider all of the possible answer choices. Don't worry if you are stuck between two that seem right. By eliminating the other two possible choices, your odds are now 50/50. Rather than wasting too much time, play the odds. You are guessing, but guessing wisely, because you've been able to knock out some of the answer choices that you know are wrong. If you are eliminating choices and realize that the answer choice you are left with is also obviously wrong, don't panic. Start over and consider each choice again. There may easily be something you missed the first time and will realize on the second pass.

WORD TYPES

The correct answer choice will contain words that are the same type of word as those in the word pair.

- Example:
- ARTIST is to PAINTBRUSH

In this example, an artist is a person, while a paintbrush is an object. The correct answer will have one word that describes a person and another word that describes an object.

- Example:
- HEDGE is to GARDENER as ROCK is to (*a.* WIND, *b.* SCULPTOR)

In this example, you could create the sentence, "Gardener cuts away at hedges." Both answer choices seem correct with this sentence, "Wind cuts away at rocks" through the process of erosion, and "sculptor cuts away at rocks" using a hammer and chisel. The difference is that a gardener is a person, as is a sculptor, while the wind is a thing, which makes answer choice B correct.

NEARLY AND PERFECT OPPOSITES

When you have determined which pair of terms you should work with, and know that the provided pair is an opposite, then you must find the opposite of the remaining unmatched term. Nearly opposite may often be more correct, because the goal is to test your understanding of the nuances, or little differences, between words. A perfect opposite may not exist, so don't be concerned if your answer choice is not a complete opposite. Focus upon edging closer to the word. Eliminate the words that you know aren't correct first. Then narrow your search. Cross out the words that are the most similar to the main word until you are left with the one that is the least similar.

PREFIXES

Take advantage of every clue that the word might include. Prefixes and suffixes can be a huge help. Usually they allow you to determine a basic meaning. Pre- means before, post- means after, pro – is positive, de- is negative. From these prefixes and suffixes, you can get an idea of the general meaning of the word and look for its opposite. Beware though of any traps. Just because con is the opposite of pro, doesn't necessarily mean congress is the opposite of progress!

POSITIVE VS. NEGATIVE

Many words can be easily determined to be a positive word or a negative word. Words such as despicable, and gruesome, bleak are all negative. Words such as ecstatic, praiseworthy, and magnificent are all positive. You will be surprised at how many words can be viewed as either positive or negative. If you recognize a positive/negative relationship between the given pair of terms, then focus in on the answer choices that would duplicate that positive/negative relationship with the remaining term.

WORD STRENGTH

When analyzing a word, determine how strong it is. For example, stupendous and good are both positive words. However, stupendous is a much stronger positive adjective than good. Also, towering or gigantic are stronger words than tall or large. Search for an answer choice with either the same or opposite strength (depending on the relationship of the matched terms) to the remaining term.

TYPE AND TOPIC

Another key is what type of word is the unmatched term. If the unmatched term is an adjective describing height, then look for the answer choice to be an adjective describing height as well. Match both the type and topic of the main word. The type refers to the parts of speech, whether the word is an adjective, adverb, or verb. The topic refers to what the definition of the word includes, such as descriptive sizes (large, small, gigantic, etc.).

FORM A SENTENCE

Many words seem more natural in a sentence. *Specious* reasoning, *irresistible* force, and *uncanny* resemblance are just a few of the word combinations that usually go together. When faced with an uncommon word that you barely understand, try to put the word in a sentence that makes sense. It will help you to understand the word's meaning and make it easier to determine its relationship. Once you have a good descriptive sentence that utilizes a main term or answer choice properly, plug in the answer choice or main term and see if a solid relationship can be established.

USE LOGIC

Ask yourself questions about each answer choice to see if they are logical.

- Example:
- AROMAS is to SMELT as POUNDINGS is to (*a.* SEEN, *b.* HEARD)

Would poundings be "seen"? Or would pounding be "heard"? It can logically be deduced that poundings are heard.

THE TRAP OF FAMILIARITY

Don't just choose a word because you recognize it. On difficult questions, you may only recognize one or two words. There won't be any made up words on the test, so don't think that just because you only recognize one word means that word must be correct. If you don't recognize three words, then focus on the one that you do recognize. Is it correct? Try your best to determine if it fits the sentence you've created that shows the relationship between terms. If it does, that is great, but if it doesn't, eliminate it. Each word you eliminate increases your chances of getting the question correct.

TOUGH QUESTIONS

If you are stumped on a problem or it appears too hard or too difficult, don't waste time. Move on! Remember though, if you can quickly check for obviously incorrect answer choices, your chances of guessing correctly are greatly improved. Before you completely give up, at least try to knock out a couple of possible answers. Eliminate what you can and then guess at the remainder before moving on.

READ CAREFULLY

Understand the analogy. Read the terms and answer choices carefully. Don't miss the question because you misread the terms. There are only a few words in each question, so you can spend time reading them carefully. Yet a happy medium must be attained, so don't waste too much time. You must read carefully, but efficiently.

BRAINSTORM

If you get stuck on a difficult analogy, spend a few seconds quickly brainstorming. Run through the complete list of possible relationships. Break down each answer choice into all of the potential combinations with the two possible analogous terms. Since there are four answer choices and each answer choice could form a pair with one of two terms, there are only eight possible relationships to test. Look at each relationship and see if it would make sense. Test with sentences to determine if any relationship can be established. By systematically going through all possibilities, you may find something that you would otherwise overlook.

AFOQT: Situational Judgment

WHAT DO SITUATIONAL JUDGMENT QUESTIONS LOOK LIKE?

All situational judgment questions will have a similar format. Test takers will be given a scenario which requires some action to be taken to solve a problem that has come up, usually involving interpersonal and/or official relationships between an officer and his subordinates and/or his superiors. The test taker will then be shown several possible actions that could be taken, and will be told to select both the **most effective** and the **least effective** of the actions listed.

WHAT ARE SITUATIONAL JUDGMENT QUESTIONS TESTING?

This is a newer section of the AFOQT, added to make the test a better predictor of success as an Air Force officer. These questions are primarily focused on testing a person in the areas of judgment and self-sufficient decision-making abilities. In order to do well on this section, test takers will need to show that they can lead subordinates and solve problems independently by using their core competencies of resource management, communication, innovation, mentoring, leadership, professionalism, and integrity.

HOW CAN I PREPARE?

Situational judgment questions aren't the kind of questions that lend themselves easily to preparation, as there really isn't any material for a person to review and memorize. However, you should keep in mind the qualities listed above (resource management, communication, innovation, mentoring, leadership, professionalism, and integrity) when answering questions. Your answers should reflect these qualities as much as possible. Also, you should avoid choosing any answer which involves going to a superior for advice or help unless there are no other viable options, or discussing a person's shortcomings behind their back no matter their rank. Officers are expected to be resourceful men and women of character.

AFOQT: Physical Science

WHAT DO PHYSICAL SCIENCE QUESTIONS LOOK LIKE?

Physical science questions primarily test your understanding of scientific terms. You won't be asked to perform complex physics calculations or balance a chemical reaction. The purpose of this section is to make sure you paid attention in high school science and retained some of the general concepts.

HOW CAN I PREPARE?

The best way to prepare for these questions is to brush up on your science terminology and concepts. We've included a glossary of terms here to give you head start, but it's a good idea to find a high school physical science textbook and look through the full glossary in there if you want a more thorough review.

A

Absolute zero: The lowest possible temperature (-273.15°C).

Atmospheric pressure: The pressure exerted by the gases in the air. Units of measurement are kilopascals (kPa), atmospheres (atm), millimeters of mercury (mm Hg) and Torr. Standard atmospheric pressure is 100 kPa, 1atm, 760 mm Hg or 760 Torr.

Atom: The smallest particle of an element; a nucleus and its surrounding electrons.

Atomic mass: The mass of an atom measured in atomic mass units (amu). An atomic mass unit is equal to one-twelfth of the atom of carbon-12. Atomic mass is now more generally used instead of atomic weight. Example: the atomic mass of chlorine is about 35 amu.

Atomic number: Also known as proton number, it is the number of electrons or the number of protons in an atom. Example: the atomic number of gold is 79.

Atomic weight: A common term used to mean the average molar mass of an element. This is the mass per mole of atoms. Example: the atomic weight of chlorine is about 35 g/mol.

B

Boiling point: The temperature at which a substance undergoes a phase change from a liquid to a gas.

C

Celsius scale (°C): A temperature scale on which the freezing point of water is at 0 degrees and the normal boiling point at standard atmospheric pressure is 100 degrees.

Change of state: A change between two of the three states of matter, solid, liquid and gas. Example: when water evaporates it changes from a liquid to a gaseous state.

Compound: A chemical consisting of two or more elements chemically bonded together. Example: Calcium can combine with carbon and oxygen to make calcium carbonate ($CaCO_3$), a compound of all three elements.

Condensation: The formation of a liquid from a gas. This is a change of state, also called a phase change.

Conduction: (i) the exchange of heat (heat conduction) by contact with another object, or (ii) allowing the flow of electrons (electrical conduction).

Convection: The exchange of heat energy with the surroundings produced by the flow of a fluid due to being heated or cooled.

D

Decay (radioactive decay): The way that a radioactive element changes into another element due to loss of mass through radiation. Example: uranium 238 decays with the loss of an alpha particle to form thorium 234.

Density: The mass per unit volume (e.g. g/cm^3).

Diffusion: The slow mixing of one substance with another until the two substances are evenly mixed. Mixing occurs because of differences in concentration within the mixture. Diffusion works rapidly with gases, very slowly with liquids.

Dissolve: To break down a substance in a solution without causing a reaction.

E

Electrical potential: The energy produced by an electrochemical cell and measured by the voltage or electromotive force (emf).

Electron: A tiny, negatively charged particle that is part of an atom. The flow of electrons through a solid material such as a wire produces an electric current.

Element: A substance that cannot be decomposed into simpler substance by chemical means. Examples: calcium, iron, gold.

Explosive: A substance which, when a shock is applied to it, decomposes very rapidly, releasing a very large amount of heat and creating a large volume of gases as a shock wave.

F

Fluid: Able to flow; either a liquid or a gas.

Freezing point: The temperature at which a substance undergoes a phase change from a liquid to a solid. It is the same temperature as the melting point. At any temperature below this point the substance will freeze.

G

Gamma rays: Waves of radiation produced as the nucleus of a radioactive element rearranges itself into a tighter cluster of protons and neutrons. Gamma rays carry enough energy to damage living cells.

Gas/gaseous phase: A form of matter in which the molecules form no definite shape and are free to move about to uniformly fill any vessel they are put in. A gas can easily be compressed into a much smaller volume.

256

Group: A vertical column in the Periodic Table. There are eight groups in the table. Their numbers correspond to the number of electrons in the outer shell of the atoms in the group. Example: Group 2 contains beryllium, magnesium, calcium, strontium, barium and radium.

H

Half-life: The time it takes for the radiation coming from a sample of a radioactive element to decrease by half.

Heat: The energy that is transferred when a substance is at a different temperature to that of its surroundings.

Heat capacity: The ratio of the heat supplied to a substance, compared with the rise in temperature that is produced.

Heat of combustion: The amount of heat given off by a mole of a substance during combustion. This heat is a property of the substance and is the same no matter what kind of combustion is involved. Example: heat of combustion of carbon is 94.05 kcal (x 4.18 kJ/kcal = 393.1 kJ).

I

Ion: An atom, or group of atoms, that has gained or lost one or more electrons and so developed an electrical charge. Ions behave differently from electrically neutral atoms and molecules. They can move in an electric field, and they can also bind strongly to solvent molecules such as water. Positively charged ions are called cations; negatively charged ions are called anions. Ions can carry an electrical current through solutions.

Isotope: One of two or more atoms of the same element that have the same number of protons in their nucleus (atomic number), but which have a different number of neutrons (atomic mass). Example: carbon-12 and carbon-14.

K

Kinetic energy: The energy an object has by virtue of its being in motion.

L

Latent heat: The amount of heat that is absorbed or released during the process of changing state between gas, liquid or solid. For example, heat is absorbed when a substance melts and it is released again when the substance solidifies.

Liquid/liquid phase: A form of matter that has a fixed volume but no fixed shape.

M

Mass: The amount of matter in an object. In everyday use the word weight is often used (somewhat incorrectly) to mean mass.

Matter: Anything that has mass and takes up space.

Melting point: The temperature at which a substance changes state from a solid phase to a liquid phase. It is the same as freezing point. At any temperature above this point the substance will melt.

Metal: A class of elements that is a good conductor of electricity and heat, has a metallic luster, is malleable and ductile, forms cations and has oxides that are bases. Metals are formed as cations held together by a sea of electrons. A metal may also be an alloy of these elements. Example: sodium, calcium, gold.

Mixture: A material that can be separated into two or more substances using physical means. Example: a mixture of copper (II) sulfate and cadmium sulfide can be separated by filtration.

Mole: 1 mole is the amount of a substance which contains Avogadro's number (about 6×10^{23}) of particles. Example: 1 mole of carbon-12 weighs exactly 12 g.

Molecule: A group of two or more atoms held together by chemical bonds. Example: O_2.

N

Neutron: A particle inside the nucleus of an atom that is neutral and has no charge.

Newton (N): The unit of force required to give one kilogram an acceleration of one meter per second every second (1 m/s^2).

Noble gases: The members of Group 8 of the Periodic Table: helium, neon, argon, krypton, xenon, and radon. These gases are almost entirely unreactive.

Nucleus: The small, positively charged particle at the centre of an atom. The nucleus is responsible for most of the mass of an atom.

P

Period: A row in the Periodic Table.

Periodic Table: A chart organizing elements by atomic number and chemical properties into groups and periods.

Phase: A particular state of matter. A substance may exist as a solid, liquid or gas and may change between these phases with addition or removal of energy. Examples: ice, liquid and vapor are the three phases of water. Ice undergoes a phase change to water when heat energy is added.

Photon: A parcel of light energy.

Potential energy: The energy an object has by virtue of its position or orientation, most commonly its height above some reference point, or amount of compression as with a spring.

Pressure: The force per unit area measured in Pascals.

Proton: A positively charged particle in the nucleus of an atom that balances out the charge of the surrounding electrons.

R

Radiation: The exchange of energy with the surroundings through the transmission of waves or particles of energy. Radiation is a form of energy transfer that can happen through space; no intervening medium is required (as would be the case for conduction and convection).

S

Solid/solid phase: A rigid form of matter which maintains its shape, whatever its container.

AFOQT: Table Reading

WHAT ARE THESE QUESTIONS TESTING?

The table reading section tests your ability to quickly and accurately locate information stored in a table. The questions require you to find a particular number in a table given a set of coordinates.

WHAT IS THE QUESTION FORMAT?

The questions will be given in groups of around 5 questions, where each group will refer to a table of numbers, with column and row headers. Each question will give an ordered pair of numbers that indicate the location in the table where the correct answer can be found. The ordered pair is given in the form (x, y), where x is the column number and y is the row number.

The questions will be presented like this:

	-3	-2	-1	0	1	2	3
3	41	39	84	77	35	42	37
2	75	57	95	16	93	16	15
1	34	54	50	89	26	19	94
0	66	89	65	23	13	42	20
-1	15	97	86	76	76	58	92
-2	80	92	78	52	90	11	56
-3	88	81	61	79	35	64	52

1. (3, -2)
- a. 56
- b. 39
- c. 64
- d. 11
- e. 92

To answer the question, look at the ordered pair. It indicates that the number you are looking for is in the column labeled 3, and the row labeled -2. In this table, that number is 56, answer choice A.

WHAT STRATEGIES CAN I USE TO ANSWER THE QUESTIONS QUICKLY AND ACCURATELY?

The best way to approach these questions is methodically. Take the first number in the ordered pair and find it on the column headers. Keep your finger on that number while you take the second number of the ordered pair and locate it on the row headers. Put another finger on that number. Drag the first finger straight down the column until you get to the row that your other finger is on. The number at the intersection of the indicated column and row is your answer.

If you find yourself staring at the table for too long trying to be sure that you've selected the right number, you may find it helpful to draw lines on the graph, or take two pieces of scratch paper and line up their edges with the column and row numbers given in the question so that the number you are looking for appears at the corner where the two pieces of paper come together.

WHAT ARE THE COMMON MISTAKES TO AVOID?

Since the process for answering these questions is very straightforward, most errors are the result of trying to go too quickly. The more you practice these sorts of questions, the faster you will be able to accurately answer them. Once you've practiced for a while, you'll be able to get a feel for how fast you can go while accurately answering all the questions. On test day, force yourself to go no faster than this.

One common mistake made on these questions is taking the ordered pair in the question to be ordinal coordinates rather than numbers referencing the column and row labels. For example, suppose a question asks for the ordered pair (1, 2). Under the pressure of the test, many people will instinctively go to the first column and second row, and take that number. Don't succumb to pressure on the test. Just follow the procedure and work through the questions at your ideal speed.

AFOQT: Instrument Comprehension

WHAT ARE THESE QUESTIONS TESTING?

These questions are designed to test your familiarity with and understanding of common instruments.

WHAT IS THE QUESTION FORMAT?

The question format will vary depending on the types of instruments that the test covers. This section of the book will focus on the compass and the artificial horizon, two instruments commonly used in airplanes.

Test questions related to these instruments will illustrate a compass and an artificial horizon inside an airplane cockpit. Based on the readings of both of these instruments, you will have to determine the position and orientation of the airplane.

HOW DO I READ THE COMPASS AND ARTIFICIAL HORIZON INSTRUMENTS?

The compass, a relatively intuitive instrument with which many people are familiar, shows which direction a person or vehicle is facing. When a person is facing north, for example, the needle on the compass points toward the "N." If the person is facing a direction between south and southeast, the needle will point between "S" and "SE."

The artificial horizon is an instrument that shows how the nose and wings of a plane are tilted. For most people, the artificial horizon is less intuitive and less familiar than the compass. However, if you imagine yourself actually flying in a plane, the artificial horizon becomes easier to read and understand.

The artificial horizon has two components that illustrate how the nose of an airplane is tilted with respect to the ground: the miniature wings and the horizon bar. The miniature wings represent the actual wings of the aircraft, and the horizon bar represents the horizon, the imaginary line that divides the ground and the sky from the pilot's point of view. When the miniature wings are level with the horizon bar, the plane is level. When the miniature wings are above the horizon bar, the plane is tilted upward, and when the miniature wings are below the horizon bar, the plane is tilted downward. These categories of nose tilt are shown in the drawing below.

To illustrate how the wings are tilted from side to side, the artificial horizon instrument also has a dial with degree marks representing the bank angle. A needle on the dial indicates the exact bank angle, and the horizon bar is tilted accordingly, as shown in the picture below. If the left wing of the plane is tilted downward, the needle will be to the right of the center of the dial; if the right wing is tilted downward; the needle will be to the left of the center. Note that the tilted horizon bar reflects the pilot's point of view: if the left wing of the plane is tilted downward, the horizon will appear to be tilted in the opposite direction.

To answer the questions on this test, you will have to use information from both the compass and artificial horizon to determine how the plane is oriented. If the plane is flying north, it will appear to fly into the page in the illustrations.

For example, based on the compass and artificial horizon shown below, which of the answer choices represents the orientation of the plane?

ANSWER: The answer is A. First, notice that the compass is pointing in a west-southwest direction. If a north-flying plane is facing into the page, then a westbound plane will be facing left. The compass indicates that the plane is flying somewhere between west and southwest, so the illustration will show a plane that appears to be facing left and just slightly out of the page.

Second, notice that the miniature wings in the artificial horizon are above the horizon line, and the needle on the dial is to the left of the center. From this information, you know that 1) the nose of the plane is tilted upward, and 2) the left wing of the plane is tilted upward, and the right wing is tilted downward. Because only the plane illustrated in choice A fits this description, it is the correct answer.

HOW CAN I IMPROVE MY ABILITY TO READ THE COMPASS AND ARTIFICIAL HORIZON?

Most people don't encounter these instruments on an everyday basis, so the best way to improve your ability to read them is simply to do the practice question in this section. However, although the artificial horizon is not commonly found outside of aircraft, you might want to practice using a real compass if you are still having trouble with these questions. You can find a reasonably-priced compass at most outdoor or sporting goods stores.

AFOQT: Block Counting

WHAT ARE THESE QUESTIONS TESTING?

These questions are designed to test your spatial, geometric, and logical abilities.

WHAT IS THE QUESTION FORMAT?

The test will show a drawing of a three-dimensional arrangement of blocks with the same size and shape, and ask you to identify how many other blocks a particular block is touching. Typically, the blocks are arranged in irregular shapes, and some of the blocks are hidden. You will have to use spatial intuition and reasoning to determine how many blocks are touching the block in question.

HOW DO I KNOW HOW MANY BLOCKS ARE TOUCHING THE PARTICULAR BLOCK?

First, it is important to know which blocks qualify as "touching" the other block. If at least part of a face of one block touches at least part of a face of another block, those blocks are considered to touch each other. However, if a block shares only a corner or an edge with another block, the two blocks do not touch.

The example below illustrates the difference between touching and non-touching blocks. Block A is touching blocks 1, 2, and 3 because part of a face of block A is touching each of these blocks. However, blocks 4 and 5 do *not* touch block A because they only contact block A at an edge; that is, they share no area with any faces of block A. Therefore, block A is touching three blocks in this picture.

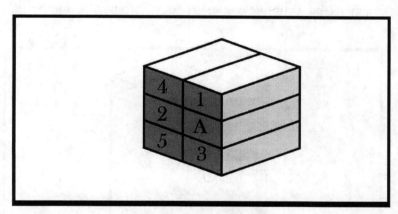

Sometimes, the blocks may be positioned so that certain blocks are hidden from view. In these cases, you will have to use basic spatial intuition and logic to determine the number of blocks touching a particular block.

In the example below, try to figure out how many blocks are touching block A.

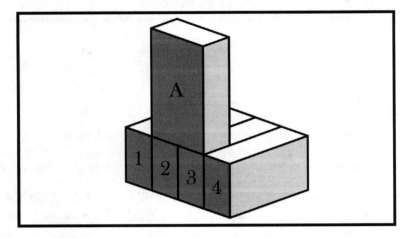

Answer: There are two blocks touching block A. Even though blocks 1 and 4 each share an edge with block A, they do not "touch" block A, as the word is used in the context of the test. Only blocks 2 and 3 actually touch a face of block A, so block A is only touching two blocks.

ARE THERE ANY WAYS TO MAKE IT EASIER TO COUNT THE NUMBER OF TOUCHING BLOCKS?

Remember that for a block to count as "touching," it much contact a face of that block. Therefore, it might help to count the number of blocks that are touching each face of the block in question.

Try to apply this strategy to the example below, in order to count the number of blocks touching block A.

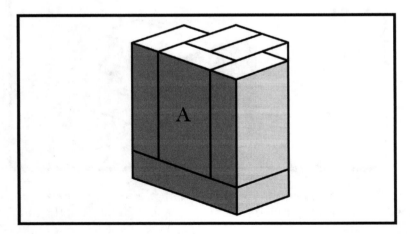

Answer: The back face of block A is touching two blocks. The left face of block A is touching one block, as is the right side. The bottom face is touching one block. Therefore, block A is touching a total of five blocks.

If you are still having trouble with the practice questions, it might help to try to re-create the example problems with a set of rectangular blocks. Practicing with physical blocks will make it easier to visualize hidden blocks when the blocks are drawn on paper.

AFOQT: Aviation Information

WHAT ARE THESE QUESTIONS TESTING?

The aviation information section tests your knowledge of basic aviation information. This includes a variety of things including aircraft terminology, the basic physics involved in flight, and common airport information.

HOW CAN I IMPROVE MY ABILITY TO ANSWER THESE QUESTIONS?

Since these are all knowledge-based questions, you can improve your success rate here by reading up on aircraft operation and airport information. The section below is an overview of the basics in these areas.

FIXED-WING AIRCRAFT

There are six basic components of a fixed-wing aircraft: wings; fuselage; tail assembly; landing gear; powerplant; and flight controls and control surfaces.

WINGS

The **wings** are the primary airfoils of the plane. An airfoil is anything designed to produce lift when it moves through the air. The leading edge of an airfoil is thicker and rounder than the trailing edge, and the top surface of the airfoil has a greater curve than the bottom. The result is that air flows more quickly over the top of the wing, and the greater air pressure beneath pushes the wing, and thus the plane, upwards.

The wings connect to either side of the fuselage. Planes are designated as high-, mid-, and low-wing, depending on where the wings are attached. The wings themselves are described as either cantilever or semi-cantilever. A cantilever wing has sufficient internal support structures to keep it steady in its location. A semi-cantilever wing, on the other hand, requires additional external support structures. The trailing edge of a wing typically has two control surfaces attached by means of a hinge: flaps run from the fuselage to the middle of the wing, and ailerons run from the middle of the wing to the tip. By raising and lowering the flaps and ailerons, the pilot can roll the plane. The plane will roll when the ailerons and flaps are pointed in opposite directions. When the plane is cruising, however, these control surfaces are aligned with the rest of the wing. During takeoff and landing, both surfaces are extended, which increases the lift.

The distance from one wingtip to the other is the wingspan, and the distance from the leading edge to the trailing edge is called the chord. The chord line runs through the wing from leading edge to trailing edge: it divides the wing into upper and lower surfaces. The mean camber line runs along the inside of the wing, such that the parts of the wing above and below it are equal in thickness. The camber is the curvature of the airfoil: if an airfoil is heavily curved, it has a high camber. The thickness of a wing is measured at its greatest point. The shape of the wings when viewed from overhead is known as the planform.

When the wings are not attached parallel to the horizontal plane, the angle they make with the horizontal plane is called the dihedral angle. A positive dihedral wing angle (wings angling above the horizontal plane) keeps the plane stable when it rolls, as it will encourage the plane to return to its original position. This does diminish the maneuverability of the plane, which is why the wings of fighter jets are usually horizontal or even pointed slightly downwards (anhedral).

The shape of the wings has a major influence on the handling, maneuverability, and speed of the plane. Today's planes generally have a straight, sweep, or delta shape. Straight wings may be rectangular, elliptical (rounded), or tapered. They are commonly found on sailplanes, gliders, and other low-speed aircraft.

A swept wing provides better handling at high speeds, but makes the plane slightly less stable at low speeds. Since most modern aircraft are designed to operate at high speeds, this is the most commonly used wing style. Wings may be swept forward or back, though forward-swept wings are rarely seen. In general, a higher angle of sweep is used for planes that are meant to travel faster and be more maneuverable; however, more extreme sweeps require much greater speeds for takeoff and landing.

The delta wing shape is triangular, so that the leading edge of the wing has a high sweep angle while the trailing edge is mostly, if not completely, straight. A delta shape enables the plane to travel but also requires very high takeoff and landing speeds. Many of the earliest supersonic aircraft used the delta wing shape, as did the space shuttles.

FUSELAGE

The **fuselage** is the main body of the airplane. The basic features of the fuselage are the cockpit, cabin, cargo area, and attachment points for external components, like the wings and landing gear. Some planes designed for specific purposes may not have all of these components; for instance, a fighter jet will not have a cabin for passengers or a cargo area, since it needs to be light and maneuverable. The fuselage may be described as either truss or monocoque, depending on whether its strength is created by triangular arrangements of steel or aluminum tubing or by bulkheads, stringers and formers. A stringer is a support structure that runs the length of the fuselage, while a former runs perpendicular.

TAIL ASSEMBLY

The **tail assembly**, or empennage, includes the vertical and horizontal stabilizers, elevators, rudders, and trim tabs. The stabilizers are fixed (non-adjustable) surfaces that extend from the back end of the fuselage. The elevators are positioned along the trailing edges of the horizontal stabilizers; the pilot can move them to raise or lower the nose of the plane. The rudders are connected to the trailing edge of the vertical stabilizer, and are used to move the nose of the plane to the left or right, typically in combination with the ailerons. The **trim tabs** are movable surfaces that extend off the trailing edges of the rudder, elevators, and ailerons and are used to make smaller adjustments.

LANDING GEAR

The **landing gear** usually consists of three sets of wheels used for takeoffs and landings, though some planes have special non-wheel landing gear for landing on snow or water. Landing gear is commonly retractable, meaning that it is pulled up inside the plane during flight to reduce drag. In a typical arrangement, wheel sets are positioned either under each wing or on the sides of the fuselage, with the third wheel set being under the nose or the tail. The most common arrangement on modern aircraft is the **tricycle** arrangement, which has the third wheel set under the nose, but having the third wheel set under the tail is still known as the **conventional** arrangement. Whether located under the tail or the nose, the third wheel will typically be able to rotate so that the plane can turn while traveling on the ground. The addition of extra wheels to each set allows the plane to handle a greater weight.

POWERPLANT

In aviation, the **powerplant** is the part of the plane that supplies the thrust. A jet engine operates by compressing the air that comes in the front, burning it along with fuel, and then blasting it out the back. There are different methods for compressing the air, but most jet engines do so by slowing it down with a set of small rotating blades. This greatly increases the air pressure at the front of the engine. The compressed air is then forced into a different section, where it is mixed with fuel and burned. As it then expands, it is pushed at great force through a series of turbines, the turning of which moves the compressor blades at the front of the engine, supplying both power and air. The exhausted air then passes out the back of the engine, which propels the plane forward. Some jet engines have afterburners, which feed extra fuel into the area between the turbines and the rear exhaust, increasing forward thrust.

In a propeller plane, on the other hand, the powerplant is the propellers and the engine. The propellers have tilted blades, which push air backwards and thereby push the plane forward. There are two types of propeller: fixed-pitch or variable-pitch. The blade angle of a fixed-pitch propeller cannot be adjusted by the pilot. Variable-pitch propellers allow the pilot, usually indirectly via the plane's control systems, to adjust the pitch of the propeller blades to alter the amount of thrust being generated. Some variable-pitch propellers are designed to operate only at a single rotational speed, allowing the engine to be much simpler and more efficient, so the amount of thrust is controlled entirely by the pitch of the blades. These are known as constant-speed propellers.

The engines of a propeller plane turn the crankshafts, which turn the propellers. The engines also are responsible for powering the plane's electrical system. The location of the engines on a propeller plane may vary. Single-engine planes typically have their engines in front of the fuselage, while multi-engine planes usually have their engines underneath the wings. Some multi-engine planes have engines in both locations.

FLIGHT ENVELOPE

During flight, there are four forces a pilot must manage: lift, gravity, thrust, and drag. These forces act downward (gravity), upward (lift), forward (thrust), and backward (drag). The collective input of these forces is known as the flight envelope.

GRAVITY

The weight of a plane is the primary force that must be overcome for flight to take place. The force of **gravity** on a given object is the same, regardless of orientation, though it varies slightly with large changes in altitude.

Aviation experts distinguish between different types of weight. The basic weight includes the aircraft and any internal or external equipment that will remain a part of the plane during flight. The operating weight is the basic weight plus the crew and any other nonexpendable items not included in the basic weight. The gross weight is the total weight of the aircraft and all contents at any given time. The weight of the airplane when it has no usable fuel is called the zero-fuel weight.

LIFT

In order to overcome gravity, the plane must generate **lift**. Lift is the upward force of air pressure on the aircraft, primarily the wings, that allows it to achieve and maintain altitude. In order to generate lift, the plane typically must be traveling forward at considerable speed.

If the wing tilts too far back the airflow may stop over the wing's upper surface, which will result in a rapid loss of altitude and often control of the plane. This is known as a stall, and it may be avoided by decreasing the angle of attack, so that normal airflow over the top of the wing is not interrupted.

THRUST

The speed required for generating lift is provided by the aircraft's **thrust**. It ensures that the aircraft is able to continue moving forward at sufficient speed to generate lift. As was discussed in the previous section, thrust is generated by the powerplant of the aircraft, usually one or more jet engines or propellers.

DRAG

An aircraft's thrust is countered by **drag**, the resistance to forward movement provided by the air that the aircraft is traveling through. At anything above normal walking or running speeds, air resistance is a noticeable hindrance to motion, and it only increases as airspeed goes up. The primary implication that this has on aircraft is that the faster the aircraft goes, the more thrust is required just to overcome the drag and maintain a constant speed.

There are two types of drag: profile drag and induced drag. Profile drag is the drag that exists when any object moves through the air. It is the result of the plane pushing air aside as it moves. Profile drag can be minimized by designing the aircraft to have a better wind profile. Induced drag, on the other hand, is drag that results from the wings generating lift. Part of the process of generating lift involves the wings redirecting the oncoming air downward (think Newton's third law), and this causes additional drag.

ATMOSPHERIC CONDITIONS

The flight envelope is significantly affected by the atmospheric conditions, primarily the density of the surrounding air and the speed and direction of any wind. The density is turn determined by the temperature, pressure, and humidity of the air. Lower temperatures, higher pressures, and lower humidity are all associated with higher density air. Denser air will produce greater lift, but will also produce more drag. Air pressure is most closely associated with altitude. In general, pressure decreases with altitude, so as you go higher up, the pressure of the surrounding air decreases.

With regard to wind, flying into the wind (headwind) has a similar type of impact to flying in denser air, though of much greater magnitude. In a headwind, the aircraft will have a higher speed relative to the surrounding air, which means it will experience greater drag and lift forces. Similarly, if the aircraft is flying the same direction as the wind (tailwind), it will have a lower speed relative to the surrounding air, and will experience reduced drag and lift.

FLIGHT CONCEPTS AND TERMINOLOGY
FLIGHT ATTITUDE

The flight attitude is described in terms of three axes, all of which meet at the plane's center of mass.

The **longitudinal** axis is the axis that extends from the center forward toward the nose and rearward toward the tail. The **lateral** axis extends from the center out to the right and left, perpendicular to the longitudinal axis. Typically, the lateral axis passes through (over/under) the wings. Both of these axes are in the horizontal plane when the aircraft is level. The **vertical** axis meanwhile extends straight upward and downward from the aircraft's center, perpendicular to the horizontal plane of the other two axes. The motion of the aircraft can be described in relation to these axes: Rotation about the longitudinal axis is called roll; rotation about the lateral axis is called pitch; rotation about the vertical axis is called yaw. In turn, these three types of motion are controlled by three sets of flight control surfaces. Roll is controlled by the ailerons, pitch by the elevators, and yaw by the rudder. This information is summarized in the table below, and is expanded upon in the following section.

Axis	Motion	Control surface
Longitudinal	Roll	Ailerons
Lateral	Pitch	Elevators
Vertical	Yaw	Rudder

FLIGHT CONTROLS

Flight controls are divided into primary and secondary groups.

PRIMARY

The primary **flight control surfaces** are the ailerons, rudder, and elevator.

The **ailerons** are responsible for the roll, or movement around the longitudinal axis. The ailerons extend from the trailing edges of the wings as shown in the figure below. They can be manipulated by the pilot to cause the wing to either dip below or elevate above the horizontal plane.

The joystick (or control wheel) controls the roll of the aircraft. By pushing the stick (or turning the wheel) to the left, the pilot raises the left aileron and lowers the right aileron, causing the left wing to dip and the right wing to elevate.

The **elevators** control the plane's pitch, or movement around the lateral axis. They are attached to the trailing edges of the horizontal stabilizers at the rear of the aircraft. Depending on the design of the plane, there may be one elevator that extends across the length of the horizontal stabilizer, or

271

there may be two elevators, divided by the vertical stabilizer, as shown in the figure below. When the elevators are undivided, they are sometimes referred to as a stabilator.

The joystick also controls the pitch of the aircraft. By pulling the stick back, the pilot raises the elevators, causing the tail of the plane to experience downward force, thus raising the nose of the plane. Pushing the stick forward will have the opposite effect on the elevators and will result in the nose of the plane dropping as the tail is pushed upward.

The **rudder** is a large flap attached by a hinge to the vertical stabilizer. It controls the motion of the plane around its vertical axis. The rudder can swing to the right or the left, causing the plane to turn (yaw) in either direction.

The rudder is controlled with two pedals: when the pilot pushes on the right pedal, the rudder swings out to the right, causing leftward pressure on the tail of the aircraft. This results in the nose of the plane turning to the right. Similarly, if the pilot pushes on the left pedal, the rudder will swing to the left, causing the tail to move right, and the nose to turn left.

The pilot also controls the amount of power or thrust being produced by the engines by manipulating the **throttle**. It is considered a primary flight control because the pilot must manage the thrust to ensure that the plane will be able to accomplish its intended maneuvers. With all three of the primary control surfaces, it is important to remember that the speed of the aircraft relative to the surrounding air determines the magnitude of the aircraft's response to the control. A plane that is traveling at 300 mph will roll much more quickly than one that is traveling at 200 mph in response to the same amount of aileron manipulation. The same is true of the other two types of motion.

Flight maneuvers usually involve the use of multiple controls. To make a proper turn, for instance, the pilot will need to employ the rudder, ailerons, and elevators. The bank is established by raising and lowering the ailerons, and the rudder pedals counteract any adverse yaw that occurs. Adverse yaw is the drifting of the nose caused by the extra drag on the downward-pointing aileron. Also, because extra lift is needed during a turn, the pilot must increase the angle of attack by applying downward elevator pressure. The amount of back elevator pressure required will be in proportion to the sharpness of the turn. This will be discussed in greater detail in the section on flight maneuvers.

SECONDARY

The secondary flight control surfaces include the flaps and leading-edge devices, spoilers, and trim systems.

The **flaps** are connected to the trailing edges of the wings; they are raised or lowered to adjust the lift or drag. The retractable flaps on modern airplanes make it possible to cruise at a high speed and land at a low speed. On the opposite end of the wing, **leading-edge devices** accomplish much the same purpose, they can increase camber, lift, or airflow, depending on the device. Both flaps and leading-edge devices reduce stall speed. There are a number of different leading-edge devices: fixed slats, moveable slats, and leading-edge flaps.

Spoilers are attached to the wings of some airplanes in order to diminish the lift and increase the drag. Spoilers can also be useful for roll control, in part because they reduce adverse yaw. This is accomplished by raising the spoiler on the side of the turn. This reduces the lift and creates more drag on that side, which causes that wing to drop and the plane to bank and yaw to that side. If both of the spoilers are raised at the same time, the plane can descend without increasing its speed. Raising the spoilers also improves the performance of the brakes, because they eliminate lift and push the plane down onto its wheels.

Trim systems exist mainly to ease the work of the pilot. They are attached to the trailing edges of one or more of the primary control surfaces. Small aircraft often have a single trim tab attached to the elevator. This tab is adjusted with a small wheel or crank, and its position is displayed in the cockpit. When the tab is deflected upwards, the trailing edge of the elevator is forced downward and the tail is pushed up, which lowers the nose of the plane.

Typically, a pilot first will achieve the desired pitch, power, attitude, and configuration, and then use the trim tabs to resolve the remaining control pressures. There are control pressures generated by any change in the flight condition, so trimming is necessary after any change. Trimming is complete when the pilot has eliminated any heaviness in the nose or tail of the plane.

FLIGHT MANEUVERS

The four basic maneuvers in flight are straight-and-level flight, turning, climbing, and descending. As the name suggests, **straight-and-level flight** involves keeping the aircraft headed in a particular direction at a particular altitude. Maintaining straight-and-level flight requires frequent adjustment, much the same way as the driver of a car has to make frequent adjustments to maintain a straight path on a windy day or when driving on a rough uneven road.

Making a smooth **turn** requires the use of all four primary controls: the throttle is set to achieve a speed suitable to the desired type of turn, the ailerons bank the wings and the elevators raise the nose to establish the rate of turn, and the rudder is employed to counter any undesired yaw resulting from the effects of the other controls or to introduce desired yaw.

There are three classes of turn: shallow, medium, and deep. A shallow turn has a bank of less than 20 degrees. At angles this shallow, most planes will tend to try to stabilize themselves back to a level angle, so the pilot must maintain some pressure on the stick to ensure that the plane doesn't pull out of the bank prematurely. A medium turn has a bank of roughly 20 to 45 degrees. Most planes will tend to stay in a medium bank until the pilot makes an adjustment. Finally, a steep turn is one in which the bank is greater than 45 degrees. For angles this steep, most planes will tend to try to increase the banking angle even further unless the pilot counters that tendency by maintaining some pressure on the stick in a stabilizing direction.

While the pilot is getting the plane to the desired bank angle, he will also be pulling back on the stick to ensure that the nose of the plane does not dip during the bank. This also serves to increase the rate at which the plane turns its heading. In general, the steeper the bank, the more sharply the pilot must pull back on the stick to maintain altitude. Because the lowered aileron on the raised wing generally creates more drag than the raised aileron on the lowered wing, the airplane tends to yaw in the direction opposite to the turn. For this reason, the pilot must at the same time apply rudder pressure in the direction of the turn.

To initiate a **climb**, an aircraft's nose is angled upward so that it gains altitude. Several things that remain constant while the aircraft is flying level change when the nose of the plane is raised. The two most significant are the effective angle of gravity and the angle of attack of the wings.

When the aircraft is level, gravity acts entirely in the direction of the vertical axis of the plane. When the plane angles upward, the force of gravity, which still acts straight down like before, now has a component in the longitudinal direction, since the rear of the plane is now pointed slightly toward the ground. Additionally, since raising the noise of the aircraft increases the angle of attack of the wings, the amount of **drag** the aircraft experiences goes up considerably during a climb. This means that, in order to maintain flight, the thrust must now overcome both an increased amount of drag and part of the force of gravity.

If the nose of the aircraft is raised too quickly or without a sufficient increase in thrust to account for the changing flight conditions, the aircraft may **stall**. The most common cause of a stall is the plane not generating enough thrust to maintain air speed, which means that the lift being generated by the wings is not sufficient to keep the plane in the air, so the plane ceases to fly in a practical sense and instead begins to fall. To correct a stall, the pilot must angle the nose of the aircraft steeply downward and increase the throttle to generate enough airspeed in the forward direction so that the control surfaces are effective in controlling the flight of the plane again, and pull out of the dive. As should be apparent from this description, recovering from a stall involves significant loss of altitude, which makes stalling at low altitudes extremely dangerous.

There are a few different styles of controlled **descent**, but they all involve manipulation of the same two factors: **pitch** and **thrust**. By angling the nose of the plane downward, the pilot reduces the angle of attack of the wings and consequently reduces the amount of lift generated by the wings. This causes the plane to lose altitude. Similarly, by pulling back on the throttle, the pilot reduces the amount of thrust being generated, which in turn reduces the plane's air speed and the amount of lift generated by the wings, also resulting in a loss of altitude.

A **glide** is a controlled descent in which little or no engine power is used, and the plane drifts downward at a regular pace. The pilot manages a glide by balancing the forces of lift and gravity as they act on the plane.

When a pilot is executing a **landing**, the nose of the plane will actually be angled upward, but the throttle will be pulled far back to ensure that the plane continues its descent all the way to the ground.

HELICOPTERS

In many ways, the operation of a helicopter is based on the same fundamentals as airplane flight. A helicopter is subject to the same four fundamental forces of lift, weight, thrust, and drag. Unlike an airplane, however, a helicopter applies most of its thrust vertically. When a helicopter flies at a constant speed in a stable horizontal path, the lift is equal to the weight and the forward thrust is equal to the drag. The helicopter will increase its horizontal speed if the thrust is greater than the drag, and will increase its altitude if the lift is greater than the weight. If the helicopter is hovering (i.e., not moving at all), there is no drag or forward thrust; only gravity and vertical thrust or lift, which are balanced.

The manner in which a helicopter generates lift is considerably different from that of an airplane. Whereas a plane derives its lift from the natural flow of air over the wing, the helicopter spins its "wing" rapidly and at a variable angle, giving it a variety of options for angles of attack. Because the main rotor of the helicopter is being torqued with such great force, it exerts the same amount of torque back on the fuselage of the helicopter but in the opposite direction (Newton's third law again). This necessitates a tail rotor to provide the force required to the keep the fuselage from spinning around while in flight. This function of the tail rotor is called **torque control**. Manipulation of the tail rotor is also used to change the heading of the helicopter.

HELICOPTER CONTROLS

Piloting a helicopter requires the use of three controls: the cyclic (stick), the collective, and the directional control system. The cyclic controls the longitudinal and lateral movement of the helicopter by adjusting the tilt of the main rotor. Moving the stick forward tilts the rotor forward, which in turn pushes the helicopter forward.

The collective is a tube running up from the cockpit floor to the left of the pilot. It has a handle that may be raised or lowered to affect the pitch, as well as a throttle that wraps around the handle and can be used to alter the engine torque. The collective controls the angle of the main rotor blades. If the handle is pulled up, the leading edge of the rotor blade lifts relative to the trailing edge.

The directional control system is a pair of pedals the pilot uses to alter the pitch of the tail rotor blades. Pressing one or the other of the pedals will cause the tail rotor to exert more or less force on the fuselage, which will in turn affect the heading of the helicopter.

A helicopter pilot must use all three of the controls at the same time. The cyclic and collective adjust the action of the main rotor, which must be compensated for with adjustment to the tail rotor. For instance, if the speed of the main rotor increases during a climb, the pilot will need to increase the amount of force generated by the tail rotor to ensure the fuselage does not begin to rotate.

If the helicopter loses engine power for some reason, the pilot will need to rely on autorotation, or the spinning of the rotors that is generated by airflow rather than the engine. The amount of torque on the fuselage will be smaller during autorotation, but it will still be enough to require the use of the tail rotor.

UNIQUE FORCES

A helicopter generates some other forces that distinguish it from an airplane. **Translational lift** is extra lift a helicopter experiences when traveling in a forward direction.

The **Coriolis force** is another physical phenomenon related to helicopters. The Coriolis force is the increase in rotational speed that occurs when the weight of a spinning object moves closer to the rotation center. In the case of a helicopter, having a greater portion of the weight closer to the base of the blade will cause the rotor to move faster, or to require less power to move at the same rotational speed.

If the main rotor increases the flow of air over the rear part of the main rotor disc, then the rear part will have a smaller angle of attack. The result of this will be less lift in the rear part of the rotor disc. This is called the **transverse flow effect**. However, when a force is applied to a spinning disc, the effects will occur ninety degrees later. This phenomenon is known as gyroscopic precession.

AIRPORT INFORMATION

At an **airport**, the areas controlled by the aircraft traffic controller are called the movement (or maneuvering) areas. These include the runways and taxiways. Runways may be composed of all different materials, ranging from grass and dirt to asphalt and concrete. At a general aviation airport, the runways may be as little as 800 feet long and 26 feet wide, while an international airport may have runways that are 18,000 feet long and 260 feet across. The markings on a runway are white, but are usually outlined in black so that they may be better seen. Taxiways and areas not meant to be traveled by aircraft are marked in yellow.

There are three basic types of runways: visual, nonprecision instrument, and precision instrument. **Visual runways** are typical of small airports: they have no markings, though the boundaries and center lines may be indicated in some way. They are called visual runways because the pilot must be able to see the ground in order to land. It is not possible to land a plane on a visual runway with only the use of instruments.

With a **nonprecision instrument runway**, a pilot may be able to make his approach using instruments. Specifically, this sort of runway can provide feedback on the horizontal position of the plane as it nears. Nonprecision instrument runways are commonly found at small and medium airports. These runways may have threshold markings, centerlines, and designators. These runways may also have a special mark, called an aiming point, between 1000 and 1500 feet long along the centerline of the runway.

Medium and large airports will have **precision instrument runways**, which give the pilot feedback on both horizontal and vertical position when the plane is on instrument approach. A precision instrument runway includes thresholds, designators, centerlines, aiming points, blast pads, stopways, and touchdown zone marks every 500 feet from the 500 foot to the 3000-foot mark.

Runways are named according to their **direction** on the compass, ranging from 01 to 36. So, for instance, due south would be runway 18 ("one-eight"), and due west would be runway 27 ("two-seven"). In North America, the runways are named in accordance with geographic (grid) north, rather than magnetic north. Of course, a runway may have two names, one for each direction in which it is used. The same runway may be referred to as runway 05 ("zero-five") or runway 23 ("two-three") depending on the direction it is being used on a given day. In most cases, fixed-wing aircraft take off and land against the wind, because the extra amount of air over the wing will increase lift (and reduce the required ground speed).

In the event that **multiple runways** travel in the same direction, they will be distinguished from each other by their relative positions according to an observer on approach from the appropriate direction: left or right runway if there are only two; left, right, or center runway if there are three. Of course, a runway that is on the right when travelling in one direction will be on the left when it is being used in the opposite direction.

In most cases, **runway lights** are operated by the airport control tower. There are a number of different components to a runway lighting system. A Runway Centerline Lighting System is a line of white lights mounted every fifty feet along the centerline. When the approaching plane gets within 3000 feet of the runway, the lights begin to blink red and white; when the plane gets within 1000 feet, the lights become solid red. Precision instrument runways have runway end lights and edge lights. Runway end lights run the width of both ends of the runway: from the ground these lights appear red, while they appear green from above. Runway edge lights run the length of the runway on both sides. This lighting typically changes color as well when the plane gets within a certain distance of the front end of the runway. There are similar lights marking the boundaries of taxiways. An Approach Lighting System is a set of strobelights and/or lightbars that indicate the end of the runway from which descending aircraft should arrive. Runway end identification lights are synchronized lights that flash at the runway thresholds. At some airports these lights face in every direction, while at others they only face the direction from which planes approach. Runway end identification lights are useful when the runway doesn't stand out from the surrounding area, or when visibility is poor.

Some big airports also have **Visual Approach Slope Indicators**, which give the incoming pilot useful information. In a typical VASI system, white lights indicate the lower glide path limits and red lights indicate the upper. The VASI should be visible for twenty miles at night, and for three to five miles during the day under normal conditions. An effective VASI should keep the plane clear of obstructions so long as it remains within approximately ten degrees of the extended runway centerline and within four nautical miles of the runway threshold.

ASVAB Practice Test

General Science

1. What is the name for any substance that stimulates the production of antibodies?

    a. collagen
    b. hemoglobin
    c. lymph
    d. antigen

2. Which of the following correctly lists the cellular hierarchy from the simplest to the most complex structure?

    a. tissue, cell, organ, organ system, organism
    b. organism, organ system, organ, tissue, cell
    c. organ system, organism, organ, tissue, cell
    d. cell, tissue, organ, organ system, organism

3. If a cell is placed in a hypertonic solution, what will happen to the cell?

    a. It will swell.
    b. It will shrink.
    c. It will stay the same.
    d. It does not affect the cell.

4. Which group of major parts and organs make up the immune system?

    a. lymphatic system, spleen, tonsils, thymus, and bone marrow
    b. brain, spinal cord, and nerve cells
    c. heart, veins, arteries, and capillaries
    d. nose, trachea, bronchial tubes, lungs, alveolus, and diaphragm

5. The rate of a chemical reaction depends on all of the following except

    a. temperature.
    b. surface area.
    c. presence of catalysts.
    d. amount of mass lost.

6. Which of the answer choices provided best defines the following statement?

For a given mass and constant temperature, an inverse relationship exists between the volume and pressure of a gas.

    a. Ideal Gas Law
    b. Boyle's Law
    c. Charles' Law
    d. Stefan-Boltzmann Law

7. Which of the following statements correctly compares prokaryotic and eukaryotic cells?

    a. Prokaryotic cells have a true nucleus, eukaryotic cells do not.
    b. Both prokaryotic and eukaryotic cells have a membrane.
    c. Prokaryotic cells do not contain membrane-bound organelles, eukaryotic cells do.
    d. Prokaryotic cells are more complex than eukaryotic cells.

8. What is the role of ribosomes?

    a. make proteins
    b. waste removal
    c. transport
    d. storage

9. If an organism is *AaBb*, which of the following combinations in the gametes is impossible?

    a. AB
    b. aa
    c. aB
    d. Ab

10. What is the oxidation number of hydrogen in CaH_2?

    a. +1
    b. −1
    c. 0
    d. +2

11. Which hormone stimulates milk production in the breasts during lactation?

    a. norepinephrine
    b. antidiuretic hormone
    c. prolactin
    d. oxytocin

12. What is the typical result of mitosis in humans?

    a. two diploid cells
    b. two haploid cells
    c. four diploid cells
    d. four haploid cells

13. Which of the following does *not* exist as a diatomic molecule?

    a. boron
    b. fluorine
    c. oxygen
    d. nitrogen

14. Which of the following structures has the lowest blood pressure?

    a. arteries
    b. arteriole
    c. venule
    d. vein

15. How does water affect the temperature of a living thing?

    a. Water increases temperature.
    b. Water keeps temperature stable.
    c. Water decreases temperature.
    d. Water does not affect temperature.

16. What is another name for aqueous HI?

    a. hydroiodate acid
    b. hydrogen monoiodide
    c. hydrogen iodide
    d. hydriodic acid

17. Which of the heart chambers is the most muscular?

    a. left atrium
    b. right atrium
    c. left ventricle
    d. right ventricle

18. Which of the following is _not_ a product of the Krebs cycle?

    a. carbon dioxide
    b. oxygen
    c. adenosine triphosphate (ATP)
    d. energy carriers

19. What is the name for the reactant that is entirely consumed by the reaction?

    a. limiting reactant
    b. reducing agent
    c. reaction intermediate
    d. reagent

20. Which part of the brain interprets sensory information?

    a. cerebrum
    b. hindbrain
    c. cerebellum
    d. medulla oblongata

21. What kind of bond connects sugar and phosphate in DNA?

    a. hydrogen
    b. ionic
    c. covalent
    d. overt

22. What is the mass (in grams) of 7.35 mol water?

    a. 10.7 g
    b. 18 g
    c. 132 g
    d. 180.6 g

23. Which of the following proteins is produced by cartilage?

    a. actin
    b. estrogen
    c. collagen
    d. myosin

24. How are lipids different than other organic molecules?

a. They are indivisible.
b. They are not water soluble.
c. They contain zinc.
d. They form long proteins.

25. Which of the following orbitals is the last to fill?

a. 1s
b. 3s
c. 4p
d. 6s

26. Which component of the nervous system is responsible for lowering the heart rate?

a. central nervous system
b. sympathetic nervous system
c. parasympathetic nervous system
d. distal nervous system

27. Which of the following is *not* a steroid?

a. cholesterol
b. estrogen
c. testosterone
d. hemoglobin

28. What is the name of the binary molecular compound NO_5?

a. nitro pentoxide
b. ammonium pentoxide
c. nitrogen pentoxide
d. pentnitrogen oxide

29. In which of the following muscle types are the filaments arranged in a disorderly manner?

a. cardiac
b. smooth
c. skeletal
d. rough

30. Which hormone is produced by the pineal gland?

a. insulin
b. testosterone
c. melatonin
d. epinephrine

Arithmetic Reasoning

1. A man buys two shirts. One is $7.50 and the other is $3.00. A 6% tax is added to his total. What is his total?

   a. $10.50
   b. $11.13
   c. $14.58
   d. $16.80

2. If a chef can make 25 pastries in a day, how many can he make in a week?

   a. 32
   b. 74
   c. 126
   d. 175

3. A woman must earn $250 in the next four days to pay a traffic ticket. How much will she have to earn each day?

   a. $45.50
   b. $62.50
   c. $75.50
   d. $100.50

4. A car lot has an inventory of 476 cars. If 36 people bought cars in the week after the inventory was taken, how many cars will remain in inventory at the end of that week?

   a. 440
   b. 476
   c. 484
   d. 512

5. A woman has $450 in a bank account. She earns 5% interest on her end-of-month balance. How much interest will she earn for the month?

   a. $5.00
   b. $22.50
   c. $427.50
   d. $472.50

6. Three children decide to buy a gift for their father. The gift costs $78.00. One child contributes $24.00. The second contributes $15.00 less than the first. How much will the third child have to contribute?

   a. $15.00
   b. $39.00
   c. $45.00
   d. $62.00

7. Two women have credit cards. One earns 3 points for every dollar she spends. The other earns 6 points for every dollar she spends. If they each spend $5.00, how many combined total points will they earn?

    a. 15
    b. 30
    c. 45
    d. 60

8. A company employing 540 individuals plans to increase its workforce by 13%. How many people will the company employ after the expansion?

    a. 527
    b. 547
    c. 553
    d. 610

9. A 13 story building has 65 apartments. If each floor has an equal number of apartments, how many apartments are on each floor?

    a. 2
    b. 3
    c. 4
    d. 5

10. If 5 people buy 3 pens each and 3 people buy 7 pencils each, what is the ratio of the total number of pens to the total number of pencils?

    a. 5:7
    b. 3:7
    c. 5:3
    d. 1:1

11. A man earns $15.23 per hour and gets a raise of $2.34 per hour. What is his new hourly rate of pay?

    a. $12.89
    b. $15.46
    c. $17.57
    d. $35.64

12. How many people can travel on 6 planes if each carries 300 passengers?

    a. 1800
    b. 1200
    c. 600
    d. 350

13. In a town, the ratio of men to women is 2:1. If the number of women in the town is doubled, what will be the new ratio of men to women?

    a. 1:2
    b. 1:1
    c. 2:1
    d. 3:1

14. A woman weighing 250 pounds goes on a diet. During the first week, she loses 3% of her body weight. During the second week, she loses 2%. At the end of the second week, how many pounds has she lost?

    a. 12.50
    b. 10
    c. 12.35
    d. 15

15. A woman is traveling to a destination 583 km away. If she drives 78 km every hour, how many hours will it take for her to reach her destination?

    a. 2.22
    b. 3.77
    c. 5.11
    d. 7.47

16. If one gallon of paint can paint 3 rooms, how many rooms can be painted with 28 gallons of paint?

    a. 10
    b. 25
    c. 56
    d. 84

17. Five workers earn $135/day. What is the total amount earned by the five workers?

    a. $675
    b. $700
    c. $725
    d. $750

18. A girl scores a 99 on her math test. On her second test, her score drops by 15. On the third test, she scores 5 points higher than she did on her second. What was the girl's score on the third test?

    a. 79
    b. 84
    c. 89
    d. 99

19. A man goes to the mall with $50.00. He spends $15.64 in one store and $7.12 in a second store. How much does he have left?

    a. $27.24
    b. $34.36
    c. $42.88
    d. $57.12

20. 600 students must share a school that has 20 classrooms. How many students will each classroom contain if there are an equal number of students in each class?

    a. 15
    b. 20
    c. 25
    d. 30

21. Four workers at a shelter agree to care for the dogs over a holiday. If there are 48 dogs, how many must each worker look after?

   a. 8
   b. 10
   c. 12
   d. 14

22. One worker has an office that is 20 feet long. Another has an office that is 6 feet longer. What is the combined length of both offices?

   a. 26 feet
   b. 36 feet
   c. 46 feet
   d. 56 feet

23. Four friends go shopping. They purchase items that cost $6.66 and $159.23. If they split the cost evenly, how much will each friend have to pay?

   a. $26.64
   b. $39.81
   c. $41.47
   d. $55.30

24. A 140-acre forest is cut in half to make way for development. What is the size of the new forest's acreage?

   a. 70
   b. 80
   c. 90
   d. 100

25. A farmer has 360 cows. He decides to sell 45. Shortly after, he purchases 85 more cows. How many cows does he have?

   a. 230
   b. 315
   c. 400
   d. 490

26. A couple plans to buy a car. They have $569 in a joint bank account. The man has $293 in additional cash and the woman has $189. What is the most expensive car they will be able to afford?

   a. $482
   b. $758
   c. $862
   d. $1051

27. The temperature of a cup of coffee is 98 degrees. If its temperature decreases by 2 degrees per minute, what will its temperature be after 4 minutes?

   a. 100 degrees
   b. 98 degrees
   c. 94 degrees
   d. 90 degrees

28. A man's lawn grass is 3 inches high. He mows the lawn and cuts off 30% of its height. How tall will the grass be after the lawn is mowed?

    a. 0.9 inches
    b. 2.1 inches
    c. 2.7 inches
    d. 2.9 inches

29. Three outlets are selling concert tickets. One ticket outlet sells 432; another outlet sells 238; the third outlet sells 123. How many concert tickets were sold in total?

    a. 361
    b. 555
    c. 670
    d. 793

30. A boy has a bag with 26 pieces of candy inside. He eats 8 pieces of candy, then divides the rest evenly between two friends. How many pieces of candy will each friend get?

    a. 7
    b. 9
    c. 11
    d. 13

Word Knowledge

1. <u>Generous</u> most nearly means

    a. giving
    b. truthful
    c. selfish
    d. harsh

2. The math test was quite <u>challenging.</u>

    a. reasonable
    b. lengthy
    c. difficult
    d. simple

3. <u>Instructor</u> most nearly means

    a. pupil
    b. teacher
    c. survivor
    d. dictator

4. The audience applauded after the woman <u>concluded</u> her presentation.

    a. delivered
    b. prepared
    c. attended
    d. finished

5. <u>Residence</u> most nearly means

    a. home
    b. area
    c. plan
    d. resist

6. The company <u>instantly</u> agreed to the terms of the contract.

    a. reluctantly
    b. eventually
    c. immediately
    d. definitely

7. <u>Gigantic</u> most nearly means

    a. small
    b. great
    c. huge
    d. scary

8. The new car was very <u>costly.</u>

    a. expensive
    b. cheap
    c. attractive
    d. rare

9. Opportunity most nearly means

    a. event
    b. plan
    c. direction
    d. chance

10. The woman's response to the question was correct.

    a. hesitation
    b. answer
    c. decision
    d. concern

11. Frequently most nearly means

    a. difficulty
    b. freely
    c. often
    d. easy

12. He observed the eagles with binoculars.

    a. watched
    b. hunted
    c. scared
    d. sold

13. Purchased most nearly means

    a. sold
    b. bargained
    c. complained
    d. bought

14. She is having difficulties with her new computer.

    a. experiences
    b. solutions
    c. pleasures
    d. problems

15. Entire most nearly means

    a. whole
    b. divide
    c. tired
    d. basic

16. The woman's performance was superior to the man's.

    a. short
    b. similar
    c. better
    d. weak

17. **Remark** most nearly means
   a. rebuke
   b. comment
   c. lecture
   d. replace

18. **Selecting** the best person for the job was difficult.
   a. locating
   b. contacting
   c. choosing
   d. informing

19. **Commence** most nearly means
   a. begin
   b. progress
   c. finish
   d. comment

20. The fox ran **swiftly** after its prey.
   a. surely
   b. quickly
   c. slowly
   d. lightly

21. **Overdue** most nearly means
   a. overall
   b. early
   c. punctual
   d. late

22. She felt intense **anguish** when her parents divorced.
   a. loneliness
   b. confusion
   c. anger
   d. sorrow

23. **Solitary** most nearly means
   a. single
   b. solid
   c. sturdy
   d. stoic

24. The class **chuckled** when the professor dropped his notes.
   a. helped
   b. commented
   c. laughed
   d. chose

25. Depart most nearly means

    a. leave
    b. describe
    c. arrive
    d. portion

26. The child was unable to locate his toy.

    a. buy
    b. find
    c. enjoy
    d. share

27. Soiled most nearly means

    a. dirty
    b. sullen
    c. sultry
    d. dainty

28. The bear slumbered in its cave.

    a. hunted
    b. fed
    c. slept
    d. explored

29. Puzzled most nearly means

    a. admired
    b. retired
    c. confused
    d. understand

30. The woman desired a new car.

    a. purchased
    b. wanted
    c. described
    d. intended

31. Cheap most nearly means

    a. cheer
    b. doubtfully
    c. cheat
    d. inexpensive

32. She is a very intelligent lady.

    a. pretty
    b. nice
    c. smart
    d. mysterious

33. <u>Object</u> most nearly means

    a. disagree
    b. state
    c. concur
    d. relate

34. The workers <u>constructed</u> the home over a three-month period.

    a. purchased
    b. explored
    c. improved
    d. built

35. <u>Required</u> most nearly means

    a. needed
    b. wished
    c. studied
    d. wanted

Paragraph Comprehension

1. Mitosis refers to the process of cell division that occurs in most higher life forms. During interphase, all of the genetic material within the cell is replicated. Then, the strands that contain the genetic material, which are known as chromatin, become compacted and condensed. Centrosomes then move to opposite ends of the cells, after which the nucleus contained in the original single cell disintegrates.

Immediately before the chromatin becomes compacted,

    a. the genetic material in the cell is copied.
    b. the centrosomes move to opposite ends of the cell.
    c. the nucleus inside of the cell disintegrates.
    d. the process of mitosis takes place.

2. Obesity in the Western world has reached epidemic levels. While exercise is important to maintaining a healthy weight, healthy eating is even more important. Even the most active people cannot burn off hundreds of excess calories if they are consumed on a daily basis.

It can be concluded that

    a. most people need to exercise more.
    b. many people do not practice healthy eating.
    c. obesity would not be a problem if people were active.
    d. most people do not know how to choose healthy foods.

3. Racism is still a widespread problem in North America. For example, one man of Arab descent was held at an airport for hours for no apparent reason. The man said he was later told that officials thought he was carrying a bomb. An African-American woman was passed over for a promotion. She says the job went to a less qualified applicant.

The author is constructing her argument by

    a. relying on studies conducted by others.
    b. relying on the self-reported experiences of others.
    c. relying on events that she personally witnessed.
    d. relying on accepted facts and proven statistics.

4. *Beowulf* is an epic poem that is important because it is often viewed as the first significant work of English literature. Although it was first written in 700A.D., it is thought to be even hundreds of years older than that. It is believed that the story of *Beowulf* was told for centuries before it ever made its way on to paper. It is still taught today in various schools and universities.

***Beowulf* is a significant poem because**

    a. it was first written down in 700A.D.
    b. it was told for centuries before it was written down.
    c. it is still taught today in academic settings.
    d. it is the first important work of English literature.

5. Cats are by far a superior pet compared to dogs. They are perfect for the working person, as they don't mind being left alone during the day. In addition, they are very easy to litter train. They require little care or effort, and are much cheaper to feed compared to dogs.

The author's purpose in writing this passage is

  a. to compare cats and dogs.
  b. to convince the reader that cats are better pets.
  c. to show why cats are cheaper to feed.
  d. to explain why cats are preferred to dogs.

6. Malaria is a dangerous disease that is still common in many countries. It is carried and transmitted to humans by female mosquitoes. When they bite humans or animals, the malaria parasite is introduced into the human's or animal's bloodstream. The parasites travel to the liver. There, they multiply, and soon they infect red blood cells. Malaria symptoms like fever will begin to be experienced at this point.

After the malaria parasites infect the red blood cells

  a. symptoms like fever occur.
  b. the parasites multiply.
  c. the parasites travel to the liver.
  d. malaria is transmitted by mosquitoes.

7. Many people feel that summer water sports are dangerous. While accidents do occur, the vast majority are preventable. For example, boating is a relatively safe activity, provided that life vests are worn and a reasonable speed is maintained. When diving, it's important to know the area well and be certain that water is deep enough. Finally, alcohol should never be consumed while engaging in water sports or activities. Following these simple tips would prevent many accidents.

The main idea expressed in the passage is

  a. summer sports are dangerous.
  b. many people who engage in water activities are careless.
  c. boating is a safe activity if precautions are followed.
  d. summer water activities aren't necessarily dangerous.

8. At one time, people who wanted to be writers had to write a query letter to a magazine and then wait weeks, sometimes months, for a response, which was usually a rejection. Today, with blogs, virtually anybody can put their work out there for others to view. It's as easy as setting up your blog, naming it, and posting anything you want: opinions, poems, short stories, news articles, etc. Of course, while people who have blogs may choose to call themselves writers or journalists, it's unlikely they are making a living by putting their random thoughts out there into cyberspace.

It can be concluded that

  a. it is easier to make a living as a writer now.
  b. there are more people who want to be writers now.
  c. most people do not submit query letters to magazines anymore.
  d. there is no approval process for getting a blog.

9. Organic food has become quite popular in the last number of years, but the price of organic foods still prevents many people from eating them on a regular basis. People choose to buy organic foods because they are becoming more concerned about what types of chemicals, fertilizers, and pesticides are in their food. Organic food is usually relatively easily obtained by visiting a grocery store or a farmer's market, and the selection of foods is also quite good.

People don't eat organic food because

    a.   it's hard to find.
    b.   it contains chemicals.
    c.   the selection is poor.
    d.   it's too expensive.

10. Studies have shown again and again that birth order strongly influences the person one will eventually become. Oldest children have been shown to be more responsible and perform better in school. Younger children tend to do less well in school and be more free spirited. Cindy is a good example. She graduated on the Dean's list, and her parents report she always did her chores as a child.

It can be concluded that

    a.   Cindy was an oldest child.
    b.   Cindy was a youngest child.
    c.   There have been no studies done on middle children.
    d.   Birth order only matters if there are exactly two children.

11. Weddings put a substantial amount of stress on the bride, the groom, and their families. There is a large amount of planning that goes into a wedding, but the expenses are the major source of grief. The cake, the dress, and meals must all be purchased. The hall must be rented, the dj hired, and the invitations bought. By the time all is said and done, even a relatively simple wedding can cost in excess of $10,000.

The main idea expressed in the passage is

    a.   weddings are stressful.
    b.   weddings require a lot of planning.
    c.   weddings are a source of grief.
    d.   weddings are expensive.

12. According to the laws of supply and demand, consumers will demand less of a good if the price is higher and more if it is lower. Conversely, suppliers will produce more of a good when the price is higher and less when it is lower.

If a supplier wanted to sell more of a good, they would

    a.   reduce the supply.
    b.   reduce the price.
    c.   raise the price.
    d.   increase the supply.

13. North America is currently dealing with a crisis. People have accumulated substantial amounts of debt. While consumers are partially to blame, much of the blame lies with the companies who actually granted the credit to consumers. This crisis wouldn't have happened if loans were not granted to people who could not afford them.

Many people in North America are in debt because

    a. they choose not to pay their debts.
    b. they borrowed money they couldn't repay.
    c. companies refused to grant credit.
    d. they dealt with serious personal crises.

14. Knowing how to perform CPR properly can save another person's life. If you come across someone who is in trouble, call 911 right away. Then, lay them on their back. Next, open their airway by raising the chin. After this, but before beginning mouth to mouth, spend a few moments to determine whether they are breathing. If not, mouth to mouth and chest compressions will be necessary.

Before checking to see whether a person is breathing

    a. open their airway.
    b. begin mouth to mouth.
    c. learn how to perform CPR.
    d. begin chest compressions.

15. Using animals for fur is a barbaric practice that should be stopped. All across the world, animals are killed every day just to provide fashionable clothing. Fur is no longer necessary as it may once have been. There are now synthetic materials that can keep people just as warm during the winter months. In addition, the conditions on many fur farms are inhumane. Considering that fur-bearing animals are suffering to provide unnecessary luxury items, it is impossible to justify this sort of cruelty to animals.

The main idea expressed in this passage is

    a. nobody needs fur.
    b. fur animals are treated badly.
    c. fur is a luxury item.
    d. other materials are warmer than fur.

Mathematics Knowledge

1. A rectangle has a width of 7 cm and a length of 9 cm. What is its perimeter?

    a.   16 cm
    b.   32 cm
    c.   48 cm
    d.   62 cm

2. In the following inequality, solve for q.
$$-3q + 12 \geq 4q - 30$$

    a. $q \geq 6$
    b. $q = 6$
    c. $q \neq 6$
    d. $q \leq 6$

3. If $x - 6 = 0$, then x is equal to

    a.   0
    b.   3
    c.   6
    d.   9

4. If $x = -3$, calculate the value of the following expression:
$$3x^3 + (3x + 4) - 2x^2$$

    a.   -104
    b.   -58
    c.   58
    d.   104

5. If $3x - 30 = 45 - 2x$, what is the value of x?

    a.   5
    b.   10
    c.   15
    d.   20

6. Solve for x in the following inequality.
$$\frac{1}{4}x - 25 \geq 75$$

    a. $x \geq 400$
    b. $x \leq 400$
    c. $x \geq 25$
    d. $x \leq 25$

7. If $x^2 - 5 = 20$, what is one possible value of x?

    a.   5
    b.   10
    c.   12.5
    d.   15

8. What is the area of a square that has a perimeter of 8 cm?

    a. 2 cm^2
    b. 4 cm^2
    c. 32 cm^2
    d. 64 cm^2

9. If $x = 4$ and $y = 2$, what is the value of the following expression:

$$3xy - 12y + 5x$$

    a. -4
    b. 10
    c. 12
    d. 20

10. If $0.65x + 10 = 15$, what is the value of x?

    a. 4.92
    b. 5.78
    c. 6.45
    d. 7.69

11. Simplify the following:

$$(3x + 5)(4x - 6)$$

    a. $12x^2 - 38x - 30$
    b. $12x^2 + 2x - 30$
    c. $12x^2 - 2x - 1$
    d. $12x^2 + 2x + 30$

12. Simplify the following expression:

$$\frac{50x^{18}t^6w^3z^{20}}{5x^5t^2w^2z^{19}}$$

    a. $10x^{13}t^3wz$
    b. $10x^{13}t^4wz$
    c. $10x^{12}t^4wz$
    d. $10x^{13}t^4wz^2$

13. The quantity $n!$ (n-factorial) is defined as the product of all positive integers between n and zero (i.e., $n \times (n - 1) \times (n - 2) \times ... \times 3 \times 2 \times 1$). The quantity 4! (four-factorial) is equal to

    a. 4
    b. 12
    c. 16
    d. 24

14. If a cube is 5 cm long, what is the volume of the cube?

    a. 15 cm^3
    b. 65 cm^3
    c. 105 cm^3
    d. 125 cm^3

15. Solve for *x* by factoring:

$$x^2 - 13x + 42 = 0$$

    a. $x = 6, 7$
    b. $x = -6, -7$
    c. $x = 6, -7$
    d. $x = -6, 7$

16. A triangle has a base measuring 12 cm and a height of 12 cm. What is its area?

    a. 24 cm^2
    b. 56 cm^2
    c. 72 cm^2
    d. 144 cm^2

17. Simplify the following expression:

$$(3x^2 7x^7) + (2y^3 9y^{12})$$

    a. $21x^{14} + 18y^{26}$
    b. $10x^9 + 11y^{15}$
    c. $21x^{14} + 18y^{15}$
    d. $21x^9 + 18y^{15}$

18. If $\frac{x}{3} + 27 = 30$, what is the value of *x*?

    a.   3
    b.   6
    c.   9
    d.   12

19. What is the slope of a line with points A (4,1) and B (-13,8)?

    a. $\frac{7}{17}$
    b. $-\frac{7}{17}$
    c. $-\frac{17}{7}$
    d. $\frac{17}{7}$

20. If *x* is 20% of 200, what is the value of *x*?

    a.   40
    b.   80
    c.   100
    d.   150

21. If a bag of balloons consists of 47 white balloons, 5 yellow balloons, and 10 black balloons, what is the probability that a balloon chosen randomly from the bag will be black?

    a.   19%
    b.   16%
    c.   21%
    d.   33%

22. A raffle game has a single grand prize that will be drawn randomly from among all the tickets. A total of 500 tickets are sold. If a man buys 25 tickets, what is the probability that he will win the grand prize?

    a. 1 in 2
    b. 1 in 5
    c. 1 in 10
    d. 1 in 20

23. What is the volume of a rectangular prism with a height of 10 cm, a length of 5 cm, and a width of 6 cm?

    a. 30 cm^3
    b. 60 cm^3
    c. 150 cm^3
    d. 300 cm^3

24. What is the midpoint of point A (6, 20) and point B (10, 40)?

    a. (30, 8)
    b. (16, 60)
    c. (8, 30)
    d. (7, 15)

25. If $5x + 60 = 75$, what is the value of x?

    a. 3
    b. 4
    c. 5
    d. 6

Electrical Information

1. Which of the following is true regarding current and voltage?

    a.   Current is potential energy
    b.   Voltage is kinetic energy
    c.   Current is the buildup of charge
    d.   Voltage is the potential energy difference between two charged terminals

2. What is the voltage across a 3 Ω resistor if the ammeter reads 4 A?

    a.   0.75 V
    b.   7 V
    c.   12 V
    d.   1.33 V

3. Which of the following demonstrates the correct associations between the components of Ohm's law and their units of measure?

    a.   Current (Amps); Voltage (Ohms)
    b.   Resistance (Ohms); Voltage (Volts)
    c.   Current (Ohms); Resistance (Amps)
    d.   Resistance (Amps); Current (Volts)

Use this image to answer the following two questions.

4. If the current at point 1 in the series circuit above is 3 A and the voltage drop across the first, second, and third resistors is 2 V, 3 V, and 4 V, respectively, what is the total resistance of the circuit?

    a.   6 Ω
    b.   3 Ω
    c.   9 Ω
    d.   0.33 Ω

5. If the current at point three in the series circuit above is 4 A, the resistance of R_1 is 0.5 Ω, the resistance of R_2 is 1 Ω, and the voltage drop across R_3 is 6 V, what is the size of the battery of the circuit?

    a.   12 V
    b.   1.5 V
    c.   9 V
    d.   3 V

Use this image to answer the following three questions.

6. In the above circuit, what is the current at points 4 and 6 if the battery is 20 V, $R_2 = 4\,\Omega$, and $R_3 = 2\,\Omega$?

    a. $I_4 = 10$ A; $I_6 = 15$ A
    b. $I_4 = 20$ A; $I_6 = 20$ A
    c. $I_4 = 10$ A; $I_6 = 10$ A
    d. $I_4 = 15$ A; $I_6 = 5$ A

7. In the above circuit, what is the equivalent resistance if $R_1 = 4\,\Omega$, $R_2 = 4\,\Omega$, and $R_3 = 2\,\Omega$?

    a. $10\,\Omega$
    b. $3.33\,\Omega$
    c. $1\,\Omega$
    d. $32\,\Omega$

8. In the above circuit, if two resistors in series were in place of R_1 and 3 resistors in series were in place of R_3, what is the order of steps necessary to solve the problem?

    a.   Treat all resistors as if they were in parallel
    b.   Find the equivalent resistance of the series resistors, then add the parallel resistors together
    c.   Add all resistors together
    d.   Add the series resistors together, then find the equivalent resistance of the parallel resistors

9. If a 60-Watt lightbulb is used in a flashlight with a 9 V battery, what is the current between them?

    a.   540 A
    b.   6.66 A
    c.   69.7 A
    d.   0.15 A

10. All of the following are true regarding alternating current except:

    a.   Alternating current periodically reverses direction.
    b.   Alternating current is used to transport electricity over land.
    c.   Alternating current is used to supply electricity to homes.
    d.   Alternating current is produced by batteries.

11. Alternating current is commonly used in which of the following places?

    a.   Cell phones
    b.   Ships
    c.   Homes
    d.   Airplanes

12. Which of the following commonly serves as a ground?

    a. The earth
    b. Car tires
    c. A house
    d. Lightning

13. Which of the following is true of p-type semiconductors?

    a. They have an excess of electrons
    b. When an electric field is applied, a positive pole is formed
    c. They can result from silicon being doped with antimony
    d. They can result from antimony being doped with boron

14. What is the purpose of a diode?

    a. Serve as a high-functioning resistor
    b. Step up or step down input voltage
    c. Allow current to pass in only one direction
    d. Create a magnetic field

15. Transistors are used in all of the following applications except:

    a. Radio
    b. Television
    c. Computer memory chips
    d. Light bulbs

16. Which of the following is a correct pairing of the function and an application of capacitors?

    a. They allow current to pass in only one direction and can be used as computer chips.
    b. They convert mechanical energy to electrical energy and can be used as a motor.
    c. They store charge and can be used to protect sensitive components during a power surge.
    d. They generate current and can be used as transformers.

17. Which of the following is not true of inductors and capacitors?

    a. Direct current flows through inductors but not capacitors
    b. They are used for electrical storage.
    c. The oppose electrical change.
    d. They can be used interchangeably.

18. What is the purpose of transformers?

    a. Serve as a high-functioning resistor
    b. Step up or step down input voltage
    c. Allow current to pass in only one direction
    d. Amplify electrical signals

19. What is the difference between motors and generators?

    a. Motors convert electrical energy to mechanical energy
    b. Generators convert electrical energy to mechanical energy
    c. Motors convert mechanical energy to electrical energy
    d. Motors are a type of generator

20. Which of the following is not true of generators?

    a.   They generate alternating current.
    b.   They can be used to generate direct or alternating current.
    c.   They use electromagnetic induction.
    d.   Their function is the opposite of motors.

Shop and Auto Information

1. What is the correct order of the steps in the four-stroke engine cycle?

 a. Intake, power, compression, exhaust
 b. Intake, compression, power, exhaust
 c. Intake, exhaust, compression, power
 d. Intake, compression, exhaust, power

2. What component supplies electricity to a vehicle while it runs?

 a. Battery
 b. Engine
 c. Alternator
 d. Starter motor

3. In older vehicles, what was the function of the carburetor?

 a. Mix air and fuel before combustion
 b. Supply electricity to the spark plugs
 c. House the combustion reaction
 d. Filter exhaust before it reached the tail pipe

4. Spark plugs use electricity to create a spark in the:

 a. Transmission
 b. Motor
 c. Alternator
 d. Engine

5. Which of the following can lead to spark plug fouling?

 a. Driving on the highway
 b. Driving long distances
 c. Driving on dusty roads
 d. City driving

6. Which of the following will occur as a result of failing piston rings?

 a. Engine smoking
 b. Car won't start
 c. Backfiring
 d. Poor fuel economy

7. Which of the following is true about the exhaust system?

 a. The exhaust manifold converts pollutants to water vapor and carbon dioxide
 b. The muffler collects gas byproducts from the engine for transport to the manifold
 c. The catalytic converter primarily dampens engine noise
 d. Exhaust flows from the combustion chamber through the exhaust valve, to the exhaust manifold, to the catalytic converter, to the muffler, and out the tail pipe

8. Which of the following is not a function of motor oil?

 a. Lubricate the engine
 b. Prevent corrosion
 c. Fuel the engine
 d. Prevent overheating

9. What happens when the thermostat gets stuck open?

    a. The engine will overheat.
    b. The engine will run cold and have bad gas mileage.
    c. The engine will flood with coolant and will stall.
    d. The air conditioning system will freeze and eventually fail.

10. A transaxle is found most commonly in which drivetrain configuration?

    a. Rear wheel drive (RWD)
    b. Front wheel drive (FWD)
    c. All wheel drive (AWD)
    d. Four-wheel drive (4WD)

11. What is a strut?

    a. Center point of each wheel that connects to the control arms
    b. Connecting point of frame to suspension system
    c. Combination of springs and shocks
    d. Component to prevent the vehicle from rolling over when turning

12. Which of the following is the least likely to cause steering problems?

    a. Worn brake pads
    b. Low or leaking power steering fluid
    c. Faulty power steering pump
    d. Worn control arm bushings

13. Which of the following is not associated with disc brakes?

    a. Brake pads
    b. Brake shoes
    c. Rotor
    d. Master cylinder

14. Which of the following describes the process of cutting wood parallel to the grain?

    a. Cross cut
    b. Rip cut
    c. Bevel cut
    d. Miter cut

15. What type of chisel is this?

    a. Mortise chisel
    b. Paring chisel
    c. Beveled edge chisel
    d. Japanese bench chisel

16. What type of wrench is this?

    a. Ratcheting wrench
    b. Socket wrench
    c. Combination wrench
    d. Torque wrench

17. Which of the following describes correct pairs?
    a. Allen wrench: hexagon; Phillips-head: simple wedge
    b. Allen wrench: cross; Phillips-head: simple wedge
    c. Flat head: hexagon; Phillips-head: cross
    d. Flat head: simple wedge; Allen wrench: hexagon

18. Which of the following correctly describes the difference between welding and soldering?
    a. Soldering uses much higher heat than welding
    b. Soldering is used in jobs that are much larger in size
    c. Welding involves melting of the base metal
    d. Welding is commonly used to connect electrical components on a circuit

19. Which of the following is true of rivets?
    a. They support shear and tensile loads
    b. They support tensile loads only
    c. They support compressive loads only
    d. They support compressive and shear loads

20. The pliers below are called:

    a. Diagonal pliers
    b. Slip joint pliers
    c. Tongue and groove pliers
    d. Crimping pliers

21. Which tool can be considered a combination of a clamp and pliers?
    a. G-clamp
    b. Vice-grips
    c. Tongue and groove pliers
    d. Speed clamp

22. What is the difference between drilling and boring?

a. Drilling produces blind holes, which do not pass completely through a workpiece; boring does not.

b. Boring produces blind holes, which do not pass completely through a workpiece; drilling does not.

c. Only boring can be done using hand tools.

d. Drilling creates new holes in workpieces; boring enlarges existing holes.

23. Which of the following is the most portable?

a. Miter saw

b. Oscillating saw

c. Table saw

d. Vertical band saw

24. Which of the following is true for files and rasps?

a. Rasps are overall coarser

b. Rasps are hand tools, files are not

c. Files have different grades of coarseness, rasps have just one grade of coarseness

d. Rasps are ideal for woodworking, especially for soft woods

25. Which of the following is not a type of grinder?

a. Angle grinder

b. Orbital grinder

c. Belt grinder

d. Bench grinder

Mechanical Comprehension

1. A cannon fires off a ship up towards a mountain range. Neglecting air resistance, where will the velocity of the projectile be greatest?

    a.   Exiting the muzzle
    b.   Halfway to the mountains
    c.   As it impacts the mountains

2. These pulleys are connected by belts. Which pulley travels the fastest?

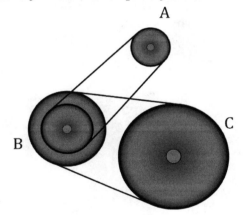

    a.   Pulley A
    b.   Pulley B
    c.   Pulley C

3. If Gear A is traveling at 10 rpm, how many times will Gear C rotate in 3 minutes?

    a. 1.7 times
    b. 3 times
    c. 30 times

4. Where should the fulcrum be located to balance this beam?

    a. closer to the large mass
    b. closer to the small mass
    c. exactly between the two masses

5. Which orientation will require more force to pull?

    a. with the rope at an angle to the table
    b. with the rope parallel to the table
    c. both orientations are equal

6. The larger piston has four times as much horizontal area as the smaller piston. If the small piston is compressed 8 inches, how far will the larger piston move?

    a. 8 inches
    b. 2 inches
    c. 32 inches

7. A wing in flight has a set of pressures causing the overall forces on the top and bottom of the wing. Where will the total force on the wing point?

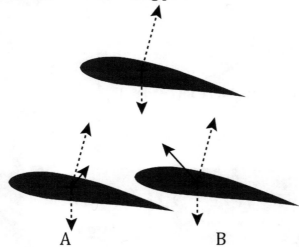

    a. up and to the right
    b. up and to the left
    c. neither A nor B

8. River water enters a section where the water spreads out into a wide, deep area. Is the water likely to speed up, slow down, or remain at a constant speed?

a. speed up
b. slow down
c. remain at a constant speed

9. A magnet is placed in the middle of two identical, anchored magnets. Which direction will the magnet go?

a. towards magnet 1
b. towards magnet 2
c. the magnet won't move

10. A solid substance melts at -21°C. If the object is known to change phase at 81°C, will the object be a solid, liquid, or gas at 90°C?

a. solid
b. liquid
c. gas

11. If the resistors in the circuits are identical, which circuit will have the greatest overall resistance?

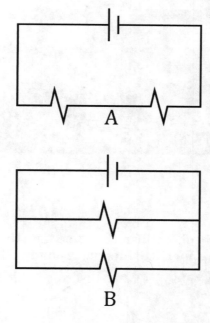

   a.   circuit A
   b.   circuit B
   c.   circuit A and B have the same overall resistance

12. A pendulum swings back and forth once per second. The pendulum is shortened by removing half of the string. The new frequency is 1.4 Hz (Hz=1/sec). How often will the pendulum swing back and forth in a minute?

   a.   84
   b.   92
   c.   72

13. Two identical pistons are connected by a pipe. What is the mechanical advantage of the piston system?

    a. 0.5
    b. 1
    c. 2

14. A ball is thrown horizontally off a cliff at the same time that an identical ball is dropped off a cliff. How long after the dropped ball hits the ground will the thrown ball hit?

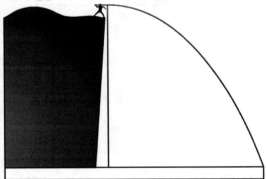

    a. approximately 1 second after
    b. approximately 2 seconds after
    c. they will hit at the same time

15. The cam rotates at 5 rpm. How many times will the follower (needle) move up and down in a minute?

   a. 20
   b. 72
   c. 140

16. Which of the following are not ways to increase the torque applied to a wrench?

   a. increase the length from the center to the applied force
   b. increase the force
   c. angle the force toward the center

17. A ball is pushed down into a vertical spring. The ball is released and flies upward. Which best describes the states of energy the ball underwent?

 a. convective energy to potential energy
 b. potential energy to kinetic energy
 c. kinetic energy to potential energy

18. A vacuum tank is held by weights at a depth of 50 feet underwater. If the tank is raised to a depth of 25 feet, will the pressure on the walls of the tank increase, decrease, or stay the same?

 a. increase
 b. decrease
 c. stay the same

19. Adding salt to water raises its density. Will salt water have a lower, higher, or the same specific gravity than 1?

a. lower
b. higher
c. the same

20. Which of the following is an example of convective heat transfer?

A   B   C

a. a man burns his hand on a hot pot
b. a man burns his hand in steam
c. a man gets a sun burn

21. Which of the following is the electrical component which holds a voltage across a gap between two conductive materials?

a. resistor
b. inductor
c. capacitor

22. **Which of these wrenches is likely to provide the greatest torque with a set force?**

A   B

    a.   wrench A
    b.   wrench B
    c.   both wrenches will provide the same torque

23. **Which of the following is true of this circuit?**

    a.   the voltage is the same everywhere
    b.   the current is the same everywhere
    c.   there is no current

24. **Which device does not measure current in an electrical system?**

    a.   ammeter
    b.   multimeter
    c.   voltmeter

25. A ball is thrown straight into the air with an initial kinetic energy of 100 ft-lb. What is the potential energy of the ball at half of the height of the flight path?

    a.   33 ft-lb
    b.   50 ft-lb
    c.   66 ft-lb

26. An increase in mechanical advantage with a set motion for the load and a set applied force necessitates an increase in _____ the applied force?
    a.   the distance traveled by
    b.   the angle of action of
    c.   the potential energy behind

27. A windlass drum has two sections with different circumferences. When winding the drum, one side of the rope winds around the large section and the other unwinds from the small section. If the large section of the drum has a circumference of 3.5 ft and the other section has a circumference of 1 ft, how far will the weight lift with two full turns of the drum?

    a.   2.5 feet
    b.   9 feet
    c.   4.5 feet

28. Which type of situation will lead to condensation on the outside of pipes?

a. hot liquid in the pipe and cold air outside the pipe
b. cold liquid in the pipe and colder air outside the pipe
c. cold liquid in the pipe and hot air outside the pipe

29. Which color will absorb the most radiation?

a. black
b. green
c. dark yellow

30. Two gears (30 and 18 teeth) mesh. If the smaller gear rotates 3 times, how many times will the larger gear rotate?

a. 1.6 times
b. 1.8 times
c. 3 times

Assembling Objects

For this practice test section, assume that shapes may be translated or rotated but not reflected unless otherwise specified.

1. Which of the following configurations represents how the following objects might appear if they are rearranged?

a.   b.   c.   d.

2. Which of the following configurations represents how the following object might appear if its components are rearranged?

a.   b.   c.   d.

3. Which of the following configurations represents how the following objects might appear if they are rearranged?

a.   b.   c.   d.

4. Which figure best shows how the objects might be connected if a line is drawn from one point to the other?

a.   b.   c.   d.

5. Which of the following configurations represents how the following object might appear if its components are rearranged?

a.   b.   c.   d.

6. Which of the following configurations represents how the following objects might appear if they are rearranged?

a.   b.   c.   d.

322

7. Which figure best shows how the objects might be connected if a line is drawn from one point to the other?

a.   b.   c.   d.

8. Which of the following configurations represents how the following objects might appear if they are rearranged?

a.   b.   c.   d.

9. If the objects below are translated along the path indicated by the line, keeping in mind that a dotted line corresponds to a place on the side of the object that cannot be seen, how might the final image appear? (Note: the images may not be rotated)

a.   b.   c.   d.

10. Which figure best shows how the objects might be connected if a line is drawn from one point to the other?

a.   b.   c.   d.

11. Which of the following configurations represents how the following objects might appear if they are rearranged?

a.   b.   c.   d.

12. Which of the following configurations represents how the following objects might appear if they are rearranged?

a.   b.   c.   d.

13. Which figure best represents what might result if the shapes shown on the left are cut out of the shape on the right?

a.   b.   c.   d.

14. Which of the following configurations represents how the following objects might appear if they are rearranged?

a.   b.   c.   d.

15. Which of the following configurations represents how the following object might appear if its components are rearranged?

a.   b.   c.   d.

325

16. Which of the following configurations represents how the following objects might appear if they are rearranged?

a.   b.   c.   d.

17. Which of the following configurations represents how the following object might appear if its components are rearranged?

a.   b.   c.   d.

18. Which figure best represents what might result if the shapes shown on the left are cut out of the shape on the right?

a.   b.   c.   d.

19. Which of the following configurations represents how the following objects might appear if they are rearranged?

a.   b.   c.   d.

20. If the objects below are translated COMPLETELY along the path indicated by the line, keeping in mind that a dotted line corresponds to a place on the side of the object that cannot be seen, how might the final image appear? (Note: the images may not be rotated)

a.   b.   c.   d.

21. Which figure best shows how the objects might be connected if a line is drawn from one point to the other?

a.   b.   c.   d.

22. Which of the following configurations represents how the following objects might appear if they are rearranged?

a.

b.

c.

d.

23. Which figure best shows how the objects will be attached if you were to connect the two shapes at the indicated points?

a.

b.

c.

d.

24. Which figure best shows how the objects might be connected if a line is drawn from one point to the other?

a.

b.

c.

d.

25. Which figure best shows how the objects will be attached if A is connected to B and C is connected to D?

a.

b.

c.

d.

Answer Key and Explanations

General Science

1. D: The name for a substance that stimulates the production of antibodies is an *antigen*. An antigen is any substance perceived by the immune system as dangerous. When the body senses an antigen, it produces an antibody. *Collagen* is one of the components of bone, tendon, and cartilage. It is a spongy protein that can be turned into gelatin by boiling. *Hemoglobin* is the part of red blood cells that carries oxygen. In order for the blood to carry enough oxygen to the cells of the body, there has to be a sufficient amount of hemoglobin. *Lymph* is a near-transparent fluid that performs a number of functions in the body: It removes bacteria from tissues, replaces lymphocytes in the blood, and moves fat away from the small intestine. Lymph contains white blood cells.

2. D: The cellular hierarchy starts with the cell, the simplest structure, and progresses to organisms, the most complex structures.

3. B: A hypertonic solution is a solution with a higher particle concentration than in the cell, and consequently lower water content than in the cell. Water moves from the cell to the solution, causing the cell to experience water loss and shrink.

4. A: The immune system consists of the lymphatic system, spleen, tonsils, thymus and bone marrow.

5. D: The rate at which a chemical reaction occurs does not depend on the amount of mass lost, since the law of conservation of mass (or matter) states that in a chemical reaction there is no loss of mass.

6. B: Boyle's law states that for a constant mass and temperature, pressure and volume are related inversely to one another: $PV = c$, where c = constant.

7. C: Prokaryotic cells are simpler cells that do not have membrane-bound organelles, whereas eukaryotic cells have several membrane-bound organelles.

8. A: A ribosome is a structure of eukaryotic cells that makes proteins.

9. B: It is impossible for an *AaBb* organism to have the *aa* combination in the gametes. It is impossible for each letter to be used more than one time, so it would be impossible for the lowercase *a* to appear twice in the gametes. It would be possible, however, for *Aa* to appear in the gametes, since there is one uppercase *A* and one lowercase *a*. Gametes are the cells involved in sexual reproduction. They are germ cells.

10. B: The oxidation number of the hydrogen in CaH_2 is –1. One of the general rules for determining oxidation states applies specifically to hydrogen: when hydrogen is bonded to a nonmetal, its oxidation state is +1, but when hydrogen is bonded to a metal, its oxidation state is –1. An ion is a charged version of an element. The oxidation number for an atom is also referred to as the oxidation state. It can be used to describe the number of electrons that must be added or removed from an atom in order to convert the atom to its elemental form.

11. C: *Prolactin* stimulates the production of breast milk during lactation. *Norepinephrine* is a hormone and neurotransmitter secreted by the adrenal gland that regulates heart rate, blood pressure, and blood sugar. *Antidiuretic hormone* is produced by the hypothalamus and secreted by the pituitary gland. It regulates the concentration of urine and triggers the contractions of the arteries and capillaries. *Oxytocin* is a hormone secreted by the pituitary gland that makes it easier to eject milk from the breast and manages the contractions of the uterus during labor.

12. A: The typical result of mitosis in humans is two diploid cells. *Mitosis* is the division of a body cell into two daughter cells. Each of the two produced cells has the same set of chromosomes as the parent. A diploid cell contains both sets of homologous chromosomes. A haploid cell contains only one set of chromosomes, which means that it only has a single set of genes.

13. A: Boron does not exist as a diatomic molecule. The other possible answer choices, fluorine, oxygen, and nitrogen, all exist as diatomic molecules. A diatomic molecule always appears in nature as a pair: the word *diatomic* means "having two atoms." With the exception of astatine, all of the halogens are diatomic. Chemistry students often use the mnemonic BrINClHOF (pronounced "brinkelhoff") to remember all of the diatomic elements: bromine, iodine, nitrogen, chlorine, hydrogen, oxygen, and fluorine. Note that not all of these diatomic elements are halogens.

14. D: Of the given structures, veins have the lowest blood pressure. *Veins* carry oxygen-poor blood from the outlying parts of the body to the heart. An *artery* carries oxygen-rich blood from the heart to the peripheral parts of the body. An *arteriole* extends from an artery to a capillary. A *venule* is a tiny vein that extends from a capillary to a larger vein.

15. B: Water stabilizes the temperature of living things. The ability of warm-blooded animals, including human beings, to maintain a constant internal temperature is known as *homeostasis*. Homeostasis depends on the presence of water in the body. Water tends to minimize changes in temperature because it takes a while to heat up or cool down. When the human body gets warm, the blood vessels dilate and blood moves away from the torso and toward the extremities. When the body gets cold, blood concentrates in the torso. This is the reason why hands and feet tend to get especially cold in cold weather.

16. D: Hydriodic acid is another name for aqueous HI. In an aqueous solution, the solvent is water. Hydriodic acid is a polyatomic ion, meaning that it is composed of two or more elements. When this solution has an increased amount of oxygen, the *-ate* suffix on the first word is converted to *-ic*.

17. C: Of the four heart chambers, the left ventricle is the most muscular. When it contracts, it pushes blood out to the organs and extremities of the body. The right ventricle pushes blood into the lungs. The atria, on the other hand, receive blood from the outlying parts of the body and transport it into the ventricles. The basic process works as follows: Oxygen-poor blood fills the right atrium and is pumped into the right ventricle, from which it is pumped into the pulmonary artery and on to the lungs. In the lungs, this blood is oxygenated. The blood then reenters the heart at the left atrium, which when full pumps into the left ventricle. When the left ventricle is full, blood is pushed into the aorta and on to the organs and extremities of the body.

18. B: Oxygen is not one of the products of the Krebs cycle. The *Krebs cycle* is the second stage of cellular respiration. In this stage, a sequence of reactions converts pyruvic acid into carbon dioxide. This stage of cellular respiration produces the phosphate compounds that provide most of the energy for the cell. The Krebs cycle is also known as the citric acid cycle or the tricarboxylic acid cycle.

19. A: A limiting reactant is entirely used up by the chemical reaction. Limiting reactants control the extent of the reaction and determine the quantity of the product. A reducing agent is a substance that reduces the amount of another substance by losing electrons. A reagent is any substance used in a chemical reaction. Some of the most common reagents in the laboratory are sodium hydroxide and hydrochloric acid. The behavior and properties of these substances are known, so they can be effectively used to produce predictable reactions in an experiment.

20. A: The *cerebrum* is the part of the brain that interprets sensory information. It is the largest part of the brain. The cerebrum is divided into two hemispheres, connected by a thin band of tissue called the corpus callosum. The *cerebellum* is positioned at the back of the head, between the brain stem and the cerebrum. It controls both voluntary and involuntary movements. The *medulla oblongata* forms the base of the brain. This part of the brain is responsible for blood flow and breathing, among other things. The *hindbrain* refers to a section of the brain including the medulla oblongata, pons, and cerebellum.

21. C: The sugar and phosphate in DNA are connected by covalent bonds. A *covalent bond* is formed when atoms share electrons. It is very common for atoms to share pairs of electrons. Hydrogen bonds are used in DNA to bind complementary bases together, such as adenine with thymine or guanine with cytosine. An *ionic bond* is created when one or more electrons are transferred between atoms. *Ionic bonds*, also known as *electrovalent bonds*, are formed between ions with opposite charges. There is no such thing as an *overt bond* in chemistry.

22. C: The mass of 7.35 moles of water is 132 grams. You should be able to find the mass of various chemical compounds when you are given the number of moles. The information required to perform this function is included on the periodic table. To solve this problem, find the molecular mass of water by finding the respective weights of hydrogen and oxygen. Remember that water contains two hydrogen molecules and one oxygen molecule. The molecular mass of hydrogen is roughly 1, and the molecular mass of oxygen is roughly 16. A molecule of water, then, has approximately 18 grams of mass. Multiply this by 7.35 moles, and you will obtain the answer 132.3, which is closest to answer choice C.

23. C: *Collagen* is the protein produced by cartilage. Bone, tendon, and cartilage are all mainly composed of collagen. *Actin* and *myosin* are the proteins responsible for muscle contractions. Actin makes up the thinner fibers in muscle tissue, while myosin makes up the thicker fibers. Myosin is the most numerous cell protein in human muscle. *Estrogen* is one of the steroid hormones produced mainly by the ovaries. Estrogen motivates the menstrual cycle and the development of female sex characteristics.

24. B: Unlike other organic molecules, lipids are not water soluble. Lipids are typically composed of carbon and hydrogen. Three common types of lipid are fats, waxes, and oils. Indeed, lipids usually feel oily when you touch them. All living cells are primarily composed of lipids, carbohydrates, and proteins. Some examples of fats are lard, corn oil, and butter. Some examples of waxes are beeswax and carnauba wax. Some examples of steroids are cholesterol and ergosterol.

25. D: Of these orbitals, the last to fill is 6s. Orbitals fill in the following order: 1s, 2s, 2p, 3s, 3p, 4s, 3d, 4p, 5s, 4d, 5p, 6s, 4f, 5d, 6p, 7s, 5f, 6d, and 7p. The number is the orbital number, and the letter is the sublevel identification. Sublevel s has one orbital and can hold a maximum of two electrons. Sublevel p has three orbitals and can hold a maximum of six electrons. Sublevel d has five orbitals and can hold a maximum of 10 electrons. Sublevel f has seven orbitals and can hold a maximum of 14 electrons.

26. C: The parasympathetic nervous system is responsible for lowering the heart rate. It slows down the heart rate, dilates the blood vessels, and increases the secretions of the digestive system. The central nervous system is composed of the brain and the spinal cord. The sympathetic nervous system is a part of the autonomic nervous system; its role is to oppose the actions taken by the parasympathetic nervous system. So, the sympathetic nervous system accelerates the heart, contracts the blood vessels, and decreases the secretions of the digestive system.

27. D: *Hemoglobin* is not a steroid. It is a protein that helps to move oxygen from the lungs to the various body tissues. Steroids can be either synthetic chemicals used to reduce swelling and inflammation or sex hormones produced by the body. *Cholesterol* is the most abundant steroid in the human body. It is necessary for the creation of bile, though it can be dangerous if the levels in the body become too high. *Estrogen* is a female steroid produced by the ovaries (in females), testes (in males), placenta, and adrenal cortex. It contributes to adolescent sexual development, menstruation, mood, lactation, and aging. *Testosterone* is the main hormone produced by the testes; it is responsible for the development of adult male sex characteristics.

28. C: Nitrogen pentoxide is the name of the binary molecular compound NO_5. The format given in answer choice C is appropriate when dealing with two nonmetals. A prefix is used to denote the number of atoms of each element. Note that when there are seven atoms of a given element, the prefix *hepta-* is used instead of the usual *septa-*. Also, when the first atom in this kind of binary molecular compound is single, it does not need to be given the prefix *mono-*.

29. B: Smooth muscle tissue is said to be arranged in a disorderly fashion because it is not striated like the other two types of muscle: cardiac and skeletal. Striations are lines that can only be seen with a microscope. *Smooth* muscle is typically found in the supporting tissues of hollow organs and blood vessels. *Cardiac* muscle is found exclusively in the heart; it is responsible for the contractions that pump blood throughout the body. *Skeletal* muscle, by far the most preponderant in the body, controls the movements of the skeleton. The contractions of skeletal muscle are responsible for all voluntary motion. There is no such thing as *rough* muscle.

30. C: *Melatonin* is produced by the pineal gland. One of the primary functions of melatonin is regulation of the circadian cycle, which is the rhythm of sleep and wakefulness. *Insulin* helps regulate the amount of glucose in the blood. Without insulin, the body is unable to convert blood sugar into energy. *Testosterone* is the main hormone produced by the testes; it is responsible for the development of adult male sex characteristics. *Epinephrine*, also known as adrenaline, performs a number of functions: It quickens and strengthens the heartbeat and dilates the bronchioles. Epinephrine is one of the hormones secreted when the body senses danger.

Arithmetic Reasoning

1. B: First, find the total before taxes:

$$\$7.50 + \$3.00 = \$10.50$$

Then, calculate 6% of the total:

$$\$10.50 \times 0.06 = \$0.63$$

Finally, add the tax to find the total cost:

$$\$10.50 + \$0.63 = \$11.13$$

2. D: There are 7 days in a week. Knowing that the chef can make 25 pastries in a day, the weekly number can be calculated:

$$25 \times 7 = 175$$

3. B: The woman has four days to earn $250. To find the amount she must earn each day, divide the amount she must earn ($250) by 4:

$$\frac{\$250}{4} = \$62.50$$

4. A: To find the number of cars remaining, subtract the number of cars that were sold from the original number:

$$476 - 36 = 440$$

5. B: Calculate 5% of $450:

$$\$450 \times 0.05 = \$22.50$$

This is the amount of interest she will earn.

6. C: First, figure out how much the second child contributed:

$$\$24.00 - \$15.00 = \$9.00$$

Then, calculate how much the first two children contributed in total:

$$\$24.00 + \$9.00 = \$33.00$$

Finally, figure out how much the third child will have to contribute:

$$\$78.00 - \$33.00 = \$45.00$$

7. C: First, figure out how many points the first woman will earn:

$$3 \times 5 = 15$$

Then, figure out how many points the second woman will earn:

$$6 \times 5 = 30$$

Then, add these two values together:

$$30 + 15 = 45 \text{ points total}$$

8. D: First, calculate 13% of 540:

$$540 \times 0.13 = 70.2 \text{ (round to 70)}$$

Then, add this value onto the original number of workers:

$$540 + 70 = 610$$

610 is the number of people that the company will employ after the expansion.

9. D: To find the number of apartments on each floor, divide the total number of apartments by the number of floors:

$$\frac{65}{13} = 5$$

10. A: First, find the total number of pens:

$$5 \times 3 = 15$$

Then, find the total number of pencils:

$$3 \times 7 = 21$$

Finally, express it as a ratio: 15:21 or 5:7.

11. C: To calculate his new salary, add his raise to his original salary:

$$\$15.23 + \$2.34 = \$17.57$$

12. A: To find the total number of passengers, multiply the number of planes by the number of passengers each can hold:

$$6 \times 300 = 1800$$

13. B: Currently, there are two men for every woman. If the number of women is doubled, then the new ratio is 2:2. This is equivalent to 1:1.

14. C: First, calculate 3% of 250 pounds:

$$250 \times 0.03 = 7.5 \text{ lb}$$

Calculate how much she weighs at the end of the first week:

$$250 - 7.5 = 242.5 \text{ lb}$$

Calculate 2% of 242.5:

$$242.5 \times 0.02 = 4.85 \text{ lb}$$

Add the two values together to get the total:

$$7.5 + 4.85 = 12.35$$

15. D: Divide the total distance she must travel (583 km) by the number of kilometers she drives each hour (78 km) to figure out how many hours it will take to reach her destination:

$$\frac{583 \text{ km}}{78 \text{ km/hr}} = 7.47 \text{ hours}$$

16. D: One gallon of paint can paint three rooms, so to find out how many 28 gallons can do, that number must be multiplied by 3:

$$28 \times 3 = 84 \text{ rooms}$$

17. A: Each earns $135, so to find the total earned, that amount must be multiplied by the number of workers:

$$\$135 \times 5 = \$675$$

18. C: First, calculate her score on the second test:

$$99 - 15 = 84$$

Then, calculate her score on the third test:

$$84 + 5 = 89$$

19. A: To find out how much he has remaining, both numbers must be subtracted from the original amount ($50.00):

$$\$50.00 - \$15.64 - \$7.12 = \$27.24$$

20. D: Divide the number of students (600) by the number of classrooms they will share (20):

$$\frac{600}{20} = 30$$

21. C: To calculate this value, divide the number of dogs (48) by the number of workers that are available to care for them (4):

$$\frac{48}{4} = 12$$

22. C: First, calculate the length of the second office:

$$20 + 6 = 26 \text{ feet}$$

Then, add both values together to get a combined length:

$$26 + 20 = 46 \text{ feet}$$

23. C: Find the total cost of the items:

$$\$6.65 + \$159.23 = \$165.88$$

Then, calculate how much each individual will owe:

$$\frac{\$165.88}{4} = \$41.47$$

24. A: To answer this question, simply calculate half of 140 acres:

$$\frac{140}{2} = 70 \text{ acres}$$

25. C: First, calculate how many he has after selling 45:

$$360 - 45 = 315$$

Then, calculate how many he has after buying 85:

$$315 + 85 = 400$$

26. D: Calculate the total amount of money the couple has available to spend, which is the amount in the joint bank account and the amount that each has:

$$\$569 + \$293 + \$189 = \$1051$$

27. D: First, find out what the total temperature decrease will be after 4 minutes:

$$2 \times 4 = 8 \text{ degrees}$$

Then, subtract that from the original temperature:

$$98 - 8 = 90 \text{ degrees}$$

28. B: First, calculate 30% of 3 inches:

$$3 \times 0.3 = 0.9 \text{ inches}$$

Then, subtract this value from the original length:

$$3 - 0.9 = 2.1$$

29. D: Add the number of tickets that were sold at each location to get the total number of tickets sold:

$$432 + 238 + 123 = 793$$

30. B: First, figure out how many pieces of candy are in the bag before they are divided:

$$26 - 8 = 18$$

Then, figure out how many pieces each friend will get by dividing by 2:

$$\frac{18}{2} = 9$$

Word Knowledge

1. A: When it is said that someone is generous, it usually means they are giving and unselfish.

2. C: When something is described as challenging, it usually means that it is difficult or demanding.

3. B: A teacher provides instruction and information to an individual or group of individuals. An instructor functions in the same capacity, that is, in the practice of teaching.

4. D: When something is concluded, it means that it is finished or completed.

5. A: A residence is a place where a person lives; the term is often used to refer to someone's home.

6. C: To say something was done instantly means that it was done immediately and without hesitation.

7. C: Something that is described as gigantic is extremely large, or huge, in size.

8. A: Something that is costly is expensive. It costs a lot of money.

9. D: An opportunity is a chance to do something. For example, saying someone was given the *opportunity* to go to school or saying somebody was given the *chance* to go to school conveys the same meaning.

10. B: A response is also commonly known as an answer. A response to a question carries the same meaning as an answer to a question.

11. C: To say that something is done frequently implies that it is done regularly or often.

12. A: Something that is being observed is being watched. Binoculars are used to see things more clearly, so it makes sense that the man would be observing or watching eagles with binoculars.

13. D: Saying that somebody purchased something and saying they bought something conveys the same meaning.

14. D: The word difficulty implies hardship. When it is said that somebody is having difficulties with another person or thing, it usually means they are experiencing problems.

15. A: Entire is an amount. It usually means the whole amount. For example, if someone says they ate an entire apple, it is the same as saying they ate a whole apple.

16. C: To say something is superior to something else usually implies that it is better.

17. B: A remark is a spoken statement, also commonly known as a comment. To say somebody made a remark conveys the same meaning as saying they made a comment.

18. C: When a selection is being made, it involves making a choice between several options. Selecting something is the same as choosing something.

19. A: To commence something is to begin or start something.

20. B: When something is done swiftly, it means that it is done fast or quickly.

21. D: When something is overdue, it means that it is late. For example, when a bill is overdue, it means that it has not been paid on time.

22. D: Somebody who is experiencing or feeling anguish is experiencing sorrow or sadness.

23. A: Solitary can mean a number of different things, but one meaning is single. For example, if you said there was a solitary tree in a yard, you would mean that there was a single tree.

24. C: Chuckled is a synonym for laughed. To say somebody chuckled or to say that somebody laughed conveys the same meaning.

25. A: If somebody or something is departing from somewhere, it means they are leaving. For example, to say the train departed from the station is the same as saying the train left the station.

26. B: To locate something that is lost or misplaced is to find it. For example, the child could not locate (find) his toy.

27. A: Something that is soiled is stained or dirty. When somebody says their clothing is soiled, it is the same as saying their clothing is dirty.

28. C: Slumber is another word for sleep. Saying someone slumbered is the same as saying they slept.

29. C: If somebody is puzzled about something, it implies confusion or bewilderment. For example, to say that a man was puzzled by the woman's reaction means that the man was confused by her reaction.

30. B: To desire something is to want something. Saying that a woman desired a new car has the same meaning as saying the woman wanted a new car.

31. D: Something that is cheap does not cost a substantial amount of money. Saying something is cheap and saying that something is inexpensive conveys the same meaning.

32. C: When somebody is described as intelligent, it usually means that they are smart.

33. A: When somebody objects to something, it means that they disagree with it. A person who objects to the expression of a specific political opinion may be said to disagree with it.

34. D: Constructed most nearly means built. If you say a home is constructed out of wood, for example, it conveys the same meaning as saying the home is built out of wood.

35. A: Something that is required is needed. For example, if you say you require ten dollars to buy lunch, it implies that you need ten dollars for lunch.

Paragraph Comprehension

1. A: The passage states: "During interphase, all of the genetic material within the cell is replicated. Then, the strands that contain the genetic material, which are known as chromatin, become compacted and condensed." According to the passage, the material in the cell is copied (replicated) before the chromatin becomes compacted into strands.

2. B: The conclusion that many people do not practice healthy eating can be made based on two points in the passage. First, we are told that many people are obese. Second, it is stated that healthy eating is more important to maintaining a healthy weight than exercise activity. Therefore, if a large number of people are overweight, and eating unhealthy foods is the major contributor to obesity, it can be concluded that many people do not practice healthy eating.

3. B: The author is relying on experiences that were reported by others. This is evident through the use of such phrases as "he said that he was later told" and "she says the job went to a less qualified applicant."

4. D: The work is important because "it is often viewed as the first significant work of English literature."

5. B: The purpose of the passage is to convince the reader that cats are better pets than dogs. This is stated in the opening sentence when the author states "Cats are by far a superior pet compared to dogs." Also, the remainder of the passage describes the advantages of cats as pets. Any time cats are compared to dogs, cats are described as superior pets.

6. A: After the malaria parasites infect the red blood cells, symptoms like fever occur. The passage states that "There, they multiply, and soon they infect red blood cells. Malaria symptoms like fever will begin to be experienced at this point."

7. D: The main idea in this passage is that water sports don't have to be dangerous. The passage states "Many people feel that summer time water sports are dangerous. While accidents do occur, the vast majority are preventable." Also, the rest of the passage focuses on outlining what precautions can be taken to ensure that water sports are less risky.

8. D: This can be concluded based on the section of the passage that states "Today, with blogs, virtually anybody can put their work out there for others to view. It's as easy as setting up your blog, naming it, and posting anything you want."

9. D: Many people still do not buy organic food because it is too expensive. The passage states "the price of organic foods still prevents many people from eating them on a regular basis."

10. A: It is reasonable to conclude that the author mentioned Cindy because it would strengthen the argument that birth order affects personality traits. The passage states that oldest children are more responsible and perform better in school. Since Cindy was on the Dean's list (good academic performance) and did her chores as a child (a sign of responsibility), it is reasonable to assume that Cindy was an oldest child.

11. D: The main idea discussed in the passage is that weddings are expensive. The author states that the expense of a wedding is a major source of stress. Then, the author discusses many of the expenses involved, finally providing an example of the high cost of a simple wedding.

12. B: A supplier should reduce the price of a good if they want to sell more of it because, according to the passage, "consumers will demand less of a good if the price is higher *and more if it is lower*."

13. B: According to the passage, many people are in debt in North America because they borrowed money they could not afford to repay. The passage states that "much of the blame lies with the companies who actually granted the credit to consumers. This debt crisis wouldn't have happened if loans were not granted to people who could not afford them."

14. A: The person's airway should be opened before checking whether they are breathing. The passage advises the rescuer to "open their airway by raising the chin. After this, but before beginning mouth to mouth, spend a few moments to determine whether they are breathing." Mouth to mouth and chest compressions are only done if the person is not breathing.

15. A: The main idea of the passage is that fur is an unnecessary material good. The author provides two statements to support the main theme. First, the author notes that there are synthetic materials which can keep people warm, so fur is no longer necessary. Second, the author states that fur is used to produce luxury items which are not really needed by anyone.

Mathematics Knowledge

1. B: The perimeter of a figure is the sum of all of its sides. Since a rectangle's width and length will be the same on opposite sides, the perimeter of a rectangle can be calculated by using the following formula:

$$P = 2w + 2l$$

Using the numbers given in the question:

$$P = 2(7) + 2(9)$$

$$P = 14 + 18 = 32 \text{ cm}$$

2. D: First, gather the like terms on opposite sides of the equation to make it easier to solve:

$$12 + 30 \geq 4q + 3q$$

$$42 \geq 7q$$

Then, divide both sides by 7 to solve for q:

$$\frac{42}{7} \geq \frac{7q}{7}$$

$$6 \geq q \text{ or } q \leq 6$$

3. C: To solve for x, simply add 6 to both sides:

$$x - 6 + 6 = 0 + 6$$

$$x = 6$$

4. A: To calculate the value of this expression, substitute -3 for x each time it appears in the expression:

$$3(-3)^3 + (3(-3) + 4) - 2(-3)^2$$

According to the order of operations, any operations inside of brackets must be done first:

$$3(-3)^3 + (-9 + 4) - 2(-3)^2$$

$$3(-3)^3 + (-5) - 2(-3)^2$$

Then, exponential operations may be performed:

$$3(-27) + (-5) - 2(9)$$

Next, multiplication:

$$-81 - 5 - 18$$

Finally, subtraction from left to right:

$$-81 - 5 - 18 = -104$$

5. C: First, combine like terms to make the equation easier to solve:

$$3x + 2x = 45 + 30$$

$$5x = 75$$

Then, divide both sides by 5 to solve for x:

$$\frac{5x}{5} = \frac{75}{5}$$

$$x = 15$$

6. A: First, add 25 to both sides to isolate x:

$$\frac{1}{4}x - 25 + 25 \geq 75 + 25$$

$$\frac{1}{4}x \geq 100$$

Then, multiply both sides by 4 to solve for x:

$$4 \times \frac{1}{4}x \geq 4 \times 100$$

$$x \geq 400$$

7. A: First, add 5 to both sides to isolate x:

$$x^2 - 5 + 5 = 20 + 5$$

$$x^2 = 25$$

Then, take the square root of both sides to solve for x:

$$\sqrt{x^2} = \sqrt{25}$$

$$x = \pm 5$$

8. B: First, we must calculate the length of one side of the square. Since we know the perimeter is 8 cm, and that a square has 4 equal sides, the length of each side can be calculated by dividing the perimeter (8 cm) by 4:

$$\frac{8 \text{ cm}}{4} = 2 \text{ cm}$$

The formula for the area of a square is length squared:

$$A = 2^2 = 4 \text{ cm}^2$$

9. D: To find the value of this expression, substitute the given values for x and y into the expression and simplify:

$$3(4)(2) - 12(2) + 5(4) = 24 - 24 + 20 = 20$$

10. D: First, subtract 10 from both sides to isolate x:

$$0.65x + 10 - 10 = 15 - 10$$

$$0.65x = 5$$

Then, divide both sides by 0.65 to solve for x:

$$\frac{0.65x}{0.65} = \frac{5}{0.65}$$

$$x = 7.69$$

11. B: Use the FOIL method (first, outside, inside, and last) to expand the polynomial:

$$12x^2 - 18x + 20x - 30$$

Then, combine like terms to simplify the expression:

$$12x^2 - 18x + 20x - 30$$

$$12x^2 + 2x - 30$$

12. B: To simplify this expression, recall the law of exponents for division:

$$\frac{x^n}{x^m} = x^{n-m}$$

Apply to each variable in the expression:

$$\frac{x^{18}}{x^5} = x^{13}; \frac{t^6}{t^2} = t^4; \frac{w^3}{w^2} = w; \frac{z^{20}}{z^{19}} = z$$

Combine to simplify:

$$10x^{13}t^4wz$$

13. D: To calculate 4 factorial, take the product of all the integers between 1 and 4:

$$4! = 4 \times 3 \times 2 \times 1 = 24$$

14. D: Because it is a cube, we can find the volume by taking the cube of any side length:

$$5 \times 5 \times 5 = 125 \text{ cm}^3$$

15. A: First, factor this equation to make solving for x easier:

$$x^2 - 13x + 42 = (x - 6)(x - 7) = 0$$

The expression on the left side of the equation is equal to zero when either $(x - 6)$ or $(x - 7)$ equals zero. Thus:

$$x = 6, 7$$

16. C: The area of a triangle can be calculated by using the following formula:

$$A = \frac{1}{2}bh$$

Therefore, by using the values given in the question:

$$A = \frac{1}{2}(12)(12) = 72 \text{ cm}^2$$

17. D: To simplify this expression, recall the law of exponents for multiplication:

$$x^n x^m = x^{n+m}$$

Apply to each variable in the expression:

$$x^7 x^2 = x^9; y^{12}y^3 = y^{15}$$

$$(3x^2 7x^7) + (2y^3 9y^{12}) = 21x^9 + 18y^{15}$$

18. C: First, subtract 27 from both sides to isolate x:

$$\frac{x}{3} + 27 - 27 = 30 - 27$$

$$\frac{x}{3} = 3$$

Next, multiply both sides by 3:

$$\frac{x}{3} \times 3 = 3 \times 3$$

$$x = 9$$

19. B: The slope of a line can be calculated by dividing the change in the y-coordinate by the change in the x-coordinate:

$$Y_{change} = 8 - 1 = 7$$

$$X_{change} = -13 - 4 = -17$$

$$Slope = \frac{Y_{change}}{X_{change}} = -\frac{7}{17}$$

20. A: To solve for x, calculate the value of 20% of 200:

$$20\% \times 200 = 0.2 \times 200 = 40$$

$$x = 40$$

21. B: The odds of a black balloon being chosen at random from a bag of balloons is calculated as:

$$P = \frac{\# \text{ black balloons}}{\# \text{ total balloons}}$$

The total number of balloons is found by adding up the number of each color:

$$47 + 5 + 10 = 62$$

There are ten black balloons, so calculate the probability of selecting a black balloon:

$$P = \frac{10}{62} = 16\%$$

22. D: Each ticket has the same odds of being the winning ticket:

$$1 \text{ in } 500 \ or \ \frac{1}{500}$$

If a man buys 25 tickets, his odds of winning are now multiplied by 25:

$$25 \text{ in } 500 \ or \frac{25}{500}$$

We can reduce this ratio by dividing both numbers by 25:

$$\frac{25}{25} = 1; \frac{500}{25} = 20$$

$$1 \text{ in } 20 \ or \frac{1}{20} = 5\%$$

23. D: To find the volume of a rectangular prism, the formula is $V = L \times W \times H$. For the prism described in this question:

$$V = 5 \text{ cm} \times 6 \text{ cm} \times 10 \text{ cm} = 300 \text{ cm}^3$$

24. C: To calculate the midpoint of a line, take the average of both the x- and y-coordinates. The x-coordinate of the midpoint can be calculated as follows:

$$\frac{6 + 10}{2} = 8$$

The y-coordinate of the midpoint can be calculated as follows:

$$\frac{20 + 40}{2} = 30$$

Therefore, the midpoint is (8, 30).

25. A: First, subtract 60 from both sides:

$$5x + 60 - 60 = 75 - 60$$

Then divide both sides by 5:

$$\frac{5x}{5} = \frac{15}{5}$$

$$x = 3$$

Electrical Information

1. D: Voltage is the potential energy difference between two charged terminals, and current is the rate of flow of charge past a given point.

2. C: 12 V. Using Ohm's Law, $V = I \times R$ and the given current ($I = 4$ A) and resistance ($R = 3\ \Omega$):

$$12\ V = 4\ A \times 3\ \Omega$$

3. B: Resistance is measured in ohms, current in amps, and voltage in volts. Ohmmeters, Ammeters, and Voltmeters can take readings of those respective measurements.

4. B: $3\ \Omega$. This series circuit can be solved 2 ways. First, by looking at the circuit as a whole:

$$\Delta V_{total} = \Delta V_1 + \Delta V_2 + \Delta V_3 \qquad I_{total} = I_1 = I_2 = I_3 = I_4 \qquad \text{Ohm's Law: } \Delta V_{total} = I_{total} \times R_{total}$$
$$\Delta V_{total} = 2\ V + 3\ V + 4\ V \qquad I_{total} = 3\ A$$
$$= 9\ V \qquad\qquad R_{total} = (9\ V)/(3\ A) = 3\ \Omega$$

Alternatively, the resistance of each resistor could be found and summed:

$$R_{R_\#} = \Delta V_{R_\#}/I_{R_\#} \qquad\qquad R_{total} = R_{R_1} + R_{R_2} + R_{R_3}$$
$$R_{R_1} = (2\ V)/(3\ A) = 0.66\ \Omega \qquad R_{total} = 0.66\ \Omega + 1\ \Omega + 1.33\ \Omega = 3\ \Omega$$
$$R_{R_2} = (3\ V)/(3\ A) = 1\ \Omega$$
$$R_{R_3} = (4\ V)/(3\ A) = 1.33\ \Omega$$

5. A: 12 V. Using Ohm's Law with a circuit in series:

$$I_{total} = I_1 = I_2 = I_3 = I_4 \qquad R_{total} = R_{R_1} + R_{R_2} + R_{R_3} \qquad \text{Ohm's Law: } \Delta V_{total} = I_{total} \times$$
$$I_{total} = 4\ A \qquad\qquad R_{total} = 0.5\ \Omega + 1\ \Omega + 1.5\ \Omega \qquad\qquad R_{total}$$
$$= 3\ \Omega \qquad\qquad \Delta V_{total} = 4\ A \times 3\ \Omega = 12\ V$$

6. A: $I_4 = 10$ A; $I_6 = 15$ A. Because the battery is 20 V, $R_2 = 4\ \Omega$, $R_3 = 2\ \Omega$, and the resistors are in parallel:

$$\Delta V_{battery} = \Delta V_2 = \Delta V_3 = 20\ V \qquad\qquad I_{R_2} = \Delta V_{R_2}/R_2 = (20\ V)/(4\ \Omega) = 5\ A$$

$$I_4 = I_{R_3} = \Delta V_{R_3}/R_3 \qquad\qquad I_6 = I_{R_2} + I_{R_3} = 10\ A + 5\ A = 15\ A$$
$$= (20\ V)/(2\ \Omega)$$
$$= 10\ A$$

7. C: 1 Ω. If $R_1 = 4\ \Omega$, $R_2 = 4\ \Omega$, and $R_3 = 2\ \Omega$, equivalent resistance (R_{eq}) can be found using:

$$\frac{1}{R_{eq}} = \frac{1}{R_1} + \frac{1}{R_2} + \frac{1}{R_3}$$
$$\frac{1}{R_{eq}} = \frac{1}{4} + \frac{1}{4} + \frac{1}{2}$$
$$\frac{1}{R_{eq}} = \frac{4}{4}$$
$$R_{eq} = 1$$

8. D: To solve a circuit with both series and parallel components, first add resistors that are found in series, then solve for the equivalent resistance of the parallel resistors. For example, in the pictured circuit, add the two resistors that would be in series in place of R_1 and add the three resistors that would be in series in place of R_3 before solving for equivalent resistance of the simplified resistors.

9. B. 6.66 A. Using $P = I \times V$ to solve for current (I), where $P = 60$ watts and $V = 9$ V:

$$I = (60\ \text{W})/(9\ \text{V}) = 6.66\ \text{A}$$

10. D: Alternating current is produced by generators, periodically changes direction of flow, can be transported over long distances without losing power, and is used to supply electricity to homes. Direct current is produced by batteries, flows only in one direction, and is used on ships and airplanes.

11. C: Direct current is used in ships, planes, and cell phones. Alternating current is used in homes to power appliances and lights.

12. A: The earth commonly serves as a ground because it can infinitely donate or accept electrons without mathematically significant changes to its net charge. In cars, the negative terminal of the car battery serves as the ground. Lightning rods allow for the high-voltage current of lightning to ground to the earth safely. Home wiring is also grounded to the earth.

13. B: P-type semiconductors have a shortage of electrons; when an electric field is applied, a positive pole forms (example: Silicon doped with boron). N-type semiconductors have an excess of electrons as a result of the doping process; when an electric field is applied, a negative pole forms due to the buildup of negatively charged electrons (example: Silicon doped with antimony).

14. C: Diodes allow current to pass in only one direction. P-n junction diodes are made up of fused p- and n-type semiconductors and are considered solid-state diodes because electricity flows through solid material rather than a vacuum.

15. D: Transistor applications include radio, television, computer chips, and early hearing aids.

16. C: Capacitors store electric charge and can be used to protect sensitive components during a power surge.

17. D: Capacitors store charge and oppose voltage change across the two plates. Direct current can charge a capacitor but cannot flow through it. Inductors store energy and oppose the rate of change of alternating current flowing through them; however, direct current passes through easily. They are not interchangeable components.

18. B: Transformers step voltage up or down and are applied so that power can be generated safely at low voltages, transported at high voltages, and distributed at lower, useful voltages.

19. A: Motors convert electrical energy (electricity) to mechanical energy (motion), and generators convert mechanical energy to electrical energy.

20. B: Generators use electromagnetic induction to convert mechanical energy to electrical energy. AC generators mechanically turn a coil in a magnetic field to produce voltage output and induce alternating current.

Shop and Auto Information

1. B: Most gasoline engines operate with reciprocating pistons in cylinders, and most automobiles in the United States utilize the four-stroke cycle. Four piston strokes make up the four-stroke cycle: intake, compression, power, and exhaust. In one cycle, the piston moves down and back up twice.

2. C: While the battery is used to start the vehicle, the alternator supplies electricity to the vehicle while it is running and recharges the battery as it turns.

3. A: Carburetors (in older vehicles) and fuel injectors (in newer vehicles) mix air and fuel before combustion. Fuel injectors complete the process with the help of a computer, and allow for greater fuel efficiency.

4. D: Combustion occurs in the engine, and in gasoline engines, a spark from a spark plug ignites the fuel-air mixture in the cylinder to begin combustion.

5. D: One of the most common ignition problems is spark plug fouling, which occurs when carbon builds up at the ignition point; it will cause engine misfiring and increased carbon emissions. Driving at highway speeds is good for spark plugs because the increased temperature of the engine helps burn off the excess fuel or ash. Spark plug fouling is more common with prolonged idling and city driving because the engine doesn't get as hot.

6. A: Failing piston rings will result in engine smoking because oil from the crankcase will leak into the combustion chamber and smoke when combusted.

7. D: Exhaust from the combustion chamber is released by the exhaust valve towards the exhaust manifold, which collects gas byproducts from each cylinder and helps with noise control. Through the exhaust pipe, gas travels to the catalytic converter, which filters out pollutants and converts them to water vapor and carbon dioxide. From the catalytic converter, exhaust travels through the exhaust pipe to the muffler, which further reduces noise. From the muffler, the tail pipe releases gas away from the vehicle.

8. C: Motor oil is not consumed by the engine and is not used in combustion, so it does not act as fuel. It does lubricate the gears and prevent overheating and corrosion.

9. B: The thermostat helps control engine temperature by sending coolant either to the engine or to the radiator if it needs to be cooled further. A thermostat stuck open will cause the engine to run cold and result in bad gas mileage; a thermostat stuck closed will cause the engine to overheat.

10. B: Front wheel drive (FWD) is found in most modern economy or compact cars; the transaxle combines the functionality of the transmission, front axle, and differential into one component.

11. C: Springs, installed between the chassis or frame and the axels, absorb the impact of the road on the vehicle. Shocks (shock absorbers or dampers) oppose the oscillating motion of the springs and dampen road vibration. Struts are a combination of springs and shocks. The anti-roll bar or sway bar keeps the vehicle from rolling over when turning and allows for better handling. The spindles, which should be parallel to the ground, are the center point of each wheel that connects to the upper and lower control arms via a sealed and greased ball joint. Control arms connect the suspension system to the frame of the vehicle through bushings, which are insulated joint linings that protect the jointed components from vibration or wear.

12. A: Low or leaking power steering fluid, a problem with the power steering pump, and even some suspension problems such as worn control arm bushings can result in difficulty turning the steering wheel and steering the vehicle. Improper alignment can also cause passive steering problems: when the steering wheel is temporarily released, the vehicle will pull to one side.

13. B: When the brake pedal is depressed, brake fluid is pushed from the master cylinder through the brake lines to each wheel's brake caliper. The fluid pressure causes friction in the brake systems (disc or drum), which forces the wheels to stop turning. Disc brakes utilize brake pads and a disc rotor; drum brakes also utilize a rotor, but brake shoes are unique to drum brakes.

14. B: Ripping wood is the process of cutting it parallel to the grain. Cross cuts are perpendicular to the grain. Bevel cuts are angled across the depth of the wood, and miter cuts are angled across the wide face of the workpiece.

15. C: Beveled edge chisels have three beveled edges; mortise chisels only have one. Japanese bench chisels are less beveled than Western chisels, and paring chisels, while beveled, are very thin and nearly flexible.

16. A: At least one end of the ratcheting wrench contains a ratcheting device so that loosening or tightening doesn't require a complete circular motion or removing and resetting the wrench if something is in the way. These wrenches are helpful in tight spaces. Manual and digital torque wrenches help prevent overtightening because they can be calibrated in accordance with manufactured specifications. Socket wrenches have a drive (the square-shaped fitting) attached to a ratchet on one end; various sockets can be attached to the drive to accommodate different size bolt heads. A combination of box-ended and open-ended wrenches, combination wrenches have an open and a closed end.

17. D: The Phillips-head screwdriver forms a cross at the end of the screwdriver; The flat head screwdriver is a simple wedge shape; Allen wrenches are hexagonal.

18. C: Soldering involves applying heat measuring roughly 600-840°F, is commonly used in electrical circuits, and is usually used in relatively smaller jobs than welding. Welding uses extreme heat (6500°F) to melt the base metal to fuse the two work pieces; soldering joins two separate metals with an alloy.

19. A: Rivets support tensile loads (force that occurs in opposite directions along the same axis) and shear loads (force that produces sliding, which is a failure in the plane parallel to direction of force), and the most common modern applications include: residential gutter construction, HVAC duct work, and aircraft manufacturing.

20. C: Various grooves on the upper jaw of tongue and groove pliers (also called Channel Locks) allow for an adjustable, locking fulcrum and a highly versatile tool. Diagonal pliers, also called wire cutters, have acutely angled jaws that enable cutting of wire and nails. Crimping pliers have specialized jaws to allow for breaking plastic coating on wire and crimping wires together; this makes them ideal for telecommunications technicians. Slip joint pliers are highly versatile, smaller than tongue and groove pliers, and the adjustable fulcrum allows the corrugated jaws to lock at varying widths.

21. B: Vise-grips (which can also be spelled vice-grips), also known as locking pliers, are part clamp and part pliers. With handles, corrugated jaws, and a fulcrum between the two like pliers, they can also be locked into a clamped position. A lever in one of the handles allows for the release of the clamping action.

22. D: Drilling creates new holes in workpieces; boring enlarges existing holes. Both processes can pertain to either blind or pass-through holes in a workpiece.

23. B: Oscillating saws are the smallest and most portable of the given list. Vertical band saws and table saws are stationary, and miter saws are able to be mounted to a workbench.

24. A: Files and rasps are manual, hand-held tools used for removing material from workpieces, most commonly of wood or metal. Files produce a finer finish but cut more slowly than rasps. Both files and rasps are available in varying grades of coarseness.

25. B: Angle grinders are the most common form of grinders and are highly versatile. They can be used to clean metal (with the wire brush attachment); cut metal bolts (with the metal cutoff wheel attachment); cut masonry (with the diamond wheel attachment); and sharpen blades (with the grinding wheel). Belt grinders can be used to finish surfaces and sharpen metal blades, among other things, using an abrasive belt. Bench grinders can be mounted on a work bench and are used for grinding off large amounts of material or rust, sharpening metal blades, buffing and polishing surfaces, and cutting wood and other hard materials. Orbital grinders do not exist; orbital sanders are hand-held power tools used for relatively delicate sanding.

Mechanical Comprehension

1. A: The velocity is made up of two components, the x and y components. The x component is not changing during flight, but the weight of the projectile decreases the positive y component of the velocity. Thus, the total velocity will be greatest before the y component has decreased.

2. A: Because the linear speed of two connected pulleys is the same, the pulley with the smaller radius spins faster. The largest pulley will spin slower than the middle pulley. The smallest pulley will spin faster than the middle pulley, making it the fastest pulley.

3. C: Gear A and gear C have the same number of teeth. Thus, gears A and C will have the same speed. Since gear C is rotating at 10 rpm, the total number of rotations is calculated by multiplying the rpm by the number of minutes.

4. A: Because the large mass will produce a greater torque at the same distance from the fulcrum as the small mass, the distance from the large mass to the fulcrum should be shortened. Then, the torque produced by the large mass will decrease and the torque produced by the small mass will increase.

5. A: When the rope is not parallel to the intended path of motion, the force is divided into useful force (x direction) and not useful force (y direction). If only some of the force is useful, then the man will need to apply more force to achieve the same pulling force as if the rope were parallel to the table.

6. B: Because the volume of the liquid doesn't change, when the small piston is compressed, the volume decrease in one piston is the volume increase in the other piston. As the volume is the area times the height, the height of the larger piston only needs to raise one fourth the height that the small piston moved.

7. A: The downward force decreases part of the y component of the top force, but does not affect the x component of the force. Thus, the resultant force is up and to the right.

8. B: Because the same volume of water has to flow through all parts of the river, the water will slow down to fill the wide section.

9. C: The negative side of magnet 2 will be attracted to the positive side of magnet 1. The positive side of magnet 2 will be attracted to the negative side of magnet 3 with the same force. Because the magnitudes of the forces are equal and the directions are opposite, the sum of the forces will be zero.

10. C: The first phase change is from solid to liquid at -21°C. The next phase change is from liquid to gas at 81°C. 90°C is only slightly higher than 81°C, making it safe to say that the substance is still a gas.

11. A: Substitute token values for the resistors to solve. Using 1 Ω resistors, the resistance of circuit A, having resistors in series, is the simple sum of the two resistors: 2 Ω. Because the resistors in circuit B are in parallel, the resistance of circuit B is the reciprocal of the sum of the reciprocals of the resistances, or $\frac{1}{\frac{1}{1}+\frac{1}{1}}$. The result is 1/2 Ω.

12. A: To find the number of swings in a time period from the frequency, multiply the frequency times the time period, after converting the time period into seconds to match the frequency. The final calculation is $\frac{1.4\ \text{swings}}{\text{second}} \times 1\ \text{minute} \times \frac{60\ \text{seconds}}{1\ \text{minute}} = 84\ \text{swings}$

13. B: The mechanical advantage is calculated by the output force divided by the input force. Because both pistons are the same size, the output force will equal the input force, resulting in a mechanical advantage of one.

14. C: Because the horizontal component of the thrown ball's velocity will not affect the vertical component, the vertical component of the thrown ball's velocity will be identical to the dropped ball's velocity. The balls will hit at the same time.

15. A: The cam has four bumps on it. The needle will move up and down for each bump. The cam will rotate five times in the time period of one minute. The total times the needle will move up and down will be five times four.

16. C: Torque is the product of a force perpendicular to the arm and the length of the arm. Options A and B each increase one part of the torque calculation. However, angling the force towards the center would decrease the part of the force that is acting perpendicular to the arm, as some of the force will be acting inward.

17. B: When the ball is compressed into the spring, the ball has potential energy stored in the spring. When the ball is flying upwards, the ball has kinetic energy associated with the motion.

18. B: Pressure increases with depth in water. When the tank was lower it experienced more pressure. Thus, when the tank is higher it experiences less pressure.

19. B: Specific gravity can be calculated as the ratio of the density of the liquid in question to the density of water. Because salt water has a higher density than water, the ratio will be greater than one.

20. B: Convective heat transfer deals with the transfer of heat by fluids (including gas). Steam is a fluid which transfers heat to objects, like a hand, with lower temperatures than it.

21. C: A capacitor stores voltage across a gap between two conductive materials.

22. A: Torque is the product of a force perpendicular to the arm and the length of the arm. Wrench A, with the longer arm, will be able to achieve greater amounts of torque with a set force.

23. B: Because the circuit only has one path and the two resistors are in series, the current is the same everywhere in the circuit. The voltage will drop over both resistors. Also, because the circuit is complete, there is current in the circuit.

24. C: Ammeters measure current (think amps). Multimeters measure current and voltage. Voltmeters only measure voltage.

25. B: When the ball is flying upwards, the kinetic energy is being converted into potential energy. Potential energy increases linearly with height, meaning that an object at 2 feet over the ground has twice the potential energy of the object at 1 foot over the ground. Thus, if all of the energy of the ball will be converted from kinetic energy, and half of the energy will be converted at half the height, the potential energy of the ball will be 50 ft-lb.

26. A: Because mechanical advantage is the ratio of output force to input force, an increase in mechanical advantage means, in this case, that the output force will be increasing. However, energy in simple machines is conserved. This means that the work, or force times distance, done to the input will need to increase, while keeping the force the same. Increasing the distance of the applied force will increase the work, allowing for an increased force for the output.

27. A: As the drum spins one full turn, the hanging rope increases length by 1 foot and decreases length by 3.5 feet. Thus, every spin decreases the rope length by 2.5 feet. In two turns, the rope will decrease length by 5 feet. The pulley makes the weight lift half the distance that the rope decreased. Thus, the weight raises 2.5 feet.

28. C: Condensation from the air occurs when the water vapor in the air cools down enough to change phase from vapor to liquid water. If a pipe is cold and the air is warm, the water vapor will condense on the pipe.

29. A: The color, black, will absorb the most heat from radiation.

30. B: The gear ratio between the small and large gears is 18/30 or 3/5. Multiply the number of rotations of the small gear times the gear ratio to get (3 rotations) × (3/5) = 1.8 rotations.

Assembling Objects

Question	Answer
1	B
2	D
3	D
4	B
5	A
6	C
7	C
8	D
9	A
10	D
11	C
12	B
13	B
14	A
15	C
16	A
17	D
18	B
19	B
20	B
21	B
22	C
23	D
24	A
25	C

OAR Practice Test

Math Skills Test

1. If $16x + 4 = 100$, what is the value of x?

   a. 6
   b. 7
   c. 8
   d. 9

2. Expand the following expression: $(2x - 20)(5x + 10)$

   a. $10x^2 - 80x - 200$
   b. $70x - 200$
   c. $10x^2 - 80x + 200$
   d. $10x^2 - 120x - 200$

3. Which of the following are complementary angles?

   a. $71°$ and $19°$
   b. $90°$ and $90°$
   c. $90°$ and $45°$
   d. $15°$ and $30°$

4. Simplify the following expression: $\left(2x^4\right)^3 + 2\left(y^5\right)^5$

   a. $8x^{64} + 2y^{3125}$
   b. $6x^7 + 2y^{10}$
   c. $6x^{12} + 2y^{25}$
   d. $8x^{12} + 2y^{25}$

5. If the measures of the three angles in a triangle are $2 : 6 : 10$, what is the measure of the smallest angle?

   a. 20 degrees
   b. 40 degrees
   c. 60 degrees
   d. 80 degrees

6. If a circle has a diameter of 12 cm, what is its approximate area?

   a. 38 cm^2
   b. 113 cm^2
   c. 276 cm^2
   d. 452 cm^2

7. The length of a square is 15cm. What is its area?

   a. 30 cm^2
   b. 60 cm^2
   c. 150 cm^2
   d. 225 cm^2

8. A rectangular solid measures 12cm by 3cm by 9cm. What is its volume?

 a. 36 cm^3
 b. 108 cm^3
 c. 324 cm^3
 d. 407 cm^3

9. If $2x^2 = -4x^2 + 216$, which of the following is a possible value of x?

 a. 4
 b. 5
 c. 6
 d. 7

10. The perimeter of a square is 24 m. What is its area?

 a. 30 m^2
 b. 36 m^2
 c. 42 m^2
 d. 24 m^2

11. If a rectangle has a length of 5cm and a width of 7cm, what is its area?

 a. 24 cm^2
 b. 35 cm^2
 c. 42 cm^2
 d. 56 cm^2

12. On a six-sided die, each side has a number between 1 and 6. What is the probability of throwing a 3 or a 4?

 a. 1 in 6
 b. 1 in 3
 c. 1 in 2
 d. 1 in 4

13. Solve for y in the following inequality: $-2y \geq 24 + 6$

 a. $y \leq 15$
 b. $y \geq 15$
 c. $y \leq -15$
 d. $y \geq -15$

14. If $2x = 5x - 30$, what is the value of x?

 a. 10
 b. -10
 c. 4.3
 d. -4.3

15. Given the functions, $f(x) = 3x + 6$ and $g(x) = 2x - 8$, what is the solution of the equation, $f(x) = g(x)$?

 a. $x = -12$
 b. $x = -8$
 c. $x = -14$
 d. $x = -10$

16. Suppose the area of the square in the diagram to the right is 64 in². (The square is not shown actual size.) What is the area of the circle?

   a. 16π in²
   b. 64π in²
   c. $\frac{64}{\pi}$ in²
   d. $(64 + \pi)$ in²

17. Solve for x in the following inequality: $4x + 23 > -3x - 6$

   a. $x > -4.14$
   b. $x < -4.14$
   c. $x > 4.14$
   d. $x < 4.14$

18. If $2x + 5x = 3x + x + 30$, what is the value of x?

   a. 2.72
   b. 4.29
   c. 6
   d. 10

19. What is the value of $3x^2y + y/2 - 6x$, if $x = 4$ and $y = 10$?

   a. 221
   b. 461
   c. 872
   d. 1916

20. At a school carnival, three students spend an average of $10. Six other students spend an average of $4. What is the average amount of money spent by all nine students?

   a. $5
   b. $6
   c. $7
   d. $8

21. If $w = 7$, calculate the value of the following expression: $8w^2 - 12w + (4w - 5) + 6$

   a. 279
   b. 285
   c. 337
   d. 505

22. If $x/3 + 7 = 35$, what is the value of x?

    a. 9.33
    b. 14
    c. 84
    d. 126

23. In the following equation, solve for x by factoring: $2x^2 - 7x = x^2 - 12$

    a. $x = -3, -4$
    b. $x = 3, 4$
    c. $x = 3, -4$
    d. $x = -3, 4$

24. If x is 25% of 250, what is the value of x?

    a. 62.5
    b. 100
    c. 1000
    d. 6250

25. Which of the following inequalities is correct?

    a. $\frac{1}{3} < \frac{2}{7} < \frac{5}{12}$
    b. $\frac{2}{7} < \frac{1}{3} < \frac{5}{12}$
    c. $\frac{5}{12} < \frac{2}{7} < \frac{1}{3}$
    d. $\frac{5}{12} < \frac{1}{3} < \frac{2}{7}$

26. If the volume of a cube is 8 cm³, what is the length of the side of the cube?

    a. 1 cm
    b. 2 cm
    c. 3 cm
    d. 4 cm

27. Simplify the following expression: $(2x^2 + 3)(2x - 1)$

    a. $4x^3 - 2x^2 + 6x - 3$
    b. $2x^2 + 6x - 3$
    c. $4x^3 - 2x^2 + 6x + 3$
    d. $4x^3 - 2x^2 - 6x - 3$

28. Simplify the following expression: $(2x^4 y^7 m^2 z) \times (5x^2 y^3 m^8)$

    a. $10x^6 y^9 m^{10} z$
    b. $7x^6 y^{10} m^{10} z$
    c. $10x^5 y^{10} m^{10} z$
    d. $10x^6 y^{10} m^{10} z$

29. A classroom contains 13 boys and 18 girls. If a student's name is chosen randomly, what is the probability it will be a girl's name?

    a. 36%

    b. 42%

    c. 58%

    d. 72%

30. What is 10% of 40%?

    a. 4%

    b. 30%

    c. 50%

    d. 400%

Reading Comprehension Test

Use the passage below to answer the following two questions:

Inside the cockpit, three key items to be checked are: (1) battery and ignition switches—off, (2) control column locks—removed, (3) landing gear control— down and locked.

The fuel selectors should be checked for proper operation in all positions—including the OFF position. Stiff selectors, or ones where the tank position is hard to find, are unacceptable. The primer should also be exercised. The pilot should feel resistance when the primer is both pulled out and pushed in. The primer should also lock securely. Faulty primers can interfere with proper engine operation. The engine controls should also be manipulated by slowly moving each through its full range to check for binding or stiffness.

The airspeed indicator should be properly marked, and the indicator needle should read zero. If it does not, the instrument may not be calibrated correctly. Similarly, the vertical speed indicator (VSI) should also read zero when the airplane is on the ground. If it does not, a small screwdriver can be used to zero the instrument. The VSI is the only flight instrument that a pilot has the prerogative to adjust. All others must be adjusted by an FAA certificated repairman or mechanic.

1. According to the passage, which of the following setting configurations is correct?

   a.
Battery and ignition switches: On
Control column locks: Removed
Landing gear control: Down and locked
Airspeed Indicator needle: 0
   b.
Battery and ignition switches: Off
Control column locks: Removed
Landing gear control: Up and locked
Airspeed Indicator needle: 0
   c.
Battery and ignition switches: On
Control column locks: In place
Landing gear control: Up and locked
Airspeed Indicator needle: 0
   d.
Battery and ignition switches: Off
Control column locks: Removed
Landing gear control: Down and locked
Airspeed Indicator needle: 0

2. In the passage, what does the word *primer* mean?

   a. Short, introductory guide
   b. Small fuel pump
   c. Painted binding agent
   d. Explosive ignition cap

Use the passage below to answer the following question:

Radial engines were widely used during World War II and many are still in service today. With these engines, a row or rows of cylinders are arranged in a circular pattern around the crankcase. The main advantage of a radial engine is the favorable power-to-weight ratio. In-line engines have a comparatively small frontal area, but their power-to-weight ratios are relatively low. In addition, the rearmost cylinders of an air-cooled, in-line engine receive very little cooling air, so these engines are normally limited to four or six cylinders. V-type engines provide more horsepower than in-line engines and still retain a small frontal area.

3. According to this passage, how much use did in-line engines get during World War II?
 a. None at all
 b. A limited amount of use
 c. Quite a bit of use
 d. The article doesn't say

Use the passage below to answer the following question:

It takes only one harrowing experience to clarify the distinction between minimum practical knowledge and a thorough understanding of how to apply the procedures and techniques used in instrument flight. Your instrument training is never complete; it is adequate when you have absorbed every foreseeable detail of knowledge and skill to ensure a solution will be available if and when you need it.

4. In this passage, harrowing means:
 a. Rapidly descending
 b. Extremely disturbing
 c. Extremely unprepared
 d. Last minute

Use the passage below to answer the following two questions:

One disadvantage of the float-type carburetor is its icing tendency. Carburetor ice occurs due to the effect of fuel vaporization and the decrease in air pressure in the venturi, which causes a sharp temperature drop in the carburetor. If water vapor in the air condenses when the carburetor temperature is at or below freezing, ice may form on internal surfaces of the carburetor, including the throttle valve. The reduced air pressure, as well as the vaporization of fuel, contributes to the temperature decrease in the carburetor. Ice generally forms in the vicinity of the throttle valve and in the venturi throat. This restricts the flow of the fuel/air mixture and reduces power. If enough ice builds up, the engine may cease to operate. Carburetor ice is most likely to occur when temperatures are below 70 degrees Fahrenheit (°F) or 21 degrees Celsius (°C) and the relative humidity is above 80 percent. Due to the sudden cooling that takes place in the carburetor, icing can occur even with temperatures as high as 100 °F (38 °C) and humidity as low as 50 percent. This temperature drop can be as much as 60 to 70 °F (15 to 21 °C). Therefore, at an outside air temperature of 100 °F (37 °C), a temperature drop of 70 °F (21 °C) results in an air temperature in the carburetor of 30 °F (-1 °C).

5. Which set of conditions would allow carburetor icing to occur?

    a.   50 degrees Fahrenheit and 50% relative humidity
    b.   90 degrees Fahrenheit and 40% relative humidity
    c.   75 degrees Fahrenheit and 60% relative humidity
    d.   80 degrees Fahrenheit and 30% relative humidity

6. In which set of conditions would carburetor icing be most likely to occur?

    a.   50 degrees Fahrenheit and 75% relative humidity
    b.   60 degrees Fahrenheit and 85% relative humidity
    c.   75 degrees Fahrenheit and 60% relative humidity
    d.   850 degrees Fahrenheit and 30% relative humidity

Use the passage below to answer the following question:

It is impossible to emphasize too strongly the necessity for forming correct habits in flying straight and level. All other flight maneuvers are in essence a deviation from this fundamental flight maneuver. Many flight instructors and students are prone to believe that perfection in straight-and-level flight will come of itself, but such is not the case. It is not uncommon to find a pilot whose basic flying ability consistently falls just short of minimum expected standards, and upon analyzing the reasons for the shortcomings to discover that the cause is the inability to fly straight and level properly.

7. Which of these human activities would most closely correlate to straight-and-level flying?

    a.   Crawling
    b.   Walking
    c.   Jogging
    d.   Running

Use the passage below to answer the following question:

The National Airspace System (NAS) is the network of United States airspace: air navigation facilities, equipment, services, airports or landing areas, aeronautical charts, information/services, rules, regulations, procedures, technical information, manpower, and material. Included are system components shared jointly with the military. The system's present configuration is a reflection of the technological advances concerning the speed and altitude capability of jet aircraft, as well as the complexity of microchip and satellite-based navigation equipment. To conform to international aviation standards, the United States adopted the primary elements of the classification system developed by the International Civil Aviation Organization (ICAO).

8. Which of these would not be considered part of the National Airspace System?

    a.   Airports
    b.   Private Flight schools
    c.   FAA
    d.   Air traffic controllers

Use the passage below to answer the following question:

The effect of free stream density and velocity is a necessary consideration when studying the development of the various aerodynamic forces. Suppose that a particular shape of airfoil is fixed at a particular angle to the airstream. The relative velocity and pressure distribution will be determined by the shape of the airfoil and the angle to the airstream. If the same airfoil shape is placed at the same angle to an airstream with twice as great a dynamic pressure the magnitude of the pressure distribution will be twice as great but the relative shape of the pressure distribution will be the same.

9. Which of these is closest to the meaning of velocity in this passage?
   a. Attitude
   b. Thrust
   c. Speed
   d. Altitude

Use the passage below to answer the following question:

Using a supercharger, at 8,000 feet a typical engine may be able to produce 75 percent of the power it could produce at mean sea level (MSL) because the air is less dense at the higher altitude. The supercharger compresses the air to a higher density allowing a supercharged engine to produce the same manifold pressure at higher altitudes as it could produce at sea level. Thus, an engine at 8,000 feet MSL could still produce 25 "Hg of manifold pressure whereas without a supercharger it could produce only 22 "Hg. Superchargers are especially valuable at high altitudes (such as 18,000 feet) where the air density is 50 percent that of sea level. The use of a supercharger in many cases will supply air to the engine at the same density it did at sea level. With a normally aspirated engine, it is not possible to have manifold pressure higher than the existing atmospheric pressure. A supercharger is capable of boosting manifold pressure above 30 "Hg.

10. According to this passage, if an engine using a supercharger can produce 22 "Hg of manifold pressure at 8,000 feet, approximately how much manifold pressure can it produce at MSL?
   a. 29
   b. 32
   c. 16
   d. 27

Use the passage below to answer the following question:

Learning to manage the many information and automation resources now available to you in the cockpit is a big challenge. Specifically, you must learn how to choose which advanced cockpit systems to use, and when. There are no definitive rules. In fact, you will learn how different features of advanced cockpit avionics systems fall in and out of usefulness depending on the situation. Becoming proficient with advanced avionics means learning to use the right tool for the right job at the right time. In many systems, there are multiple methods of accomplishing the same function. The competent pilot learns all of these methods and chooses the method that works best for the specific situation, environment, and equipment. This handbook will help you get started in learning this important skill.

11. With which of these statements would the author agree?
   a. Choosing an advanced aviation system method is a personal decision best left to each pilot.
   b. Any decent advanced aviation system method will do just fine in most situations.
   c. There is no advanced aviation system method that is a one size fits all solution.
   d. Advanced aviation systems are somewhat overrated.

Use the passage below to answer the following question:

Keeping track of primary flight information is critical at all times, and pilots must become very familiar with their PFD. Flight instrument presentations on a PFD differ from conventional instrumentation not only in format, but sometimes in location as well. Airspeed and altitude indications are presented on vertical tape displays that appear on the left and right sides of the display. The vertical speed indicator is depicted using conventional analog presentation. Turn coordination is shown using a segmented triangle near the top of the attitude indicator. The rate-of-turn indicator appears as a curved line display at the top of the heading/navigation instrument in the lower half of the PFD.

12. In this passage, PFD most likely stands for:
   a. Pilot Flight Details
   b. Power and Features Display
   c. Pilot Flight Display
   d. Primary Flight Display

Use the passage below to answer the following question:

Turbochargers increase the pressure of the engine's induction air, which allows the engine to develop sea level or greater horsepower at higher altitudes. A turbocharger is comprised of two main elements: a compressor and turbine. The compressor section houses an impeller that turns at a high rate of speed. As induction air is drawn across the impeller blades, the impeller accelerates the air, allowing a large volume of air to be drawn into the compressor housing. The impeller's action subsequently produces high-pressure, high-density air, which is delivered to the engine. To turn the impeller, the engine's exhaust gases are used to drive a turbine wheel that is mounted on the opposite end of the impeller's drive shaft. By directing different amounts of exhaust gases to flow over the turbine, more energy can be extracted, causing the impeller to deliver more compressed air to the engine. The waste gate, essentially an adjustable butterfly valve installed in the exhaust system, is used to vary the mass of exhaust gas flowing into the turbine. When closed, most of the exhaust gases from the engine are forced to flow through the turbine. When open, the exhaust gases are allowed to bypass the turbine by flowing directly out through the engine's exhaust pipe.

13. High-density air is delivered to the engine after being produced by the:
   a. Impeller
   b. Inductor
   c. Turbocharger
   d. Butterfly valve

Use the passage below to answer the following two questions:

One of the biggest safety concerns in aviation is the surface movement accident. As a direct result, the Federal Aviation Administration (FAA) has rapidly expanded the information available to pilots, including the addition of taxiway and runway information in FAA publications, particularly the IFR U.S. Terminal Procedures Publication (TPP) booklets and Airport/Facility Directory (A/FD) volumes. The FAA has also implemented new procedures and created educational and awareness programs for pilots, ATC, and ground operators. By focusing resources to attack this problem head on, the FAA hopes to reduce and eventually eliminate surface movement accidents.

Airport sketches and diagrams provide pilots of all levels with graphical depictions of the airport layout. Aeronautical Information Systems (AIS), formerly known as Aeronautical Products (AeroNav), provide an airport sketch on the lower left or right portion of every instrument approach chart. This sketch depicts the runways, their length, width and slope, the touchdown zone elevation, the lighting system installed on the end of the runway, and taxiways. Graphical depictions of NOTAMS are also available for selected airports as well as for temporary flight restriction (TFRs) areas on the defense internet NOTAM service (DINS) website.

For select airports, typically those with heavy traffic or complex runway layouts, AIS also prints an airport diagram. The diagram is located in the IFR TPP booklet following the instrument approach chart for a particular airport. It is a full-page depiction of the airport that includes the same features of the airport sketch plus additional details, such as taxiway identifiers, airport latitude and longitude, and building identification. The airport diagrams are also available in the A/FD and on the AIS website, located at www.aeronav.faa.gov.

14. Which of the following acronyms is not defined by this passage?
    a. TPP
    b. A/FD
    c. NOTAMS
    d. AeroNav

15. Which of the following provides the airport sketches of the airport layout?
    a. AeroNav
    b. AIS
    c. TFR
    d. A/FD

Use the passage below to answer the following question:

Although the regulations specify minimum requirements, the amount of instructional time needed to earn an instrument rating is determined not by the regulation, but by the individual's ability to achieve a satisfactory level of proficiency. A professional pilot with diversified flying experience may easily attain a satisfactory level of proficiency in the minimum time required by regulation. Your own time requirements will depend upon a variety of factors, including previous flying experience, rate of learning, basic ability, frequency of flight training, type of aircraft flown, quality of ground school training, and quality of flight instruction, to name a few. The total instructional time you will need, the scheduling of such time, is up to the individual most qualified to judge your proficiency—the instructor who supervises your progress and endorses your record of flight training.

16. Which of these is not a factor in determining how long it takes a pilot to earn an instrument rating?
    a. Make and model of plane used
    b. Age of pilot
    c. Whether someone is a fast or slow learner
    d. How good the instructor is

Use the passage below to answer the following two questions:

Flight deck crews almost seamlessly launch, recover and deploy aircraft and people all over the flight deck? Did you ever wonder how we do this? Simply put, because we have very dedicated professionals doing their job. However, whether we realize it or not, the success of those individuals who are just "doing their job" hinges upon thorough application of Operational Risk Management on three levels—in depth, when our leadership and acquisition folks provide the equipment, training and guidance for flight deck operations; deliberate, when we plan and brief for the events or operations of the day; and time critical, when we actually apply the risk controls or use the resources provided to us for getting the job done.

17. Which of the following best expresses the meaning of *seamlessly* in this passage?
a. Without a hitch
b. Around the clock
c. Non-stop
d. Automatically

18 Which of the following is closest in meaning to *deploy*?
a. Retire from active service
b. Disguise by using camouflage
c. Move into position
d. Recruit or enlist someone into military service

Use the passage below to answer the following question:

Displacing the cyclic forward causes the nose to pitch down initially, with a resultant increase in airspeed and loss of altitude. Aft cyclic causes the nose to pitch up initially, slowing the helicopter and causing it to climb; however, as the helicopter reaches a state of equilibrium, the horizontal stabilizer levels the helicopter airframe to minimize drag, unlike an airplane. Therefore, the helicopter has very little pitch deflection up or down when the helicopter is stable in a flight mode. The variation from absolutely level depends on the particular helicopter and the horizontal stabilizer function. Increasing collective (power) while maintaining a constant airspeed induces a climb while decreasing collective causes a descent. Coordinating these two inputs, down collective plus aft cyclic or up collective plus forward cyclic, results in airspeed changes while maintaining a constant altitude. The pedals serve the same function in both a helicopter and a fixed-wing aircraft, to maintain balanced flight. This is done by applying a pedal input in whichever direction is necessary to center the ball in the turn and bank indicator.

19. According to this article, what is one of the main factors when it comes to variation from absolute level?
a. The horizontal stabilizer
b. The direction of the wind
c. The speed of the wind
d. Whether the weight of passengers and cargo is properly balanced

Use the passage below to answer the following question:

Making good choices sounds easy enough. However, there are a multitude of factors that come into play when these choices, and subsequent decisions, are made in the aeronautical world. Many tools are available for pilots to become more self-aware and assess the options available, along with the impact of their decision. Yet, with all the available resources, accident rates are not being reduced. Poor decisions continue to be made, frequently resulting in lives being lost and/or aircraft damaged or destroyed. The Risk Management Handbook discusses aeronautical decision-making (ADM) and single-pilot resource management (SRM) in detail and should be thoroughly read and understood. While progress is continually being made in the advancement of pilot training methods, aircraft equipment and systems, and services for pilots, accidents still occur. Historically, the term "pilot error" has been used to describe the causes of these accidents. Pilot error means an action or decision made by the pilot was the cause of, or a contributing factor that led to, the accident. This definition also includes the pilot's failure to make a decision or take action. From a broader perspective, the phrase "human factors related" more aptly describes these accidents since it is usually not a single decision that leads to an accident, but a chain of events triggered by a number of factors. The poor judgment chain, sometimes referred to as the "error chain," is a term used to describe this concept of contributing factors in a human factors related accident. Breaking one link in the chain is often the only event necessary to change the outcome of the sequence of events.

20. Which of the following statements would the author be most likely to agree with?
  a. The problem of aircraft accidents has never been worse.
  b. Realistically, the number of aircraft accidents is probably as low as it's ever going to be.
  c. There is still much room for improvement when it comes to reducing aircraft accidents.
  d. Great strides have been made in recent years in reducing the number of aircraft accidents.

Use the passage below to answer the following question:

When an operator requests a Minimum Equipment List (MEL), and a Letter of Authorization (LOA) is issued by the FAA, then the use of the MEL becomes mandatory for that helicopter. All maintenance deferrals must be accomplished in accordance with the terms and conditions of the MEL and the operator-generated procedures document. Exercise extreme caution when hovering near buildings or other aircraft. The use of an MEL for rotorcraft operated under part 91 also allows for the deferral of inoperative items or equipment. The primary guidance becomes the FAA-approved MEL issued to that specific operator and N-numbered helicopter. The FAA has developed master minimum equipment lists (MMELs) for rotorcraft in current use. Upon written request by a rotorcraft operator, the local FAA Flight Standards District Office (FSDO) may issue the appropriate make and model MMEL, along with an LOA, and the preamble. The operator then develops operations and maintenance (O&M) procedures from the MMEL. This MMEL with O&M procedures now becomes the operator's MEL. The MEL, LOA, preamble, and procedures document developed by the operator must be on board the helicopter when it is operated. The FAA considers an approved MEL to be a supplemental type certificate (STC) issued to an aircraft by serial number and registration number. It therefore becomes the authority to operate that aircraft in a condition other than originally type certificated. With an approved MEL, if the position lights were discovered inoperative prior to a daytime flight, the pilot would make an entry in the maintenance record or discrepancy record provided for that purpose. The item is then either repaired or deferred in accordance with the MEL. Upon confirming that daytime flight with inoperative position lights is acceptable in accordance with the provisions of the MEL, the pilot would leave the position lights switch OFF, open the circuit breaker (or whatever action is called for in the procedures document), and placard the position light switch as INOPERATIVE.

21. What resource would a pilot use to determine if an inoperative part or system rendered daytime flight unacceptable?
  a. LOA
  b. O&M
  c. FSDO
  d. MEL

Use the passage below to answer the following question:

It is important to understand the three levels of Operational Risk Management, because each level plays a role in improving our chance of completing the mission successfully. In particular, the controls developed at each level are resources we can tap into to accomplish our job or mission during its execution. These resources make it easier to do our job and help catch errors that might be detrimental to task or mission success. Beyond the equipment itself and our fellow shipmates, there are other resources we can tap to help mitigate the risks associated with the hazards of the flight deck.

22. Which of the following is closest in meaning to mitigate?
   a. Eliminate
   b. Control
   c. Reduce
   d. Understand

Use the passage below to answer the following question:

Today, helicopters are quite reliable. However, emergencies do occur, whether as a result of mechanical failure or pilot error, and should be anticipated. Regardless of the cause, the recovery needs to be quick and precise. By having a thorough knowledge of the helicopter and its systems, a pilot is able to handle the situation more readily. Helicopter emergencies and the proper recovery procedures should be discussed and, when possible, practiced in flight. In addition, by knowing the conditions that can lead to an emergency, many potential accidents can be avoided. Emergencies should always be anticipated. Knowledge of the helicopter, possible malfunctions and failures, and methods of recovery can help the pilot avoid accidents and be a safer pilot. Helicopter pilots should always expect the worst hazards and possible aerodynamic effects and plan for a safe exit path or procedure to compensate for the hazard.

23. Which of the following best sums up this passage?
   a. Planning ahead is the best way to prepare for emergencies.
   b. Many helicopter emergencies are due to faulty equipment.
   c. In helicopter emergencies, there is little margin for error.
   d. Helicopter emergencies can arise at any time and for a variety of reasons.

Use the passage below to answer the following question:

Medium-frequency vibrations (1,000–2,000 cycles per minute) range between the low frequencies of the main rotor (100–500 cycles per minute) and the high frequencies (2,100 cycles per minute or higher) of the engine and tail rotor. Depending on the helicopter, medium-frequency vibration sources may be engine and transmission cooling fans, and accessories such as air conditioner compressors, or driveline components. Medium-frequency vibrations are felt through the entire airframe, and prolonged exposure to the vibrations will result in greater pilot fatigue. Most tail rotor vibrations fall into the high-frequency range (2,100 cycles per minute or higher) and can be felt through the tail rotor pedals as long as there are no hydraulic actuators to dampen out the vibration. This vibration is felt by the pilot through his or her feet, which are usually "put to sleep" by the vibration. The tail rotor operates at approximately a 6:1 ratio with the main rotor, meaning for every one rotation of the main rotor the tail rotor rotates 6 times. A main rotor operating rpm of 350 means the tail rotor rpm would be 2,100 rpm. Any imbalance in the tail rotor system is very harmful as it can cause cracks to develop and rivets to work loose. Piston engines usually produce a normal amount of high-frequency vibration, which is aggravated by engine malfunctions, such as spark plug fouling, incorrect magneto timing, carburetor icing and/or incorrect fuel/air mixture. Vibrations in turbine engines are often difficult to detect as these engines operate at a very high rpm. Turbine engine vibration can be at 30,000 rpm internally, but common gearbox speeds are in the 1,000 to 3,000 rpm range for the output shaft. The vibrations in turbine engines may be short lived as the engine disintegrates rapidly when damaged due to high rpm and the forces present.

24. Which frequencies can result in the pilot experiencing numbness in the pilot's leg?
   a. Low frequency vibrations
   b. Medium frequency vibrations
   c. High frequency vibrations
   d. Both medium and high frequency vibrations

Use the passage below to answer the following question:

Rigid rotor systems tend to behave like fully articulated systems through aerodynamics, but lack flapping or lead/ lag hinges. Instead, the blades accommodate these motions by bending. They cannot flap or lead/lag but they can be feathered. As advancements in helicopter aerodynamics and materials continue to improve, rigid rotor systems may become more common because the system is fundamentally easier to design and offers the best properties of both semirigid and fully articulated systems. The rigid rotor system is very responsive and is usually not susceptible to mast bumping like the semirigid or articulated systems because the rotor hubs are mounted solid to the main rotor mast. This allows the rotor and fuselage to move together as one entity and eliminates much of the oscillation usually present in the other rotor systems. Other advantages of the rigid rotor include a reduction in the weight and drag of the rotor hub and a larger flapping arm, which significantly reduces control inputs. Without the complex hinges, the rotor system becomes much more reliable and easier to maintain than the other rotor configurations. A disadvantage of this system is the quality of ride in turbulent or gusty air. Because there are no hinges to help absorb the larger loads, vibrations are felt in the cabin much more than with other rotor head designs. There are several variations of the basic three rotor head designs. The bearingless rotor system is closely related to the articulated rotor system, but has no bearings or hinges. This design relies on the structure of blades and hub to absorb stresses. The main difference between the rigid rotor system and the bearingless system is that the bearingless system has no feathering bearing— the material inside the cuff is twisted by the action of the pitch change arm. Nearly all bearingless rotor hubs are made of fiber-composite materials.

25. The author of this passage would probably agree most strongly with which statement about rigid rotor systems?
   a. They are less popular than they used to be.
   b. They result in fewer vibrations than semirigid and fully articulated systems.
   c. Overall, they're superior to semirigid and fully articulated systems.
   d. They are not as safe as semirigid and fully articulated systems.

Use the passage below to answer the following question:

The roots of aviation are firmly based on curiosity. Where would we be today had it not been for the dreams of Leonardo da Vinci, the Wright Brothers, and Igor Sikorsky? They all were infatuated with flight, a curiosity that led to the origins of aviation. The tale of aviation is full of firsts: first flight, first helicopter, first trans-Atlantic flight, and so on. But, along the way there were many setbacks, fatalities, and lessons learned. Today, we continue to learn and investigate the limits of aviation. We've been to the moon, and soon beyond. Our curiosity will continue to drive us to search for the next challenge. However, curiosity can also have catastrophic consequences. Despite over 100 years of aviation practice, we still see accidents that are caused by impaired judgment formed from curious behavior. Pilots commonly seek to determine the limits of their ability as well as the limits of the aircraft. Unfortunately, too often this leads to mishaps with deadly results. Inquisitive behavior must be harnessed and displayed within personal and material limits. Deadly curiosity may not seem as obvious to some as it is to others. Simple thoughts such as, "Is visibility really as bad as what the ATIS is reporting?" or "Does the 20-minute fuel light really indicate only 20 minutes' worth of fuel?" can lead to poor decisions and disastrous outcomes. Some aviators blatantly violate rules and aircraft limitations without thinking through the consequences. "What indications and change in flight characteristics will I see if I fly this helicopter above its maximum gross weight?" or "I've heard this helicopter can do aerobatic flight. Why is it prohibited?" are examples of extremely harmful curiosity. Even more astounding is their ignoring the fact that the damage potentially done to the aircraft will probably manifest later in the aircraft's life, affecting other crews. Spontaneous excursions in aviation can be deadly. Curiosity is natural, and promotes learning. Airmen should abide by established procedures until proper and complete hazard assessment and risk management can be completed.

26. Which of these statements most closely matches the theme of this passage?
   a. Fortune favors the bold.
   b. An ounce of prevention is worth a pound of cure.
   c. Curiosity killed the cat.
   d. Fools rush in where angels fear to tread.

Use the passage below to answer the following question:

Although helicopters were developed and built during the first half-century of flight, some even reaching limited production; it was not until 1942 that a helicopter designed by Igor Sikorsky reached full-scale production, with 131 aircraft built. Even though most previous designs used more than one main rotor, it was the single main rotor with an antitorque tail rotor configuration design that would come to be recognized worldwide as the helicopter. In 1951, at the urging of his contacts at the Department of the Navy, Charles H. Kaman modified his K-225 helicopter with a new kind of engine, the turbo-shaft engine. This adaptation of the turbine engine provided a large amount of horsepower to the helicopter with a lower weight penalty than piston engines, heavy engine blocks, and auxiliary components. On December 11, 1951, the K-225 became the first turbine-powered helicopter in the world. Two years later, on March 26, 1954, a modified Navy HTK -1, another Kaman helicopter, became the first twin-turbine helicopter to fly. However, it was the Sud Aviation Alouette II that would become the first helicopter to be produced with a turbine engine. Reliable helicopters capable of stable hover flight were developed decades after fixed-wing aircraft. This is largely due to higher engine power density requirements than fixed-wing aircraft. Improvements in fuels and engines during the first half of the 20th century were a critical factor in helicopter development. The availability of lightweight turbo-shaft engines in the second half of the 20th century led to the development of larger, faster, and higher-performance helicopters. The turbine engine has the following advantages over a reciprocating engine: less vibration, increased aircraft performance, reliability, and ease of operation. While smaller and less expensive helicopters still use piston engines, turboshaft engines are the preferred powerplant for helicopters today.

27. Which of these is most responsible for a huge increase in the variety of helicopters in use?

    a. The military demand for helicopters in World War II
    b. The development of an antitorque tail rotor configuration design
    c. The development of turbine engine powered helicopters
    d. The development of piston engine helicopters

Mechanical Comprehension Test

1. A cannon fires off a ship up towards a mountain range. Neglecting air resistance, where will the velocity of the projectile be greatest?

    a. Exiting the muzzle
    b. Halfway to the mountains
    c. As it impacts the mountains

2. These pulleys are connected by belts. Which pulley travels the fastest?

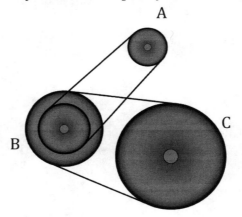

    a. Pulley A
    b. Pulley B
    c. Pulley C

3. If Gear A is traveling at 10 rpm, how many times will Gear C rotate in 3 minutes?

    a. 1.7 times
    b. 3 times
    c. 30 times

4. Where should the fulcrum be located to balance this beam?

    a.   closer to the large mass
    b.   closer to the small mass
    c.   exactly between the two masses

5. Which orientation will require more force to pull?

    a.   with the rope at an angle to the table
    b.   with the rope parallel to the table
    c.   both orientations are equal

6. The larger piston has four times as much horizontal area as the smaller piston. If the small piston is compressed 8 inches, how far will the larger piston move?

    a.   8 inches
    b.   2 inches
    c.   32 inches

7. A wing in flight has a set of pressures causing the overall forces on the top and bottom of the wing. Where will the total force on the wing point?

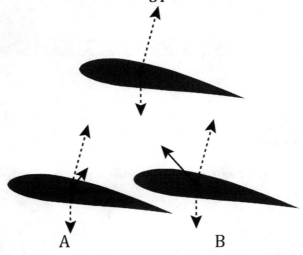

a. up and to the right
b. up and to the left
c. neither A nor B

8. River water enters a section where the water spreads out into a wide, deep area. Is the water likely to speed up, slow down, or remain at a constant speed?

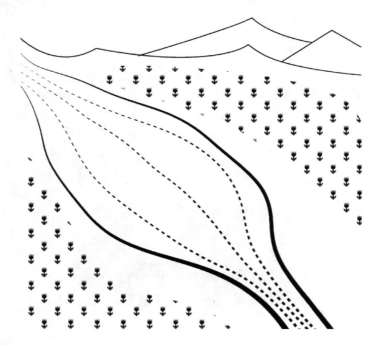

a. speed up
b. slow down
c. remain at a constant speed

9. A magnet is placed in the middle of two identical, anchored magnets. Which direction will the magnet go?

a. towards magnet 1
b. towards magnet 2
c. the magnet won't move

10. A solid substance melts at -21°C. If the object is known to change phase at 81°C, will the object be a solid, liquid, or gas at 90°C?

a. solid
b. liquid
c. gas

377

11. If the resistors in the circuits are identical, which circuit will have the greatest overall resistance?

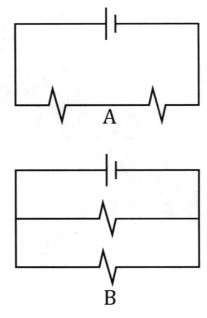

a. circuit A
b. circuit B
c. circuit A and B have the same overall resistance

12. A pendulum swings back and forth once per second. The pendulum is shortened by removing half of the string. The new frequency is 1.4 Hz (Hz=1/sec). How often will the pendulum swing back and forth in a minute?

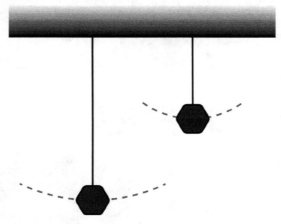

a. 84
b. 92
c. 72

13. Two identical pistons are connected by a pipe. What is the mechanical advantage of the piston system?

    a.   0.5
    b.   1
    c.   2

14. A ball is thrown horizontally off a cliff at the same time that an identical ball is dropped off a cliff. How long after the dropped ball hits the ground will the thrown ball hit?

    a.   approximately 1 second after
    b.   approximately 2 seconds after
    c.   they will hit at the same time

15. The cam rotates at 5 rpm. How many times will the follower (needle) move up and down in a minute?

a. 20
b. 72
c. 140

16. Which of the following are not ways to increase the torque applied to a wrench?

a. increase the length from the center to the applied force
b. increase the force
c. angle the force toward the center

17. A ball is pushed down into a vertical spring. The ball is released and flies upward. Which best describes the states of energy the ball underwent?

a. convective energy to potential energy
b. potential energy to kinetic energy
c. kinetic energy to potential energy

18. A vacuum tank is held by weights at a depth of 50 feet underwater. If the tank is raised to a depth of 25 feet, will the pressure on the walls of the tank increase, decrease, or stay the same?

a. increase
b. decrease
c. stay the same

19. Adding salt to water raises its density. Will salt water have a lower, higher, or the same specific gravity than 1?

a. lower
b. higher
c. the same

20. Which of the following is an example of convective heat transfer?

A   B   C

a. a man burns his hand on a hot pot
b. a man burns his hand in steam
c. a man gets a sun burn

21. Which of the following is the electrical component which holds a voltage across a gap between two conductive materials?

a. resistor
b. inductor
c. capacitor

22. Which of these wrenches is likely to provide the greatest torque with a set force?

A   B

a. wrench A
b. wrench B
c. both wrenches will provide the same torque

23. Which of the following is true of this circuit?

a. the voltage is the same everywhere
b. the current is the same everywhere
c. there is no current

24. Which device does not measure current in an electrical system?

a. ammeter
b. multimeter
c. voltmeter

25. A ball is thrown straight into the air with an initial kinetic energy of 100 ft-lb. What is the potential energy of the ball at half of the height of the flight path?

 a. 33 ft-lb
 b. 50 ft-lb
 c. 66 ft-lb

26. An increase in mechanical advantage with a set motion for the load and a set applied force necessitates an increase in _____ the applied force?

 a. the distance traveled by
 b. the angle of action of
 c. the potential energy behind

27. A windlass drum has two sections with different circumferences. When winding the drum, one side of the rope winds around the large section and the other unwinds from the small section. If the large section of the drum has a circumference of 3.5 ft and the other section has a circumference of 1 ft, how far will the weight lift with two full turns of the drum?

 a. 2.5 feet
 b. 9 feet
 c. 4.5 feet

28. **Which type of situation will lead to condensation on the outside of pipes?**
    a. hot liquid in the pipe and cold air outside the pipe
    b. cold liquid in the pipe and colder air outside the pipe
    c. cold liquid in the pipe and hot air outside the pipe

29. **Which color will absorb the most radiation?**
    a. black
    b. green
    c. dark yellow

30. **Two gears (30 and 18 teeth) mesh. If the smaller gear rotates 3 times, how many times will the larger gear rotate?**

    a. 1.6 times
    b. 1.8 times
    c. 3 times

Answer Key and Explanations

Math Skills Test

1. A: First, subtract 4 from both sides to isolate the variable, Then, divide both sides by 16 to solve for x:

$$16x + 4 - 4 = 100 - 4$$
$$16x = 96$$
$$16x/16 = 96/16$$
$$x = 6$$

2. A: Start with the FOIL method to evaluate the multiplication and then combine like terms:

$$(2x - 20)(5x + 10) = 10x^2 + 20x - 100x - 200$$
$$= 10x^2 - 80x - 200$$

3. A: Complementary angles are two angles that add to 90°.

4. D: To simplify this expression, the law of exponents that states that $(x^m)^n = x^{m \times n}$ must be observed:

$$(2x^4)^3 + 2(y^5)^5 = 2^3 x^{4 \times 3} + 2(y^{5 \times 5})$$
$$= 8x^{12} + 2y^{25}$$

5. A: The sum of the measures of the three angles of any triangle is 180. The equation of the angles of this triangle can be written as $2x + 6x + 10x = 180$, or $18x = 180$. Therefore, $x = 10$. Therefore, the measure of the smallest angle is 20.

6. B: The formula for the area of a circle is πr^2. The diameter of a circle is equal to twice its radius. Therefore, to find the radius, it is necessary to divide the diameter by 2: $\frac{12 \text{ cm}}{2} = 6$ cm. Then, use the formula to find the area of the circle:

$$A = \pi 6^2$$
$$= \pi \times 36$$
$$\approx 113 \text{ cm}^2$$

7. D: The general equation to find the area of a rectangle is $length \times width$. Since the length and width of a square are equal, we can calculate the area of the square described in the question:

$$A = l \times w$$
$$= (15 \text{ cm}) \times (15 \text{ cm})$$
$$= 225 \text{ cm}^2$$

8. C: To find the volume of a rectangular solid, the formula is $length \times width \times height$. Therefore:

$$V = l \times w \times h$$
$$= (12 \text{ cm}) \times (3 \text{ cm}) \times (9 \text{ cm})$$
$$= 324 \text{ cm}^3$$

9. C: First, add $4x^2$ to both sides to isolate x:

$$2x^2 + 4x^2 = -4x^2 + 4x^2 + 216$$
$$6x^2 = 216$$

Then, divide both sides by 6:

$$\frac{6x^2}{6} = \frac{216}{6}$$
$$x^2 = 36$$

Finally, take the square root of both sides to solve for x:

$$\sqrt{x^2} = \sqrt{36}$$
$$x = \pm 6$$

Even though both +6 and -6 are answers, only +6 is an option.

10. B: The 4 sides of a square are all of equal length, so the side length is $\frac{perimeter}{4} = \frac{24}{4}$ m = 6 m. Now we can calculate the area of the square described in the question:

$$A = l \times w$$
$$= (6 \text{ m}) \times (6 \text{ m})$$
$$= 36 \text{ m}^2$$

11. B: The formula for the area of a rectangle is $length \times width$. Using the measurements given in the question, the area of the rectangle can be calculated:

$$A = l \times w$$
$$= (5 \text{ cm}) \times (7 \text{ cm})$$
$$= 35 \text{ cm}^2$$

12. B: On a six-sided die, the probability of throwing any number is 1 in 6. The probability of throwing a 3 or a 4 is double that, or 2 in 6. This can be simplified by dividing both 2 and 6 by 2. Therefore, the probability of throwing either a 3 or 4 is 1 in 3.

13. C: The key thing to remember to simplify this inequality is that when both sides are divided by a negative number, the direction of the sign must be reversed:

$$-2y \geq 24 + 6$$
$$-2y \geq 30$$
$$\frac{-2y}{-2} \leq \frac{30}{-2}$$
$$y \leq -15$$

14. A: First, subtract $5x$ from both sides to get the variable to one side of the equation:

$$2x - 5x = -30$$
$$-3x = -30$$

Then, divide both sides by -3 to solve for x:

$$-3x/-3 = -30/-3$$
$$x = 10$$

15. C: The solution of $f(x) = g(x)$ can be determined by setting the two functions equal to one another. Thus, the following may be written $3x + 6 = 2x - 8$. Solving for x gives $x = -14$.

16. A: The area of a square is equal to the square of the length of one side. If the area is 64 in^2, the side length must therefore be $\sqrt{64 \text{ in}^2} = 8$ in. The circle is inscribed in the square, so the side length of the square is the same as the circle's diameter. If the circle's diameter is 8 in, then the circle's radius must be half of that, or 4 in. The area of a circle is equal to $A = \pi r^2 = \pi (4 \text{ in})^2 = 16\pi \text{ in}^2$.

17. A: First, bring the $-3x$ to the left side of the equation and the 23 to the right side of the equation to make it easier to solve:

$$4x + 23 > -3x - 6$$
$$4x + 3x > -6 - 23$$
$$7x > -29$$

Then, divide both side by 7 to solve for x:

$$7x/7 > -29/7$$
$$x > -4.14$$

18. D: First, bring all of the terms containing x to the left side of the equation to make it easier to solve:

$$2x + 5x = 3x + x + 30$$
$$2x + 5x - 3x - x = 30$$
$$7x - 4x = 30$$
$$3x = 30$$

Then, divide both sides by 3 to solve for x:

$$3x/3 = 30/3$$
$$x = 10$$

19. B: First, substitute the given values into the expression and then follow the order of operations to simplify:

$$
\begin{aligned}
3x^2y + y/2 - 6x &= 3 \times 4^2 \times 10 + 10/2 - 6 \times 4 && \text{Exponents} \\
&= 3 \times 16 \times 10 + 10/2 - 6 \times 4 && \text{Multiplication and Division} \\
&= 480 + 5 - 24 && \text{Addition and Subtraction} \\
&= 461
\end{aligned}
$$

20. B: The average is the total amount spent divided by the number of students. The first three students spend an average of $10, so the total amount they spend is $3 \times \$10 = \$30$. The other six students spend an average of $4, so the total amount they spend is $6 \times \$4 = \$24$. The total amount spent by all nine students is $\$30 + \$24 = \$54$, and the average amount they spend is $\$54 \div 9 = \$6$.

21. C: First, substitute the given value of *w* into the expression each time it appears. Then, follow the order of operations to find the result:

$$8w^2 - 12w + (4w - 5) + 6 = 8 \times 7^2 - 12(7) + (4 \times 7 - 5) + 6$$
$$= 8 \times 7^2 - 12(7) + (23) + 6$$
$$= 8 \times 49 - 84 + 23 + 6$$
$$= 392 - 84 + 23 + 6$$
$$= 337$$

22. C: First, subtract 7 from both sides to isolate *x*:

$$\frac{x}{3} + 7 = 35$$
$$\frac{x}{3} + 7 - 7 = 35 - 7$$
$$\frac{x}{3} = 28$$

Then, multiply both sides by three to solve for *x*:

$$\frac{x}{3} \times 3 = 28 \times 3$$
$$x = 84$$

23. B: First, bring all terms to the left side of the equation and combine like terms to make it easier to factor:

$$2x^2 - 7x - x^2 + 12 = 0$$
$$x^2 - 7x + 12 = 0$$
$$(x - 3)(x - 4) = 0$$

Finally, solve for *x* in both instances:

$$x - 3 = 0 \qquad\qquad x - 4 = 0$$
$$x = 3 \qquad\qquad x = 4$$
$$x = 3, 4$$

24. A: Another way of expressing the fact that *x* is 25% of 250 is: $x = (0.25)250$

Then, it is simply a matter of multiplying out the right side of the equation: $x = 62.5$

25. B: The volume of a cube is calculated by cubing the side length of the cube. In this case, where *x* can represent the length of the cube: $8 \text{ cm}^3 = x \times x \times x$. To find the length, we must figure out what number cubed equals 8. The answer is 2: $8 \text{ cm}^3 = 2 \text{ cm} \times 2 \text{ cm} \times 2 \text{ cm}$

26. B: One way to compare fractions is to convert them to equivalent fractions which have common denominators. In this case the lowest common denominator of the three fractions is $7 \times 12 = 84$. Converting each of the fractions to this denominator, $\frac{1}{3} = \frac{1 \times 28}{3 \times 28} = \frac{28}{84}, \frac{2}{7} = \frac{2 \times 12}{7 \times 12} = \frac{24}{84}$, and $\frac{5}{12} = \frac{5 \times 7}{12 \times 7} = \frac{35}{84}$. Since $24 < 28 < 35$, it must be the case that $\frac{2}{7} < \frac{1}{3} < \frac{5}{12}$.

27. A: Use the FOIL method to expand the expression:

$$(2x^2 + 3)(2x - 1) = 4x^3 - 2x^2 + 6x - 3$$

There are no like terms, so the expression cannot be simplified any further.

28. D: To simplify this expression, the law of exponents that states that $x^m \times x^n = x^{m+n}$ must be observed.

$$(2x^4y^7m^2z) \times (5x^2y^3m^8) = (2 \times 5)x^{(4+2)}y^{(7+3)}m^{(2+8)}z$$
$$= 10x^6y^{10}m^{10}z$$

29. C: First, find the total number of students in the classroom: $13 + 18 = 31$. There is an 18 in 31 chance that a name chosen randomly will be a girl's name. To express this as a percentage, divide 18 by 31, then multiply that number by 100: $18/31 \times 100\% = 58\%$

30. A: Recall that $x\%$ is the same thing as $\frac{x}{100}$, and finding $x\%$ of a number is the same as multiplying that number by $x\%$. This is true even when the number is itself a percentage. So, 10% of 40% is $40\% \times 10\% = 40\% \times \frac{10}{100} = 40\% \times \frac{1}{10} = 4\%$.

Reading Comprehension Test

1. D: Battery and ignition switches: Off

Control column locks: Removed

Landing gear control: Down and locked

Airspeed Indicator needle: 0

2. B: The primer is a small pump used to draw fuel from the tanks to vaporize it directly into the cylinders prior to starting the engine.

3. D: While the article does state that radial engines were widely used during WW II, it doesn't say how much use in-line engines got.

4. B: Harrowing means extremely disturbing

5. C: 75 degrees Fahrenheit and 60% relative humidity

6. B: 60 degrees Fahrenheit and 85% relative humidity

7. B: Walking is the fundamental way of moving for a mature human being, and jogging and running are deviations of walking, just as straight-and-level flying is the fundamental flight maneuver, and all other flight maneuvers are considered to be deviations of it.

8. B: Flight schools not affiliated with the government or the military would not be considered part of the National Airspace System. They might conduct some of their training at airports, which are part of the NAS, but the school itself would not be considered an NAS component.

9. C: Of the four answer choices, *Speed* is the closest in meaning to *velocity*.

10. A: 29. Using a supercharger, at 8,000 feet a typical engine may be able to produce 75 percent of the power it could produce at mean sea level (MSL) because the air is less dense at the higher altitude. So, if it can produce 22 "Hg at 8,000 feet, that represents 75% of its potential production at MSL. Dividing 22 by .75 gives us 29.333.

11. C: The author makes it clear that there is no advanced aviation system method that works best in every situation, and pilots need to choose the right method based on the circumstances.

12. D: Primary Flight Display. From the context, we know that PFD most likely refers to both *primary* and *display*, and D is the only answer choice that contains both words.

13. A: Impeller. The passage states that the impeller's action produces high-pressure, high-density air, which is then delivered to the engine.

14. C: NOTAMS is used in the passage, but isn't defined. It stands for Notices to Airmen. The singular is NOTAM, for Notice to Airmen. A NOTAM is a notification to pilots of factors along a flight path or at a destination that could be hazardous.

15. B: AIS stands for Aeronautical Information Systems, which is a division of the Federal Aviation Administration.

16. B: Although the passage states that how much experience a pilot has is important, the age of the pilot is not listed as a factor in how quickly one can earn an instrument rating. All of the other answer choices are listed in the passage as factors, although not in the same exact words.

17. A: *Seamlessly* in this context means *easily and without interruptions*, and *without a hitch* is another way of expressing that.

18. C: Of the four answer choices, *move into position* best expresses the meaning of *deploy*.

19. A: The passages states: "The variation from absolutely level depends on the particular helicopter and the horizontal stabilizer function."

20. C: This statement is the only one backed up by the contents of the passage.

21. D: The Minimum Equipment List (MEL) is the correct answer, based on this part of the passage: The FAA considers an approved MEL to be a supplemental type certificate (STC) issued to an aircraft by serial number and registration number. It therefore becomes the authority to operate that aircraft in a condition other than originally type certificated.

22. C: *Reduce* and *mitigate* have almost the same meaning.

23. A: The author's main point in this passage is that pilots can best prepare for emergencies by planning ahead – taking the time to master the helicopter and its systems, and anticipating emergencies and how to respond to them before they happen.

24. C: The passage states that high frequency vibrations can cause numbness in the pilot's leg.

25. C: The author says that rigid rotor systems offer the best properties of semirigid and fully articulated systems, and are easier to design, too.

26. D: Fools rush in where angels fear to tread expresses the idea that people who are new or inexperienced at something will often take dangerous chances that wiser or more experienced people would steer clear of, which most closely matches the author's theme that unbridled curiosity in a pilot can lead to disaster. He is not saying curiosity is bad in and of itself; only that it needs to have limits. That's why *Curiosity killed the cat* is incorrect.

27. D: Taking the entire passage as a whole, it shows that the development of turbine engine powered helicopters is the factor that was most responsible for a huge increase in the variety of helicopters in use.

Mechanical Comprehension Test

1. A: The velocity is made up of two components, the x and y components. The x component is not changing during flight, but the weight of the projectile decreases the positive y component of the velocity. Thus, the total velocity will be greatest before the y component has decreased.

2. A: Because the linear speed of two connected pulleys is the same, the pulley with the smaller radius spins faster. The largest pulley will spin slower than the middle pulley. The smallest pulley will spin faster than the middle pulley, making it the fastest pulley.

3. C: Gear A and gear C have the same number of teeth. Thus, gears A and C will have the same speed. Since gear C is rotating at 10 rpm, the total number of rotations is calculated by multiplying the rpm by the number of minutes.

4. A: Because the large mass will produce a greater torque at the same distance from the fulcrum as the small mass, the distance from the large mass to the fulcrum should be shortened. Then, the torque produced by the large mass will decrease and the torque produced by the small mass will increase.

5. A: When the rope is not parallel to the intended path of motion, the force is divided into useful force (x direction) and not useful force (y direction). If only some of the force is useful, then the man will need to apply more force to achieve the same pulling force as if the rope were parallel to the table.

6. B: Because the volume of the liquid doesn't change, when the small piston is compressed, the volume decrease in one piston is the volume increase in the other piston. As the volume is the area times the height, the height of the larger piston only needs to raise one fourth the height that the small piston moved.

7. A: The downward force decreases part of the y component of the top force, but does not affect the x component of the force. Thus, the resultant force is up and to the right.

8. B: because the same volume of water has to flow through all parts of the river, the water will slow down to fill the wide section.

9. C: The negative side of magnet 2 will be attracted to the positive side of magnet 1. The positive side of magnet 2 will be attracted to the negative side of magnet 3 with the same force. Because the magnitudes of the forces are equal and the directions are opposite, the sum of the forces will be zero.

10. C: The first phase change is from solid to liquid at -21°C. The next phase change is from liquid to gas at 81°C. 90°C is only slightly higher than 81°C, making it safe to say that the substance is still a gas.

11. A: Substitute token values for the resistors to solve. Using 1 Ω resistors, the resistance of circuit A, having resistors in series, is the simple sum of the two resistors: 2 Ω. Because the resistors in circuit B are in parallel, the resistance of circuit B is the reciprocal of the sum of the reciprocals of the resistances, or $\frac{1}{\frac{1}{1}+\frac{1}{1}}$. The result is 1/2 Ω.

12. A: To find the number of swings in a time period from the frequency, multiply the frequency times the time period, after converting the time period into seconds to match the frequency. The final calculation is $\frac{1.4 \text{ swings}}{\text{second}} \times 1 \text{ minute} \times \frac{60 \text{ seconds}}{1 \text{ minute}} = 84$ swings

13. B: The mechanical advantage is calculated by the output force divided by the input force. Because both pistons are the same size, the output force will equal the input force, resulting in a mechanical advantage of one.

14. C: Because the horizontal component of the thrown ball's velocity will not affect the vertical component, the vertical component of the thrown ball's velocity will be identical to the dropped ball's velocity. The balls will hit at the same time.

15. A: The cam has four bumps on it. The needle will move up and down for each bump. The cam will rotate five times in the time period of one minute. The total times the needle will move up and down will be five times four.

16. C: Torque is the product of a force perpendicular to the arm and the length of the arm. Options A and B each increase one part of the torque calculation. However, angling the force towards the center would decrease the part of the force that is acting perpendicular to the arm, as some of the force will be acting inward.

17. B: When the ball is compressed into the spring, the ball has potential energy stored in the spring. When the ball is flying upwards, the ball has kinetic energy associated with the motion.

18. B: Pressure increases with depth in water. When the tank was lower it experienced more pressure. Thus, when the tank is higher it experiences less pressure.

19. B: Specific gravity can be calculated as the ratio of the density of the liquid in question to the density of water. Because salt water has a higher density than water, the ratio will be greater than one.

20. B: Convective heat transfer deals with the transfer of heat by fluids (including gas). Steam is a fluid which transfers heat to objects, like a hand, with lower temperatures than it.

21. C: A capacitor stores voltage across a gap between two conductive materials.

22. A: Torque is the product of a force perpendicular to the arm and the length of the arm. Wrench A, with the longer arm, will be able to achieve greater amounts of torque with a set force.

23. B: Because the circuit only has one path and the two resistors are in series, the current is the same everywhere in the circuit. The voltage will drop over both resistors. Also, because the circuit is complete, there is current in the circuit.

24. C: Ammeters measure current (think amps). Multimeters measure current and voltage. Voltmeters only measure voltage.

25. B: When the ball is flying upwards, the kinetic energy is being converted into potential energy. Potential energy increases linearly with height, meaning that an object at 2 feet over the ground has twice the potential energy of the object at 1 foot over the ground. Thus, if all of the energy of the ball will be converted from kinetic energy, and half of the energy will be converted at half the height, the potential energy of the ball will be 50 ft-lb.

26. A: Because mechanical advantage is the ratio of output force to input force, an increase in mechanical advantage means, in this case, that the output force will be increasing. However, energy in simple machines is conserved. This means that the work, or force times distance, done to the input will need to increase, while keeping the force the same. Increasing the distance of the applied force will increase the work, allowing for an increased force for the output.

27. A: As the drum spins one full turn, the hanging rope increases length by 1 foot and decreases length by 3.5 feet. Thus, every spin decreases the rope length by 2.5 feet. In two turns, the rope will decrease length by 5 feet. The pulley makes the weight lift half the distance that the rope decreased. Thus, the weight raises 2.5 feet.

28. C: Condensation from the air occurs when the water vapor in the air cools down enough to change phase from vapor to liquid water. If a pipe is cold and the air is warm, the water vapor will condense on the pipe.

29. A: The color, black, will absorb the most heat from radiation.

30. B: The gear ratio between the small and large gears is 18/30 or 3/5. Multiply the number of rotations of the small gear times the gear ratio to get (3 rotations) × (3/5) = 1.8 rotations.

AFOQT Practice Test

Verbal Analogies

1. CHASTISE is to REPRIMAND as IMPETUOUS is to

    a. PUNISH
    b. RASH
    c. CONSIDERED
    d. POOR
    e. CALM

2. ARM is to HUMERUS as LEG is to

    a. ULNA
    b. CLAVICLE
    c. FEMUR
    d. MANDIBLE
    e. METACARPAL

3. MULTIPLICATION is to DIVISION as PRODUCT is to

    a. QUOTIENT
    b. DIVISOR
    c. INTEGER
    d. DIVIDEND
    e. MULTIPLIER

4. WEAR is to SWEATER as EAT is to

    a. SHIRT
    b. TOP HAT
    c. ASPARAGUS
    d. LOOKS
    e. MOUTH

5. MONEY is to IMPECUNIOUS as FOOD is to

    a. FAMISHED
    b. NAUSEATED
    c. DISTRACTED
    d. ANTAGONISTIC
    e. IMPOVERISHED

6. DENIGRATE is to MALIGN as DEMUR is to

    a. PROTEST
    b. DEFER
    c. SLANDER
    d. BENUMB
    e. BELITTLE

7. OBEISANCE is to DEFERENCE as MUNIFICENT is to

    a. BENEVOLENT
    b. MAGNIFICENT
    c. SQUALID
    d. GENEROUS
    e. AVARICE

8. GOAT is to NANNY as PIG is to

    a. SHOAT
    b. EWE
    c. CUB
    d. SOW
    e. CALF

9. CACHE is to RESERVE as DEARTH is to

    a. STOCKPILE
    b. PAUCITY
    c. CUDGEL
    d. DIRGE
    e. SOMBER

10. ARABLE is to FARMABLE as ASYLUM is to

    a. FAMINE
    b. DANGER
    c. ARID
    d. FERTILE
    e. REFUGE

11. MYRIAD is to FEW as STATIONARY is to

    a. PERIPATETIC
    b. MANY
    c. SEVERAL
    d. HALTED
    e. PARKED

12. HOUSE is to MANSION as BOTTLE is to

    a. FLAGON
    b. CONTAINER
    c. VESSEL
    d. POT
    e. FLASK

13. DICTIONARY is to DEFINITIONS as THESAURUS is to

    a. PRONUNCIATIONS
    b. SYNONYMS
    c. EXPLANATIONS
    d. PRONOUNS
    e. DEFINITIONS

14. ABSTRUSE is to ESOTERIC as ADAMANT is to

   a. YIELDING
   b. STUBBORN
   c. KEEN
   d. FORTHRIGHT
   e. FLEXIBLE

15. BEES is to HIVE as CATTLE is to

   a. SWARM
   b. POD
   c. HERD
   d. FLOCK
   e. PACK

16. LATITUDE is to LONGITUDE as PARALLEL is to

   a. STRAIT
   b. LINE
   c. EQUATOR
   d. AQUIFER
   e. MERIDIAN

17. PREVENTION is to DETERRENCE as INCITEMENT is to

   a. EXCITEMENT
   b. PROVOCATION
   c. REQUEST
   d. DISREGARD
   e. DISGUST

18. VALUE is to WORTH as MEASURE is to

   a. GAUGE
   b. ALLOWANCE
   c. DEMERIT
   d. INSIGNIFICANCE
   e. LARGE

19. ENERVATE is to ENERGIZE as ESPOUSE is to

   a. OPPOSE
   b. WED
   c. EQUINE
   d. EPISTOLARY
   e. MARRY

20. HAMMER is to CARPENTER as STETHOSCOPE is to

   a. PATIENT
   b. HEARING
   c. HEARTBEAT
   d. DOCTOR
   e. PEDOMETER

21. ARMOIRE is to BEDROOM as DESK is to

  a. CHAIR
  b. OFFICE
  c. COMPUTER
  d. WORK
  e. BUILDING

22. PLANKTON is to WHALES as BAMBOO is to

  a. PREDATORS
  b. GRASSES
  c. PANDAS
  d. FAST-GROWING
  e. CHINA

23. TUNDRA is to ARCTIC as SAVANNA is to

  a. PRAIRIE
  b. LUSH
  c. TROPIC
  d. GEORGIA
  e. JUNGLE

24. THIRSTY is to PARCHED as HUNGRY is to

  a. FAMISHED
  b. FED
  c. SATIATED
  d. SATISFIED
  e. FULL

25. FELICITY is to SADNESS as IGNOMINY is to

  a. SHAME
  b. SLANDER
  c. CRIME
  d. INDICT
  e. HONOR

Arithmetic Reasoning

1. A man buys two shirts. One is $7.50 and the other is $3.00. A 6% tax is added to his total. What is his total?

    a. $10.50
    b. $11.13
    c. $14.58
    d. $16.80
    e. $18.21

2. If a chef can make 25 pastries in a day, how many can he make in a week?

    a. 32
    b. 74
    c. 126
    d. 175
    e. 250

3. A woman must earn $250 in the next four days to pay a traffic ticket. How much will she have to earn each day?

    a. $45.50
    b. $62.50
    c. $75.50
    d. $100.50
    e. $125.00

4. A car lot has an inventory of 476 cars. If 36 people bought cars in the week after the inventory was taken, how many cars will remain in inventory at the end of that week?

    a. 440
    b. 476
    c. 484
    d. 512
    e. 536

5. A woman has $450 in a bank account. She earns 0.5% interest on her end-of-month balance. How much interest will she earn for the month?

    a. $0.50
    b. $2.25
    c. $4.28
    d. $4.73
    e. $6.34

6. Three children decide to buy a gift for their father. The gift costs $78. One child contributes $24. The second contributes $15 less than the first. How much will the third child have to contribute?

    a. $15
    b. $39
    c. $45
    d. $62
    e. $69

7. Two women have credit cards. One earns 3 points for every dollar she spends. The other earns 6 points for every dollar she spends. If they each spend $5.00, how many combined total points will they earn?

    a. 15
    b. 30
    c. 45
    d. 60
    e. 75

8. A company employing 540 individuals plans to increase its workforce by 13%. How many people will the company employ after the expansion?

    a. 527
    b. 547
    c. 553
    d. 570
    e. 610

9. A 13 story building has 65 apartments. If each floor has an equal number of apartments, how many apartments are on each floor?

    a. 2
    b. 3
    c. 4
    d. 5
    e. 6

10. If 5 people buy 3 pens each and 3 people buy 7 pencils each, what is the ratio of the total number of pens sold to the total number of pencils sold?

    a. 7:3
    b. 3:7
    c. 5:7
    d. 1:1
    e. 5:3

11. A man earns $15.23 per hour and gets a raise of $2.34 per hour. What is his new hourly rate of pay?

    a. $12.89
    b. $15.46
    c. $17.57
    d. $23.40
    e. $35.64

12. How many people can travel on 6 planes if each carries 300 passengers?

    a. 1,800
    b. 1,200
    c. 600
    d. 350
    e. 300

13. In a town, the ratio of men to women is 2 : 1. If the number of women in the town is doubled, what will be the new ratio of men to women?

  a. 1 : 2
  b. 1 : 1
  c. 2 : 1
  d. 3 : 1
  e. 4 : 1

14. A woman weighing 250 pounds goes on a diet. During the first week, she loses 3% of her body weight. During the second week, she loses 2% of her new body weight. At the end of the second week, how many pounds has she lost?

  a. 12.5
  b. 10
  c. 12.35
  d. 15
  e. 17.5

15. A woman is traveling to a destination 600 km away. If she drives 80 km every hour, how many hours will it take for her to reach her destination?

  a. 2.0
  b. 3.5
  c. 5.0
  d. 7.5
  e. 8.5

16. If one gallon of paint can paint 3 rooms, how many rooms can be painted with 28 gallons of paint?

  a. 10
  b. 25
  c. 56
  d. 84
  e. 92

17. Five workers each earn $135/day. What is the total amount earned by the five workers?

  a. $675
  b. $700
  c. $725
  d. $750
  e. $775

18. A girl scores a 99 on her math test. On her second test, her score drops by 15. On the third test, she scores 5 points higher than she did on her second. What was the girl's score on the third test?

  a. 79
  b. 84
  c. 89
  d. 99
  e. 104

19. A man goes to the mall with $50.00. He spends $15.64 in one store and $7.12 in a second store. How much does he have left?

a. $27.24
b. $32.76
c. $34.36
d. $42.80
e. $57.12

20. 600 students must share a school that has 20 classrooms. How many students will each classroom contain if there are an equal number of students in each class?

a. 10
b. 15
c. 20
d. 25
e. 30

21. Four workers at a shelter agree to care for the dogs over a holiday. If there are 48 dogs, how many must each worker look after?

a. 8
b. 10
c. 12
d. 14
e. 16

22. One worker has an office that is 20 feet long. Another has an office that is 6 feet longer. What is the combined length of both offices?

a. 26 feet
b. 36 feet
c. 46 feet
d. 56 feet
e. 66 feet

23. Four friends go shopping. They purchase items that cost $6.65 and $159.23. If they split the cost evenly, how much will each friend have to pay?

a. $26.64
b. $39.81
c. $41.47
d. $55.30
e. $82.95

24. A 140-acre forest is cut in half to make way for development. What is the size of the new forest's acreage?

a. 70
b. 80
c. 90
d. 100
e. 120

25. A farmer has 360 cows. He decides to sell 45. Shortly after, he purchases 85 more cows. How many cows does he have?

    a. 230
    b. 315
    c. 400
    d. 490
    e. 530

Word Knowledge

1. SPOILED
   a. Ruined
   b. Splendid
   c. Told
   d. Believed
   e. Hated

2. OATH
   a. Delivery
   b. Promise
   c. Statement
   d. Criticism
   e. Threat

3. INQUIRE
   a. Invest
   b. Ask
   c. Tell
   d. Release
   e. Inquest

4. COMPREHEND
   a. Learn
   b. Speak
   c. Understand
   d. Appreciate
   e. Commemorate

5. APPARENT
   a. Clear
   b. Occasional
   c. Angry
   d. Applied
   e. Father

6. SILENCE
   a. Darkness
   b. Excitement
   c. Quiet
   d. Mood
   e. Quaint

7. ABSOLUTELY
   a. Assuredly
   b. Rapidly
   c. Never
   d. Weakly
   e. completely

8. MODIFIED

a. Checked
b. Shortened
c. Considered
d. Changed
e. Lengthened

9. DELICATE

a. Fragile
b. Sturdy
c. Loud
d. Soft
e. Lovely

10. FESTIVITIES

a. Commitments
b. Celebrations
c. Crowds
d. Dates
e. Funeral

11. EXHAUSTED

a. Excited
b. Tired
c. Worried
d. Energized
e. Animated

12. CLEANSED

a. Examined
b. Washed
c. Touched
d. Dried
e. Motivated

13. BATTLED

a. Fought
b. Attempt
c. Bold
d. Saw
e. Excited

14. WANDERED

a. Looked
b. Shopped
c. Roamed
d. Searched
e. Lived

15. ABRUPTLY
a. Homely
b. Commonly
c. Wisely
d. Ugly
e. Suddenly

16. TRICKED
a. Conned
b. Begged
c. Convinced
d. Nagged
e. Criticized

17. EXTREMELY
a. Almost
b. Slightly
c. Very
d. Clearly
e. Happily

18. DOUBTFUL
a. Uncertain
b. Panicked
c. Pondering
d. Indifferent
e. Confused

19. PECULIAR
a. Original
b. Novel
c. Dull
d. Strange
e. Awesome

20. COURTEOUS
a. Handsome
b. Polite
c. Inconsiderate
d. Odd
e. Unrelenting

21. TROUBLED
a. Relieved
b. Satisfied
c. Bothered
d. Relaxed
e. Persistent

22. PERSPIRATION

a. Sweat
b. Work
c. Help
d. Advice
e. Job

23. TREMBLED

a. Spoke
b. Shook
c. Wept
d. Ducked
e. Cowered

24. ADHERED

a. Stuck
b. Went
c. Spoke
d. Altered
e. Stunk

25. TIDY

a. Furnished
b. Warm
c. Locked
d. Neat
e. Inviting

Mathematics Knowledge

1. A rectangle has a width of 7 cm and a length of 9 cm. What is its perimeter?

    a. 16 cm
    b. 32 cm
    c. 48 cm
    d. 62 cm
    e. 63 cm

2. In the following inequality, solve for q.

$$-3q + 12 \geq 4q - 30$$

    a. $q \geq 6$
    b. $q = 6$
    c. $q \neq 6$
    d. $q \leq 6$
    e. q does not exist

3. If $x - 6 = 0$, then x is equal to

    a. 0
    b. 3
    c. 6
    d. 9
    e. 12

4. If $x = -3$, calculate the value of the following expression:

$$3x^3 + (3x + 4) - 2x^2$$

    a. -104
    b. -58
    c. 58
    d. 104
    e. 0

5. If $3x - 30 = 45 - 2x$, what is the value of x?

    a. 5
    b. 10
    c. 15
    d. 20
    e. 25

6. Solve for x in the following inequality.

$$\frac{1}{4}x - 25 \geq 75$$

    a. $x \geq 400$
    b. $x \leq 400$
    c. $x \geq 25$
    d. $x \leq 25$
    e. $x \geq 50$

7. If $x^2 - 5 = 20$, what is one possible value of x?

    a. 5
    b. 10
    c. 12.5
    d. 15
    e. 25

8. What is the area of a square that has a perimeter of 8 cm?

    a. 2 cm^2
    b. 4 cm^2
    c. 32 cm^2
    d. 64 cm^2
    e. 160 cm^2

9. If $x = 4$ and $y = 2$, what is the value of the following expression:

$$3xy - 12y + 5x$$

    a. -4
    b. 10
    c. 12
    d. 20
    e. 24

10. If $\frac{2}{3}x + 10 = 16$, what is the value of x?

    a. 6
    b. 7
    c. 8
    d. 9
    e. 10

11. Simplify the following:

$$(3x + 5)(4x - 6)$$

    a. $12x^2 - 38x - 30$
    b. $12x^2 + 2x - 30$
    c. $12x^2 - 2x - 1$
    d. $12x^2 + 2x + 30$
    e. $12x^2 + 7x - 30$

12. Simplify the following expression:

$$\frac{50x^{18}t^6w^3z^{20}}{5x^5t^2w^2z^{19}}$$

    a. $10x^{13}t^3wz$
    b. $10x^{13}t^4wz$
    c. $10x^{12}t^4wz$
    d. $10x^{13}t^4wz^2$
    e. $10x^{12}t^3w^2z^2$

13. The quantity $n!$ (n-factorial) is defined as the product of all positive integers between n and zero. (i.e., $n \times (n-1) \times (n-2) \times ... \times 3 \times 2 \times 1$). The quantity 4! (four-factorial) is equal to

    a. 4
    b. 12
    c. 16
    d. 20
    e. 24

14. If one side of a cube is 5 cm long, what is the volume of the cube?

    a. 15 cm^3
    b. 65 cm^3
    c. 105 cm^3
    d. 125 cm^3
    e. 225 cm^3

15. Solve for x by factoring:

$$x^2 - 13x + 42 = 0$$

    a. $x = 6,7$
    b. $x = -6,-7$
    c. $x = 6,-7$
    d. $x = -6,7$
    e. $x = 7$ only

16. A triangle has a base measuring 12 cm and a height of 12 cm. What is its area?

    a. 24 cm^2
    b. 56 cm^2
    c. 72 cm^2
    d. 144 cm^2
    e. 288 cm^2

17. Simplify the following expression:

$$(3x^2 7x^7) + (2y^3 9y^{12})$$

    a. $21x^{14} + 18y^{26}$
    b. $10x^9 + 11y^{15}$
    c. $21x^{14} + 18y^{15}$
    d. $21x^9 + 18y^{15}$
    e. $10x^{14} + 11y^{26}$

18. If $\frac{x}{3} + 27 = 30$, what is the value of x?

    a. 3
    b. 6
    c. 9
    d. 12
    e. 27

19. What is the slope of a line with points A $(4, 1)$ and B $(-13, 8)$?

    a. $\dfrac{7}{17}$

    b. $-\dfrac{7}{17}$

    c. $-\dfrac{17}{7}$

    d. $\dfrac{17}{7}$

    e.   None of the above

20. If x is 20% of 200, what is the value of x?

    a.   40

    b.   80

    c.   100

    d.   150

    e.   180

21. If a bag of balloons consists of 37 white balloons, 8 yellow balloons, and 15 black balloons, what is the probability that a balloon chosen randomly from the bag will be black?

    a.   29%

    b.   25%

    c.   21%

    d.   17%

    e.   13%

22. A raffle game has a single grand prize that will be drawn randomly from among all the tickets. A total of 500 tickets are sold. If a man buys 25 tickets, what is the probability that he will win the grand prize?

    a.   1 in 2

    b.   1 in 5

    c.   1 in 10

    d.   1 in 20

    e.   1 in 40

23. What is the volume of a rectangular prism with a height of 10 cm, a length of 5 cm, and a width of 6 cm?

    a. 30 cm^3

    b. 60 cm^3

    c. 150 cm^3

    d. 240 cm^3

    e. 300 cm^3

24. What is the midpoint of a line segment that runs from point A $(6, 20)$ to point B $(10, 40)$?

    a. $(30, 8)$

    b. $(16, 60)$

    c. $(8, 30)$

    d. $(7, 15)$

    e. $(15, 8)$

25. If $5x + 60 = 75$, what is the value of x?

    a.   3
    b.   4
    c.   5
    d.   6
    e.   7

Reading Comprehension

Passage 1

Since air is a gas, it can be compressed or expanded. When air is compressed, a greater amount of air can occupy a given volume. Conversely, when pressure on a given volume of air is decreased, the air expands and occupies a greater space. That is, the original column of air at a lower pressure contains a smaller mass of air. In other words, the density is decreased. In fact, density is directly proportional to pressure. If the pressure is doubled, the density is doubled, and if the pressure is lowered, so is the density. This statement is true only at a constant temperature.

Increasing the temperature of a substance decreases its density. Conversely, decreasing the temperature increases the density. Thus, the density of air varies inversely with temperature. This statement is true only at a constant pressure. In the atmosphere, both temperature and pressure decrease with altitude and have conflicting effects upon density. However, the fairly rapid drop in pressure as altitude is increased usually has the dominant effect. Hence, pilots can expect the density to decrease with altitude.

The preceding paragraphs are based on the presupposition of perfectly dry air. In reality, it is never completely dry. The small amount of water vapor suspended in the atmosphere may be negligible under certain conditions, but in other conditions humidity may become an important factor in the performance of an aircraft. Water vapor is lighter than air; consequently, moist air is lighter than dry air. Therefore, as the water content of the air increases, the air becomes less dense, increasing density altitude and decreasing performance. It is lightest or least dense when, in a given set of conditions, it contains the maximum amount of water vapor.

Humidity, also called relative humidity, refers to the amount of water vapor contained in the atmosphere and is expressed as a percentage of the maximum amount of water vapor the air can hold. This amount varies with the temperature; warm air can hold more water vapor, while colder air can hold less. Perfectly dry air that contains no water vapor has a relative humidity of zero percent, while saturated air that cannot hold any more water vapor has a relative humidity of 100 percent. Humidity alone is usually not considered an essential factor in calculating density altitude and aircraft performance; however, it does contribute.

The higher the temperature, the greater amount of water vapor that the air can hold. When comparing two separate air masses, the first warm and moist (both qualities making air lighter) and the second cold and dry (both qualities making it heavier), the first must be less dense than the second. Pressure, temperature, and humidity have a great influence on aircraft performance because of their effect upon density. There is no rule-of-thumb or chart used to compute the effects of humidity on density altitude, but it must be taken into consideration. Expect a decrease in overall performance in high humidity conditions.

1. The primary purpose of the passage is to

    a. Explain the qualities of air that may affect flight

    b. Explain g-force and how it works

    c. Describe the constituent elements of air

    d. Explain humidity

    e. Describe the ideal air conditions for flight

2. In the second paragraph, *inversely* most nearly means

    a. Severely

    b. Incredibly

    c. In the opposite direction

    d. In an unrelated fashion

    e. Concurrently

3. If the air temperature drops while a plane is gaining altitude, the pilot can expect

    a. The density of the air to increase

    b. The humidity of the air to increase

    c. The air pressure to increase

    d. The density of the air to decrease

    e. Aircraft performance to decrease

4. With which one of the following claims about air quality would the author most likely agree?

    a. Pilots never need to pay attention to relative humidity.

    b. For a pilot, the density of air is more important than the relative humidity.

    c. Completely dry air is very rare.

    d. Aircraft performance is unrelated to humidity.

    e. The best conditions for flying are very hot and humid.

5. What is the most likely reason why there is no chart for assessing the effects of humidity on density altitude?

    a. Humidity does not affect density altitude.

    b. It is impossible to measure humidity.

    c. Humidity does not affect flight performance very much.

    d. Humidity varies a great deal in relatively small areas.

    e. Density altitude never varies.

Passage 2

The climb performance of an aircraft is affected by certain variables. The conditions of the aircraft's maximum climb angle or maximum climb rate occur at specific speeds, and variations in speed will produce variations in climb performance. There is sufficient latitude in most aircraft that small variations in speed from the optimum do not produce large changes in climb performance, and certain operational considerations may require speeds slightly different from the optimum. Of course, climb performance would be most critical with high gross weight, at high altitude, in obstructed takeoff areas, or during malfunction of a powerplant. Then, optimum climb speeds are necessary.

Weight has a very pronounced effect on aircraft performance. If weight is added to an aircraft, it must fly at a higher angle of attack (AOA) to maintain a given altitude and speed. This increases the induced drag of the wings, as well as the parasite drag of the aircraft. Increased drag means that additional thrust is needed to overcome it, which in turn means that less reserve thrust is available for climbing. Aircraft designers go to great effort to minimize the weight since it has such a marked effect on the factors pertaining to performance.

A change in an aircraft's weight produces a twofold effect on climb performance. First, a change in weight will change the drag and the power required. This alters the reserve power available, which in turn, affects both the climb angle and the climb rate. Secondly, an increase in weight will reduce the maximum rate of climb, but the aircraft must be operated at a higher climb speed to achieve the smaller peak climb rate.

An increase in altitude also will increase the power required and decrease the power available. Therefore, the climb performance of an aircraft diminishes with altitude. The speeds for maximum rate of climb, maximum angle of climb, and maximum and minimum level flight airspeeds vary with altitude. As altitude is increased, these various speeds finally converge at the absolute ceiling of the aircraft. At the absolute ceiling, there is no excess of power and only one speed will allow steady, level flight. Consequently, the absolute ceiling of an aircraft produces zero rate of climb. The service ceiling is the altitude at which the aircraft is unable to climb at a rate greater than 100 feet per minute (fpm). Usually, these specific performance reference points are provided for the aircraft at a specific design configuration.

In discussing performance, it frequently is convenient to use the terms power loading, wing loading, blade loading, and disk loading. Power loading is expressed in pounds per horsepower and is obtained by dividing the total weight of the aircraft by the rated horsepower of the engine. It is a significant factor in an aircraft's takeoff and climb capabilities. Wing loading is expressed in pounds per square foot and is obtained by dividing the total weight of an airplane in pounds by the wing area (including ailerons) in square feet. It is the airplane's wing loading that determines the landing speed. Blade loading is expressed in pounds per square foot and is obtained by dividing the total weight of a helicopter by the area of the rotor blades. Blade loading is not to be confused with disk loading, which is the total weight of a helicopter divided by the area of the disk swept by the rotor blades.

6. Which of the following would be the best title for this passage?

    a. The Importance of Weight
    b. Climb Performance and You
    c. Power Loading, Wing Loading, and Disk Loading
    d. Influences on Climb Performance
    e. Achieving Maximum Climb Angle

7. In the second paragraph, *pronounced* most nearly means

    a. Selective
    b. Intoned
    c. Detrimental
    d. Spoken
    e. Noticeable

8. Which of the following is NOT one of the effects of increased weight on flight performance?

    a. Diminished reserve power
    b. Decreased climb rate
    c. Lower angle of attack required to maintain altitude
    d. Diminished maximum rate of climb
    e. Increased drag

9. With which one of the following claims about climb performance would the author most likely agree?

    a. Optimal climb performance can be achieved even with heavy cargo.
    b. At the end of a long journey, a plane will have a higher maximum rate of climb.
    c. A plane can handle any amount of weight, though climb performance will be affected.
    d. Pilots have no influence over climb performance.
    e. The climb performance of a two-engine plane will remain the same even if one engine fails.

10. If a helicopter weighs two tons and its rotor blades cover an area of five hundred square feet, what is its disc loading measure?

    a. 8 pounds per square foot
    b. 125 square foot-pounds
    c. 0.125 tons per square foot
    d. 4 metric tons
    e. 8 ton-feet

Passage 3

The aerodynamic properties of an aircraft generally determine the power requirements at various conditions of flight, while the powerplant capabilities generally determine the power available at various conditions of flight. When an aircraft is in steady, level flight, a condition of equilibrium must prevail. An unaccelerated condition of flight is achieved when lift equals weight, and the powerplant is set for thrust equal to drag. The power required to achieve equilibrium in constant-altitude flight at various airspeeds is depicted on a power required curve. The power required curve illustrates the fact that at low airspeeds near the stall or minimum controllable airspeed, the power setting required for steady, level flight is quite high.

Flight in the region of normal command means that while holding a constant altitude, a higher airspeed requires a higher power setting, and a lower airspeed requires a lower power setting. The majority of aircraft flying (climb, cruise, and maneuvers) is conducted in the region of normal command.

Flight in the region of reversed command means flight in which a higher airspeed requires a lower power setting, and a lower airspeed requires a higher power setting to hold altitude. It does not imply that a decrease in power will produce lower airspeed. The region of reversed command is encountered in the low speed phases of flight. Flight speeds below the speed for maximum endurance (lowest point on the power curve) require higher power settings with a decrease in airspeed. Since the need to increase the required power setting with decreased speed is contrary to the normal command of flight, the regime of flight speeds between the speed for minimum required power setting and the stall speed (or minimum control speed) is termed the region of reversed command. In the region of reversed command, a decrease in airspeed must be accompanied by an increased power setting in order to maintain steady flight.

An airplane performing a low airspeed, high pitch attitude power approach for a short-field landing is an example of operating in the region of reversed command. If an unacceptably high sink rate should develop, it may be possible for the pilot to reduce or stop the descent by applying power. But without further use of power, the airplane would probably stall or be incapable of flaring for the landing. Merely lowering the nose of the airplane to regain flying speed in this situation, without the use of power, would result in a rapid sink rate and corresponding loss of altitude.

If during a soft-field takeoff and climb, for example, the pilot attempts to climb out of ground effect without first attaining normal climb pitch attitude and airspeed, the airplane may inadvertently enter the region of reversed command at a dangerously low altitude. Even with full power, the airplane may be incapable of climbing or even maintaining altitude. The pilot's only recourse in this situation is to lower the pitch attitude in order to increase airspeed, which will inevitably result in a loss of altitude. Airplane pilots must give particular attention to precise control of airspeed when operating in the low flight speeds of the region of reversed command.

11. The primary purpose of the passage is to

    a. Instruct pilots on proper airspeed.
    b. Discuss the interrelationships of airspeed, power, and pitch attitude.
    c. Explain reversed command.
    d. Discuss the physics of flight at low airspeeds.
    e. Persuade the reader to fly faster aircraft.

12. In the fifth paragraph, *inadvertently* most nearly means

    a. Unintentionally
    b. Indirectly
    c. Sequentially
    d. Primarily
    e. Eventually

13. In which region of command does most flight occur?

    a. Inverse command
    b. Normal command
    c. Direct command
    d. Reverse command
    e. Decreased command

14. With which one of the following statements about flight would the author most likely agree?

    a. As speed increases, the power required to descend decreases.
    b. As speed increases, the power required to descend remains constant.
    c. As speed decreases, the power required to climb remains constant.
    d. As speed increases, the power required to maintain altitude increases.
    e. As speed decreases, the power required to maintain altitude increases.

15. Which of the following would be the best title for this passage?

    a. How to Avoid Reversed Command
    b. Normal Command Flight
    c. Learning to Fly
    d. Power Requirements During Flight
    e. Reversed Command and the Modern Pilot

Passage 4

In many cases, the landing distance of an aircraft will define the runway requirements for flight operations. The minimum landing distance is obtained by landing at some minimum safe speed, which allows sufficient margin above stall and provides satisfactory control and capability for a go-around. Generally, the landing speed is some fixed percentage of the stall speed or minimum control speed for the aircraft in the landing configuration. As such, the landing will be accomplished at some particular value of lift coefficient and angle of attack (AOA). The exact values will depend on the aircraft characteristics but, once defined, the values are independent of weight, altitude, and wind.

To obtain minimum landing distance at the specified landing speed, the forces that act on the aircraft must provide maximum deceleration during the landing roll. The forces acting on the aircraft during the landing roll may require various procedures to maintain landing deceleration at the peak value.

A distinction should be made between the procedures for minimum landing distance and an ordinary landing roll with considerable excess runway available. Minimum landing distance will be obtained by creating a continuous peak deceleration of the aircraft; that is, extensive use of the brakes for maximum deceleration. On the other hand, an ordinary landing roll with considerable excess runway may allow extensive use of aerodynamic drag to minimize wear and tear on the tires and brakes. If aerodynamic drag is sufficient to cause deceleration, it can be used in deference to the brakes in the early stages of the landing roll; i.e., brakes and tires suffer from continuous hard use, but aircraft aerodynamic drag is free and does not wear out with use.

The use of aerodynamic drag is applicable only for deceleration to 60 or 70 percent of the touchdown speed. At speeds less than 60 to 70 percent of the touchdown speed, aerodynamic drag is so slight as to be of little use, and braking must be utilized to produce continued deceleration. Since the objective during the landing roll is to decelerate, the powerplant thrust should be the smallest possible positive value (or largest possible negative value in the case of thrust reversers). In addition to the important factors of proper procedures, many other variables affect the landing performance. Any item that alters the landing speed or deceleration rate during the landing roll will affect the landing distance.

The effect of gross weight on landing distance is one of the principal items determining the landing distance. One effect of an increased gross weight is that a greater speed will be required to support the aircraft at the landing AOA and lift coefficient. For an example of the effect of a change in gross weight, a 21 percent increase in landing weight will require a ten percent increase in landing speed to support the greater weight.

When minimum landing distances are considered, braking friction forces predominate during the landing roll and, for the majority of aircraft configurations, braking friction is the main source of deceleration.

The minimum landing distance will vary in direct proportion to the gross weight. For example, a ten percent increase in gross weight at landing would cause a:

- Five percent increase in landing velocity
- Ten percent increase in landing distance

A contingency of this is the relationship between weight and braking friction force.

The effect of wind on landing distance is large and deserves proper consideration when predicting landing distance. Since the aircraft will land at a particular airspeed independent of the wind, the principal effect of wind on landing distance is the change in the groundspeed at which the aircraft touches down. The effect of wind on deceleration during the landing is identical to the effect on acceleration during the takeoff.

The effect of pressure altitude and ambient temperature is to define density altitude and its effect on landing performance. An increase in density altitude increases the landing speed but does not alter the net retarding force. Thus, the aircraft at altitude lands at the same indicated airspeed as at sea level but, because of the reduced density, the true airspeed is greater. Since the aircraft lands at altitude with the same weight and dynamic pressure, the drag and braking friction throughout the landing roll have the same values as at sea level. As long as the condition is within the capability of the brakes, the net retarding force is unchanged, and the deceleration is the same as with the landing at sea level. Since an increase in altitude does not alter deceleration, the effect of density altitude on landing distance is due to the greater true airspeed.

16. The main purpose of the passage is to

a. Give some examples of near accidents during landing.
b. Improve landing skills.
c. Explain the effects of varying pressure altitudes.
d. Advocate safer protocols for landing.
e. Describe the factors that influence landing distance.

17. Why will a pilot rely on aerodynamic drag when making a normal landing?

a. To increase the rate of deceleration
b. To avoid wearing down the brakes and tires
c. To avoid unnecessary turbulence
d. To mitigate a large gross weight
e. To simplify landing procedures

18. In the fourth paragraph, *principal* most nearly means

a. Most important
b. Easiest
c. Moral
d. First
e. Value

19. Why must a heavier plane land at a higher speed?

a. To diminish fuel supplies and thereby decrease gross weight
b. To encourage a stall just before landing
c. To avoid hitting the runway with too much force
d. To improve handling on the runway
e. To allow for the longest landing distance

20. With which one of the following claims about landing performance would the author most likely agree?

a. Many landings occur without any use of the brakes.
b. Ambient temperature has no effect on minimum landing distance.
c. Gross weight and minimum landing distance are positively correlated.
d. Runway length is less important than gross weight in determining the appropriate airspeed during landing.
e. Minimum landing distance is generally consistent for aircraft of the same size.

Passage 5

For over 25 years, the importance of good pilot judgment, or aeronautical decision-making (ADM), has been recognized as critical to the safe operation of aircraft, as well as accident avoidance. The airline industry, motivated by the need to reduce accidents caused by human factors, developed the first training programs based on improving ADM. Crew resource management (CRM) training for flight crews is focused on the effective use of all available resources: human resources, hardware, and information supporting ADM to facilitate crew cooperation and improve decision-making. The goal of all flight crews is good ADM and the use of CRM is one way to make good decisions.

Research in this area prompted the Federal Aviation Administration (FAA) to produce training directed at improving the decision-making of pilots and led to current FAA regulations that require that decision-making be taught as part of the pilot training curriculum. ADM research, development, and testing culminated in 1987 with the publication of six manuals oriented to the decision-making needs of variously rated pilots.

These manuals provided multifaceted materials designed to reduce the number of decision-related accidents. The effectiveness of these materials was validated in independent studies where student pilots received such training in conjunction with the standard flying curriculum. When tested, the pilots who had received ADM training made fewer inflight errors than those who had not received ADM training. The differences were statistically significant and ranged from about 10 to 50 percent fewer judgment errors. In the operational environment, an operator flying about 400,000 hours annually demonstrated a 54 percent reduction in accident rate after using these materials for recurrency training.

Contrary to popular opinion, good judgment can be taught. Tradition held that good judgment was a natural by-product of experience, but as pilots continued to log accident-free flight hours, a corresponding increase of good judgment was assumed. Building upon the foundation of conventional decision-making, ADM enhances the process to decrease the probability of human error and increase the probability of a safe flight. ADM provides a structured, systematic approach to analyzing changes that occur during a flight and how these changes might affect a flight's safe outcome. The ADM process addresses all aspects of decision-making in the flight deck and identifies the steps involved in good decision-making.

Steps for good decision-making are:

6. Identifying personal attitudes hazardous to safe flight
7. Learning behavior modification techniques
8. Learning how to recognize and cope with stress
9. Developing risk assessment skills
10. Using all resources
11. Evaluating the effectiveness of one's ADM skills

Risk management is an important component of ADM. When a pilot follows good decision-making practices, the inherent risk in a flight is reduced or even eliminated. The ability to make good decisions is based upon direct or indirect experience and education.

Consider automotive seat belt use. In just two decades, seat belt use has become the norm, placing those who do not wear seat belts outside the norm, but this group may learn to wear a seat belt by either direct or indirect experience.

For example, a driver learns through direct experience about the value of wearing a seat belt when he or she is involved in a car accident that leads to a personal injury. An indirect learning experience occurs when a loved one is injured during a car accident because he or she failed to wear a seat belt.

While poor decision-making in everyday life does not always lead to tragedy, the margin for error in aviation is thin. Since ADM enhances management of an aeronautical environment, all pilots should become familiar with and employ ADM.

21. The primary purpose of the passage is to

    a. List the steps in good decision-making.
    b. Improve the decision-making abilities of the reader.
    c. Outline the relationship between aeronautical decision-making and crew resource management.
    d. Discuss aeronautical decision-making.
    e. Inspire the reader to make better decisions.

22. According to the passage, how is aviation safety distinguished from other forms of safety?

    a. Aviation safety is much simpler than most other areas of safety.
    b. Aviation safety is no different than most other areas of safety.
    c. Aviation safety is only important to a small percentage of the population.
    d. There is a smaller margin for error in aviation.
    e. Aviation safety can be systematized.

23. In the second paragraph, *conjunction* most nearly means

    a. Combination
    b. Linking word
    c. Opposition
    d. Collection
    e. Organization

24. With which one of the following claims about aeronautical decision-making would the author most likely agree?

    a. The body of knowledge about ADM is increasing, and this will have a positive effect on flight safety.
    b. Aeronautical decision-making is the responsibility of the pilot alone.
    c. Eventually, researchers will establish a perfect set of decision-making tools for pilots.
    d. Aeronautical decision-making is the only tool required for flight safety.
    e. Aeronautical decision-making has no applications in areas other than flight.

25. When a pilot reads the account of a recent aviation accident, this is an opportunity for a(n)

    a. Recertification
    b. Direct learning experience
    c. Implicit learning experience
    d. Reorientation of learning
    e. Indirect learning experience

Situational Judgment

SITUATION 1:

You are approached by a senior officer, who requests a private meeting with you. He asks you for your candid opinion on your immediate supervisor, who is a subordinate to the senior officer. You have a generally favorable opinion of the supervisor, but you do have a few complaints about her performance. Specifically, you feel that she does a poor job of running staff meetings.

Possible actions:

a. Decline to meet with the senior officer.
b. Meet with the senior officer, and focus on the ways your supervisor could improve staff meetings.
c. Give your candid opinion of your supervisor, including your criticisms, but emphasizing your overall positive opinion.
d. Write a letter to the senior officer, explaining your opinions about your supervisor.
e. Give the senior officer a glowing report of the supervisor, without mentioning your complaints.

1. Select the MOST EFFECTIVE action in response to the situation.

2. Select the LEAST EFFECTIVE action in response to the situation.

SITUATION 2:

While performing administrative work with another officer, you notice that he is manipulating the numbers on some reports. Specifically, the officer is inflating the amounts of time spent on certain training exercises. These reports are sent on to senior officers, who use them to assess the readiness of the airmen for more sophisticated and complicated missions. If men and women are unprepared for these more difficult missions, there is a greater risk of accident or injury, to themselves or others.

Possible actions:

a. Immediately report this infraction to your superior.
b. Wait until you can acquire clear proof of the data manipulation.
c. Say nothing at present, but keep an eye on this other officer.
d. Write an anonymous letter to the other officer, encouraging him to stop manipulating the data.
e. Go back over the other officer's work, correcting the data as necessary.

3. Select the MOST EFFECTIVE action in response to the situation.

4. Select the LEAST EFFECTIVE action in response to the situation.

SITUATION 3:

You and two of your fellow officers have been selected to interview candidates for a promotion. One of the three candidates (Candidate A) is known to be an old family friend of your commanding officer. During the interviews, Candidate A is, in your opinion, the most impressive. However, Candidate B also seems like an excellent choice for the position. Candidate C performs poorly. One of the other judges votes for Candidate A, and the other votes for Candidate B.

Possible actions:
   a. Vote for Candidate B to avoid the appearance of favoritism.
   b. Vote for Candidate C so that the decision will be passed on to another round of deliberation.
   c. Abstain from voting.
   d. Request a new set of candidates.
   e. Vote for Candidate A because you feel he is the most qualified.

5. Select the MOST EFFECTIVE action in response to the situation.

6. Select the LEAST EFFECTIVE action in response to the situation.

SITUATION 4:

You attend a meeting with two other officers. During the meeting, these officers get into a heated conflict over a possible change in policy. You have heard that they have a personal antipathy, though you are not aware of its origins. They ask you to settle their dispute.

Possible actions:
   a. Ignore the request, and instead lecture the two officers on the need for cooperation and goodwill in the military.
   b. Take the side of the officer who you believe will be the most help to you in the future.
   c. Refuse to take a side, citing the obvious personal differences between the two officers.
   d. Select the option that you think is best, leaving aside everything you know about their personal conflict.
   e. Take the side of the officer you like better.

7. Select the MOST EFFECTIVE action in response to the situation.

8. Select the LEAST EFFECTIVE action in response to the situation.

SITUATION 5:

You are asked to collaborate on an important project with an officer from a different unit. This officer is very close to retirement and appears to have lost interest in his work. Consequently, he puts very little effort into the work you two are supposed to be sharing.

Possible actions:

a. Request a different partner for the project.
b. Inform your senior officer of the situation.
c. Do your best on your work, but accept that the project probably will fail because of the poor attitude of your collaborator.
d. Do your work and the work that was supposed to be done by your partner, since the most important thing is the successful completion of the project.
e. Express your frustrations directly to your collaborator, emphasizing that the success of this project is very important to you, and agree upon a fair division of labor.

9. Select the MOST EFFECTIVE action in response to the situation.

10. Select the LEAST EFFECTIVE action in response to the situation.

SITUATION 6:

While working in a field office, you observe that one of your colleagues is being severely overworked. Despite doing an excellent job and working more than the required number of hours, she is unable to keep up with the amount of paperwork being sent to her by other offices. Her commanding officers do not seem to be aware that she is being asked to do an unfair amount of work.

Possible actions:

a. Assign one of your subordinates to assist your overworked colleague.
b. Request a meeting with your overworked colleague's commanding officer, and describe the problem to him.
c. Ignore the problem, since it does not relate to your work.
d. Express your sympathy with your overworked colleague.
e. Help your overworked colleague whenever you finish your own work.

11. Select the MOST EFFECTIVE action in response to the situation.

12. Select the LEAST EFFECTIVE action in response to the situation.

SITUATION 7:

You have become suspicious that one of your junior officers is trying to undermine your work. This junior officer is very competent and very ambitious. You have even heard from other officers that this junior officer wants to take over your job. You have not yet mentioned your suspicion directly to the junior officer.

Possible actions:

a. Meet with the junior officer and explain that you expect his full cooperation and support.
b. Publicly reprimand and humiliate the junior officer.
c. Ignore the situation, in the hopes that it will resolve itself.
d. Report this insubordination to your commanding officer.
e. Ask one of your fellow officers to talk with the junior officer and try to improve the situation.

13. Select the MOST EFFECTIVE action in response to the situation.

14. Select the LEAST EFFECTIVE action in response to the situation.

SITUATION 8:

You are extremely busy with paperwork, but a senior officer asks you to complete a set of special reports in addition to your normal work. You do not think it will be possible for you to complete this extra assignment without sacrificing the quality of your work. However, you would like to impress your senior officer by fulfilling his request.

Possible actions:

a. Tell the senior officer that you are too busy to complete extra projects.
b. Accept the extra work and resolve to complete it quickly no matter what.
c. Ask the senior officer if you can have a few days to decide whether you will complete the extra work.
d. Accept the extra work, but have a junior staff member complete it for you.
e. Decline the extra work, but offer to pass it along to another qualified member of your team.

15. Select the MOST EFFECTIVE action in response to the situation.

16. Select the LEAST EFFECTIVE action in response to the situation.

SITUATION 9:

Over the past few months, you have noticed that office supplies are being used at a much greater pace than is usual. There is no clear reason for this, but you have begun to suspect that one of your fellow officers is taking office supplies home with her at night. You have no specific evidence to support your claims, but the office supplies seem to be disappearing after shifts in which this officer is alone with access to the supply closet.

Possible actions:

a. Ignore the situation, since you know that you are not personally responsible for the thefts.
b. Tell a senior officer about your suspicions.
c. Confront the officer with your suspicions and ask for an explanation.
d. Set up a hidden surveillance camera so that you can catch the officer stealing supplies.
e. Ask some of your fellow officers if they have noticed any suspicious behavior.

17. Select the MOST EFFECTIVE action in response to the situation.

18. Select the LEAST EFFECTIVE action in response to the situation.

SITUATION 10:

You have been working in the same unit for the past two years. Although you have been successful, you are beginning to get burnt out, and you are thinking about requesting a transfer. You contact some friends and colleagues in other units, trying to determine whether you would like it there. After a few weeks, you realize that rumors about your interest in a transfer have begun to spread throughout your unit.

Possible actions:

a. In a letter to your senior officer, acknowledge the truth of the rumors and request a transfer.
b. Deny the rumors publicly, but continue to pursue a transfer.
c. Ignore the rumors, but refocus on your work with your current unit.
d. Acknowledge the rumors and refocus on your work with your current unit.
e. Request a leave of absence so that you can decide how to handle the situation.

19. Select the MOST EFFECTIVE action in response to the situation.

20 Select the LEAST EFFECTIVE action in response to the situation.

SITUATION 11:

You have been asked to attend a meeting between the senior officers in your unit and a group of local community leaders. The meeting has been called because of rumors that your military base will be shut down due to budgetary constraints. The community leaders are willing to lobby on behalf of the base, so long as they receive assurances that the military leadership will cooperate with them on some local initiatives. Specifically, the community leaders would like the airmen to help coordinate disaster relief efforts when necessary. At one point, a community leader turns to you and asks for your opinion on the subject.

Possible actions:

    a. Answer the question, but mention only the potential positive consequences of the proposal.

    b. Try to answer the question as honestly and completely as possible, but remind the community leader that you are only a junior officer.

    c. Answer the question thoroughly, even though you have little direct knowledge of the situation.

    d. Remind the community leader that you are a junior officer and cannot give your opinion.

    e. Decline to answer the question, and instead refer it to one of the senior officers.

21. Select the MOST EFFECTIVE action in response to the situation.

22. Select the LEAST EFFECTIVE action in response to the situation.

SITUATION 12:

Another officer in your section is granted a week-long leave to visit his sick grandmother. However, during this period you discover through social media that the officer is actually on a beach vacation with his girlfriend, hundreds of miles from the hospital where his grandmother was supposedly being treated.

Possible actions:

    a. Tell the officer that he has been dishonest and unethical, and that you will have to report any future episodes of this nature.

    b. Ignore the situation, since it does not really involve you.

    c. Tell the officer that you will agree to keep his misbehavior a secret if he will do your weekly reports.

    d. Immediately notify your commanding officer in person.

    e. Anonymously forward the evidence of the officer's misbehavior to your commanding officer.

23. Select the MOST EFFECTIVE action in response to the situation.

24. Select the LEAST EFFECTIVE action in response to the situation.

SITUATION 13:

One of the airmen in your unit has displayed a marked decline in her performance over the past month. She appears frustrated and burnt out with her normal duties. She is one of the more popular members of the unit, so her negative attitude has a bad influence on her fellow airmen.

Possible actions:

a. Convene a meeting of the entire unit, and use this as a chance to single out the airman for her poor performance.
b. Meet with the airman and offer whatever help you can give to improve her performance, while emphasizing the effect that her behavior has on the other airmen.
c. Reassign the airman to a different unit so that her bad attitude doesn't continue to affect the other airmen.
d. Do nothing, in the hopes that the situation will improve without your influence.
e. Inform your senior officer about the situation.

25. Select the MOST EFFECTIVE action in response to the situation.

26. Select the LEAST EFFECTIVE action in response to the situation.

SITUATION 14:

You are about to transfer to a new unit, where you will have duties in areas where you have little experience. A week before you are due to make the transfer, you receive an email from the senior officer in charge of your new unit. She reminds you that you will be entering her unit at a very important time for them, because they will be leading a set of training exercises for highly-skilled airmen. She wants to make sure that you are ready to contribute immediately to the success of the unit, and that you will not need a great deal of assistance to complete your work.

Possible actions:

a. Do not respond to the email, and assume that you will be able to move into your new role seamlessly.
b. Thank the senior officer for her message, and do some internet research on your new duties.
c. Request that the transfer be canceled, and remain with your original unit.
d. Email the senior officer back, requesting a personal meeting where you can get more information about how to make a good transition to your new role.
e. Ask one of the other officers in your new unit if he will quietly bring you up to speed when you arrive.

27. Select the MOST EFFECTIVE action in response to the situation.

28. Select the LEAST EFFECTIVE action in response to the situation.

SITUATION 15:

One of your responsibilities is to keep a set of officers briefed on some confidential activities that are taking place at your base. One day, you accidentally send an email containing some information about these confidential activities to an officer who has not received the security clearance.

Possible actions:

    a. Notify your supervisor of your mistake and let him resolve the situation.
    b. Immediately send a second email to the improper recipient, requesting that he or she destroy the email. Inform your supervisors of your mistake.
    c. Send a second email to the improper recipient, claiming that your email account has been hacked and that he should disregard any earlier messages.
    d. Wait to see if there will be any negative consequences of your mistake.
    e. Ask your supervisor if the improper recipient could be given the security clearance retroactively.

29. Select the MOST EFFECTIVE action in response to the situation.

30. Select the LEAST EFFECTIVE action in response to the situation.

SITUATION 16:

After completing your work at the base, you return to your living quarters for the evening. An hour later, you realize that you failed to affix your signature to a set of papers that are to be forwarded on to a different unit for completion. Without your signature, the papers cannot be sent. The content of the papers is not particularly urgent, but the delay will require the other unit officer to stay later than normal at his post.

Possible actions:

    a. Wait until your next shift to sign the papers, since they are not considered urgent.
    b. Call the base and ask a junior officer to forge your signature so the paperwork can be sent.
    c. Call the officer at the other base and explain that the papers will be arriving a little later than expected.
    d. Arrive for your next shift a little early and sign the papers first.
    e. Return to the base and sign the necessary papers.

31. Select the MOST EFFECTIVE action in response to the situation.

32. Select the LEAST EFFECTIVE action in response to the situation.

SITUATION 17:

Several of the airmen in your unit have yet to complete a basic training module at a nearby base. They have asked to participate in the next training session, but instead, a group of airmen from another unit have been selected. The selected airmen have not been waiting nearly as long as your airmen to complete this training module. You suspect that the director of the training session dislikes you personally, though you have no specific evidence of this.

Possible actions:

a. Request a meeting with the training director, and ask why your airmen have been passed over, emphasizing the importance of this module for their development.
b. Do nothing, in the hopes that the situation will improve on its own.
c. Ask the officer in charge of the other unit if your airmen can attend the training session instead of his.
d. Write a critical letter to the training director and your senior officer, outlining what you perceive as the injustice of the situation.
e. Ask the training director if your airmen can attend the next training session along with the selected airmen.

33. Select the MOST EFFECTIVE action in response to the situation.

34. Select the LEAST EFFECTIVE action in response to the situation.

SITUATION 18:

You have been assigned to draft an important report along with another officer in your unit. It is expected that the report will take approximately one month to complete. However, after about a week of work, the other officer falls ill and is required to go on leave. He is only supposed to be gone for about ten days, but at the end of this period he has not returned and there is no definitive word on when he will. You need the expertise of this officer in order to finish the report.

Possible actions:

a. Wait until the other officer returns from leave, even if it means delaying the report.
b. Ask for an extension, without making excuses for your failure to complete the report on time.
c. Work extra hours to complete the report as best as you can.
d. Tell your commanding officer the situation, and request assistance in completing the report.
e. Order a junior officer to assist you in the completion of the report.

35. Select the MOST EFFECTIVE action in response to the situation.

36. Select the LEAST EFFECTIVE action in response to the situation.

SITUATION 19:

Two months ago, you joined a new unit. The leader of this unit was very welcoming to you and made sure to give you as much assistance as you needed in learning your new duties and responsibilities. However, you are now feeling more comfortable in your role and would like more independence in your work.

Possible actions:

a. Request a meeting with the unit leader, thank him for his assistance, and indicate that you would like to work on your own a bit more.
b. Request that another officer be transferred to your unit so that the unit leader will divert his attention to training this new arrival.
c. Without saying anything directly, try to avoid the unit leader as much as possible.
d. Tell the unit leader's commanding officer that you need the unit leader to give you more space.
e. Keep extensive records of your work so that you can demonstrate your competence to the unit leader.

37. Select the MOST EFFECTIVE action in response to the situation.

38. Select the LEAST EFFECTIVE action in response to the situation.

SITUATION 20:

One of the other officers in your division is going to make an important presentation at the end of the week. He is nervous, but he has done good work in the past and has spent a great deal of time preparing the report. He asks you to look over his work in advance. You notice a few things that need to be changed, but the other officer disagrees with your corrections. You are certain that you are right and that the other officer will be sorry he did not listen to you.

Possible actions:

a. Let your coworker go ahead with the uncorrected presentation, but make yourself look better by mentioning the errors to a senior officer before the presentation.
b. Allow your coworker to go ahead with the presentation as is, without trying to convince him to make the corrections.
c. Discuss the matter with your senior officer, and ask him or her to mandate the corrections.
d. Contrive an excuse to be absent from the presentation.
e. Make every effort to convince your colleague to make the necessary corrections.

39. Select the MOST EFFECTIVE action in response to the situation.

40. Select the LEAST EFFECTIVE action in response to the situation.

SITUATION 21:

You have been working with a new unit for the past six weeks. During that time, you have noticed some inefficiencies in the unit's operations, and you have developed a set of proposals for eliminating them. The majority of your coworkers agree with your proposals, but the senior officer in charge of the unit does not. The senior officer believes that implementing your proposals would be too risky and would undermine the stability of the unit.

Possible actions:

a. Confront your senior officer, using the support of your coworkers as a reason to implement your proposals.
b. Create a detailed and comprehensive report outlining the potential benefits of your proposals. Deliver the report and then obey the senior officer's final decision.
c. Implement your proposals anyway, on the assumption that your senior officer will change his mind once he sees their success.
d. Accept the senior officer's decision and try to succeed within the agreed-upon structure.
e. Accept the senior officer's decision, but keep a running list of the ways your proposals could have improved performance, had they been implemented.

41. Select the MOST EFFECTIVE action in response to the situation.

42. Select the LEAST EFFECTIVE action in response to the situation.

SITUATION 22:

Six months ago, you were assigned a new assistant. Although you have been able to work successfully together, you have developed a personal dislike for this person. In your opinion, he is arrogant and too critical of the other officers. During a meeting with your senior officer, she mentions that she is considering transferring your assistant to another unit. This would represent a step up for him and would make it possible for him to achieve even more promotions in a relatively short time.

Possible actions:

a. Recommend that your assistant receive the promotion, if only to get him away from you.
b. Strongly discourage the senior officer from choosing your assistant so that he will not get a professional reward.
c. Write an anonymous letter to the senior officer, outlining your complaints about your assistant.
d. Strongly discourage the senior officer from choosing your assistant, with an emphasis on his personality flaws.
e. Avoid interfering in the senior officer's decision, but make sure that she is aware of your opinion of your assistant.

43. Select the MOST EFFECTIVE action in response to the situation.

44. Select the LEAST EFFECTIVE action in response to the situation.

SITUATION 23:

Your base uses a computer program to determine the logistics related to supply deliveries. One day, while you are coordinating the arrival and unloading of several concurrent deliveries, the computer system crashes. The computer technician tells you that it could be an hour before the system is up and running again. You can see that there is a long line of trucks waiting to deliver their goods and that the drivers are becoming impatient.

Possible actions:

a. Ask one of your assistants to inform the drivers of the situation and the likely wait time. Offer whatever accommodations you can in the interim.
b. Receive the deliveries despite the computer problems, and keep paper records so you can update the system later.
c. Call your senior officer and ask for advice.
d. Use this opportunity to take your lunch break, somewhere you are unlikely to meet any of the drivers.
e. Encourage the drivers to make any other deliveries they have and then come back later.

45. Select the MOST EFFECTIVE action in response to the situation.

46. Select the LEAST EFFECTIVE action in response to the situation.

SITUATION 24:

You have developed an idea that you believe will improve the performance of your unit. However, some of the airmen in your unit disagree with this idea, and one has gone so far as to write a letter of complaint to your senior officer without notifying you. You have not yet implemented your idea.

Possible actions:

a. Meet with the letter-writer and other critics, emphasizing that going above your head will not be tolerated in the future.
b. Abandon your idea and ask for suggestions from the airmen who were critical of it.
c. Ignore the critics in you unit, and implement your idea anyway.
d. Harshly punish the letter writer, as a warning to the other airmen.
e. Implement your idea without acknowledging the letter or the criticism of other airmen in the unit.

47. Select the MOST EFFECTIVE action in response to the situation.

48. Select the LEAST EFFECTIVE action in response to the situation.

SITUATION 25:

You received a promotion six months ago and have been excelling in your new job. However, due to forces beyond your control, the quality of your work has decreased over the past few weeks. In part, you have been undermined by recent budget cuts. Unfortunately, your commanding officer does not fully understand the consequences of the budget cuts and has expressed her displeasure with your recent work. She has even suggested that problems in your unit may be a result of poor management on your part.

Possible actions:

a. Ask the commanding officer if you can take a brief leave to refocus.
b. Do not make any excuses, but ask the advice of other officers who are dealing with the same budget constraints.
c. Ask your commanding officer for a list of her specific complaints.
d. Shift the blame for your unit's performance to your subordinates.
e. Remind the commanding officer of the budget constraints, and defend your management style to her.

49. Select the MOST EFFECTIVE action in response to the situation.

50. Select the LEAST EFFECTIVE action in response to the situation.

Physical Science

1. A long nail is heated at one end. After a few seconds, the other end of the nail becomes equally hot. What type of heat transfer does this represent?

    a. Advection
    b. Conduction
    c. Convection
    d. Entropy
    e. Radiation

2. The measure of energy within a system is called

    a. Temperature
    b. Convection
    c. Entropy
    d. Thermodynamics
    e. Heat

3. How do two isotopes of the same element differ?

    a. They have different numbers of protons.
    b. They have different numbers of neutrons.
    c. They have different numbers of electrons.
    d. They have different charges.
    e. They have different atomic numbers.

4. Which type of nuclear process features atomic nuclei splitting apart to form smaller nuclei?

    a. Fission
    b. Fusion
    c. Decay
    d. Ionization
    e. Chain reaction

5. The process whereby a radioactive element releases energy slowly over a long period of time to lower its energy and become more stable is best described as

    a. Combustion
    b. Fission
    c. Fusion
    d. Decay
    e. Radioactivity

6. What property of light explains why a pencil in a glass of water appears to be bent?

    a. Reflection
    b. Refraction
    c. The angle of incidence equals the angle of reflection
    d. Constructive interference
    e. Destructive interference

7. What unit describes the frequency of a wave?

    a. Hertz (Hz)
    b. Decibels (dB)
    c. Meters (m)
    d. Meters per second (m/s)
    e. Meters per second squared (m/s^2)

8. Which of the following is an example of kinetic energy being converted to potential energy?

    a. A child sliding down a slide
    b. A cyclist coasting on his way up a hill
    c. A pilot deploying airbrakes on approach to land
    d. A motorist swerving to avoid a deer
    e. A pair of billiard balls colliding and rebounding off each other

9. The boiling of water is an example of

    a. Sublimation
    b. Condensation
    c. Neutralization
    d. Chemical change
    e. Physical change

10. The center of an atom is called the

    a. Nucleus
    b. Nuclide
    c. Neutrino
    d. Electron cloud
    e. Electrolyte

11. When a solid is heated and transforms directly to the gaseous phases, this process is called

    a. Sublimation
    b. Fusion
    c. Diffusion
    d. Condensation
    e. Fission

12. Which scientist was responsible for developing the format of the modern periodic table?

    a. Faraday
    b. Einstein
    c. Hess
    d. Mendeleev
    e. Oppenheimer

13. The density of a material refers to its:

   a. Mass per unit volume
   b. Mass per unit length
   c. Mass per unit surface area
   d. Volume per unit surface area
   e. Volume per unit length

14. The precision of a set of experimentally obtained data points refers to

   a. How accurate the data points are
   b. How many errors the data points contain
   c. How close the data points are to the mean of the data
   d. How close the data points are to the predicted result
   e. How close the set of data is to a normal distribution

15. Current, or the amount of electricity that is flowing, is measured in

   a. Volts
   b. Watts
   c. Ohms
   d. Farads
   e. Amperes

16. A solar eclipse can only occur if

   a. The earth and the sun are on the same side of the moon.
   b. The earth is between the sun and the moon.
   c. The moon is between the earth and the sun.
   d. The sun is between the earth and the moon.
   e. The moon is full.

17. What property of motion explains why passengers in a turning car feel pulled toward the outside of the turn?

   a. Centripetal force
   b. Inertia
   c. Normal force
   d. Impulse
   e. Torque

18. According to the ideal gas law, if a certain amount of gas is being held at a constant volume, and the temperature is increased, what will happen?

   a. The mass of the gas will increase
   b. The pressure of the gas will increase
   c. The density of the gas will decrease
   d. The mass of the gas will decrease
   e. The pressure of the gas will decrease

19. What wave characteristic is related to the loudness of a sound?

    a. Frequency
    b. Amplitude
    c. Wavelength
    d. Velocity
    e. Period

20. Which of the following scenarios is NOT an example of a person applying work to a book?

    a. A book is picked up from the floor and put on a shelf.
    b. A book is pushed across a table top.
    c. A backpack holding a book is carried across the room.
    d. A book is held and then released so that it falls to the ground.
    e. A book is thrown vertically into the air.

Table Reading

For each question, select the number that appears in the table at the given coordinates. Recall that the first number in the ordered pair gives the column number, and the second gives the row number. For instance, the ordered pair (2, −1) refers to the number in column 2, row -1, which is 732 in the table.

Use the table below to answer questions 1-40.

	-12	-11	-10	-9	-8	-7	-6	-5	-4	-3	-2	-1	0	1	2	3	4	5	6	7	8	9	10	11	12
-12	987	972	433	251	462	338	836	424	131	773	809	602	261	569	550	952	216	808	891	232	316	623	986	141	488
-11	337	740	563	587	510	138	491	654	775	261	528	986	212	387	837	100	241	114	536	568	673	833	610	398	578
-10	639	122	374	648	229	692	250	767	803	337	725	838	725	144	863	542	928	232	908	809	296	852	284	963	991
-9	280	271	269	575	696	649	637	750	161	366	151	226	577	995	494	106	819	390	618	557	191	993	438	850	751
-8	586	970	977	677	988	166	748	340	833	710	631	207	464	524	279	596	990	621	752	365	355	920	544	122	185
-7	728	206	273	437	636	394	813	161	731	219	494	278	349	423	325	409	631	538	918	134	151	867	624	920	733
-6	714	817	929	377	264	974	300	999	982	348	166	859	667	762	441	226	734	692	302	688	550	589	143	169	860
-5	780	511	934	814	538	712	832	165	315	637	252	800	205	290	557	713	629	764	228	585	594	912	473	651	957
-4	278	232	882	615	475	795	492	763	943	798	519	682	314	471	338	666	996	118	712	879	663	111	593	380	907
-3	576	534	470	835	886	318	738	322	739	284	890	397	683	356	177	839	679	496	344	613	268	179	951	292	204
-2	597	806	779	782	137	601	669	599	486	562	119	331	497	848	701	602	476	253	787	785	212	734	357	810	356
-1	266	142	405	779	792	514	369	731	663	422	328	529	754	122	732	319	332	927	665	438	342	698	714	637	262
0	836	881	121	327	431	710	702	742	966	902	562	733	522	486	608	810	432	843	413	179	219	556	235	330	776
1	928	271	938	525	554	176	714	402	992	199	870	962	595	959	800	851	823	561	568	647	245	652	669	953	121
2	201	464	830	565	678	748	176	382	161	598	909	610	483	902	512	435	607	119	111	710	331	105	430	958	838
3	955	181	865	766	989	835	207	894	836	533	907	137	339	693	166	619	247	882	948	913	701	130	259	361	754
4	258	997	209	333	331	773	987	354	436	837	269	650	263	813	345	137	861	442	394	456	616	521	870	139	974
5	818	390	866	177	144	937	368	823	703	862	512	545	414	571	713	766	818	268	116	494	936	678	237	401	604
6	165	464	708	301	825	992	526	975	649	450	527	507	455	581	287	528	414	338	779	729	284	247	341	972	443
7	206	217	571	346	566	921	741	462	106	647	464	743	480	700	222	139	947	963	392	826	106	661	917	228	502
8	516	409	120	796	838	721	852	106	226	704	231	187	115	827	434	548	683	138	848	824	957	304	998	617	121
9	779	812	809	702	596	844	261	136	301	227	582	378	683	735	910	620	367	483	826	518	905	563	596	521	751
10	477	320	645	916	438	150	787	578	236	734	393	396	156	507	176	236	886	161	676	226	179	812	999	853	167
11	273	514	137	670	965	886	919	657	775	420	354	146	610	639	181	293	476	150	192	558	729	160	955	780	293
12	675	164	725	723	196	262	436	496	880	663	650	765	851	848	620	743	615	248	536	881	122	642	440	307	846

1. **(0, −1)**
   a. 529
   b. 754
   c. 733
   d. 536
   e. 486

2. **(7, −11)**
   a. 568
   b. 138
   c. 348
   d. 809
   e. 232

3. **(1, −2)**
   a. 122
   b. 356
   c. 848
   d. 331
   e. 497

4. **(−9, −11)**
   a. 648
   b. 510
   c. 587
   d. 216
   e. 563

5. **(11, 5)**
   a. 139
   b. 972
   c. 237
   d. 511
   e. 401

6. **(−9, −1)**
   a. 792
   b. 782
   c. 405
   d. 779
   e. 327

7. **(6, 9)**
   a. 848
   b. 138
   c. 826
   d. 261
   e. 618

8. **(−4, −3)**
   a. 739
   b. 322
   c. 284
   d. 943
   e. 679

9. **(2, −5)**
   a. 557
   b. 441
   c. 290
   d. 762
   e. 382

10. **(−7, −10)**
    a. 649
    b. 692
    c. 250
    d. 510
    e. 273

11. **(11, −12)**
    a. 398
    b. 578
    c. 488
    d. 972
    e. 141

12. **(4, −10)**
    a. 241
    b. 100
    c. 803
    d. 882
    e. 928

13. **(−8, 9)**
    a. 596
    b. 844
    c. 702
    d. 566
    e. 438

14. **(10, 7)**
    a. 661
    b. 917
    c. 341
    d. 998
    e. 571

15. **(−5, −11)**
    a. 424
    b. 654
    c. 803
    d. 114
    e. 511

16. **(−6, −11)**
    a. 836
    b. 536
    c. 169
    d. 491
    e. 817

17. **(3, −5)**
    a. 713
    b. 226
    c. 637
    d. 511
    e. 496

18. **(−7, 7)**
    a. 741
    b. 462
    c. 721
    d. 992
    e. 921

19. **(−4, −5)**
    a. 999
    b. 982
    c. 315
    d. 763
    e. 629

20. **(−4, −1)**
    a. 663
    b. 422
    c. 486
    d. 731
    e. 471

21. **(−5, 8)**
    a. 852
    b. 462
    c. 138
    d. 166
    e. 106

22. $(8, -1)$

   a. 212
   b. 219
   c. 792
   d. 207
   e. 342

23. $(-11, 9)$

   a. 409
   b. 809
   c. 812
   d. 320
   e. 141

24. $(8, -2)$

   a. 268
   b. 212
   c. 342
   d. 137
   e. 678

25. $(5, -2)$

   a. 253
   b. 787
   c. 927
   d. 599
   e. 557

26. $(12, -11)$

   a. 568
   b. 578
   c. 991
   d. 398
   e. 337

27. $(0, -10)$

   a. 725
   b. 151
   c. 337
   d. 838
   e. 121

28. $(8, 7)$

   a. 661
   b. 957
   c. 826
   d. 824
   e. 106

29. $(-11, 10)$

   a. 812
   b. 514
   c. 320
   d. 645
   e. 137

30. $(-3, 5)$

   a. 862
   b. 512
   c. 450
   d. 837
   e. 322

31. $(-2, -6)$

   a. 859
   b. 252
   c. 601
   d. 166
   e. 787

32. $(-11, -5)$

   a. 817
   b. 934
   c. 511
   d. 780
   e. 114

33. $(-7, 11)$

   a. 150
   b. 262
   c. 886
   d. 217
   e. 558

34. $(10, 5)$

   a. 866
   b. 161
   c. 678
   d. 237
   e. 401

35. $(3, 7)$

   a. 139
   b. 222
   c. 548
   d. 683
   e. 913

36. $(7, 3)$

   a. 710
   b. 913
   c. 701
   d. 111
   e. 613

37. $(0, 2)$

   a. 595
   b. 339
   c. 438
   d. 843
   e. 483

38. $(2, 5)$

   a. 441
   b. 762
   c. 253
   d. 599
   e. 713

39. $(6, -3)$

   a. 344
   b. 712
   c. 738
   d. 343
   e. 434

40. $(10, -12)$

   a. 610
   b. 968
   c. 986
   d. 433
   e. 440

Instrument Comprehension

1. Which of the answer choices represents the orientation of the plane?

Artificial Horizon   Compass

A	B
C	D

2. Which of the answer choices represents the orientation of the plane?

Artificial Horizon   Compass

A	B
C	D

3. Which of the answer choices represents the orientation of the plane?

Artificial Horizon   Compass

A	B
C	D

445

4. Which of the answer choices represents the orientation of the plane?

5. Which of the answer choices represents the orientation of the plane?

6. Which of the answer choices represents the orientation of the plane?

7. Which of the answer choices represents the orientation of the plane?

Artificial Horizon   Compass

8. Which of the answer choices represents the orientation of the plane?

Artificial Horizon   Compass

9. Which of the answer choices represents the orientation of the plane?

Artificial Horizon   Compass

10. Which of the answer choices represents the orientation of the plane?

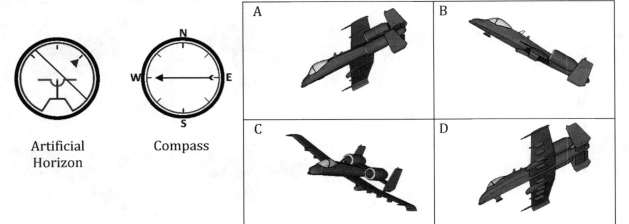

11. Which of the answer choices represents the orientation of the plane?

12. Which of the answer choices represents the orientation of the plane?

13. Which of the answer choices represents the orientation of the plane?

14. Which of the answer choices represents the orientation of the plane?

15. Which of the answer choices represents the orientation of the plane?

16. Which of the answer choices represents the orientation of the plane?

17. Which of the answer choices represents the orientation of the plane?

18. Which of the answer choices represents the orientation of the plane?

19. Which of the answer choices represents the orientation of the plane?

20. Which of the answer choices represents the orientation of the plane?

21. Which of the answer choices represents the orientation of the plane?

22. Which of the answer choices represents the orientation of the plane?

23. Which of the answer choices represents the orientation of the plane?

24. Which of the answer choices represents the orientation of the plane?

25. Which of the answer choices represents the orientation of the plane?

Artificial Horizon

Compass

Block Counting

The explanations to these problems use terms like "top," "left," and "front" to refer to the faces of the blocks. This terminology can be confusing due to the angled view of the block arrangements, so the illustration below is provided to help you keep these terms straight.

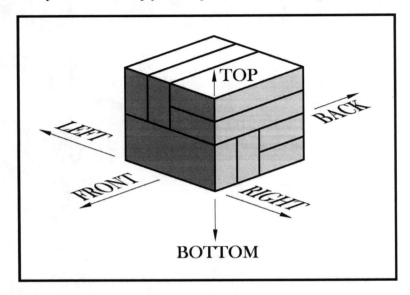

Once you understand these terms, proceed to the practice problems below. As a reminder, all the blocks in the images are intended to be the same size and shape, regardless of how much of each block is shown.

1. How many blocks are touching block 1 in the figure above?

2. How many blocks are touching block 2 in the figure above?

3. How many blocks are touching block 3 in the figure above?

4. How many blocks are touching block 1 in the figure above?

5. How many blocks are touching block 2 in the figure above?

6. How many blocks are touching block 3 in the figure above?

7. How many blocks are touching block 1 in the figure above?

8. How many blocks are touching block 2 in the figure above?

9. How many blocks are touching block 3 in the figure above?

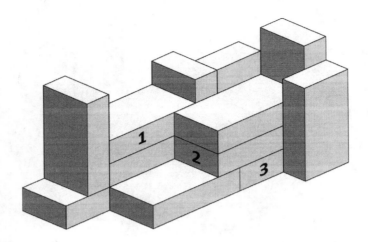

10. How many blocks are touching block 1 in the figure above?

11. How many blocks are touching block 2 in the figure above?

12. How many blocks are touching block 3 in the figure above?

13. How many blocks are touching block 1 in the figure above?

14. How many blocks are touching block 2 in the figure above?

15. How many blocks are touching block 3 in the figure above?

16. How many blocks are touching block 1 in the figure above?

17. How many blocks are touching block 2 in the figure above?

18. How many blocks are touching block 3 in the figure above?

19. How many blocks are touching block 1 in the figure above?

20. How many blocks are touching block 2 in the figure above?

21. How many blocks are touching block 3 in the figure above?

22. How many blocks are touching block 1 in the figure above?

23. How many blocks are touching block 2 in the figure above?

24. How many blocks are touching block 3 in the figure above?

25. How many blocks are touching block 1 in the figure above?

26. How many blocks are touching block 2 in the figure above?

27. How many blocks are touching block 3 in the figure above?

28. How many blocks are touching block 1 in the figure above?

29. How many blocks are touching block 2 in the figure above?

30. How many blocks are touching block 3 in the figure above?

Aviation Information

1. From approximately how far away should a Visual Approach Slope Indicator be visible at night?

    a. Five miles
    b. Ten miles
    c. Twenty miles
    d. Thirty miles
    e. Fifty miles

2. Which of the following is NOT one of the forces a pilot must manage during flight?

    a. Thrust
    b. Gravity
    c. Drag
    d. Lift
    e. Torque

3. Which control affects the angle of the main rotor blades of a helicopter?

    a. Collective
    b. Throttle
    c. Cyclic
    d. Directional control system
    e. None of the above

4. What is the flight attitude?

    a. The environment immediately around the plane
    b. The morale of the flight crew
    c. The position of the plane in motion
    d. The inclination of the elevators
    e. The positions of the ailerons

5. The curvature of an airfoil is known as the

    a. Bank
    b. Position
    c. Camber
    d. Angle
    e. Attitude

6. Which of the following is considered one of the primary flight controls?

    a. Elevators
    b. Leading edge devices
    c. Flaps
    d. Spoilers
    e. Trim tabs

7. What is the term in aviation for movement around the plane's longitudinal axis?

a. Stalling
b. Rolling
c. Pitching
d. Leaning
e. Yawing

8. What is the primary determinant of air pressure in the flight envelope?

a. The altitude at which the plane is flying
b. The camber of the wings
c. The amount of lift that the airfoils can create
d. The pitch of the elevators
e. The humidity of the air

9. A plane is said to have conventional landing gear when the third wheel is

a. Aligned with the second wheel
b. Under the tail
c. Directly behind the first wheel
d. Under the nose
e. Underneath the cockpit

10. Which of the following is NOT part of the empennage?

a. Rudder
b. Trim tab
c. Elevator
d. Aileron
e. Horizontal stabilizer

11. A glider would be most likely to have a

a. Delta wing
b. Triangular wing
c. Forward swept wing
d. Backward swept wing
e. Straight wing

12. Which of the following is NOT considered part of a plane's basic weight?

a. Crew
b. Fuel
c. External equipment
d. Internal equipment
e. Fuselage

13. The support structure that runs the length of the fuselage in a monocoque plane is called a

a. Counter
b. Former
c. Truss
d. Stringer
e. Bulkhead

14. Which control is used to manipulate the elevators on an airplane?

   a. Throttle
   b. Rudder
   c. Joystick
   d. Pedals
   e. Collective

15. Which maneuver is appropriate when a pilot needs to descend quickly onto a shorter-than-normal runway?

   a. Descent at minimum safe airspeed
   b. Idle
   c. Partial power descent
   d. Glide
   e. Stall

16. In aviation, which of the following is NOT one of the possible functions of a spoiler?

   a. Diminishing lift
   b. Raising the nose
   c. Increasing drag
   d. Reducing adverse yaw
   e. Enabling descent without speed reduction

17. The vertical axis of a plane extends upward through the plane's

   a. Cockpit
   b. Tail
   c. Landing gear
   d. Center of mass
   e. Geometric center

18. When is trimming necessary?

   a. When the plane is ascending or descending
   b. After the elevators have been deflected upwards
   c. After the ailerons have been adjusted
   d. After the elevators have been deflected downwards
   e. After any change in the flight condition

19. How far away is an approaching plane when the Runway Centerline Lighting System lights become solid red?

   a. Five hundred feet
   b. One thousand feet
   c. Three thousand feet
   d. Five thousand feet
   e. One mile

20. What is the Coriolis force?

    a.   The extra lift generated by a helicopter once it has exited its own downwash

    b.   The force that spins the rotors of a helicopter even when there is no power from the engine

    c.   The greater downwash at the rear half of the rotor disc, as compared with the front

    d.   The phenomenon in which the effects of a force applied to a spinning disc occur ninety degrees later

    e.   The change in rotational speed caused by the shift of the weight towards or away from the center of the spinning object

Answer Key and Explanations

Verbal Analogies

1. B: Rash. Chastise and reprimand are synonyms. The answer choice synonym for impetuous is rash.

2. C: Femur. The humerus is a bone in the arm; the femur is a bone in the leg.

3. A: Quotient. A quotient is the result of division as a product is the result of multiplication.

4. C: Asparagus. As a sweater is something one wears, asparagus is something one eats.

5. A: Famished. As a person who is impecunious needs money, so a person who is famished needs food.

6. A: Protest. Denigrate and malign are synonyms. The answer choice synonym for demur is protest.

7. D: Generous. Obeisance and deference are synonyms. The answer choice synonym for munificent is generous.

8. D: Sow. A female goat is a nanny and a female pig is a sow.

9. B: Paucity. Cache and reserve are synonyms. The answer choice synonym for dearth is paucity.

10. E: Refuge. Arable and farmable are synonyms. The answer choice synonym for asylum is refuge.

11. A: Peripatetic. Myriad and few are antonyms. The answer choice antonym for stationary is peripatetic.

12. A: Flagon. As a mansion is a large house, so a flagon is a large bottle.

13. B: Synonyms. As a dictionary is a collection of definitions, so a thesaurus is a collection of synonyms.

14. B: Stubborn. Abstruse and esoteric are synonyms. The answer choice synonym for adamant is stubborn.

15. C: Herd. A group of bees is called a hive, and a group of cattle is called a herd.

16. E: Meridian. A parallel is a line of latitude, while a meridian is a line of longitude.

17. B: Provocation. Prevention and deterrence are synonyms. The answer choice synonym for incitement is provocation.

18. A: Gauge. Value and worth are synonyms. The answer choice synonym for measure is gauge.

19. A: Oppose. Enervate and energize are antonyms. The answer choice antonym for espouse is oppose.

20. D: The analogy is tool to worker. A carpenter uses a hammer, just as a doctor uses a stethoscope.

464

21. B: The analogy describes characteristic location. An armoire is usually kept in a bedroom, just as a desk is usually kept in an office.

22. C: This analogy describes a food source to animal relationship. Just as plankton is a food source for whales, so is bamboo a food source for pandas.

23. C: The analogy is geographic location. Just as the tundra is located in the Arctic regions, so are savannas located in tropic regions.

24. A: This is an analogy of relative degree. *Parched* is a more intense degree of *thirsty*, just as *famished* is a more intense degree of *hungry*.

25. E: This is an analogy based on antonyms. *Felicity,* or happiness, is the opposite of *sadness,* just as *ignominy,* or disgrace, is the opposite of *honor.*

Arithmetic Reasoning

1. B: First, find the total before taxes:

$$\$7.50 + \$3.00 = \$10.50$$

Then, calculate 6% of the total:

$$\$10.50 \times 0.06 = \$0.63$$

Finally, add the tax to find the total cost:

$$\$10.50 + \$0.63 = \$11.13$$

2. D: There are 7 days in a week. Knowing that the chef can make 25 pastries in a day, the weekly number can be calculated:

$$25 \times 7 = 175$$

3. B: The woman has four days to earn $250. To find the amount she must earn each day, divide the amount she must earn ($250) by 4:

$$\frac{\$250}{4} = \$62.50$$

4. A: To find the number of cars remaining, subtract the number of cars that were sold from the original number:

$$476 - 36 = 440$$

5. B: Calculate 0.5% of $450:

$$\$450 \times 0.005 = \$2.25$$

This is the amount of interest she will earn.

6. C: First, figure out how much the second child contributed:

$$\$24.00 - \$15.00 = \$9.00$$

Then, calculate how much the first two children contributed in total:

$$\$24.00 + \$9.00 = \$33.00$$

Finally, figure out how much the third child will have to contribute:

$$\$78.00 - \$33.00 = \$45.00$$

7. C: First, figure out how many points the first woman will earn:

$$3 \times 5 = 15$$

Then, figure out how many points the second woman will earn:

$$6 \times 5 = 30$$

Then, add these two values together:

$$30 + 15 = 45 \text{ points total}$$

8. E: First, calculate 13% of 540:

$$540 \times 0.13 = 70.2 \text{ (round to 70)}$$

Then, add this value onto the original number of workers:

$$540 + 70 = 610$$

610 is the number of people that the company will employ after the expansion.

9. D: To find the number of apartments on each floor, divide the total number of apartments by the number of floors:

$$\frac{65}{13} = 5$$

10. C: First, find the total number of pens:

$$5 \times 3 = 15$$

Then, find the total number of pencils:

$$3 \times 7 = 21$$

Finally, express it as a ratio: $15:21$ which simplifies to $5:7$.

11. C: To calculate his new salary, add his raise to his original salary:

$$\$15.23 + \$2.34 = \$17.57$$

12. A: To find the total number of passengers, multiply the number of planes by the number of passengers each can hold:

$$6 \times 300 = 1,800$$

13. B: Currently, there are two men for every woman. If the number of women is doubled, then the new ratio is $2:2$. This is equivalent to $1:1$.

14. C: First, calculate 3% of 250 pounds:

$$250 \times 0.03 = 7.5 \text{ lb}$$

Calculate how much she weighs at the end of the first week:

$$250 - 7.5 = 242.5 \text{ lb}$$

Calculate 2% of 242.5:

$$242.5 \times 0.02 = 4.85 \text{ lb}$$

Add the two values together to get the total number of pounds she lost:

$$7.5 + 4.85 = 12.35$$

15. D: Divide the total distance she must travel (600 km) by the number of kilometers she drives each hour (80 km) to figure out how many hours it will take to reach her destination:

$$\frac{600 \text{ km}}{80 \text{ km/hr}} = 7.5 \text{ hours}$$

16. D: One gallon of paint can paint three rooms, so to find out how many 28 gallons can do, that number must be multiplied by 3:

$$28 \times 3 = 84 \text{ rooms}$$

17. A: Each earns $135, so to find the total earned, that amount must be multiplied by the number of workers:

$$\$135 \times 5 = \$675$$

18. C: First, calculate her score on the second test:

$$99 - 15 = 84$$

Then, calculate her score on the third test:

$$84 + 5 = 89$$

19. A: To find out how much he has remaining, both numbers must be subtracted from the original amount ($50.00):

$$\$50.00 - \$15.64 - \$7.12 = \$27.24$$

20. E: Divide the number of students (600) by the number of classrooms they will share (20):

$$\frac{600}{20} = 30$$

21. C: To calculate this value, divide the number of dogs (48) by the number of workers that are available to care for them (4):

$$\frac{48}{4} = 12$$

22. C: First, calculate the length of the second office:

$$20 + 6 = 26 \text{ feet}$$

Then, add both values together to get a combined length:

$$26 + 20 = 46 \text{ feet}$$

23. C: Find the total cost of the items:

$$\$6.65 + \$159.23 = \$165.88$$

Then, calculate how much each individual will owe:

$$\frac{\$165.88}{4} = \$41.47$$

24. A: To answer this question, simply calculate half of 140 acres:

$$\frac{140}{2} = 70 \text{ acres}$$

25. C: First, calculate how many he has after selling 45:

$$360 - 45 = 315$$

Then, calculate how many he has after buying 85:

$$315 + 85 = 400$$

Word Knowledge

1. A: Spoiled has a number of meanings, and one of them is ruined. If you said somebody spoiled your fun, it would convey the same meaning as saying somebody ruined your fun.

2. B: An oath is a promise. For example, if you make an oath to keep a secret, you are promising to keep that secret.

3. B: When you inquire about something, you are asking about it or requesting more information. For example, if you told somebody you inquired about a job, it would mean you asked about it.

4. C: If you say that you comprehend something, it is the same as saying you understand it. For example, saying you comprehend what another person is saying is the same as saying you understand them.

5. A: To say that something is apparent implies that it is clear or obvious. For example, saying that it is apparent that somebody wants a job is the same as saying it is clear they want the job.

6. C: Silent or silence indicates quiet and calm. To enjoy the silence of the night is to enjoy the complete quiet of the night.

7. E: Absolutely, when used to describe a feeling or state of mind, means completely or totally. For example, saying you are absolutely certain that you made the right decision or saying you are completely certain you made the right decision conveys the same meaning.

8. D: Something that has been modified has been changed. Saying you modified your plans or saying that you changed them conveys the same meaning.

9. A: Something that is delicate can also be described as fragile. Saying that a crystal figurine is delicate or saying it is fragile conveys the same meaning.

10. B: Festivities are commonly known as celebrations. Attending festivities implies that you are attending a celebration or party.

11. B: To say that someone is exhausted or to say that they are tired conveys a similar meaning. Usually, exhausted is a word used to describe extreme tiredness.

12. B: To cleanse something is to clean or wash it. Saying you cleansed your face or clothes is the same as saying you washed them.

13. A: To battle something is to fight it. To say that two armies battled each other and to say they fought each other conveys the same meaning.

14. C: To wander is to roam. To say someone wandered around a mall is to say they roamed or walked around aimlessly, without a specific goal or destination in mind.

15. E: Something that is done abruptly is done suddenly and without warning. For example, saying the car stopped abruptly and saying it stopped suddenly conveys the same meaning.

16. A: Somebody who has been tricked has been conned. To trick somebody is to con them, which implies that dishonest methods are used to convince another to do something they wouldn't normally do.

17. C: When used as an adjective extremely has the same meaning as very. Saying somebody is extremely happy and saying they are very happy conveys the same meaning.

18. A: To have doubts is to have uncertainties or hesitations. To say that someone is doubtful about something means that they are uncertain.

19. D: To describe something as peculiar is to say it is strange or out of the ordinary. For example, saying you are in a strange situation or saying you are in a peculiar situation conveys the same meaning.

20. B: Describing somebody as courteous implies that they are polite and well-mannered. Polite and courteous both convey the same meaning.

21. C: When somebody says they are troubled by something, they mean that they are bothered by it.

22. A: Perspiration is another word for sweat. Saying somebody is perspiring is the same as saying they are sweating.

23. B: Tremble is another word for shake. To say somebody or something trembled means that it shook or shuddered.

24. A: Adhered is often used as another word for stuck. For example, to say a piece of tape adhered to the wall conveys the same meaning as saying the piece of tape stuck to the wall.

25. D: When something is described as tidy, it usually means that it is neat and that things are in their proper place. Saying a house is tidy and saying it is neat conveys the same meaning.

Mathematics Knowledge

1. B: The perimeter of a figure is the sum of all of its sides. Since a rectangle's width and length will be the same on opposite sides, the perimeter of a rectangle can be calculated by using the following formula:

$$P = 2w + 2l$$

Using the numbers given in the question:

$$P = 2(7) + 2(9)$$

$$P = 14 + 18 = 32 \text{ cm}$$

2. D: First, gather the like terms on opposite sides of the equation to make it easier to solve:

$$12 + 30 \geq 4q + 3q$$

$$42 \geq 7q$$

Then, divide both sides by 7 to solve for q:

$$\frac{42}{7} \geq \frac{7q}{7}$$

$$6 \geq q \text{ or } q \leq 6$$

3. C: To solve for x, simply add 6 to both sides:

$$x - 6 + 6 = 0 + 6$$

$$x = 6$$

4. A: To calculate the value of this expression, substitute –3 for x each time it appears in the expression:

$$3(-3)^3 + (3(-3) + 4) - 2(-3)^2$$

According to the order of operations, any operations inside of brackets must be done first:

$$3(-3)^3 + (-9 + 4) - 2(-3)^2$$

$$3(-3)^3 + (-5) - 2(-3)^2$$

Then, exponential operations may be performed:

$$3(-27) + (-5) - 2(9)$$

Next, multiplication:

$$-81 - 5 - 18$$

Finally, subtraction from left to right:

$$-81 - 5 - 18 = -104$$

5. C: First, combine like terms to make the equation easier to solve:

$$3x + 2x = 45 + 30$$

$$5x = 75$$

Then, divide both sides by 5 to solve for x:

$$\frac{5x}{5} = \frac{75}{5}$$

$$x = 15$$

6. A: First, add 25 to both sides to isolate x:

$$\frac{1}{4}x - 25 + 25 \geq 75 + 25$$

$$\frac{1}{4}x \geq 100$$

Then, multiply both sides by 4 to solve for x:

$$4 \times \frac{1}{4}x \geq 4 \times 100$$

$$x \geq 400$$

7. A: First, add 5 to both sides to isolate x:

$$x^2 - 5 + 5 = 20 + 5$$

$$x^2 = 25$$

Then, take the square root of both sides to solve for x:

$$\sqrt{x^2} = \sqrt{25}$$

$$x = \pm 5$$

8. B: First, we must calculate the length of one side of the square. Since we know the perimeter is 8 cm and that a square has 4 equal sides, the length of each side can be calculated by dividing the perimeter (8 cm) by 4:

$$\frac{8 \text{ cm}}{4} = 2 \text{ cm}$$

The formula for the area of a square is its side length squared:

$$A = (2 \text{ cm})^2 = 4 \text{ cm}^2$$

9. D: To find the value of this expression, substitute the given values for x and y into the expression and simplify:

$$3(4)(2) - 12(2) + 5(4) = 24 - 24 + 20 = 20$$

10. D: First, subtract 10 from both sides to isolate x:

$$\frac{2}{3}x + 10 - 10 = 16 - 10$$

$$\frac{2}{3}x = 6$$

Then, multiply both sides by the reciprocal of $\frac{2}{3}$ to solve for x:

$$\frac{3}{2} \times \frac{2}{3}x = 6 \times \frac{3}{2}$$

$$x = 9$$

11. B: Use the FOIL method (first, outside, inside, and last) to expand the polynomial:

$$12x^2 - 18x + 20x - 30$$

Then, combine like terms to simplify the expression:

$$12x^2 + 2x - 30$$

12. B: To simplify this expression, recall the law of exponents for division:

$$\frac{x^n}{x^m} = x^{n-m}$$

Apply to each variable in the expression:

$$\frac{x^{18}}{x^5} = x^{13}; \frac{t^6}{t^2} = t^4; \frac{w^3}{w^2} = w; \frac{z^{20}}{z^{19}} = z$$

Combine to simplify:

$$10x^{13}t^4wz$$

13. E: To calculate 4-factorial, take the product of all the integers between 1 and 4:

$$4! = 4 \times 3 \times 2 \times 1 = 24$$

14. D: Because it is a cube, we can find the volume by taking the cube of any side length:

$$5 \times 5 \times 5 = 125 \text{ cm}^3$$

15. A: First, factor this equation to make solving for x easier:

$$x^2 - 13x + 42 = (x - 6)(x - 7) = 0$$

The expression on the left side of the equation is equal to zero when either $(x - 6)$ or $(x - 7)$ equals zero. Thus:

$$x = 6, 7$$

16. C: The area of a triangle can be calculated by using the following formula:

$$A = \frac{1}{2}bh$$

Therefore, by using the values given in the question:

$$A = \frac{1}{2}(12)(12) = 72 \text{ cm}^2$$

17. D: To simplify this expression, recall the law of exponents for multiplication:

$$x^n x^m = x^{n+m}$$

Apply to each variable in the expression:

$$x^7 x^2 = x^9; \; y^{12}y^3 = y^{15}$$

$$(3x^2 7x^7) + (2y^3 9y^{12}) = 21x^9 + 18y^{15}$$

18. C: First, subtract 27 from both sides to isolate x:

$$\frac{x}{3} + 27 - 27 = 30 - 27$$

$$\frac{x}{3} = 3$$

Next, multiply both sides by 3:

$$\frac{x}{3} \times 3 = 3 \times 3$$

$$x = 9$$

19. B: The slope of a line can be calculated by dividing the change in the y-coordinate by the change in the x-coordinate:

$$y_{change} = 8 - 1 = 7$$

$$x_{change} = -13 - 4 = -17$$

$$Slope = \frac{y_{change}}{x_{change}} = -\frac{7}{17}$$

20. A: To solve for x, calculate the value of 20% of 200:

$$20\% \times 200 = 0.2 \times 200 = 40$$

$$x = 40$$

21. B: The odds of a black balloon being chosen at random from a bag of balloons is calculated as:

$$P = \frac{\# \text{ black balloons}}{\# \text{ total balloons}}$$

The total number of balloons is found by adding up the number of each color:

$$37 + 8 + 15 = 60$$

There are ten black balloons, so calculate the probability of selecting a black balloon:

$$P = \frac{15}{60} = 25\%$$

22. D: Each ticket has the same odds of being the winning ticket:

$$1 \text{ in } 500 \text{ or } \frac{1}{500}$$

If a man buys 25 tickets, his odds of winning are now multiplied by 25:

$$25 \text{ in } 500 \text{ or } \frac{25}{500}$$

We can reduce this ratio by dividing both numbers by 25:

$$\frac{25}{25} = 1; \frac{500}{25} = 20$$

$$1 \text{ in } 20 \text{ or } \frac{1}{20} = 5\%$$

23. E: To find the volume of a rectangular prism, the formula is $V = L \times W \times H$. For the prism described in this question:

$$V = 5 \text{ cm} \times 6 \text{ cm} \times 10 \text{ cm} = 300 \text{ cm}^3$$

24. C: To calculate the midpoint of a line, take the average of both the x- and y-coordinates. The x-coordinate of the midpoint can be calculated as follows:

$$\frac{6 + 10}{2} = 8$$

The y-coordinate of the midpoint can be calculated as follows:

$$\frac{20 + 40}{2} = 30$$

Therefore, the midpoint is $(8, 30)$.

25. A: First, subtract 60 from both sides:

$$5x + 60 - 60 = 75 - 60$$

Then divide both sides by 5:

$$\frac{5x}{5} = \frac{15}{5}$$

$$x = 3$$

Reading Comprehension

1. A: Explaining the qualities of air that may affect flight is the primary purpose of the passage.

2. C: The best definition for *inversely* as it is used in the second paragraph is *in the opposite direction*. The author is indicating that the density of air decreases as the temperature rises, and increases as the temperature falls.

3. D: A pilot can expect the air density to decrease as the plane gains altitude. At the end of the second paragraph, the author states that a gain in altitude will usually lead to a decrease in air density, no matter what changes there may be in the temperature.

4. B: The author would most likely agree that air density is more important than relative humidity. Though the passage states that humidity can have an effect on aircraft performance, the author admits that it is not considered an essential factor. Indeed, humidity is just one of three factors (along with pressure and temperature) that affect air density.

5. C: The most likely reason why there is no chart for assessing the effects of humidity on density altitude is that humidity does not affect flight performance very much. The author mentions several times that flight performance is not significantly affected by humidity, and so it is seems that a special chart for this purpose would be unnecessary.

6. D: *Influences on Climb Performance* would be the best title for this passage. The passage surveys the various factors that affect climb performance and the choices made by pilots as they gain altitude, both during take-off and while the aircraft is already in flight.

7. E: The best definition for *pronounced* as it is used in the second paragraph is *noticeable*. The author is stating that the weight of an aircraft has a significant impact on aircraft performance. In this sentence *pronounced* is being used as an adjective, but it can also be used as a verb, meaning *spoke* or *said*.

8. C: An increase in weight means that the angle of attack must be higher in order to maintain altitude. Greater weight diminishes reserve power, lowers the climb rate, diminishes the maximum rate of climb, and increases drag.

9. B: The author would most likely agree that at the end of a long journey a plane will have a higher maximum rate of climb. The maximum rate of climb of a plane increases as the weight decreases, and the weight of a plane will decrease as it burns off fuel over the course of a long journey.

10. A: A helicopter that weighs two tons and has rotor blades that cover five hundred square feet would have a disc loading measure of eight pounds per square foot. Pounds per square foot is the standard measure for disc loading. There are two thousand pounds in a ton. Disc loading is calculated by dividing the weight of the helicopter by the area covered by the rotor blades.

11. B: Discussing the interrelationships of airspeed, power, and pitch attitude is the primary purpose of the passage. Answer choices *C* and *D* are partially correct, but they leave out large sections of the passage and therefore do not comprehensively describe the purpose or the content of the passage.

12. A: *Inadvertently*, as it is used in the fifth paragraph, most nearly means *unintentionally*. The author is indicating that a pilot can enter the region of reversed command without meaning to, if he or she attempts to climb out of ground effect without first attaining normal climb pitch attitude and airspeed.

13. B: Most flight occurs in the region of normal command. In the region of normal command, increasing power increases the airspeed, and decreasing power decreases the airspeed. This information is given in the last sentence of the second paragraph.

14. E: The author would most likely agree that as the speed of flight decreases, the power required to maintain altitude increases. This inverse relationship between required power and airspeed is expressed in the last sentence of the first paragraph.

15. D: The best title for this passage would be *Power Requirements During Flight*. The passage discusses how the need for and effects of changes in power are influenced by factors such as airspeed, pitch attitude, and altitude.

16. E: The primary purpose of the passage is to describe the factors that influence landing distance. The passage begins by discussing the minimum and normal landing distances and goes on to cover influences on landing distance, as for instance gross weight, wind, and density altitude.

17. B: When making a normal landing, a pilot will rely on aerodynamic drag in order to avoid wearing down the brakes and tires. This point is made several times in the third paragraph of the passage.

18. A: The best definition for *principal* as it is used in the fourth paragraph is *most important*. The author is trying to make the point that gross weight has an enormous effect on landing distance.

19. C: A heavier plane must be landed at a higher airspeed to avoid hitting the runway with too much force. This idea is explored in the fourth paragraph. In order to generate an amount of lift sufficient for a smooth landing, a higher airspeed must be maintained.

20. C: The author would most likely agree that gross weight and minimum landing distance are positively correlated. The information in the passage makes it clear that as gross weight rises, minimum landing distance increases.

21. D: The primary purpose of the article is to discuss aeronautical decision making, or ADM. The article does give some examples of decision-making strategies, but these are given in the context of a description of ADM, not as the main body of the article.

22. D: The passage explains that aviation safety is distinct from other areas of safety because there is a much smaller margin for error. In other words, even small accidents in aviation can be catastrophic, because of the risks inherent in flight.

23. A: The closest definition for *conjunction* as it is used in the second paragraph is *combination*. The author is stating that the FAA manuals worked well when combined with the usual flight training.

24. A: The author would most likely agree that the body of knowledge about ADM is increasing, and this will have a positive effect on flight safety. The article details the efforts to improve ADM and suggests that these have already improved flight safety a great deal.

25. E: For a pilot, reading the account of a recent aviation accident is an opportunity for an indirect learning experience. The passage distinguishes between direct learning experiences, which are events in one's own life, and indirect learning experiences, which are things that happen to others.

Situational Judgment

1. C (Most effective)

2. A (Least effective)

3. A (Most effective)

4. C (Least effective)

5. E (Most effective)

6. B (Least effective)

7. D (Most effective)

8. A (Least effective)

9. E (Most effective)

10. C (Least effective)

11. B (Most effective)

12. C (Least effective)

13. A (Most effective)

14. B (Least effective)

15. E (Most effective)

16. B (Least effective)

17. C (Most effective)

18. A (Least effective)

19. A (Most effective)

20. B (Least effective)

21. B (Most effective)

22. D (Least effective)

23. A (Most effective)

24. C (Least effective)

25. B (Most effective)

26. E (Least effective)

27. D (Most effective)

28. A (Least effective)

29. B (Most effective)

30. C (Least effective)

31. E (Most effective)

32. B (Least effective)

33. A (Most effective)

34. D (Least effective)

35. D (Most effective)

36. C (Least effective)

37. A (Most effective)

38. D (Least effective)

39. E (Most effective)

40. A (Least effective)

41. B (Most effective)

42. C (Least effective)

43. E (Most effective)

44. A or C (Least effective)

45. A (Most effective)

46. D (Least effective)

47. A (Most effective)

48. B (Least effective)

49. B (Most effective)

50. D (Least effective)

Physical Science

1. B: A long nail or other type of metal, substance, or matter that is heated at one end and then the other end becomes equally hot is an example of conduction. Conduction is energy transfer by neighboring molecules from an area of hotter temperature to cooler temperature.

2. E: The measure of energy within a system is called heat.

3. B: They have a different number of neutrons. The distinguishing feature of an isotope is its number of neutrons. Two different isotopes of the same element will have the same number of protons but different numbers of neutrons.

4. A: Fission is a nuclear process where atomic nuclei split apart to form smaller nuclei. Nuclear fission can release large amounts of energy, emit gamma rays and form daughter products. It is used in nuclear power plants and bombs.

5. D: The process whereby a radioactive element releases energy slowly over a long period of time to lower its energy and become more stable is best described as decay. The nucleus undergoing decay spontaneously releases energy, most commonly through the emission of an alpha particle, a beta particle, or a gamma ray.

6. B: Light within a single medium travels in a straight line. When it changes to a different medium, however, the light rays bend according to the refractive index of each substance. Light coming from the submerged portion of the pencil is refracted as it passes through the air-water barrier, giving the perception of a bent pencil.

7. A: Hertz (Hz) is a unit of measure used for frequency, often described as 1 cycle/second. In the context of wave motion, it is the number of complete waves that pass a given point in one second.

8. B: A cyclist coasting up a hill is trading his speed for increased altitude. This is an example of kinetic energy being converted to potential energy. The other options are examples of potential energy being converted to kinetic, kinetic energy being dissipated, and conservation of kinetic energy.

9. E: Phase changes such as boiling, melting, and freezing are physical changes. No chemical reaction takes place when water is boiled.

10. A: The center of an atom is known as the nucleus. It is composed of protons and neutrons.

11. A: Sublimation is the process of a solid changing directly into a gas without entering the liquid phase.

12. D: Mendeleev was able to connect the trends of the different elements' behaviors and develop a table that showed the periodicity of the elements and their relationship to each other.

13. A: Density is mass per unit volume, typically expressed in units such as g/cm^3, or kg/m^3.

14. C: The closer the data points are to each other, the more precise the data. This does not mean the data is accurate, but rather that the results are reproducible.

15. E: Current is measured in units of amperes or amps.

16. C: In order for a solar eclipse to occur, the moon must come directly between the earth and the sun, blocking the sun's light from the earth.

17. B: Inertia is the tendency of objects that are in motion to continue moving in the same direction. The turning car initiates a change in direction, but the passengers' mass wants to continue going straight, causing them to feel a pull in that direction. This phenomenon is sometimes referred to as centrifugal force.

18. B: According to the ideal gas law, when volume is held constant, the temperature of a gas is directly proportional to the pressure of the gas. Thus, when the temperature is increased, the pressure will also increase.

19. B: The amplitude of a sound wave is what determines how loud the sound is perceived by the ear.

20. D: In all of the other examples, there is a person applying work to the book, either directly, by being picked up, pushed, or thrown, or indirectly, by being carried in a backpack. In the example of a book being released so that it falls, the only work being applied to the book is being done by gravity.

Table Reading

1. B	28. E
2. A	29. C
3. C	30. A
4. C	31. D
5. E	32. C
6. D	33. C
7. C	34. D
8. A	35. A
9. A	36. B
10. B	37. E
11. E	38. E
12. E	39. A
13. A	40. C
14. B	
15. B	
16. D	
17. A	
18. E	
19. C	
20. A	
21. E	
22. E	
23. C	
24. B	
25. A	
26. B	
27. A	

Instrument Comprehension

1. B

2. C

3. C

4. A

5. C

6. C

7. A

8. B

9. B

10. A

11. C

12. A

13. D

14. B

15. D

16. B

17. C

18. A

19. A

20. D

21. C

22. B

23. A

24. A

25. C

Block Counting

1. 5: 1 on the front, 1 on the back, 3 on the right.

2. 3: 2 on the top, 1 on the bottom.

3. 5: 1 on the front, 2 on the back, 1 on the left, 1 on the top.

4. 4: 1 on the left, 1 on the top, 2 on the bottom.

5. 4: 3 on the top, 1 on the bottom.

6. 5: 1 on the back, 3 on the top, 1 on the bottom.

7. 3: 1 on the back, 1 on the right, 1 on the top.

8. 5: 2 on the front, 2 on the back, 1 on top.

9. 2: 1 on the front, 1 on the left.

10. 4: 1 on the front, 1 on the back, 1 on the right, 1 on the bottom.

11. 8: 1 on the back, 3 on the left, 1 on the right, 1 on the top, 2 on the bottom,

12. 6: 1 on the front, 1 on the back, 2 on the left, 1 on the right, 1 on the top.

13. 4: 1 on the back, 1 on the left, 2 on the top.

14. 4: 1 on the front, 1 on the back, 1 on the right, 1 on the bottom.

15. 5: 1 on the front, 1 on the back, 1 on the left, 2 on the bottom.

16. 3: 1 on the front, 2 on the right.

17. 7: 2 on the front, 1 on the back, 1 on the left, 2 on the right, 1 on top.

18. 5: 1 on the front, 1 on the back, 1 on the left, 1 on the top, 1 on the bottom.

19. 4: 2 on the back, 2 on the bottom.

20. 6: 2 on the front, 2 on the back, 2 on the right.

21. 4: 1 on the front, 2 on the back, 1 on the left.

22. 5: 4 on the top, 1 on the bottom.

23. 4: 1 on the front, 1 on the back, 1 on the right, 1 on the bottom.

24. 7: 1 on the front, 2 on the back, 2 on the top, 2 on the bottom.

25. 6: 1 on the back, 2 on the left, 1 on the right, 1 on the top, 1 on the bottom.

26. 6: 3 on the left, 2 on the top, 1 on the bottom.

27. 9: 2 on the front, 1 on the back, 2 on the left, 2 on the right, 1 on the top, 1 on the bottom.

28. 5: 1 on the back, 1 on the right, 3 on top.

29. 5: 1 on the front, 1 on the back, 1 on the right, 2 on the bottom.

30. 7: 1 on the front, 3 on the left, 2 on the right, 1 on the bottom.

Aviation Information

1. C: A Visual Approach Slope Indicator should be visible from approximately twenty miles away at night. A Visual Approach Slope Indicator (VASI) is a common feature at large airports. This system helps guide the approaching pilot to the runway. The pilot will see white lights at the lower border of the glide path, and red lights at the upper border. In normal conditions, the lights of the VASI system should be visible for three to five miles during the day and for twenty miles at night. If the VASI system is working properly, the plane will be safe so long as it stays within ten degrees of the extended runway centerline and four nautical miles of the runway threshold.

2. E: Torque is not one of the forces a pilot must manage during flight. The four forces a pilot must manage are lift, gravity, thrust, and drag. Lift pushes the plane up, gravity pulls the plane down, thrust propels the plane forward, and drag holds the plane back. The overall admixture of these forces as they operate on the plane is called the flight envelope.

3. A: The collective affects the angle of the main rotor blades of a helicopter. It is a long tube that extends from the floor of the cockpit. In most helicopters, it is situated on the pilot's left. The collective has two parts: a handle that can be raised or lowered, to control the pitch of the blades; and a throttle, to control the torque of the engine. The handle is the part that affects the angle of the main rotor blades. When it is raised, the leading edge of the blade is raised higher than the trailing edge.

4. C: The flight attitude is the position of a plane in motion. The flight attitude is described in terms of its position with respect to three axes: vertical, lateral, and longitudinal. The vertical axis runs up through the plane's center of gravity. A plane's position with respect to this axis is known as its yaw. The lateral axis of a plane runs from wingtip to wingtip, and the motion of the plane around this axis is known as pitch. The longitudinal axis, finally, is an imaginary line extending from the nose of the plane to its tail. The position of the plane in relation to the longitudinal axis is called roll. The attitude of the plane is controlled with the joystick, rudder pedals, and throttle.

5. C: The curvature of an airfoil is known as the camber. An airfoil (wing) is considered to have a high camber if it is very curved. A related piece of wing terminology is the mean camber line, which runs along the inside of the wing, such that the upper and lower wings are equal in thickness.

6. A: The elevators are considered one of the primary flight controls. The elevators are responsible for the plane's pitch, or movement around the lateral axis. The other primary flight controls are the ailerons and the rudder. The ailerons control the roll, or movement around the longitudinal axis, while the rudder controls the yaw, or movement around the vertical axis. The secondary flight controls are the flaps, spoilers, leading edge devices, and trim systems.

7. B: In aviation, the term for movement around the plane's longitudinal axis is rolling. The longitudinal axis runs from the nose of the plane to its tail. For the most part, the plane's roll is controlled by the joystick. By moving the stick to the right or left, the pilot dips the wings.

8. A: The altitude at which the plane is flying is the primary determinant of air pressure in the flight envelope. The most important elements of the flight envelope are the temperature, air pressure, and humidity. The conditions in the atmosphere have a great deal of influence over the amount of lift created by the airfoils. Greater air pressure is the same as greater air density. A plane will generate greater lift when it is in cool air, because cool air is less dense than warm air.

9. B: A plane is said to have conventional landing gear when the third wheel is under the tail. Typically, a plane's landing gear will consist of three wheels or sets of wheels. Two of these are under either wing or on opposing sides of the fuselage. In the conventional arrangement, the third wheel, or wheel set, is under the tail, while in the tricycle arrangement it is under the nose. This third wheel can rotate, which will make it possible for the plane to turn while moving on the ground.

10. D: An aileron is not part of the empennage. The empennage, otherwise known as the tail assembly, includes the elevators, vertical and horizontal stabilizers, rudders, and trim tabs. A fixed wing aircraft will typically have both vertical and horizontal stabilizers, which are immobile surfaces that extend from the back of the fuselage. The horizontal stabilizers have mobile surfaces along their trailing edges; these surfaces are called the elevators. The elevators deflect up and down to raise or lower the nose of the plane. The rudder is a single, large flap connected by a hinge to the vertical stabilizer. The rudder's back-and-forth motion controls the motion of the plane with respect to its vertical axis. The trim tabs, finally, are connected to the trailing edges of one or more of the primary flight controls (i.e., ailerons, elevators, rudder).

11. E: A glider would be most likely to have a straight wing. A straight wing may be tapered, elliptical, or rectangular. This planform (wing shape) is common in aircraft that move at extremely low speeds. A straight wing is often found on sailplanes and gliders. The swept wing, on the other hand, is appropriate for high-speed aircraft. The wing may be swept forward or back. This will make the plane unstable at low speeds, but will produce much less drag. A swept wing requires high-speed takeoff and landing. The delta wing, which is also known as the triangular wing, has a straight trailing edge and a high angle of sweep. This allows the plane to take off and land at high speeds.

12. A: The crew is not considered part of a plane's basic weight. The basic weight is the aircraft plus whatever internal or external equipment will remain on the plane during its journey. The crew is not included in the basic weight, though it is a part of the operating weight (basic weight plus crew), gross weight (total weight of the aircraft at any particular time), landing gross weight (weight of the plane and its contents upon touchdown), and zero fuel weight (weight of the airplane when it has no usable fuel).

13. D: The support structure that runs the length of the fuselage in a monocoque plane is called a stringer. In a monocoque plane, the fuselage is supported by stringers, formers, and bulkheads. Stringers and formers are generally made out of the same material, though they run perpendicular to one another (that is, formers run in circles around the width of the fuselage). Bulkheads are the walls that divide the sections of the fuselage. The other style of fuselage, known as a truss, is composed of triangular groupings of aluminum or steel tubing.

14. C: The joystick is used to manipulate the elevators. When the stick is pulled back, the elevators deflect upwards. This decreases the camber of the horizontal tail surface, which moves the nose up and pushes the tail down. Pushing the joystick forward, on the other hand, pushes the elevators down, which creates an upward force on the tail by increasing the camber of the horizontal tail surface.

15. A: When a pilot needs to descend quickly onto a shorter-than-normal runway, he or she will descend at the minimum safe airspeed. A descent at the minimum safe airspeed is achieved by slightly lifting the nose and moving the plane into the landing configuration. During such a descent, the plane should not exceed 1.3 times the stall speed. This technique is appropriate for landing quickly on a short runway because the rate of descent is much faster. However, if the rate of descent should become too great, the pilot should be ready to increase power.

16. B: Raising the nose is not one of the possible functions of a spoiler. Spoilers can diminish lift and reduce drag, which enables the plane to descend without reducing its speed. However, spoilers also control the plane's roll, partly by reducing any adverse yaw. A pilot uses the spoiler in this way by raising the spoiler on the side of the turn. That side will thereby have less lift and more drag, making it drop. The plane will then bank and yaw in the intended direction. When the pilot raises both of the spoilers at the same time, the plane will descend without losing any speed. Another incidental benefit of spoilers is improved brake performance, which occurs because the plane has lift and is pushed down towards the ground.

17. D: The vertical axis of a plane extends up through the plane's center of gravity. Movement around this axis is called yawing. The position of a plane is also described with respect to the lateral and longitudinal axes. The lateral axis extends from wingtip to wingtip. The longitudinal axis runs from the nose of the plane to its tail.

18. E: Trimming is necessary after any change in the flight condition. Trimming is the adjustment of the trim tabs, which are small flaps that extend from the trailing edges of the elevators, rudder, and ailerons. Trimming generally occurs after the pilot has achieved the desired pitch, power, attitude, and configuration. The trim tabs are then used to resolve the remaining control pressures. A small plane may only have a single tab, which is controlled with a small wheel or crank.

19. B: When the Runway Centerline Lighting System lights become solid red, an approaching plane is one thousand feet away. A Runway Centerline Lighting System is a line of white lights every fifty feet or so along the centerline. The lights change their color and pattern as the plane nears the runway. When the plane gets within 3,000 feet of the runway, the lights blink red and white. Within a thousand feet, the lights will turn solid red.

20. E: The Coriolis force is the change in rotational speed caused by the shift of the weight towards or away from the center of the spinning object. This phenomenon has an important application for helicopters, in which the rotor will move faster or will require less power to maintain its speed when the weight is closer to the base of the blade. The other answer choices are similarly related to helicopters. The extra lift generated by a helicopter once it has exited its own downwash is known as translational lift. The force that spins the rotors of a helicopter even when there is no power from the engine is autorotation. Greater downwash at the rear half of the rotor disc, as compared to the front half, is the result of applying the lateral cyclic. The phenomenon in which the effects of a force applied to a spinning disc occur ninety degrees later is called gyroscopic precession.

Image Credits

LICENSED UNDER CC BY 4.0 (CREATIVECOMMONS.ORG/LICENSES/BY/4.0/)

Leaf Spring: "Elliptic leaf spring of Galakhov" by Wikimedia user Alex Gomankov
(https://commons.wikimedia.org/wiki/File:Elliptic_leaf_spring_of_Galakhov.svg)

Simple Outside Micrometer: "Micrometer caliper parts" by Wikimedia user Three-quarter-ten
(https://commons.wikimedia.org/wiki/File:Micrometer_caliper_parts_0001.png)

Band Saw: "Delta bandsaw" by Wikimedia user Tiia Monto
(https://commons.wikimedia.org/wiki/File:Delta_bandsaw.jpg)

LICENSED UNDER CC BY-SA 4.0 (CREATIVECOMMONS.ORG/LICENSES/BY-SA/4.0/)

Jigsaw: "Jigsaw AccuMaster" by Wikimedia user Артём В.
(https://commons.wikimedia.org/wiki/File:Jigsaw_AccuMaster.jpg)

Reciprocating Saw: "AEG us 400 xe" by Wikimedia user Eladhayut
(https://commons.wikimedia.org/wiki/File:AEG_us_400_xe.jpg)

LICENSED UNDER CC BY-SA 3.0 (CREATIVECOMMONS.ORG/LICENSES/BY-SA/3.0/)

Water Level: "Schlauchwaage Schematik" by Wikimedia user Obersachse
(https://commons.wikimedia.org/wiki/File:Schlauchwaage_Schematik.svg)

Pipe Wrench: "Straight Pipe Wrench 3C by Wikimedia user TheAdcomGroup
(https://commons.wikimedia.org/wiki/File:Straight_Pipe_Wrench_3C.jpg)

Lug Wrench: "Kreuzschlüssel" by Wikimedia user Steffen Heinz Caronna
(https://commons.wikimedia.org/wiki/File:Kreuzschl%C3%BCssel.jpg)

Combination Wrench: "1933 Plomb Combination Wrench" by Wikimedia user Electron2002
(https://commons.wikimedia.org/wiki/File:1933_Plomb_Combination_Wrench.jpg)

Socket Wrench: "Socket wrench and sockets" by Wikimedia user Kae
(https://commons.wikimedia.org/wiki/File:Socket_wrench_and_sockets.JPG)

Speed Clamp: "Irwin Quick-Grip bar clamp" by Wikipedia user J.C. Fields
(https://en.wikipedia.org/wiki/File:Irwin_Quick-Grip_bar_clamp.jpg)

Vise-grips: "Locking Pliers" by Wikimedia user Duk
(https://commons.wikimedia.org/wiki/File:Locking_pliers.jpg)

Back Saw: "Backsaw" by Wikimedia user Simon A. Eugster
(https://commons.wikimedia.org/wiki/File:Backsaw.jpeg)

Chainsaw: "Chainsaw-mcculloch hg" by Wikimedia user Hgrobe
(https://commons.wikimedia.org/wiki/File:Chainsaw-mcculloch_hg.jpg)

LICENSED UNDER CC BY-2.0 (CREATIVECOMMONS.ORG/LICENSES/BY /2.0/)

Dial Caliper: "Dial Caliper" by Keith Litchfield
(https://www.flickr.com/photos/keithitchfield/21551991804)

Mortise Chisel: "mortising chisel" by David Numan
(https://www.flickr.com/photos/57813190@N00/1841488509)

Bent Nose Pliers: "IMG_2818" by Windel Oskay
(https://www.flickr.com/photos/oskay/4792522961)

C-Clamp: "Clamp compression tool on white" by Marco Verch
(https://www.flickr.com/photos/30478819@N08/33917308458)

Miter Saw: "Mitre saw white" by Ewen Roberts
(https://commons.wikimedia.org/wiki/File:Mitre_saw_white.jpg)

LICENSED UNDER CC BY-SA 2.0 (CREATIVECOMMONS.ORG/LICENSES/BY-SA/2.0/)

Vernier Caliper: "Vernier callipers" by Coshipi
(https://www.flickr.com/photos/coshipi/8789583212)

Table Saw: "Table saw" by Nottingham Hackspace
(https://www.flickr.com/photos/nottinghack/6843985536)

Drill Bit: "Twist Drill Bit" by andersen_mrjh
(https://www.flickr.com/photos/75793838@N08/6954963717)

How to Overcome Test Anxiety

Just the thought of taking a test is enough to make most people a little nervous. A test is an important event that can have a long-term impact on your future, so it's important to take it seriously and it's natural to feel anxious about performing well. But just because anxiety is normal, that doesn't mean that it's helpful in test taking, or that you should simply accept it as part of your life. Anxiety can have a variety of effects. These effects can be mild, like making you feel slightly nervous, or severe, like blocking your ability to focus or remember even a simple detail.

If you experience test anxiety—whether severe or mild—it's important to know how to beat it. To discover this, first you need to understand what causes test anxiety.

Causes of Test Anxiety

While we often think of anxiety as an uncontrollable emotional state, it can actually be caused by simple, practical things. One of the most common causes of test anxiety is that a person does not feel adequately prepared for their test. This feeling can be the result of many different issues such as poor study habits or lack of organization, but the most common culprit is time management. Starting to study too late, failing to organize your study time to cover all of the material, or being distracted while you study will mean that you're not well prepared for the test. This may lead to cramming the night before, which will cause you to be physically and mentally exhausted for the test. Poor time management also contributes to feelings of stress, fear, and hopelessness as you realize you are not well prepared but don't know what to do about it.

Other times, test anxiety is not related to your preparation for the test but comes from unresolved fear. This may be a past failure on a test, or poor performance on tests in general. It may come from comparing yourself to others who seem to be performing better or from the stress of living up to expectations. Anxiety may be driven by fears of the future—how failure on this test would affect your educational and career goals. These fears are often completely irrational, but they can still negatively impact your test performance.

> **Review Video: 3 Reasons You Have Test Anxiety**
> Visit mometrix.com/academy and enter code: 428468

491

Elements of Test Anxiety

As mentioned earlier, test anxiety is considered to be an emotional state, but it has physical and mental components as well. Sometimes you may not even realize that you are suffering from test anxiety until you notice the physical symptoms. These can include trembling hands, rapid heartbeat, sweating, nausea, and tense muscles. Extreme anxiety may lead to fainting or vomiting. Obviously, any of these symptoms can have a negative impact on testing. It is important to recognize them as soon as they begin to occur so that you can address the problem before it damages your performance.

> **Review Video: 3 Ways to Tell You Have Test Anxiety**
> Visit mometrix.com/academy and enter code: 927847

The mental components of test anxiety include trouble focusing and inability to remember learned information. During a test, your mind is on high alert, which can help you recall information and stay focused for an extended period of time. However, anxiety interferes with your mind's natural processes, causing you to blank out, even on the questions you know well. The strain of testing during anxiety makes it difficult to stay focused, especially on a test that may take several hours. Extreme anxiety can take a huge mental toll, making it difficult not only to recall test information but even to understand the test questions or pull your thoughts together.

> **Review Video: How Test Anxiety Affects Memory**
> Visit mometrix.com/academy and enter code: 609003

Effects of Test Anxiety

Test anxiety is like a disease—if left untreated, it will get progressively worse. Anxiety leads to poor performance, and this reinforces the feelings of fear and failure, which in turn lead to poor performances on subsequent tests. It can grow from a mild nervousness to a crippling condition. If allowed to progress, test anxiety can have a big impact on your schooling, and consequently on your future.

Test anxiety can spread to other parts of your life. Anxiety on tests can become anxiety in any stressful situation, and blanking on a test can turn into panicking in a job situation. But fortunately, you don't have to let anxiety rule your testing and determine your grades. There are a number of relatively simple steps you can take to move past anxiety and function normally on a test and in the rest of life.

> **Review Video: How Test Anxiety Impacts Your Grades**
> Visit mometrix.com/academy and enter code: 939819

Physical Steps for Beating Test Anxiety

While test anxiety is a serious problem, the good news is that it can be overcome. It doesn't have to control your ability to think and remember information. While it may take time, you can begin taking steps today to beat anxiety.

Just as your first hint that you may be struggling with anxiety comes from the physical symptoms, the first step to treating it is also physical. Rest is crucial for having a clear, strong mind. If you are tired, it is much easier to give in to anxiety. But if you establish good sleep habits, your body and mind will be ready to perform optimally, without the strain of exhaustion. Additionally, sleeping well helps you to retain information better, so you're more likely to recall the answers when you see the test questions.

Getting good sleep means more than going to bed on time. It's important to allow your brain time to relax. Take study breaks from time to time so it doesn't get overworked, and don't study right before bed. Take time to rest your mind before trying to rest your body, or you may find it difficult to fall asleep.

> **Review Video: The Importance of Sleep for Your Brain**
> Visit mometrix.com/academy and enter code: 319338

Along with sleep, other aspects of physical health are important in preparing for a test. Good nutrition is vital for good brain function. Sugary foods and drinks may give a burst of energy but this burst is followed by a crash, both physically and emotionally. Instead, fuel your body with protein and vitamin-rich foods.

Also, drink plenty of water. Dehydration can lead to headaches and exhaustion, especially if your brain is already under stress from the rigors of the test. Particularly if your test is a long one, drink water during the breaks. And if possible, take an energy-boosting snack to eat between sections.

> **Review Video: How Diet Can Affect your Mood**
> Visit mometrix.com/academy and enter code: 624317

Along with sleep and diet, a third important part of physical health is exercise. Maintaining a steady workout schedule is helpful, but even taking 5-minute study breaks to walk can help get your blood pumping faster and clear your head. Exercise also releases endorphins, which contribute to a positive feeling and can help combat test anxiety.

When you nurture your physical health, you are also contributing to your mental health. If your body is healthy, your mind is much more likely to be healthy as well. So take time to rest, nourish your body with healthy food and water, and get moving as much as possible. Taking these physical steps will make you stronger and more able to take the mental steps necessary to overcome test anxiety.

Mental Steps for Beating Test Anxiety

Working on the mental side of test anxiety can be more challenging, but as with the physical side, there are clear steps you can take to overcome it. As mentioned earlier, test anxiety often stems from lack of preparation, so the obvious solution is to prepare for the test. Effective studying may be the most important weapon you have for beating test anxiety, but you can and should employ several other mental tools to combat fear.

First, boost your confidence by reminding yourself of past success—tests or projects that you aced. If you're putting as much effort into preparing for this test as you did for those, there's no reason you should expect to fail here. Work hard to prepare; then trust your preparation.

Second, surround yourself with encouraging people. It can be helpful to find a study group, but be sure that the people you're around will encourage a positive attitude. If you spend time with others who are anxious or cynical, this will only contribute to your own anxiety. Look for others who are motivated to study hard from a desire to succeed, not from a fear of failure.

Third, reward yourself. A test is physically and mentally tiring, even without anxiety, and it can be helpful to have something to look forward to. Plan an activity following the test, regardless of the outcome, such as going to a movie or getting ice cream.

When you are taking the test, if you find yourself beginning to feel anxious, remind yourself that you know the material. Visualize successfully completing the test. Then take a few deep, relaxing breaths and return to it. Work through the questions carefully but with confidence, knowing that you are capable of succeeding.

Developing a healthy mental approach to test taking will also aid in other areas of life. Test anxiety affects more than just the actual test—it can be damaging to your mental health and even contribute to depression. It's important to beat test anxiety before it becomes a problem for more than testing.

> **Review Video: Test Anxiety and Depression**
> Visit mometrix.com/academy and enter code: 904704

Study Strategy

Being prepared for the test is necessary to combat anxiety, but what does being prepared look like? You may study for hours on end and still not feel prepared. What you need is a strategy for test prep. The next few pages outline our recommended steps to help you plan out and conquer the challenge of preparation.

STEP 1: SCOPE OUT THE TEST

Learn everything you can about the format (multiple choice, essay, etc.) and what will be on the test. Gather any study materials, course outlines, or sample exams that may be available. Not only will this help you to prepare, but knowing what to expect can help to alleviate test anxiety.

STEP 2: MAP OUT THE MATERIAL

Look through the textbook or study guide and make note of how many chapters or sections it has. Then divide these over the time you have. For example, if a book has 15 chapters and you have five days to study, you need to cover three chapters each day. Even better, if you have the time, leave an extra day at the end for overall review after you have gone through the material in depth.

If time is limited, you may need to prioritize the material. Look through it and make note of which sections you think you already have a good grasp on, and which need review. While you are studying, skim quickly through the familiar sections and take more time on the challenging parts. Write out your plan so you don't get lost as you go. Having a written plan also helps you feel more in control of the study, so anxiety is less likely to arise from feeling overwhelmed at the amount to cover.

STEP 3: GATHER YOUR TOOLS

Decide what study method works best for you. Do you prefer to highlight in the book as you study and then go back over the highlighted portions? Or do you type out notes of the important information? Or is it helpful to make flashcards that you can carry with you? Assemble the pens, index cards, highlighters, post-it notes, and any other materials you may need so you won't be distracted by getting up to find things while you study.

If you're having a hard time retaining the information or organizing your notes, experiment with different methods. For example, try color-coding by subject with colored pens, highlighters, or post-it notes. If you learn better by hearing, try recording yourself reading your notes so you can listen while in the car, working out, or simply sitting at your desk. Ask a friend to quiz you from your flashcards, or try teaching someone the material to solidify it in your mind.

STEP 4: CREATE YOUR ENVIRONMENT

It's important to avoid distractions while you study. This includes both the obvious distractions like visitors and the subtle distractions like an uncomfortable chair (or a too-comfortable couch that makes you want to fall asleep). Set up the best study environment possible: good lighting and a comfortable work area. If background music helps you focus, you may want to turn it on, but otherwise keep the room quiet. If you are using a computer to take notes, be sure you don't have any other windows open, especially applications like social media, games, or anything else that could distract you. Silence your phone and turn off notifications. Be sure to keep water close by so you stay hydrated while you study (but avoid unhealthy drinks and snacks).

Also, take into account the best time of day to study. Are you freshest first thing in the morning? Try to set aside some time then to work through the material. Is your mind clearer in the afternoon or evening? Schedule your study session then. Another method is to study at the same time of day that you will take the test, so that your brain gets used to working on the material at that time and will be ready to focus at test time.

STEP 5: STUDY!

Once you have done all the study preparation, it's time to settle into the actual studying. Sit down, take a few moments to settle your mind so you can focus, and begin to follow your study plan. Don't give in to distractions or let yourself procrastinate. This is your time to prepare so you'll be ready to fearlessly approach the test. Make the most of the time and stay focused.

Of course, you don't want to burn out. If you study too long you may find that you're not retaining the information very well. Take regular study breaks. For example, taking five minutes out of every hour to walk briskly, breathing deeply and swinging your arms, can help your mind stay fresh.

As you get to the end of each chapter or section, it's a good idea to do a quick review. Remind yourself of what you learned and work on any difficult parts. When you feel that you've mastered the material, move on to the next part. At the end of your study session, briefly skim through your notes again.

But while review is helpful, cramming last minute is NOT. If at all possible, work ahead so that you won't need to fit all your study into the last day. Cramming overloads your brain with more information than it can process and retain, and your tired mind may struggle to recall even previously learned information when it is overwhelmed with last-minute study. Also, the urgent nature of cramming and the stress placed on your brain contribute to anxiety. You'll be more likely to go to the test feeling unprepared and having trouble thinking clearly.

So don't cram, and don't stay up late before the test, even just to review your notes at a leisurely pace. Your brain needs rest more than it needs to go over the information again. In fact, plan to finish your studies by noon or early afternoon the day before the test. Give your brain the rest of the day to relax or focus on other things, and get a good night's sleep. Then you will be fresh for the test and better able to recall what you've studied.

STEP 6: TAKE A PRACTICE TEST

Many courses offer sample tests, either online or in the study materials. This is an excellent resource to check whether you have mastered the material, as well as to prepare for the test format and environment.

Check the test format ahead of time: the number of questions, the type (multiple choice, free response, etc.), and the time limit. Then create a plan for working through them. For example, if you have 30 minutes to take a 60-question test, your limit is 30 seconds per question. Spend less time on the questions you know well so that you can take more time on the difficult ones.

If you have time to take several practice tests, take the first one open book, with no time limit. Work through the questions at your own pace and make sure you fully understand them. Gradually work up to taking a test under test conditions: sit at a desk with all study materials put away and set a timer. Pace yourself to make sure you finish the test with time to spare and go back to check your answers if you have time.

After each test, check your answers. On the questions you missed, be sure you understand why you missed them. Did you misread the question (tests can use tricky wording)? Did you forget the information? Or was it something you hadn't learned? Go back and study any shaky areas that the practice tests reveal.

Taking these tests not only helps with your grade, but also aids in combating test anxiety. If you're already used to the test conditions, you're less likely to worry about it, and working through tests until you're scoring well gives you a confidence boost. Go through the practice tests until you feel comfortable, and then you can go into the test knowing that you're ready for it.

Test Tips

On test day, you should be confident, knowing that you've prepared well and are ready to answer the questions. But aside from preparation, there are several test day strategies you can employ to maximize your performance.

First, as stated before, get a good night's sleep the night before the test (and for several nights before that, if possible). Go into the test with a fresh, alert mind rather than staying up late to study.

Try not to change too much about your normal routine on the day of the test. It's important to eat a nutritious breakfast, but if you normally don't eat breakfast at all, consider eating just a protein bar. If you're a coffee drinker, go ahead and have your normal coffee. Just make sure you time it so that the caffeine doesn't wear off right in the middle of your test. Avoid sugary beverages, and drink enough water to stay hydrated but not so much that you need a restroom break 10 minutes into the test. If your test isn't first thing in the morning, consider going for a walk or doing a light workout before the test to get your blood flowing.

Allow yourself enough time to get ready, and leave for the test with plenty of time to spare so you won't have the anxiety of scrambling to arrive in time. Another reason to be early is to select a good seat. It's helpful to sit away from doors and windows, which can be distracting. Find a good seat, get out your supplies, and settle your mind before the test begins.

When the test begins, start by going over the instructions carefully, even if you already know what to expect. Make sure you avoid any careless mistakes by following the directions.

Then begin working through the questions, pacing yourself as you've practiced. If you're not sure on an answer, don't spend too much time on it, and don't let it shake your confidence. Either skip it and come back later, or eliminate as many wrong answers as possible and guess among the remaining ones. Don't dwell on these questions as you continue—put them out of your mind and focus on what lies ahead.

Be sure to read all of the answer choices, even if you're sure the first one is the right answer. Sometimes you'll find a better one if you keep reading. But don't second-guess yourself if you do immediately know the answer. Your gut instinct is usually right. Don't let test anxiety rob you of the information you know.

If you have time at the end of the test (and if the test format allows), go back and review your answers. Be cautious about changing any, since your first instinct tends to be correct, but make sure you didn't misread any of the questions or accidentally mark the wrong answer choice. Look over any you skipped and make an educated guess.

At the end, leave the test feeling confident. You've done your best, so don't waste time worrying about your performance or wishing you could change anything. Instead, celebrate the successful completion of this test. And finally, use this test to learn how to deal with anxiety even better next time.

Important Qualification

Not all anxiety is created equal. If your test anxiety is causing major issues in your life beyond the classroom or testing center, or if you are experiencing troubling physical symptoms related to your anxiety, it may be a sign of a serious physiological or psychological condition. If this sounds like your situation, we strongly encourage you to seek professional help.

How to Overcome Your Fear of Math

Not again. You're sitting in math class, look down at your test, and immediately start to panic. Your stomach is in knots, your heart is racing, and you break out in a cold sweat. You're staring at the paper, but everything looks like it's written in a foreign language. Even though you studied, you're blanking out on how to begin solving these problems.

Does this sound familiar? If so, then you're not alone! You may be like millions of other people who experience math anxiety. Anxiety about performing well in math is a common experience for students of all ages. In this article, we'll discuss what math anxiety is, common misconceptions about learning math, and tips and strategies for overcoming math anxiety.

What Is Math Anxiety?

Psychologist Mark H. Ashcraft explains math anxiety as a feeling of tension, apprehension, or fear that interferes with math performance. Having math anxiety negatively impacts people's beliefs about themselves and what they can achieve. It hinders achievement within the math classroom and affects the successful application of mathematics in the real world.

SYMPTOMS AND SIGNS OF MATH ANXIETY

To overcome math anxiety, you must recognize its symptoms. Becoming aware of the signs of math anxiety is the first step in addressing and resolving these fears.

NEGATIVE SELF-TALK

If you have math anxiety, you've most likely said at least one of these statements to yourself:

- "I hate math."
- "I'm not good at math."
- "I'm not a math person."

The way we speak to ourselves and think about ourselves matters. Our thoughts become our words, our words become our actions, and our actions become our habits. Thinking negatively about math creates a self-fulfilling prophecy. In other words, if you take an idea as a fact, then it will come true because your behaviors will align to match it.

AVOIDANCE

Some people who are fearful or anxious about math will tend to avoid it altogether. Avoidance can manifest in the following ways:

- Lack of engagement with math content
- Not completing homework and other assignments
- Not asking for help when needed
- Skipping class
- Avoiding math-related courses and activities

Avoidance is one of the most harmful impacts of math anxiety. If you steer clear of math at all costs, then you can't set yourself up for the success you deserve.

LACK OF MOTIVATION

Students with math anxiety may experience a lack of motivation. They may struggle to find the incentive to get engaged with what they view as a frightening subject. These students are often overwhelmed, making it difficult for them to complete or even start math assignments.

PROCRASTINATION

Another symptom of math anxiety is procrastination. Students may voluntarily delay or postpone their classwork and assignments, even if they know there will be a negative consequence for doing so. Additionally, they may choose to wait until the last minute to start projects and homework, even when they know they need more time to put forth their best effort.

PHYSIOLOGICAL REACTIONS

Many people with a fear of math experience physiological side effects. These may include an increase in heart rate, sweatiness, shakiness, nausea, and irregular breathing. These symptoms make it difficult to focus on the math content, causing the student even more stress and fear.

STRONG EMOTIONAL RESPONSES

Math anxiety also affects people on an emotional level. Responding to math content with strong emotions such as panic, anger, or despair can be a sign of math anxiety.

LOW TEST SCORES AND PERFORMANCE

Low achievement can be both a symptom and a cause of math anxiety. When someone does not take the steps needed to perform well on tests and assessments, they are less likely to pass. The more they perform poorly, the more they accept this poor performance as a fact that can't be changed.

FEELING ALONE

People who experience math anxiety feel like they are the only ones struggling, even if the math they are working on is challenging to many people. Feeling isolated in what they perceive as failure can trigger tension or nervousness.

FEELING OF PERMANENCY

Math anxiety can feel very permanent. You may assume that you are naturally bad at math and always will be. Viewing math as a natural ability rather than a skill that can be learned causes people to believe that nothing will help them improve. They take their current math abilities as fact and assume that they can't be changed. As a result, they give up, stop trying to improve, and avoid engaging with math altogether.

LACK OF CONFIDENCE

People with low self-confidence in math tend to feel awkward and incompetent when asked to solve a math problem. They don't feel comfortable taking chances or risks when problem-solving because they second-guess themselves and assume they are incorrect. They don't trust in their ability to learn the content and solve problems correctly.

PANIC

A general sense of unexplained panic is also a sign of math anxiety. You may feel a sudden sense of fear that triggers physical reactions, even when there is no apparent reason for such a response.

CAUSES OF MATH ANXIETY

Math anxiety can start at a young age and may have one or more underlying causes. Common causes of math anxiety include the following:

THE ATTITUDE OF PARENTS OR GUARDIANS

Parents often put pressure on their children to perform well in school. Although their intentions are usually good, this pressure can lead to anxiety, especially if the student is struggling with a subject or class.

Perhaps your parents or others in your life hold negative predispositions about math based on their own experiences. For instance, if your mother once claimed she was not good at math, then you might have incorrectly interpreted this as a predisposed trait that was passed down to you.

TEACHER INFLUENCE

Students often pick up on their teachers' attitudes about the content being taught. If a teacher is happy and excited about math, students are more likely to mirror these emotions. However, if a teacher lacks enthusiasm or genuine interest, then students are more inclined to disengage.

Teachers have a responsibility to cultivate a welcoming classroom culture that is accepting of mistakes. When teachers blame students for not understanding a concept, they create a hostile classroom environment where mistakes are not tolerated. This tension increases student stress and anxiety, creating conditions that are not conducive to inquiry and learning. Instead, when teachers normalize mistakes as a natural part of the problem-solving process, they give their students the freedom to explore and grapple with the math content. In such an environment, students feel comfortable taking chances because they are not afraid of being wrong.

Students need teachers that can help when they're having problems understanding difficult concepts. In doing so, educators may need to change how they teach the content. Since different people have unique learning styles, it's the job of the teacher to adapt to the needs of each student. Additionally, teachers should encourage students to explore alternate problem-solving strategies, even if it's not the preferred method of the educator.

FEAR OF BEING WRONG

Embarrassing situations can be traumatic, especially for young children and adolescents. These experiences can stay with people through their adult lives. Those with math anxiety may experience a fear of being wrong, especially in front of a group of peers. This fear can be paralyzing, interfering with the student's concentration and ability to focus on the problem at hand.

TIMED ASSESSMENTS

Timed assessments can help improve math fluency, but they often create unnecessary pressure for students to complete an unrealistic number of problems within a specified timeframe. Many studies have shown that timed assessments often result in increased levels of anxiety, reducing a student's overall competence and ability to problem-solve.

Debunking Math Myths

There are lots of myths about math that are related to the causes and development of math-related anxiety. Although these myths have been proven to be false, many people take them as fact. Let's go over a few of the most common myths about learning math.

MYTH: MEN ARE BETTER AT MATH THAN WOMEN

Math has a reputation for being a male-dominant subject, but this doesn't mean that men are inherently better at math than women. Many famous mathematical discoveries have been made by women. Katherine Johnson, Dame Mary Lucy Cartwright, and Marjorie Lee Brown are just a few of the many famous women mathematicians. Expecting to be good or bad at math because of your gender sets you up for stress and confusion. Math is a skill that can be learned, just like cooking or riding a bike.

MYTH: THERE IS ONLY ONE GOOD WAY TO SOLVE MATH PROBLEMS

There are many ways to get the correct answer when it comes to math. No two people have the same brain, so everyone takes a slightly different approach to problem-solving. Moreover, there isn't one way of problem-solving that's superior to another. Your way of working through a problem might differ from someone else's, and that is okay. Math can be a highly individualized process, so the best method for you should be the one that makes you feel the most comfortable and makes the most sense to you.

MYTH: MATH REQUIRES A GOOD MEMORY

For many years, mathematics was taught through memorization. However, learning in such a way hinders the development of critical thinking and conceptual understanding. These skill sets are much more valuable than basic memorization. For instance, you might be great at memorizing mathematical formulas, but if you don't understand what they mean, then you can't apply them to different scenarios in the real world. When a student is working from memory, they are limited in the strategies available to them to problem-solve. In other words, they assume there is only one correct way to do the math, which is the method they memorized. Having a variety of problem-solving options can help students figure out which method works best for them. Additionally, it provides students with a better understanding of how and why certain mathematical strategies work. While memorization can be helpful in some instances, it is not an absolute requirement for mathematicians.

MYTH: MATH IS NOT CREATIVE

Math requires imagination and intuition. Contrary to popular belief, it is a highly creative field. Mathematical creativity can help in developing new ways to think about and solve problems. Many people incorrectly assume that all things are either creative or analytical. However, this black-and-white view is limiting because the field of mathematics involves both creativity and logic.

MYTH: MATH ISN'T SUPPOSED TO BE FUN

Whoever told you that math isn't supposed to be fun is a liar. There are tons of math-based activities and games that foster friendly competition and engagement. Math is often best learned through play, and lots of mobile apps and computer games exemplify this.

Additionally, math can be an exceptionally collaborative and social experience. Studying or working through problems with a friend often makes the process a lot more fun. The excitement and satisfaction of solving a difficult problem with others is quite rewarding. Math can be fun if you look for ways to make it more collaborative and enjoyable.

MYTH: NOT EVERYONE IS CAPABLE OF LEARNING MATH

There's no such thing as a "math person." Although many people think that you're either good at math or you're not, this is simply not true. Everyone is capable of learning and applying mathematics. However, not everyone learns the same way. Since each person has a different learning style, the trick is to find the strategies and learning tools that work best for you. Some people learn best through hands-on experiences, and others find success through the use of visual aids. Others are auditory learners and learn best by hearing and listening. When people are overwhelmed or feel that math is too hard, it's often because they haven't found the learning strategy that works best for them.

MYTH: GOOD MATHEMATICIANS WORK QUICKLY AND NEVER MAKE MISTAKES

There is no prize for finishing first in math. It's not a race, and speed isn't a measure of your ability. Good mathematicians take their time to ensure their work is accurate. As you gain more experience and practice, you will naturally become faster and more confident.

Additionally, everyone makes mistakes, including good mathematicians. Mistakes are a normal part of the problem-solving process, and they're not a bad thing. The important thing is that we take the time to learn from our mistakes, understand where our misconceptions are, and move forward.

MYTH: YOU DON'T NEED MATH IN THE REAL WORLD

Our day-to-day lives are so infused with mathematical concepts that we often don't even realize when we're using math in the real world. In fact, most people tend to underestimate how much we do math in our everyday lives. It's involved in an enormous variety of daily activities such as shopping, baking, finances, and gardening, as well as in many careers, including architecture, nursing, design, and sales.

Tips and Strategies for Overcoming Math Anxiety

If your anxiety is getting in the way of your level of mathematical engagement, then there are lots of steps you can take. Check out the strategies below to start building confidence in math today.

FOCUS ON UNDERSTANDING, NOT MEMORIZATION

Don't drive yourself crazy trying to memorize every single formula or mathematical process. Instead, shift your attention to understanding concepts. Those who prioritize memorization over conceptual understanding tend to have lower achievement levels in math. Students who memorize may be able to complete some math, but they don't understand the process well enough to apply it to different situations. Memorization comes with time and practice, but it won't help alleviate math anxiety. On the other hand, conceptual understanding will give you the building blocks of knowledge you need to build up your confidence.

REPLACE NEGATIVE SELF-TALK WITH POSITIVE SELF-TALK

Start to notice how you think about yourself. Whenever you catch yourself thinking something negative, try replacing that thought with a positive affirmation. Instead of continuing the negative thought, pause to reframe the situation. For ideas on how to get started, take a look at the table below:

Instead of thinking...	Try thinking...
"I can't do this math." "I'm not a math person."	"I'm up for the challenge, and I'm training my brain in math."
"This problem is too hard."	"This problem is hard, so this might take some time and effort. I know I can do this."
"I give up."	"What strategies can help me solve this problem?"
"I made a mistake, so I'm not good at this."	"Everyone makes mistakes. Mistakes help me to grow and understand."
"I'll never be smart enough."	"I can figure this out, and I am smart enough."

PRACTICE MINDFULNESS

Practicing mindfulness and focusing on your breathing can help alleviate some of the physical symptoms of math anxiety. By taking deep breaths, you can remind your nervous system that you are not in immediate danger. Doing so will reduce your heart rate and help with any irregular breathing or shakiness. Taking the edge off of the physiological effects of anxiety will clear your mind, allowing your brain to focus its energy on problem-solving.

DO SOME MATH EVERY DAY

Think about learning math as if you were learning a foreign language. If you don't use it, you lose it. If you don't practice your math skills regularly, you'll have a harder time achieving comprehension and fluency. Set some amount of time aside each day, even if it's just for a few minutes, to practice. It might take some discipline to build a habit around this, but doing so will help increase your mathematical self-assurance.

USE ALL OF YOUR RESOURCES

Everyone has a different learning style, and there are plenty of resources out there to support all learners. When you get stuck on a math problem, think about the tools you have access to, and use them when applicable. Such resources may include flashcards, graphic organizers, study guides, interactive notebooks, and peer study groups. All of these are great tools to accommodate your individual learning style. Finding the tools and resources that work for your learning style will give you the confidence you need to succeed.

REALIZE THAT YOU AREN'T ALONE

Remind yourself that lots of other people struggle with math anxiety, including teachers, nurses, and even successful mathematicians. You aren't the only one who panics when faced with a new or challenging problem. It's probably much more common than you think. Realizing that you aren't alone in your experience can help put some distance between yourself and the emotions you feel about math. It also helps to normalize the anxiety and shift your perspective.

ASK QUESTIONS

If there's a concept you don't understand and you've tried everything you can, then it's okay to ask for help! You can always ask your teacher or professor for help. If you're not learning math in a traditional classroom, you may want to join a study group, work with a tutor, or talk to your friends. More often than not, you aren't the only one of your peers who needs clarity on a mathematical concept. Seeking understanding is a great way to increase self-confidence in math.

REMEMBER THAT THERE'S MORE THAN ONE WAY TO SOLVE A PROBLEM

Since everyone learns differently, it's best to focus on understanding a math problem with an approach that makes sense to you. If the way it's being taught is confusing to you, don't give up. Instead, work to understand the problem using a different technique. There's almost always more than one problem-solving method when it comes to math. Don't get stressed if one of them doesn't make sense to you. Instead, shift your focus to what does make sense. Chances are high that you know more than you think you do.

VISUALIZATION

Visualization is the process of creating images in your mind's eye. Picture yourself as a successful, confident mathematician. Think about how you would feel and how you would behave. What would your work area look like? How would you organize your belongings? The more you focus on something, the more likely you are to achieve it. Visualizing teaches your brain that you can achieve whatever it is that you want. Thinking about success in mathematics will lead to acting like a successful mathematician. This, in turn, leads to actual success.

FOCUS ON THE EASIEST PROBLEMS FIRST

To increase your confidence when working on a math test or assignment, try solving the easiest problems first. Doing so will remind you that you are successful in math and that you do have what it takes. This process will increase your belief in yourself, giving you the confidence you need to tackle more complex problems.

FIND A SUPPORT GROUP

A study buddy, tutor, or peer group can go a long way in decreasing math-related anxiety. Such support systems offer lots of benefits, including a safe place to ask questions, additional practice with mathematical concepts, and an understanding of other problem-solving explanations that may work better for you. Equipping yourself with a support group is one of the fastest ways to eliminate math anxiety.

REWARD YOURSELF FOR WORKING HARD

Recognize the amount of effort you're putting in to overcome your math anxiety. It's not an easy task, so you deserve acknowledgement. Surround yourself with people who will provide you with the positive reinforcement you deserve.

Remember, You Can Do This!

Conquering a fear of math can be challenging, but there are lots of strategies that can help you out. Your own beliefs about your mathematical capabilities can limit your potential. Working toward a growth mindset can have a tremendous impact on decreasing math-related anxiety and building confidence. By knowing the symptoms of math anxiety and recognizing common misconceptions about learning math, you can develop a plan to address your fear of math. Utilizing the strategies discussed can help you overcome this anxiety and build the confidence you need to succeed.

Tell Us Your Story

We at Mometrix would like to extend our heartfelt thanks to you for letting us be a part of your journey. It is an honor to serve people from all walks of life, people like you, who are committed to building the best future they can for themselves.

We know that each person's situation is unique. But we also know that, whether you are a young student or a mother of four, you care about working to make your own life and the lives of those around you better.

That's why we want to hear your story.

We want to know why you're taking this test. We want to know about the trials you've gone through to get here. And we want to know about the successes you've experienced after taking and passing your test.

In addition to your story, which can be an inspiration both to us and to others, we value your feedback. We want to know both what you loved about our book and what you think we can improve on.

The team at Mometrix would be absolutely thrilled to hear from you! So please, send us an email at tellusyourstory@mometrix.com or visit us at mometrix.com/tellusyourstory.php and let's stay in touch.

Additional Bonus Material

Due to our efforts to try to keep this book to a manageable length, we've created a link that will give you access to all of your additional bonus material.

Please visit https://www.mometrix.com/bonus948/officercand to access the information.